ANGELS TAPPING AT THE WINE-SHOP'S DOOR

RUDI MATTHEE

Angels Tapping at the Wine-Shop's Door

A History of Alcohol in the Islamic World

HURST & COMPANY, LONDON

First published in the United Kingdom in 2023 by
C. Hurst & Co. (Publishers) Ltd.,
New Wing, Somerset House, Strand, London, WC2R 1LA

Copyright © Rudi Matthee, 2023

The right of Rudi Matthee to be identified as the author of
this publication is asserted by him in accordance with the
Copyright, Designs and Patents Act, 1988.

A Cataloguing-in-Publication data record for this book
is available from the British Library.

ISBN: 9781787388154

www.hurstpublishers.com

Every effort has been made to trace copyright-holders and to obtain their
permission for the use of copyrighted material. The publisher apologises for
any errors or omissions and would be grateful if notified of any corrections
that should be incorporated in future reprints or editions of this book.

Printed and bound in Great Britain by Bell and Bain Ltd, Glasgow.

CONTENTS

CONTENTS

LIST OF ILLUSTRATIONS

ACKNOWLEDGEMENTS

As with all my writings on drugs and stimulants, my first expression of gratitude goes to Nikki Keddie. It was she who awakened my interest in the topic back in 1988, when the late Roy Porter invited her to London to participate in a one-day conference on drugs. In my capacity as Nikki's research assistant, I wrote a draft of a paper. She then graciously suggested that I should go to London in her stead and present my findings. I did, and the result was my first publication on drugs in the early modern world.

In retrospect, my subsequent work on the topic, which mainly concentrated on Iran, in some ways served as preparatory work for the current, more comprehensive, study. The following friends and colleagues deserve my special thanks for assisting me with this project. Houchang Chehabi read all nine chapters and discussed the contents with me during as many Zoom meetings. Devin Stewart went over the entire manuscript as well, and was especially helpful with the parts on Islamic law and jurisprudence. Edhem Eldem and François Georgeon inspected what I wrote about the Ottoman Empire and modern Turkey. Owen White, my colleague at University of Delaware, made many valuable suggestions about the parts on North Africa. I am indebted to Dick Davis for checking the chapter on painting and literature, but above all for providing the title of this book, 'Angels Tapping at the Wine-shop's Door', from his translation of the beautiful opening line from Hafez. I am also immensely grateful to Eralp Erdoğan for helping me to finally gain enough reading knowledge of Turkish to be able to read modern texts with some fluency.

Other friends and colleagues who were kind enough to read individual chapters with a critical eye are Beth Baron, Sheila Canby, Maziyar Ghiabi, Ranin Kazemi, Hugh Kennedy, and Afshin Matin-Asgari.

The following colleagues deserve my thanks for improving this study with their keen observations and suggestions: Rula Abisaab, Masoud Amini, Mohsen Ashtiyani, Sussan Babaie, Alda Benjamen, Andrew Scott Cooper, Maribel Fierro, Jorge Flores, Jürgen Wasim Frembgen, Jaihan Garan, Ali Gheissari, Gottfried Hagen, Jane Hathaway, Yakup Karaşahan, Ahmad Karimi-Hakkak, Linda Komaroff, Daniel-Joseph Macarthur-Seal, Mary McWilliams, Ikram Masmoudi, Abbas Milani, Amy Mills, Farrokh Mostowfi, Mehdi Mousavi, Carl Petry, Lawrence Potter, Siavush Randjbar-Daemi, Yann Richard, Kristina Richardson, Jan-Jaap de Ruiter, Sunil Sharma, Miroslav Šedivý, Nina Studer, Nugzar Ter-Oganov, Denis Volkov, Arnoud Vrolijk, John Woods, Riza Yildirim, Hasan Zandiyeh, and Nessim Znaien. Any errors they did not catch are naturally mine. I am also grateful to Masoud Amini, Sussan Babaie, Sheila Canby, Philippe Chaudat, Massumeh Farhad, Aimée Froom, François Georgeon, Farrokh Mostowfi, and Abolala Soudavar for their assistance with illustrations.

I am indebted to the staff of the many archives and libraries where I have worked in the past few decades for their unfailing efficiency and kindness. I am also grateful to the Institute for Advanced Study in Princeton, where I spent the spring of 2017 as the Agnes Gund and Daniel Shapiro Fellow drafting two initial chapters of the book. And, as always, my deeply felt appreciation goes to the John and Dorothy Munroe family of Delaware for facilitating my research in the past decade. I thank Alice Clarke, Michael Eckhardt, and Daisy Leitch at Hurst for their expert editorial assistance.

My wonderful Fariba, who decided that—after working in our basement for a decade or more—I deserved a proper library and made it happen, has, once again, my special thanks and love. My brother-in-law, Mohammad, finally, did not live to see the publication of this book. I dedicate it to his memory, out of respect for his humanity, his deep knowledge of Iranian history, and his unremitting struggle for a free and democratic Iran.

A NOTE ON TRANSLITERATION

Faced with multiple languages and different alphabets, I have tried to keep the transliteration as simple and user-friendly as possible. For Arabic and Persian, I have opted for the *IJMES* style, which inevitably results in some awkwardness in the rendering of modern Persian names and terms. I have kept diacritical marks to a minimum, though, omitting any dots and only differentiating between the short a and the long a, ā, in titles and terms unfamiliar to the non-specialized reader. Ottoman-Turkish terms and titles follow modern standard Turkish orthography. For Russian, I use the Library of Congress system. Terms commonly encountered in English appear the way they tend to be spelled: thus Koran, not Qur'an; Kaaba, not Ka'ba; ulama, not 'ulama or ulema; Mossadegh, not Musaddiq; and Khomeini, not Khumayni. In the case of North Africa, I use conventional French spelling in names such as Moulay and terms such as *boukha*.

INTRODUCTION

I first set foot in the Islamic world in the summer of 1974, following two years of studying Arabic and Persian at Utrecht University. Having hitchhiked through Spain, from Madrid to Algeciras via Toledo, Jaén, Malaga, and, with a detour, Ronda, I took the ferry across the Strait of Gibraltar to the Spanish enclave of Ceuta, and from there entered Tetouan, the first town in Morocco proper. Overwhelmed by the colors and smells of this captivating, edgy city, I was soon lured into a back alley by someone in a burnoose and within minutes found myself with a glass of brandy in my hand. My memory about the incident is fuzzy; I remember little more than that I was charged a hefty sum for what initially appeared like hospitality. Looking back on it, I admit to hopeless naivety.

A year later, in the summer of 1975, having finished my BA in Oriental Languages and Cultures, I decided to go to Egypt with Henk, the same classmate who had joined me on my Morocco trip in Tangier the year before. We first traveled to Greece, and after a few days in Athens we took an overnight boat from Piraeus to Alexandria. Upon arrival the next morning, someone came up to us at the quay and offered us a very reasonably priced bottle of Johnnie Walker Red Label, capped and wax-sealed. Still gullible, we purchased the bottle thinking we had made a good deal, only to find out in our hotel room that it was filled with water.

Some twenty years ago, then a professor and (I like to think) no longer susceptible to such tricks, I flew to Shiraz, Iran, to attend a

1

meeting celebrating the creation of a Persianate study center at the local university. Upon arrival at the airport, my host asked me what I wanted to drink. I demurred, saying that I had not come to Iran to 'drink'. He insisted, though, and when I hesitantly said beer, he asked me what kind of beer I fancied—Dutch beer, German beer, Danish beer? I opted for German, only to be prodded about the type of German beer I wanted, as anything could be delivered within a half-hour by the (Armenian) *payk*, the neighborhood delivery man.

A final incident involving alcohol in a Muslim context occurred in 2015, during a conference in Warsaw commemorating 600 years of Polish-Turkish relations. As part of the event, a trip had been organized to two lovely wooden Tatar mosques, dating back to the seventeenth century, near the border of Belarus. Near the town of Białystok, the bus pulled up at a rest stop. One of the Turkish scholars had managed to acquire a bottle of Polish vodka from the convenience store without paying for it. After arriving at the first of the two mosques, he was the one who most ostentatiously bowed down to pray.

Alcohol, these anecdotes suggest, plays a conspicuous role in the Islamic world; it does and has always done so. Etymology suggests a primordial connection. The very word alcohol is Arabic in origin, deriving from *al-kuhl*, pulverized antimony used to darken the eye lines. The common word 'booze' in English likely comes from a word of possibly Turkic origins referring to a drink called *booza*, or *buza*, a barley or millet drink found in premodern times in a region ranging from the Crimea to Egypt.[1] Muslim alchemists, most notably the Iranian Abu Bakr Muhammad—b. Zakariyya al-Razi (865–925), a.k.a. Rhazes—are credited with the invention of the process of distillation. Another polymath, Ibn Sina, known in the West as Avicenna (980–1037), discusses the medicinal benefits of wine in his *Qānun al-tibb*, a medical encyclopedia whose Latin translation remained a key text in Europe's leading medical schools well into the seventeenth century.[2] Many if not most caliphs, sultans, and shahs who ruled the Muslim world after the death of the Prophet in 632 are known to have imbibed, often in excess, giving the lie to the notion that binge drinking started in late medieval Germany.[3]

Arabic has more than 100 terms for wine.[4] It also has separate verbs for drinking in the late evening, *al-ightibāq*, drinking in the morning, *al-istibāh*, and drinking as early as possible in the morning, *al-mubākara*; and, for good measure, the language has a term for a midday drink, *al-qayl*, while it calls a midnight swill a *fahma*.[5] Classical Arabic poetry knows a widely practiced genre called *khamriyya*, or wine poetry. Called the *'arus* ('bride') of poetry, wine serves as the life blood of the rich Persian poetic tradition, symbolizing earthy pleasure, esthetic refinement, and the intoxication that stands for the self-effacing quality of the bond between the mystic and the divine. Medieval Islamic manuals of etiquette, known as 'Mirrors for Princes', too, invariably include prescriptions for when to drink and how to do so in style. Muhammad b. Ya'qub al-Firuzabadi (d. 1415), included 357 terms for wine in his lexicography.[6] Wine before the onset of the modern age was ubiquitous, not just in poetry and painting or the normative *adab* literature, but in real life as well—especially among the elite. It would be perfectly possible to write a history of at least the eastern half of the lands that originally fell under the sway of Islam as the history of *razm-u-bazm*, of royal fighting and feasting, producing the equivalent of *Vodka Politics*, the title of a recent study of the history of Russia seen through the prism of its leaders' disturbing drinking habits.[7]

Nor was—or is—alcohol just the province of the elite, who clearly thought water and fruit juice inferior to wine. The examples of ordinary Muslims violating their religion's ban on drinking, past and present, are too numerous to count. Statistics about current alcohol consumption tell the story for modern times: whereas the intake of alcohol in most European countries is declining, in the Islamic world it went up by some 25 percent between 2005 and 2010—the result of 'modernization' involving youth, lifestyle, freedom, and tourism—so that international beer companies are now looking at the Middle East as a serious growth market.[8]

Yet Islam and alcohol do not go together; or so we are told. Islam bans alcohol. A pious Muslim does not drink! Consequently, all modern majority-Muslim countries—with the partial exception of Lebanon, Turkey, some African Sahel countries, and the fledgling nations that emerged from the former Soviet Union—are 'dry' in the sense that they outlaw or at least restrict the sale and consumption of alcohol. Historically, water, in addition to a variety of sweetened beverages—and, after *c.* 1600, coffee and tea—was the beverage of choice for Muslims, and in parts of the early modern Islamic world, such as in some regions in Afghanistan and in the interior of the Arabian Peninsula, virtually no one seems to have consumed alcohol. Although rising in some countries, the per-capita consumption of alcohol among Muslims continues to be low. From Morocco to Indonesia, all countries with a majority Muslim population, except those that were part of the Soviet Union until the 1990s, the annual per-capita intake in 2010 was less than 2.5 liters. Again with the partial exception of the Central Asian Muslim countries, drinking in the Muslim world is not socially approved of, not integrated into social life, not part of the code of sociability and hospitality. The tradition of having a drink after work, of enjoying a beer with one's friends, of alcohol as a rite of passage marking the entry into adulthood is largely absent in the Islamic world. The liquid that lubricates life and its ceremonial key moments is tea or coffee rather than beer, wine, or vodka.

Islam is the only major world faith that challenges the juggernaut that alcohol has proven to be in human history. Judaism considers wine a holy drink, accepts it in diluted form, and accords it a significant role in its various ceremonies. Christianity goes further. It embraces wine, indeed integrates it into the very core of the faith by turning it into the metaphorical blood of Christ as celebrated in the Eucharist. Islam, by contrast, rejects the fermented juice of the grape. Of all the proscriptions of Islam, the one on alcohol is, after the rejection of pork, the most emphatic one. Yet for all its outcast status, alcohol tends to be the first taboo Muslims violate when given a chance—the consumption of pork being the last. Just as bans on prostitution throughout history have never put an end to the phenomenon, drinking is bound up with Islamic history and culture in intricate ways. The lure is clearly as strong as the rejection, and the intensity of the two are arguably entwined. Pork has never given anyone a 'high'; eating it gives a lot of people pleasure, but addiction to it is unknown and abstaining from it has thus always been much easier than resisting the temptation of alcohol.

In modern Iran, of all places, a glass of vodka or homemade wine is often the third offering, after tea and a plethora of fruit, presented to guests in middle-class homes. As one modern scholar puts it: 'An examination of sources from the pre-modern Islamic world shows that abstemiousness was often the exception rather than the rule and that Muslims throughout history employed a variety of techniques to justify or legitimate their drinking theologically or, alternatively, to absolve themselves after the fact.'[9]

The paradox, then, is that alcohol is integral to the constitution of Islamic culture by its 'absence' as much as by its presence, putting it at the center of Islam, making it almost its defining issue.[10] Wine, in the words of one modern scholar, is the 'Islamic beverage *par excellence*'.[11] The author of a recent study of the eighth-century Arab poet Abu Nuwas similarly calls it a 'permanent fixture of the Islamic universe'.[12]

This very fact of presence through absence creates problems of communicability, making it difficult to have an honest discourse about alcohol in Islam. The formal ban on alcohol in the faith combined with the obvious violations of that same ban has left it in the shadows in both traditional Islamic historiography and modern scholarship. Premodern Muslim chroniclers are quite open about elite drinking, focusing on the courts of the ruler, the khan, the sultan, or the shah, who were allowed to engage in revelry for reasons that this book will discuss. But drinking outside the royal palace or the mansions of the ruling classes remains largely unmentioned in their works, in part because it often involved non-Muslims, who by definition did not merit much attention, but mostly because the lives of common people rarely feature in narrative sources in general. Rather, they focus on bans passed by new rulers intent on establishing their legitimacy at their accession or keen to propitiate the divine in the face of war, political crisis, or natural disaster, with the implication that they were successful, that they rooted out the problem—until a new ruler arrived and issued a new ban.

The result is that modern research on alcohol in the Islamic world is far less extensive than one might imagine, and what exists often extrapolates practices and policies from proclamations. General histories of alcohol tend to pay scant attention to Islam and the

Muslim world, and studies of Islam reciprocate by rarely addressing alcohol beyond the complexity of the Koranic stance on it or the trope of wine in the poetic tradition.[13] The former either leave out the Islamic world altogether or limit themselves to observing that wine originated in the Middle East but that the region's vinous tradition was interrupted by the advent of Islam. Some authors, digging deeper, add that Islam—beginning with the Koran itself— shows some ambiguity about drinking, but that, on balance, alcohol came to be forbidden, even though some countries in the modern Middle East conditionally allow for its consumption. The message often implied by this is that drinking in the Islamic world is both rather inconsequential and a matter of hypocritical behavior. Several recent works on the global history of alcohol thus dedicate no more than a page or two to the Islamic world.[14] Westerners, little familiar with Islam's past manifestations of openness and toleration—and weaned on the narrow, scripturalist version of the faith that has been getting headlines since the late 1970s—may be excused for believing that there is little more to Islam and alcohol than that they are mutually exclusive. Ayatollah Khomeini's famous pronouncement, 'God did not create man so that he could have fun', seamlessly aligns with such perceptions.[15]

Examples of this type of approach abound. In his *The Wet and the Dry: A Drinker's Journey*, published in 2013, British novelist and travel writer Lawrence Osborne uses the Muslim world as a backdrop to a series of witty and wistful musings on the psychology of the itinerant alcoholic. Osborne visits Beirut and the Bekaa Valley in Lebanon, the Pakistani capital Islamabad, the United Arab Emirates, the heavily Muslim southern parts of Thailand, as well as Malaysia and Egypt. Whenever he is not in Christian (or Druze) company, as in Lebanon, or ensconced in the bar of some international hotel frequented by expats, as in Dubai, the atmosphere he depicts is furtively nostalgic and melancholic, as in Cairo, or grimly clandestine, as in Pakistan. 'You can get a drink in most Islamic countries,' Osborne concludes, 'but it is either not easy, sometimes even for a foreign national, or one has to find a (dwindling) non-Muslim recess of society.'[16]

If a lazy reliance on received wisdom accounts for the lack of attention given by Western writing to drinking in Islam, a combination of ignorance, dismissive denial, and taboo thinking plays a role in the dearth of serious research on the topic coming out of the modern Islamic world. The Yemeni novelist ʿAli al-Muqri opens his book on alcohol—serially published as four (redacted) chapters in the cultural supplement of the Yemeni newspaper *al-Jumhuriyya*—by noting that, when people around him learned about his project, they asked him if he had nothing else to talk about and what he intended to achieve by taking on the topic.[17]

To my knowledge, al-Muqri's work remains the only serious book-length study on alcohol in modern Arabic writing. In the Islamic world, a tradition that was intimately interwoven with life and literature in premodern times now generally falls beyond the realm of subjects worth investigating. As German journalist and Islam-critic Samuel Schirmbeck puts it, these days who in the Arab world (or, for that matter, in Muslim-dominated quarters of European cities) would risk bringing the juxtaposition of wine and the Koran found in the Bacchic poetry of Abu Nuwas out into the open? Indeed, who even knows about Abu Nuwas and his verse filled with alcohol-fueled deviance and defiance? Who, in an environment where alcohol is associated with mental and physical deficiency leading to depravity and social malaise—that is, Western decadence—is willing to speak honestly about the fact that the main consumers of alcohol in majority-Muslim countries are, and have historically been, Muslims? Just as the West's former association of Islam with (sexual) indulgence has been supplanted by a buttoned-up image of stern morality, so the openness with which Islamic cultures used to talk about sex and stimulants—alcohol, opium, and hashish—is concealed by modern Muslims, rarely talked about, and censored if need be. In societies where an increasingly strict halal/haram dichotomy has gained ground, ambiguity and doubt having gone underground, most people just retreat, submitting to social pressure, while in secret, plagued by guilt, they continue to drink (and make love without a wedding ring).[18] Modern Muslim fundamentalists exclusively focus on the textual dimension of Islam, as if they had inherited colonialism's ignorance of the religion's history of diversity and tolerance.[19] One Muslim critic goes so far as to characterize Islam in the face of the modern world as 'j'ai peur, donc je crois' ('I am afraid, therefore I believe').[20] An Egyptian song censored in its country of origin in 2020, branded for promoting immorality because it featured the line *'ashrab khumur wa-hashish'* ('I will drink wine and smoke hashish [if you leave me]'), seems to prove the point.[21]

The notion that a pious Muslim does not drink, coupled with the reality that many Muslims do drink, raises the obvious question: what is a pious Muslim? Moreover, what is Islam, what does it stand for, what does it require of its adherents? The conventional answer, given by Westerners and Muslims alike, points to a scripturalist religion, a creed of unambiguous uniformity consisting of a series of beliefs and practices that are based on a shared history grounded in a sacred text, the Koran, and complemented by the *hadith*, the sayings and actions of the Prophet and his companions as orally transmitted by subsequent generations. Muslims, or at least 'good' Muslims, are people who organize their lives according to both texts, who pray five times a day and observe the rules of fasting—and do not drink alcohol.

Since they began engaging with it as an object of study in the nineteenth century, Western scholars have seen Islam primarily in such terms: as a rule-bound, legalistic faith represented by its clerics, the ulama, and its legal scholars, the *fuqahā*. In 1974, the American scholar Marshall Hodgson broke with that perception in a magisterial three-volume study titled *The Venture of Islam*, in which he separated Islam as faith from Islam as culture, especially as it pertains to philosophy and art. He called the latter, ambient sphere, 'Islamicate'. This distinction has since gained wide traction among scholars, albeit often implicitly, with few adopting the ungainly term 'Islamicate', which may also be one reason why the distinction has not crossed over into general works on Islam and its history.

A more recent interpretation of Islam takes issue with Hodgson's distinction between Islam as belief and Islam as culture by insisting that Islam, rather than a faith or a faith plus culture, is a capacious universe of multifarious, variable, and mutable beliefs and practices. German scholar of Islam Thomas Bauer submits that Islam is fluid, embraces paradox and ambiguity, and this begins with the Koran itself, the ambiguous text *par excellence*.[22] Bauer also revisits the hoary notion that, unlike Christianity, Islam knows no distinction between the sacred and the secular, between religion and state. He makes a claim for a vast arena of practice and behavior in its history not informed and regulated by 'religious' enjoinment and proscription. The notion that belief and practice are inextricably entwined in Islam, he asserts, first took hold in the nineteenth century, the age of Western intrusion. Islam has been 'Islamized' ever since, first in Europe and then in the actual Muslim world, and entire swathes of what used to be 'secular' life have been 'sacralized' in the process.[23]

The late Shahab Ahmed goes further in his celebrated *What Is Islam?*, arguing that Islam is whatever Muslims claim and show it to be in their words and actions. Ahmed dismisses the distinction between religion and culture outright, positing that there are no clear criteria for separating the two.[24] He even rejects the very term 'Islam' as a useless moniker, given the multitude of variations it covers. 'Religion' to him is '*hermeneutical engagement*, that is … engagement by an actor or agent with a source of object of (potential) meaning in a way that ultimately *produces meaning for the actor* by way of the source'. In the case of Islam, this means interactive engagement with what Ahmed calls the Pre-Text, being the traditions that preceded Islam; the Text, being the Muslim revelation, the Koran, and the prophetic *hadith*; and the Con-Text, being the 'entire accumulated lexicon of means and meanings of Islam that has been historically generated and recorded up to any given moment'.[25] Echoing Bauer, he contends that if Islam appears to us as a dogmatic, scriptural faith that rejects a distinction between the sacred and the profane, this is a modern interpretation, the result of a defensive reaction to the intrusion of the arrogantly secularizing West, inculcated by the agents of modernity, colonial administrators and Western scholars.

There is something attractive, even compelling about this interpretative revisionism. Bauer's proposition that ambiguity and paradox are inherent in Islam evokes a premodern sensibility attuned to multiplicity in religious thought and practice—*any* religious thought and practice—a multiplicity which the modern world has narrowed, rendered suspect and relegated to strictly separate domains. It is hard to disagree with his complaint that it is absurd to label any artifact found in the Middle East dating from the seventh century onward as automatically 'Islamic' once it is displayed in a museum.[26] As for Ahmed, the notion that Islam is malleable, that its seemingly contradictory qualities are not part of its cultural ambiance but rather intrinsic to it, and that these do nothing to make it lose its overarching cohesion and coherence, makes sense. The same author is also right to say that an emphasis on the prescriptive dimension of Islam and the orthodoxy it preaches misses the point.[27]

Bauer's and Ahmed's arguments directly bear on our topic— alcohol in Islam. Bauer's argument that ambiguity is deeply embedded in Islam, it will be seen in this book, is fully borne out by the complex ways in which Muslims have always approached alcohol. Bauer's explication of ambiguity and Islam is both nuanced and complex. It is not, he submits, a matter of contrasting the ultimate Koranic ban on drinking with the ubiquity of drinking in Islam; it is not, in other words, a question of the norm and violating it, but rather a matter of parallel normative systems. One he calls *zarf*, refinement, worldliness, sophistication; the other is *zuhd*, asceticism, piety. The first was the province of the elite, the court, members of the literary classes; the other was supposed to inform the behavior of the religious estate, and of ordinary people. Yet, Bauer argues, no strict division existed between these two: by the tenth century, *zarf*— mostly expressed in lyrical poetry celebrating nature, love, and wine—had become quintessential to the notion of good breeding, and even entered the purview of the religious leaders, the ulama. Poets might juxtapose verse extolling asceticism with erotic poetry, leaving it up to the reader to interpret meaning.[28]

Behavior in violation of the rules, Ahmed concurs with Bauer, is still Islamic. Wine-drinking, for instance, must qualify as Islamic because there has been a 'mutually-constitutive relationship between wine and Islam in history' by way of the ban that exists on it.[29] Abstinence is a basic element in the construction of identity for Muslims, a way of situating oneself in the world as a Muslim. But so is drinking, as a way of challenging and resisting the same abstinence as imposed identity-forming behavior. Drinking is thus part of the 'full historical vocabulary of Islam at any given moment'. A wine-cup is Islamic precisely because of the (contradictory) values and meanings, negative and positive, that are made for wine in the hermeneutical engagement by Muslims with Pre-Text, Text, and Con-Text.[30] This allows Ibn Sina to be a good Muslim even as he prescribes alcohol as a remedy for certain ailments, and for entertainment after studying for hours.

This study subscribes to these notions involving capaciousness expressed as ambiguity, with some qualifications and caveats. Bauer overstates his case, contrasting too starkly a presumed premodern Islamic penchant for ambiguity and the flexibility that results from it with what he sees as a contemporary Western tendency to emphasize linearity and uniformity. He also draws his examples almost exclusively from the Arab world, and more particularly the Mamluk period in Egypt (1250–1517), and largely disregards the traditional eastern Islamic 'Persianate' world, which arguably is even more given to ambiguity than the Arab lands.

Ahmed's all-enveloping interpretive scheme has problems, too. We should no doubt include *zarf*, expressed in poetry as well as in the Mirror for Princes literature, in any definition of Islam. But by classifying everything that Muslims have done over time as 'Islam' without regard for intentionality, he ends up casting a net that is too capacious to be meaningful—or historically applicable. As critics have pointed out, Ahmed's theoretical framework elides a historical reality in which those who defied the norm often suffered terrible punishment rather than acceptance under a tolerant rubric.[31]

Ahmed's insistence that no functional division existed in Islam until the 'West' created one is debatable as well, as a modern political apologetic view. Today's dichotomy in Islam between the 'religious' and the 'secular' is not just a function of Western categories imposed by colonialism or having entered the Muslim world as part of the adoption of 'modernity'. It is also an outgrowth of an authentic, preexisting binary, one that conceptually as well as practically differentiated between 'religion' and the 'world'—*din wa-dunyā*, the spiritual and the profane—in ways that allowed both to exist side by side.[32] This made it possible for things that are enjoyable, if religiously questionable, to enter the realm of the acceptable, the argument being that they are beneficial, useful for human health and wellbeing.

With Bauer and Ahmed, I proceed from several premises in this study. One is that Islam is both words and actions, both scripture and practice, that it has to be both: the one cannot exist without the other. Texts not performed, unexecuted, ignored, or negated, wither. Performance unmoored from texts providing guiding principles becomes inchoate. Ambiguity, in turn, should not be confused with toleration, much less with tolerance. Ambiguity is inherent to Islam, as it must be in any faith seeking to survive beyond the lifetime of its founder and his immediate disciples. No evolving religion can effectively do so without multiplicity, without the ability to live with aporia, unresolvable contradictions. Yet no religion which takes itself seriously *presents* itself as a series of ambiguities. Indeed, absolutism, the obverse of ambiguity, is inherent in the way religions view and present themselves, the monotheistic ones more so than others.

That the Islamic world, combining theory and practice, is exceedingly diverse and complex and filled with paradox—apparent contradiction—is simply observable. Only those who have never been to the Middle East would lump all people inhabiting the region together. Arabs, Iranians, and Turks, to name only the three largest ethno- linguistic groups in the Muslim Middle East, inhabit different universes. Within the Arab world, Morocco, Egypt, and Syria—to name but three countries—pair a shared religio-cultural idiom to a particularism shaped by different historical experience, including a distinct colonial past. Within modern countries like Iran and Turkey one finds a great deal of diversity: between Shi'is—the majority in Iran—and Sunnis; between Turks, Kurds, and Alevis, followers of a heterodox branch of Islam found in eastern Turkey that has made wine part of its rituals. The astonishing variety and multiplicity of the Islamic experience in the Muslim territories of the former Soviet Union offers another striking example of the religion's chameleon-like quality, its ability to absorb elements from adjacent cultures.

History points up similar types of diversity and complexity. The heartland of the 'Islamic world' has never been just 'Islamic', but deeply enmeshed with pre-Islamic, pagan, Hellenistic, and Roman antecedents, as much as with the Jewish, Zoroastrian, and Christian Greek-Byzantine world that Islam would ultimately conquer. These substrata did not just dissolve in a Muslim universe. They rather became subsumed under an evolving amalgamation that we call

Islamic but that remained a layered composite. From the death of
the Prophet in 632 until the end of the traditional caliphate in 1258,
more non-Muslims lived in the caliphate than Muslims. Until the
First World War, fully half of the population of Istanbul was non-
Muslim Greek and Armenian. Most of the people of the Balkans
living under Ottoman control never converted to Islam. The history
of the Mediterranean Sea overlaps with the history of Islam. Its
shores—from Western Anatolia and islands such as Chios, Kos,
Rhodes, Crete, and Cyprus to modern-day Tunisia—always retained
a cultural flavor markedly different from that of the interior, inner
Anatolia, Syria beyond the coast, Iraq, the Arabian Peninsula; and
one of its signifiers has been the cultivation and consumption of
wine. The 'Levant'—the eastern seaboard of the Mediterranean
comprising the modern countries of Syria, Lebanon, Israel-Palestine,
and Egypt—continues to be home to a significant, albeit decreasing,
Christian population.

Mystical or charismatic Islam—as opposed to scriptural
Islam—points up a wholly different facet of the Islamic faith and
civilization—one that remains poorly known among the public in
the West. Sufis, Islamic mystics, often drank, and their writings are
filled with wine imagery. In poetry, the most eloquent expression
of mystical thought, wine reveals a universe beyond good and evil,
a treasure box of eternal wisdom and truth. This level of truth, as
exciting as it is dangerous, is beyond the reach of ordinary people.
As the late fifteenth-century Persian poet Baba Fighani proclaimed:
'What's not in the treasury of both worlds is in the tavern'.[33]

For all the diversity of Islam, one is also struck by the similarities
throughout its history and across the lands where it came to prevail
in the manifestations of drinking and the ambivalent approach to
alcohol, most clearly expressed in attempts to keep up the appearance
of sobriety in the face of reality. These include hypocrisy—the
inevitable byproduct of the ban on a commodity that has proved to be
irrepressible the world over—including among those who fulminate
against said hypocrisy while indulging themselves in secret.

At the heart of this book is the simultaneity of an oft-proclaimed
singular Islam, clear and unambiguous, and the great diversity and
multiplicity of its real-life manifestations. It builds its main argument

on a series of paradoxes. Historically, most people, and certainly Muslims, inhabiting the world where Islam spread and became the dominant faith, did not drink. This was in accordance with Islam's formal proscription of the consumption of alcohol and the draconian punishment potentially awaiting violators of the ban— eighty lashes; forty for women and slaves.[34] Water has always been their main beverage, women as a rule never drank, and fermented or distilled drinks were generally not readily available, least of all in the respectable public sphere. Throughout Islamic history, radical bans on drinking have often followed the rise to power of puritanical regimes: the North African Almoravids and Almohads in eleventh- and thirteenth-century Spain, respectively; the Wahhabis who haunted the Arabian Peninsula and ransacked the Shi'i shrines of Iraq in the early nineteenth century and whose creed informs the Islam of modern Saudi Arabia; more recently, the clerics of the Islamic Republic of Iran and the Taliban in Afghanistan.

Yet, the formal ban on the consumption of alcohol in Islam notwithstanding, Muslims throughout history have been known to drink, and often to drink in excess. The issue of consuming alcohol in an Islamic environment thus was never clear-cut, simply conforming to the presumed straightforwardness of religiously prescribed and proscribed behavior. Consuming alcohol in an Islamic environment sounds oxymoronic but in reality has always been part of the multiplicity of life, officially banned but effectively tolerated at the margins, the beneficiary of a certain 'perspectivism' which does reflect a greater tolerance for practical ambiguity than that found in contemporary Western societies, which emphasized (the need for) linearity and uniformity to a far greater degree much earlier. Indeed, rather than following the conventional notion that Islam is all uncompromising law and that whatever does not fit that mold is not Islam but mystical Islam, outside of Islam or 'secular Islam'— denoting deviance rather than the norm—this study surveys a premodern world extending from the Balkans to Bengal as well as from the Maghreb to Central Asia, to discern, with Ahmed, a vast land of dazzling diversity, of far greater ethnic, linguistic, and religious variety than post-Roman Europe ever exhibited. A universe of intrinsic pluralism and complexity, yet unified in a common paradigm of life and thought, traditional Islam was indeed capacious, capable of embracing contradiction.

Nor was, or is, drinking just a matter of morality. The idiom always was and continues to be Islamic; the references are invariably the Koran and the *hadith*. But power and money has invariably played a role in the production and consumption of alcohol. Chroniclers justified the drinking of sultans and shahs by invoking their special status; people of wealth and influence had ways to keep their consumption private. And behind it all there was money in the form of tax revenue for perennially underfunded states, which typically prevailed in decisions to leave the alcohol trade undisturbed, even if it could never be officially presented as such.

It is important, finally, to state what this book does not intend to be. Navigating between the Scylla of Orientalism and the Charybdis of nostalgia, it does not see the formal rejection of alcohol as a manifestation of 'absence' and 'deficiency' in Islamic society, or as a way simply to expose rampant 'hypocrisy'. The formal rejection, we will see, is just that: formal. As for hypocrisy, all societies have their share of loose living and censorious philistinism. Pointing out that in Islam the difference between 'is' and 'ought' is stark when it comes to alcohol is merely stating the obvious given the clash between its demonization in Islam and its near-universal irresistibility. Nor does this study equate the consumption of alcohol with inherent Islamic debauchery and decadence, as would appear from the high-volume drinking that took place at most caliphal and sultanic courts. If many Muslim rulers and high officials were frequently deep in their cups, often shockingly so, they were little different from political leaders in early modern Europe and beyond, and not just the Russian elites. In the West, too, 'inebriated escape' has been customary for as long as alcohol has been consumed.[35] Only consider English rulers and statesmen, from James I through George IV, and William Pitt the Younger, to Churchill, whose drinking habits have recently become the object of serious scholarly investigation.[36]

Nor, finally, is this study meant as an elegy about a lost world. It does portray a past far more open to drinking, engaging in it, talking about it, than the present; yet I do not intend to idealize or romanticize that past in the way scholarship on the Middle

15

East, seeking to offset the bleak present with evidence of a lost 'cosmopolitanism' with its connotation of tolerance and social diversity, has long hailed Andalusia for its *convivencia*, its presumed cultural coexistence under Muslim rule. Similarly, this work does not follow those historians and authors of diasporic exile literature who lament the vanished world of Levantine 'minorities'—Greeks, Armenians, Jews, European expatriates—'citizens of the world' who once inhabited the urban centers and in particular the port cities of the eastern Mediterranean.[37]

Sources, Geography and Organization

Documenting and analyzing the incidence of Muslim drinking through history is fraught with problems. The obvious one is that drinking was religiously illegitimate and, almost invariably, officially illegal and thus subject to imprecise and inherently deficient documentation. Few people engaged in legally forbidden or morally suspect behavior advertise their habits, and Muslim drinkers past and present are no exception to this truism. Indeed, one is confronted with a serious imbalance regarding the sources, between 'internal' and 'external' ones; that is, the ones written in 'Islamic' languages (Arabic, Persian, and Turkish) and the ones composed by foreigners, usually European residents and visitors. I use 'indigenous' sources whenever they are available, either in the original or in translation, supplemented by a host of observations and descriptions by foreigners, in a multitude of languages.

First-person narratives describing alcohol use in neutral terms do exist, but these are quite rare.[38] Muslim historiographers in classical times often openly write about the drinking habits of the rulers they cover, from the assumption that shahs and sultans have the right to consume (large amounts of) alcohol. But most of the 'internal' sources on drinking broadly fall into two categories: *belles lettres*, including wine poetry, and official edicts launching anti-vice campaigns. The first are generally positive about drinking, hailing it as part of the divinely ordained order or as an integral ingredient of joyous living; the second are by definition negative, accusatory, or just ignore the use of alcohol, leaving it unmentioned. Both to some extent are also idealized, failing to separate the imagined and the normative from the real—whether celebratory or censorious—prescriptive rather than descriptive.[39] The recurrent references to alcohol in the 'celebratory' or 'exculpatory' sources point to the existence of a flourishing drinking culture but also distort it in the sense that they sensationalize, giving the impression that the incidence of drinking was much greater and more widespread than in reality it often was. The 'incriminating' sources, on the other hand, tend to obfuscate. They also underreport toleration. Bans are more spectacular than connivance, and for that reason are more likely to have been recorded by authors intent on enthralling their readers. They are also performative, obligatory acts for the pious ruler bound to combat vice. 'Pragmatic tolerance', which was often the status quo, could hardly be publicized as official policy, after all. Taxation, institutionalizing, and legitimizing the status quo is underreported for the same reason: it was not supposed to be practiced, for it would condone what cannot be condoned. After all, levying taxes on sin effectively means legalizing sin.[40]

With few exceptions, none of the 'internal' sources match the documentation, either in quantity or in expository quality, provided by external sources—the observations and comments made by Western visitors and residents, merchants, monks, diplomats—beginning in the fifteenth century.[41] However, these external sources pose their own problems. The most important one is the very outsider status of those who observed. Foreigners often consorted mainly with fellow foreigners or members of the religious minorities, typically Christians. Yet external reporting is not to be rejected out of hand as flawed and prejudiced, and not just because many foreigners did mingle with Muslims. Indeed, the outside voice has clear advantages. The foreign observer often discerns aspects of life that are too familiar to be noticed by the insider, the participant. In past and present, the best studies of societies have often been written by foreigners for precisely this reason. More relevant to the topic at hand, the external view throws light onto societal phenomena that indigenous voices cannot articulate and publicize other than by omission, or in disparaging and dismissive terms. As importantly, the Europeans (and the few Americans) who visited or lived in the

Islamic Middle East before the twentieth century—the travelers, monks, merchants, and, beginning in the nineteenth century, colonial agents, missionaries, diplomats, and educationalists— looked at Islam less as a strictly normative religion than as a way of life. To be sure, they recognized that Islam was bound by rules, but they primarily perceived a faith leavened by a practice of evading or defying official strictures, a social and political environment in which a religiously justified, harshly punitive regime alternated with a live-and-let-live approach at least as latitudinarian as what existed in contemporary Europe.

Faced with a swath of territory spanning some 13,000 kilometers (9,000 miles) and encompassing nearly forty modern countries, from Morocco to Indonesia and the Philippines, I have had to make geographical choices. This study examines the central lands where Islam became the dominant faith after its great conquests of the seventh and eighth centuries; the area included in the first two Islamic empires, the Umayyads (661–750) and the Abbasids (750–1258); and the lands that were part of the three great early modern empires, the Ottomans, the Safavids, and the Mughals. The breakup of these overarching states in the eighteenth and nineteenth centuries led to fragmentation, colonial incorporation, and, ultimately, the formation of the modern nation-state. The coverage in the modern period thus will be more selective, consisting of much (not all) of today's Arab world, as well as Turkey and Iran, with forays into North Africa west of Egypt, the Maghreb—Tunisia, Algeria, and Morocco—the Indian subcontinent and, in modern times, Pakistan. This focus on the 'heartland' means that vast swathes of the Muslim world such as Islamic Central Asia under Russian and Soviet domination, the Horn of Africa, and today's most populous Islamic nation, Indonesia— home to some 225 million Muslims—as well as a host of smaller majority-Muslim countries remain undiscussed.

1

ISLAM AND ALCOHOL

Introduction: Alcohol in Pre-Islamic West Asia

Long before Islam made its appearance and spread across West Asia and North Africa in the seventh century CE, much of the region was awash in alcohol. The world's earliest wine culture, going back some 9,000 years, is believed to have existed in the heart of the ancient world, in the borderlands of today's Iran, Iraq, Turkey, and the countries of the southern Caucasus, Armenia, and Georgia. Jars from 5,400 to 5,000 BCE containing what likely are remnants of wine have been found at Hajji Firuz Tepe in the Iranian Zagros Mountains. More recent findings of bowls and goblets dating to *c*. 7,000 BCE point to southeastern Anatolia and today's Georgia as the earliest sites of viticulture.[1] In the fourth millennium BCE, wine, now domesticated, spread to the shores of the Mediterranean, Syria, Palestine, and Egypt, as well as to Mesopotamia, where it became a luxury item for Sumerian and Babylonian royalty. Central Asia seems to have developed its viticulture no later than the third millennium BCE.[2]

Beer, too, originated in the Middle East. The ancient craft of beer-making can be traced back to Sumer. The oldest depiction of beer drinking is found on a 6,000-year-old clay tablet showing people sipping the beverage through straws from a communal bowl.

A 3,900-year-old poem honoring Nikasi, the goddess of brewing, contains the world's oldest known beer recipe. The ancient Egyptian pharaohs had their own breweries five millennia ago.[3]

Given such origins, it is no surprise that alcohol in the form of (red) wine plays an important role in the mythology of the various religious traditions that sprang from the soil of the same region before the advent of Islam: Judaism, Zoroastrianism, and Christianity. Each ascribes various practical applications as well as symbolic meaning to wine. Wine was known for its medicinal qualities throughout antiquity.[4] The vine and wine are prominent throughout the Abrahamic tradition. The Hebrew Bible mentions wine 280 times. The vine is frequently used as a metaphor in it, at times a sexual one, the unripe grape being likened to a virgin. In the story about Noah in the Book of Genesis 9:20–21, wine is associated with danger and impudence—as presented in the story where Noah's son discovers him naked in a drunken stupor. The Bible's opinion on inebriation is further exemplified in the story of Lot and his daughters who make him drunk before sleeping with him to create offspring, and by David attempting to get Uriah drunk to have intercourse with his wife, Bathsheba.[5] The story of Joseph in the Old Testament links wine to agriculture and fertility, and specifically to good harvests, symbolizing prosperous times after lean years. In Joseph's dreams, wine bridges the gap between the terrestrial and the divine.[6]

Alcohol plays an important role in the ancient Iranian tradition as well. In Zoroastrianism, Iran's original religion, wine symbolized liquid gold and the flowing fire of the radiant sun, and as such had a ritual function, expressed in the libation ritual, in which it stood in as a substitute for blood, the ultimate life force. Pre-Islamic Iran also provides the earliest historical record about drinking. The Achaemenid kings, who ruled from the early sixth century BCE until 330 BCE, drank copiously, except for the dynasty's founder, Cyrus 'the Great' (r. 600–580 BCE), who apparently did not indulge. His successors made up for this. Cambyses (r. 580–59 BCE) in particular was a real toper. The ephemeral Xerxes II (r. 423 BCE) is said to have been soused at the time of his assassination, and Darius II (r. 423–04/5 BCE) insisted that mention of his ability to hold his liquor be engraved on his tomb.[7] Herodotus famously claimed that the Persians were in the habit of deliberating on important matters in a state of drunkenness and revisiting on the following day the points on which they had agreed while intoxicated.[8] Iran's subsequent ruling houses were little different. The Parthians (a.k.a. Arsacids, r. 247 BCE–224 CE) and the Sasanians (224–630s CE), too, imbibed with gusto. The Roman emperor Tiberius (r. 14–37 CE)) is said to have learned to drink on an empty stomach and to have meals preceded by a draught of wine from the Parthians.[9] A plethora of wine rhytons, wine horns, and wine boats has come to us from Sasanian times.[10] Sasanian rulers reportedly engaged in wine drinking every second or third day.[11] Since landowners, *dihqāns*, at the time often owned large vineyards, the term *dihqān* became almost synonymous with vintner (*razbān* in Persian).[12] How widespread wine consumption was in pre-Islamic Iran is suggested by the fact that the Arab armies found wine in every home when they took Isfahan in 749.[13]

Wine may not generally be a 'drink of the desert', but that fact by itself does not account for the marginalization of alcohol in Islam.[14] Grapes were cultivated in the shadow of palm groves, and wine was known in various parts of the peninsula in pre-Islamic times.[15] Pre-Islamic poetry is replete with wine. The Ghassanids, an originally Yemenite tribe enlisted by the Byzantines to patrol the northern Arabian *limes*, are said to have been partial to the wines of Maqadd, an unidentified location in Arabia.[16] Christian and Jewish merchants supplied Syrian wine to the monasteries that dotted the Arabian Peninsula.[17] References to alcohol are found in South Arabic, Palmyrene, and Nabataean inscriptions bearing terms such as *mizr*, a fermented drink made of cereals mixed in with honey, and *bit'*, a beverage made from honey as well. Most of these point to Yemen, Arabia Felix, which produced wine in abundance and where wine drinking seems to have been common.[18] For the northern parts of the peninsula, adjacent to Syria and Iraq, too, we have information about viticulture, wine shops, and taverns.[19]

The Koran and Alcohol

The Koran reproduces much of the information about the main characters known from the Bible. It retells their stories, often in

21

considerable detail, although typically in a less linear fashion. We thus read the account of Joseph as it occurs in the Old Testament, complete with the dreams, the wine, Joseph's position as the Pharaoh's cupbearer, with only minor differences. Yet when it comes to the Biblical patriarchs, the Koran tends to leave out the most compromising information about their association with alcohol. Noah's drunkenness during which he passes out in a state of nakedness as it is told in Genesis, for instance, has no place in the Koranic version of the story, which depicts him, rather than as an inebriated man, as 'a man possessed'. There is wine in the Koranic story of Lot, but the focus is on alcohol as an aspect of the depravity of the doomed people of Sodom. Lot himself is presented as a paragon of morality and righteousness; there is no mention of the incest with his daughters he commits in a state of intoxication, as narrated in Genesis 18–19. Such bowdlerization continues in the way the Koran retells the New Testament, omitting the many references to wine in connection with Jesus. God's messengers, in sum, mostly appear as idealized figures, untainted by human flaw and failure.

Like the Bible, the Koran discusses wine mostly as a cautionary tale, warning against overindulgence and the loss of discernment it produces. Yet, whereas Judaism and Christianity (and Zoroastrianism) preached moderation, Islam decreed a ban. It arrived at this verdict in a circuitous way, though. Indeed, the Koran appears to be ambivalent about alcohol, evincing a 'progressively negative sequence' in a series of 'discreet, evocative statements' regarding its properties and its consumption, clearly 'in response to a particular set of human circumstances'.[20]

The aggregate of Koranic references to alcohol indeed suggests that Islam does not reject alcohol unconditionally and categorically, as it does pork, carrion, and blood. Unlike pork, which carries the connotation of being impure in the sense of being dirty and disease-ridden, wine, according to many jurists, is in and of itself not impure; it is the effect—loss of rational control by way of intoxication, or *sukr*—that makes it objectionable. As Muslims and Western scholars have long argued, the reason for the Prophet to move against it was the drinking habits of the people of Medina, in particular Muhammad's companions, and the divisions this created.

There is some (retroactive) evidence for this. Early commentaries suggest that the people in Muhammad's entourage engaged in drinking parties, causing them to perform their prayers in a less than sober state.[21]

Viewed as an historical source, the Koran allows one to see a trajectory in the non-linear way in which it deals with alcohol (and is structured in general). Sura 16:66–7 confers a positive meaning on wine by hailing it as good nourishment and one of God's special signs to the community of true believers. Muhammad's initial warning against the misuse of wine is reflected in Sura 2:219, which insists that the risk of wine leading to sin is greater than its usefulness. As his followers apparently paid no heed to this warning, a new revelation came down in the form of Sura 4:46, which admonishes the believer not to engage in prayer in a state of drunkenness. An outright call to avoidance—referring to grape wine, or *khamr*, and gambling as satanic enticements—only appears in Sura 5:90–1.[22]

The Koran's tendency to sublimate reality by projecting it onto an idealized world finds its ultimate manifestation in the way it makes the enjoyment of wine acceptable in the afterlife. Islam clearly is not averse to pleasure. Some pleasures are just better deferred lest they disturb the social order. As if to make up for the deprivation caused by a ban on alcohol in this world, God promises (non-intoxicating) wine to the elect in paradise. Immortally youthful cupbearers will serve them under shady palm trees, and indulging will bring clear-headedness rather than befuddlement (Sura 54:17–24). The Koran thus distinguishes between terrestrial wine (impure and to be avoided) and heavenly wine (pure and divinely sanctioned). Praising wine as God's gift and recognizing it as a source of enjoyment, the Koran 'etherealizes' it by giving it a place in paradise—an ideal world without worries about corruption and decay—where, shorn of its blameworthiness, it can be enjoyed without harm or guilt.[23]

After the Prophet: Debates Among Legal Scholars

For the first three centuries of its existence, Christianity lived under a well-developed legal order—that of the Romans—and thus never generated its own separate legal system. Conversely, Islam created an empire before it appropriated several others, initially ruling over uncontested legal terrain, and thus developed a new, divinely ordained law and polity all its own, set off from the previous period of *jāhiliyya*, 'ignorance'.[24]

The Koran, only a small part of which has direct legal bearing, is unspecific about the consequences for those who violate the ban on alcohol. The treatment of drinking as one of the so-called *hadd* (pl. *hudud*) crimes—offenses against God Himself, such as murder, fornication, and serious forms of theft—would come later, under the four so-called rightly guided caliphs, and more specifically under 'Umar (r. 634–44), the second one, who is said to have played a crucial role in the institutionalization of the emerging Islamic polity. Faced with a community that persisted in its drinking habits, 'Umar, who was instrumental in the creation of an incipient judicial system, doubled the forty lashes that both the Prophet and the first caliph, Abu Bakr (r. 632–34), had decreed as suitable punishment, to eighty.[25] Conviction requiring two witnesses who attest that they have smelled the breath of the perpetrator came later as well. All this suggests a process that unfolded in stages.

Beyond the Koran, the community relied and relies for guidance on the *hadith* (pl. *ahādith*)—the corpus of traditions and presumed sayings by the Prophet and his followers that were gathered, memorized, and memorialized by later generations—which often reflect conditions at the time of their enunciation. In its attempt to organize the world as an orderly, stable universe, the *hadith* replaced the lyricism of the Koran as reflected in its tantalizing promise of wine in the afterlife, with prosaic lists of proscribed substances. The quintessential *hadith* is the one that invokes the Prophet who, responding to questions about the use of alcohol, is said to have ruled that any inebriating drink is prohibited. Wine thus became the mother of all evil, *umm al-khabā'ith*. Anyone consuming it without repenting will not enter paradise; those who drink, buy, sell, or cause others to drink it shall be cursed; and God will not accept their prayer for at least forty days. A grim fate awaits those who persist in the habit without atonement: they will die of thirst and remain parched for eternity. Their stomachs will writhe with hellfire; their heads will be covered by a crown of fire; scorpions will crowd at their feet, and snakes will coil around their necks. They will appear on Judgment Day with their faces blackened, tongues hanging out, and saliva flowing down their backs.[26]

Shiʻism, a branch of Islam that privileges the family of the Prophet, with a particular focus on the lineage through his cousin and son-in-law, ʻAli ibn Abi Talib, tends to be even more vehement than Sunni Islam in its rejection of *khamr*. For Sunnis, divine intervention in the world ended with God's final messenger, the Prophet, and his message, the Koran, which contains a moral blueprint for all time. By contrast, Shiʻis view humans as inherently prone to sin, incapable of following the rules without active guidance, and revelation therefore must be continuous, channeled through the Imams, the direct descendants of ʻAli, and especially the twelfth and last one.[27] The line between order that is God-willed as opposed to human-caused is razor-thin, and preventing the breakdown of the societal order necessitates perpetual vigilance. The Shiʻi *hadith* and law regarding alcohol are thus more explicit, their description of the punishment awaiting offenders more graphic. The repeat offender should be killed not after four but after three times, and no Shiʻi *hadith* refers to paradisical wine. In the Shiʻi imagination of hell, drinkers will be treated to *tinat al-khabal*—a pus that bleeds from fornicators and oozes from the pudenda of prostitutes.[28]

Interpretive Schools and Their Stance on Alcohol

The *hadith* ostensibly eliminates any ambivalence found in the Koran by making life conform to what is ontologically true: God and the universe He designed. Yet, following the expansion of the Muslim state beyond the confines of the Arabian Peninsula, religious exegetes continued to wrestle with the task of how to deal with a substance that was formally banished yet too seductive to be simply mandated away, the way pork was relegated to the realm of the categorically impermissible without too much resistance from either a preexisting tradition or a class of connoisseurs. Faced with a combination of textual ambiguity and alcohol's persistent lure in the newly developing community, they debated what separates fermented from non-fermented liquids and whether wine really counts as a proscribed drink if it is made from other than fermented grapes. *Nabidh* (a beverage made from fruit, usually dates, that might become mildly intoxicating through fermentation) in particular became the object of much speculation, since it is not explicitly mentioned in the Koran. Ancillary questions involved the status of vinegar and the use of cooking and storage vessels. The stance vis-à-vis such issues came to vary according to the four interpretive schools (*madhāhib*, sing. *madhhab*) of Sunni Islam.

Three of these legal traditions—the Hanbalis, the Malikis, and the Shafiʿis—reject not just grape wine (*khamr*) but any intoxicating drink regardless of the quality and origin of the product or the quantity of the intake. To arrive at this verdict, Maliki jurists relied on analogy (*qiyās*) with respect to beverages not directly specified in the Koran, or not mentioned because they were unknown at the time of its revelation. The Shafiʿis, in turn, stood out for their textual analysis of the Koran and the *hadith*, with some arguing that Koran 16:66–7 had been abrogated by 5:90–1. The Hanafis, who originated in Iraq and who came to form the majority in the Turkic world, are the most lenient of the four schools of Sunni Islam with respect to alcohol. For them, inebriation rather than the actual intoxicant (other than *khamr*) is the central issue. They differ from the other three by distinguishing between *khamr*, expressly forbidden in the Koran, and other alcoholic drinks such as *nabidh*, which are only proscribed by implication. The Hanafis point to the fact that the Prophet himself drank an undefined type of *nabidh* prepared for him by his wives. Or they referred to the wine consumed by Noah, Lot, and Jesus in the Hebrew Bible and New Testament to justify their own drinking.[29] Some Hanafi jurists took the position that if no smell is detected, no proof of intoxication exists. Other consented to the moderate use of intoxicating drinks other than *khamr*, considering only the last drink before the onset of inebriation impermissible. Or they considered *muthallath*, wine boiled down to one-third of its original volume, permissible, arguing that in the process it turns to a new substance. In later times, the Hanafis moved closer to the position of the other schools, perhaps to draw a clearer line between Muslims and non-Muslims. Yet they remained the most lenient of the four schools.[30] As we will see, their stance would have major repercussions once

European spirits began to enter the Middle Eastern market. In the late Ottoman Empire and in early republican Turkey, for instance, beer was not even classified as an alcoholic drink, and many Hanafi legal scholars countenanced the consumption of what would become Turkey's national drink, raki, if taken in moderation.

Shi'i legal scholars agree with their Sunni colleagues that the consumption of *khamr* and really of any alcoholic drink is forbidden.[31] In their preoccupation with the ritual purity of food and drink— and in particular the issue of whether one would be prevented from performing one's prayers in clothes previously soiled by alcohol—they spilled much ink over the question whether alcohol as a substance is pure, like water, or impure (*najis*), like urine and menstrual blood.[32]

Legal scholars also had different opinions about the permissibility of non-Muslims producing, consuming, and selling wine. Most agreed that Christians, Jews, and Zoroastrians have the right to manufacture and consume alcohol for their own purposes but cannot drink it in public and are not allowed to sell it to Muslims. Some argued that pouring out wine owned by a Christian is unlawful. Others did not make any distinction between Muslims and non-Muslims on this issue, arguing that, regardless of ownership, wine detected in public should be destroyed and punishment should depend on the attendant circumstances and the demands of the public interest.[33]

Aside from the four legal schools, there arose other interpretive schools in the early Islamic period, less in competition with the *madhāhib* than in parallel to them. One is that of the Murji'ites, early Islamic latitudinarians who tended to refrain from judging people's behavior, with the argument that only God knows what is in a man's heart. Consequently, the ultimate judgment about one's conduct will be rendered at Judgment Day, and it is not up to humans to preempt His verdict. While the Murji'ites did not advocate drinking, they naturally left the door open to salvation for those who did imbibe.

Another current was that of the Mu'tazilites, early Islamic rationalists who sought to reconcile the philosophical tradition of the ancient Greeks with the truth of divine revelation. Some condoned the consumption of alcohol, with the argument that God has created the world as a reflection of the celestial word and that drinking thus provides a foretaste of the wine promised to us in the hereafter.[34]

All along, there was also the tradition of 'profane ethical thought', which continued the legacy of Greek philosophy and the practical counsel of the pre-Islamic Persian tradition.[35] Here, too, it was not a question of either one or the other. A Muslim jurist might subscribe to one of the four schools and simultaneously be a follower of originally Greek, rational thinking. This interpretation has relevance for the use of alcohol as a healing substance in the Galenic tradition, which views alcohol as a medicinal agent with curative power. Numerous *ahādith* reject the use of medicinal use of alcohol. But over time, many Muslim philosophers and physicians—most notably Ibn Sina and Abu Bakr al-Razi (Rhazes, 1150–1210)—weighing the Koranic prohibition against potential health benefits, argued that alcohol could be beneficial and as such was legitimately used as a medicine.[36]

Practical Applications: Repentance and Privacy

Islamic law is often presented as a rigid system, conspicuous for its myriad theoretical minutiae that bear no real relationship to social reality or cultural context. There is an element of truth in this. *Fiqh* (Islamic jurisprudence) is essentially idealist from the outset, and its practitioners, the *fuqahā*, have tended to lose themselves in highly theoretical and hypothetical issues, self-referentially generating commentaries upon commentaries that increasingly deviate from real life. The underlying theoretical model thus continued to inform jurisprudence.[37] Yet theory inevitably was tested against reality and, as modern scholars have come to recognize, *fiqh* is thus not totally impervious to cultural context. Two features are relevant in this regard. One is that the Islamic legal system is premised on the notion that truth—other than the ultimate, ontological Truth, God—is contingent, situational, relative, and contextual. This makes for a great deal of flexibility, as is evidenced in the multiple ways in which legal scholars justified drinking alcohol other than *khamr*. The other is that, as Lawrence Rosen puts it, 'Muslim judges do not uphold the principle, or even the technicalities of the law; they uphold the social order'.[38] As already foreshadowed in the Koran, this means that, in practice, the use of alcohol is less tied to the inner level of permissibility than to its effect on the social equilibrium.

Drinking in Islam became the ultimate target of the injunction to 'command right and forbid wrong' (*al-amr bi'l ma'ruf wa'l-nahy 'an al-munkar*), which occurs eight times in the Koran and which each righteous believer is bound to engage in.[39] Yet commanding right and combating wrong is less a matter of moral absolutism than it appears to be at first glance. From the outset, the injunction was subject to several caveats and provisos, depending on circumstances. It should, if possible, take place with the 'hand'—that is, be enacted by the worldly rulers—but, failing this, it falls to the tongue—the legal scholars—and the heart—the common people—to act. Yet, in the opinion of most, zealotry, especially zealotry in invading people's private spheres, is to be avoided. Actively prying and looking for contraband, even in places where it is likely to be found, is not allowed under the maxim 'not to investigate what is not out in the open'.[40] In other words, the law pursues public problems; it does not go looking for private ones.

Personal risk is to be eschewed as well, especially if the target is a powerful ruler who might retaliate. Endangering one's life by pointing out the misdeeds of such a ruler is probably better avoided; admonition and counsel are preferable to outright rebuke. Nor should combating evil lead to evil greater than that caused by the original infraction.[41] The command thus is not necessarily to be interpreted as part of a doctrine of rebellion, where the sword comes into play. Enforcing the law through violence, after all, might lead to disorder, chaos, *fitna*; and *fitna* in standard Muslim political philosophy is among the ultimate causes of evil and thus must be avoided at all cost.[42] Other provisos include the advice only to engage in forbidding if the offender can be expected to heed the rebuke, and to perform this duty with civility, preferably in private so as not to cause embarrassment.[43] These qualifications occur in Sunni as well as in Shi'i Islam.[44]

There is also relief of a different kind for those who transgress. They can take comfort in the notion that sin can be expiated through repentance (*tawba*). The term, which occurs frequently in the Koran, connotes the idea of the individual who seeks to attain salvation and God's forgiveness by repudiating sin and embracing righteousness.[45] Sin, after all, is not innate in Islam but the willful act of turning one's back to God, which means that the act can be reversed, that the sinner can 'return' to God. As the Koran 5:39 says, 'Whoever turns (in repentance) after his evildoing and sets (things) right—surely God will turn to him'.[46] Drinking is bad, but it does not turn the drinker into a heretic, excluding him irrevocably from the community of believers or from paradise and its enjoyments. Rather, it is heretical to consider it permissible to drink alcohol.[47] It also helps if the alcohol one consumes is manufactured by non-Muslims, as this absolves the person who drinks at least to some extent from the intentionality of the offense.[48] Drinking, in sum, is not an irredeemable act.

A powerful way to redeem oneself through repentance is by foreswearing alcohol in a private moment of contrition. According to a prophetic *hadith*, a Muslim can repent and receive forgiveness 'so long as the death rattle has not occurred'.[49] It is thus not surprising that repentance in old age is a recurring literary motif. Debauchery and drinking go along with youth, but old age demands renunciation, as articulated in this poem by Abu Nuwas (*c.* 756–*c.* 814):

> Blessed be with rain my idle days when we used to revel in youthful inclinations,
> The days when my passion served as a horse, running in the field of my pleasures,
> A variety of love surrounded us, with different kinds of libertinism.
> There is nothing good in life if you're not laid down by gazelles, goblets (*wa-kasati*),
> Fragrant citrons and apples, and drinking glasses of wine (*bi-ka'sati*)
> When old age sets in, it is time to make up one's account.[50]

The context is the way authors such as Ibn Sina divided the human life cycle from the cradle to the grave into four phases. Following a pre-Islamic Hippocratic Greek model, they distinguished between 1) growth and physical development (*hadātha*), which lasts between birth and age fifteen or twenty; 2) maturity (*sibāh*) or the prime of life (*shabāb*), which lasts from age twenty until *c*. forty; 3) decline (*kuhula*), up until *c*. sixty, when some strength remains; and 4) old age (*shaykhukha*), until the end. These biological stages correspond to the four seasons, spring (temperate), summer (hot and dry), autumn (cold and dry), and winter (cold and moist).[51]

This scheme is reflected in a Koranic verse 46:15, which reads:

> We have charged each person (to do) good to his parents. His mother bore him with difficulty—his bearing and weaning are thirty months—until, when he reaches maturity, and reaches forty years, he says, 'My Lord, (so) dispose me that I may be thankful for your blessings with which You have blessed me and my parents, and that I may do righteousness pleasing to You, and do right by me concerning my descendants. Surely I turn to you (in repentance), and surely I am one of those who submit.'[52]

A man, according to this scheme, attains full strength at the age of forty. At that point he should thank God for the favors bestowed on him as well as reassess his commitments and responsibilities. He should ask God for forgiveness for his wrongdoings and engage in repentance, vowing to abandon all wrongful acts and blameworthy forms of behavior and make a renewed effort to stay on the straight path. Repentance at forty (or fifty) is the cathartic moment marking the existential realization that life is finite, that youth and the behavior that goes with it of needs must end.[53] This is the onset of what the Arabs call *al-bukā 'ala'l-shabāb*, weeping over lost youth, wistfully and nostalgically looking back on youthfulness and its vitality, when one may have been ignorant and naïve but also carefree, blithely engaged in the pleasures of drink and sex. A tradition in *al-Kafi*, a prominent *hadith* collection by the Shi'i theologian Muhammad b. Ya'qub al-Kulayni (864–941), connects this sequence to God's grace, stating that at fifty, Allah makes a man's accounting for his deeds light, and at sixty He grants him acceptance of his repentance.[54]

The (unrepentant) imbiber, finally, is offered a place of refuge of sorts in the form of the respect Islam has always shown for the privacy of the inner home, the sanctuary of a family's honor. A strong Islamic, prophetically underwritten injunction about the impermissibility of prying into people's private lives to seek out hidden sin—so as not to bring shame on them—has often provided some legal shelter against the intrusion of the state by way of a morality police.[55] The Koran 24:27–29 itself states, 'Do not enter houses other than your own, until you have asked permission and greeted those in them'. Exposing and shaming a Muslim is a great taboo, since social solidarity and communal cohesion are important virtues in traditional Islamic culture. In other words, so long as drinking and other proscribed activities remained confined to the private sphere, the community was satisfied to 'keep up appearances' by pretending that no infringement was taking place.[56] The *muhtasib* was there to check on public behavior and enforce public conformity, not to intrude into people's private lives by spying on them.

Privacy is, of course, a cultural construct. 'Privacy' was never recognized in traditional Muslim societies the way it is in the modern world, as a self-contained and autonomous category. Yet Islam's legal scholars did acknowledge and leave room for a person's need for a sphere free from intrusion. If anything, the notion of privacy in this sense only expanded over time in the Islamic world. In the early history of Islam, privacy appears to have been bound up with property rights, making approaching a legally occupied house unlawful—even, at times, when it was known as a place of misconduct, provided the misconduct did not spill into the open and threaten the stability of the community by creating a public nuisance. As of the ninth century, however, the concept of privacy evolved into a much more expansive and sophisticated, morally defined category. A measure of privacy came to signify security and peace of mind, thus undergirding a healthy society, making the mere act of closing the door signal to the outside world that the action inside is off-limits to prying eyes, with the justification that God is the ultimate arbiter of one's actions. This led prominent religious scholars such as al-Mawardi (972–1058) and al-Ghazali (1058–1111), among others, to declare spying on a person engaged in a sinful act behind closed doors unlawful.[57]

All this encouraged—and still encourages—discretion, provided a measure of protection, and fostered an unwritten albeit officially acknowledged separation between the private and the public spheres. Privacy ended up being built into subsequent legal doctrine, creating a Muslim tradition in which 'private sins lie beyond the reach of earthly judges'.[58] Even a well-known hardline jurist like the thirteenth-century Ibn Taymiyya (1263–1328) argued that 'manifest' wrongs—that is, publicly visible ones—must be acted against, whereas 'hidden' ones are a matter of individual divine punishment.[59]

Class and Status Distinctions

Keen to bring the world under the rule of transparent principles, Muslim jurists turned the ambiguities surrounding alcohol into straightforward precepts, so that over time the distinction between drinking and abstemiousness became a quasi-fixed line. Practically, though, these casuistic endeavors had to compete with reality. The actual incidence of drinking was governed less by legal matters than by power relations: the state's control mechanisms or lack thereof, perennial fiscal exigencies, and, in general, far more lax attitudes vis-à-vis personal behavior than exist in the modern world. That does not mean that legal issues were not important. They were often invoked, and punishment was at times meted out accordingly.

But other customs and traditions, some of them holdovers from pre-Islamic times, existed as well. One involves the element of class or status. An important marker of distinction in the Muslim world, though an under-researched one, is 'class' in the Weberian sense of status group. Class played a role in the consumption of alcohol. Those who drank in the Middle East hailed predominantly from the high end of the social spectrum. Piety, and with it abstemiousness, was most prevalent among the urban middle classes. The typical term used for the elite in Arabic and Persian sources, *khāssa* (pl. *khawāss*), covers a wide spectrum. It usually refers to 'a ruler's entourage or, in a more restrictive sense, the caliphal family'. But, yoking together wealth, proper education, and good breeding, it also encompasses 'people of merit and quality' and 'rich and cultivated people'.[60] This finds justification not just in the ruler who dwelled in his own moral universe, but even in the perspectivism articulated by someone like al-Ghazali, who saw authority not just as prescriptive but also as explorative, and thus advocated finding the truth by one's own investigations, arguing that a position, *madhhab*, is changeable and opens up a range of possible meanings; it varies from person to person according to what each individual can comprehend.[61]

Regarding alcohol, in almost all uses of the term, the underlying notion of the 'deserving' privileged those who legitimately enjoy a particular lifestyle. The upper classes, it will be seen in subsequent chapters, drank from a sense of entitlement, enjoying alcohol as a 'right', one of the privileges traditionally granted to the *khawāss*, in Islamic lands. Abstention was something for commoners, the *'āmma* (pl. *'awāmm*), ordinary folk, the people less well endowed with mental faculties and talent who were unable to restrain themselves. This segmented elite system is not part of official Islam; quite the contrary, the faith preaches radical egalitarianism. Such distinctions belong to an older political and social set of conventions and practices, and as such are explicitly articulated in the literature of the Middle East known as *adab*, which will be discussed in Chapter 3. Prescriptive and concerned with manners and morals, *adab* literature makes a clear distinction between the elite, the literate, the ranks of the discerning on the one hand, and the common people on the other.[62] Commoners are typically dismissed as *ra'iyat*, sheep, obedient underlings, or *awbāsh* or *radhā'il*, rabble, riffraff, the urban mob.

In sum, as with other aspects of life and society, the issue of drinking in an Islamic environment was never clear-cut, simply conforming to a presumed straightforwardness of religiously prescribed behavior. It was rather part of the multiplicity of life, officially proscribed but effectively tolerated at the margins; the beneficiary of a certain perspectivism reflecting a great tolerance for practical ambiguity.[63] The following chapters discuss how this ambiguity played out in historical time.

2

ALCOHOL IN THE PREMODERN ISLAMIC WORLD
(*c*. 600 TO *c*. 1400)

Introduction

In the heart of the Arabian Peninsula, Islam's formal ban on alcohol made from grapes was of little economic consequence. Elsewhere, particularly in lands that had been under Christian domination prior to the arrival of the faith, this rejection was ruinous to viniculture. Thus, 3,500 years of wine cultivation and production in Palestine wound down following the Arab conquest of the region in the 630s.[1] In Egypt, too, the wineries of Lake Mariotis (Buhayrat Maryut), famous in antiquity, declined with the coming of Islam.[2] Yet that does not mean that alcohol disappeared altogether from the vast area that fell under Muslim domination. On the contrary: from Andalusia in the far west to Khorasan on the eastern marches of the Islamic empire, drinking remained common following the Arab conquests. In Egypt, the consumption of wine, most of it produced in the Fayyum Oasis, seems in fact to have gone up after the Arabs took over.[3] Early Muslims are known to have been fascinated by Christian ceremony and its use of wine. Many visited monasteries in Iraq, Arabia, and Egypt for devotional reasons, but more often, it seems, to engage in forms of 'entertainment and licentiousness',

35

(*lahw wa-khalā'a*)—including drinking—not permitted in their own religion.[4] Christian celebrations, from saint festivals to weddings, also provided opportunities for Muslims to indulge.[5] As a result, many (newly converted) Muslims continued to consume alcohol with an alacrity barely dimmed by a guilty conscience.

They did so from the very beginning of the spread of Islam, the reign of the four so-called 'rightly guided' caliphs, who presided over the fledgling Islamic polity for some three decades following the death of the Prophet Muhammad in 632, during which time Egypt, Syria, and much of urban Iran was brought under their control. They continued to do so under the dynasty that took over in 661, that of the Umayyads, who definitively moved out of the Arabian Peninsula and closer to the original epicenter of late-antique viticulture by making Damascus in Syria their capital. Little changed under subsequent regimes, beginning with the Abbasids, who replaced the Umayyads in 750, nominally reigning from Baghdad until the Mongols swept in from Inner Asia, sacked the city, and ended their rule in 1258. If anything, drinking habits became more varied with the emergence of an assortment of successor regimes that held sway over much of the Islamic periphery between the ninth and the twelfth centuries. In North Africa and Egypt, these included the Fatimids (909–1171), the Ayyubids (1171–1250), and the Mamluks (1250–1517), all of whom relied on slave soldiers recruited in large part from the Caucasus and Central Asia, lands where drinking was indigenous and common. More directly influential on the world of Islam were the Persianate dynasties that emerged in the ninth and tenth centuries in what is today Afghanistan: the Samanids (819–999), the Saffarids (861–1003), and the Buyids (934–1062). Even more consequential were the Ghaznavids (977–1186), a Persian ruling house of Turkic slave origins, and the Seljuqs, a Turkic dynasty with roots in Central Asia that took control of Islam's eastern marches in the new millennium.

The Umayyads, 661–750

Most of the sources about the Umayyads were written under the dynasty that overthrew them, the Abbasids, who were obviously keen to defame their predecessors. That may be why we are relatively well informed about Umayyad drinking habits. Yet even if some of the stories in the Abbasid sources may have been exaggerated, it is clear that many Umayyad caliphs did imbibe with gusto, beginning with the second one, Yazid b. Mu'awiyya (r. 680–83), who, born of a Christian mother, proudly defied his father's admonishments to abstain, until he finally agreed not to drink any longer during daylight hours. Yazid is said to have drunk wine with the monkeys and played with the dogs, throwing parties with dancers and singers where he himself would perform until he collapsed, all of which earned him the reputation of *Yazid al-khumur* (Yazid the drunkard).[6]

Caliph 'Umar II (r. 717–20), like his namesake 'Umar I, known for his piety, banned alcohol from his court, ordered taverns destroyed and bottles broken in the newly conquered territories, and forbade *dhimmi*s from bringing booze into the Muslim army camps.[7] 'Umar II, however, was an exception to what would become an overall pattern. Following a royal Sasanian custom, some Umayyad rulers apparently drank at intervals, on alternate days, every third day, or once a week. This includes the fifth caliph, 'Abd al-Malik b. Marwan (r. 685–705), who used emetics to aid his monthly carousing; al-Walid I (r. 705–15), who held drinking parties every other day; his successor, Sulayman b. 'Abd al-Malik (r. 715–17), who indulged every third day; and even the otherwise stern and frugal Hisham b. 'Abd al-Malik (r. 724–43), who reportedly succumbed to the habit once a week.[8] The Arab theologian-littérateur al-Jahiz (776–868/9) claims that some Umayyad caliphs were not ashamed to dance or even get undressed in front of their drinking pals.[9] They might also relax with musicians and dancing girls in various hunting lodges and pleasure palaces in the Jordanian desert, sites such as Qusay 'Amra, whose walls were bedecked with frescoes of naked women.[10]

Caliphal sobriety did not necessarily include the members of his household. Hisham b. 'Abd al-Malik (r. 724–43) by all accounts was sober and austere. His favorite wife, Umm Hakim, by contrast, was a notorious drunk, her addiction symbolized by a legendary cup she owned, made of green glass mounted with a gold handle and weighing nearly 3.5 kg. This goblet was immortalized in a poem composed by al-Walid in which he mocks his detractor, Yazid, one of Umm Hakim's sons, by contrasting him, a wimp, with his vigorous mother:

Pure water fills the weakling's cup, a cup
Not like the cup of Umm Hakim ...[11]

Yazid's mother, the poet continues, imbibes such strong 'nectar' that a camel or even an elephant would be rendered 'insensible' if they drank from her cup.

No Umayyad ruler comes close to Hisham's successor, the sybaritic Caliph al-Walid II (r. 743–44), in his unbridled hedonism. The Arab historian-littérateur al-Mas'udi (896–956) called him the first caliph to summon musicians from far and wide to offer entertainment at his orgies.[12] No Umayyad ruler is said to have been given as much to wine and song as al-Walid, who more than as an ephemeral caliph, is known as a gifted poet.[13] Presented in the sources as *al-fāsiq* (the debauched one) and *sāhib sharāb* (given to wine), al-Walid has long been known as a religious deviant and incompetent ruler, a 'hopeless drunk who cavorted with singing girls and poets'. He justified his extravagant lifestyle by claiming caliphal prerogative.[14] Recent scholarly efforts to rehabilitate him have softened his religious heresy, turning him into a 'sophisticated religious thinker', yet have done little to diminish his reputation as a drunken playboy. The debauchery of the comely al-Walid indeed remains undisputed, his unholy lifestyle preceding his tenure as caliph. In 735, the reigning caliph, Hisham (r. 724–43), sought to block al-Walid's, his nephew's, succession to the caliphate by charging him with the organization of the Hajj caravan in hopes that he would disgrace himself in the process. Al-Walid did, and in fact he exceeded Hisham's expectations, turning the event into a party. He equipped the pilgrimage caravan with hunting dogs, a consignment of wine, and singing girls. Most shockingly, upon his arrival in Mecca he turned Islam's holiest shrine, the Kaaba, into a tavern by putting a tent next to it, so that he could enjoy his wine in the shade. While encamped in Mecca, he summoned the best Hijazi singers to perform for him, rewarding them handsomely.

The height of this excess came when al-Walid, now caliph, had a special bath constructed in his desert palace at Khirbat al-Mafjar, near Jericho in the Jordan Valley, filling it with wine and bathing in it. During one boozy evening, he reportedly was offered seventy cups of wine by his singing girls. He also regularly visited Christian monasteries to engage in private drinking.[15] No wonder that his son, al-Walid III (r. 744), was a model of sobriety and restraint. However, Walid III's successor, Marwan, the last of the Umayyad caliphs (r. 744–50), again stood out for his love of fun for as long as he was not engaged in war.[16]

The Abbasid Dynasty, 750–1258

In 750, a movement supportive of the Abbasids, originating in northeastern Iran, revolted against the Umayyads by hoisting their black flags of sedition, accusing the Umayyads of having betrayed the tenets of Islam. They marched on Damascus and overthrew their enemies in a welter of violence, killing all members of the family except for one, 'Abd al-Rahman, who managed to escape to Spain, where the Umayyads continued their rule until 1030.

Under the Abbasids, the center of gravity of the Islamic empire shifted eastward, away from Syria and toward Iraq, where in 762 their second caliph, Abu Ja'far 'Abdallah b. Muhammad al-Mansur (r. 754–75), established a new capital: Madinat al-Salam, the City of Peace, which in time became known as Baghdad. The Abbasids nominally reigned until 1258, when the Mongols seized and sacked Baghdad. Centuries earlier, however, they had become puppets of various emerging dynasties—most notably the Buyids and the Turkic Seljuqs—which at the turn of the millennium settled in the heartland of Islam and took actual power.

The early Abbasid rulers, as self-styled religious revolutionaries bound to show their devoutness and thus practice sobriety (in public), are said to have kept their boon companions (nudamā, sing. nadim) at arms' length by having them separated by a curtain. This custom, which went back to the Parthian and Sasanian dynasts, is said to have been introduced by the first Abbasid caliph, Abu'l-'Abbas al-Saffah (r. 750–54). Al-Mansur continued it. An emblem of piety, al-Mansur prayed regularly and often oversaw the Friday prayer personally. No one ever saw him drink anything but water. He did not serve wine to his guests either and is known to have disliked music.[17]

Aside from their first caliphs, the Abbasids proved to be worthy successors to the Umayyads in terms of the way that most of their caliphs caroused with their boon companions. The Abbasid palace, like the residences of upper-class families in general, included a *sharāb-khāna* (wine cellar) overseen by a *sāhib sharāb* (wine steward).[18] The *bon viveur* image of the cultured courtier did not just include the actual quaffing of wine but presupposed knowledge about when and how to consume it and, of course, how to come to terms with the fact that it is formally forbidden in Islam.

As was true for the Umayyads, Abbasid rulers varied in the way and the extent to which they imbibed, in a kind of generational alternation, with an indulgent ruler often succeeded by an abstemious son and vice versa. Thus, al-Mansur's successor, al-Mahdi (r. 775–85), was fond of music and poetry. He ended the seclusion established by his grandfather and mingled with his *nudamā*, stating that 'one derives more pleasure from being with and beholding them'.[19] The boon companion reached a new level of respectability at the court of Harun al-Rashid (r. 786–809), whose reign represents the high water mark of Abbasid rule. He became the constant companion of the caliph, his drinking buddy and raconteur, his confidant and conduit to society, able to keep secrets, allowing the ruler at once to lower his guard and to hear things he might not hear otherwise. For the better part of the ninth century, the office remained the monopoly of two important families, the Banu Munajjim and the Banu Hamdun.[20]

Variable information exists on the eating and drinking habits of the Abbasid caliphs over the next hundred years or so. Of al-Amin (r. 808–13), the son and successor of Harun al-Rashid, it is said that he initially cultivated an image of piousness but after four years fell into hedonistic habits including gluttony, pederasty, and drunkenness. Some of this negative portrayal may have been a matter of later historians blaming his fall and death on his bad conduct. Yet, given the fact that the libertine poet Abu Nuwas was among his boon companions, al-Amin likely did lead a rather frivolous lifestyle.[21] His son, Abu 'Ali, was much given to boozing as well.[22]

Subsequent caliphs, al-Mu'tasim (833–42), al-Wathiq bi'llah (r. 842–47), and al-Mutawakkil (r. 847–61) all employed Ahmad b. Ibrahim b. Dawud b. Hamdun as their *nadim*.[23] Al-Mu'tasim, whose reign saw the introduction of Turkish slave soldiers employed as a praetorian guard at the court, was little given to intellectual pursuits. We are short on biographical data for his son and successor, al-Wathiq, but he seems to have been given to indolence and the pleasures of court life. A poet himself, al-Wathiq patronized fellow versifiers as well as singers and musicians.[24] We are better informed about his brother and successor, al-Mutawakkil. Al-Mutawakkil frequented the Christian monasteries of Iraq and was known for his building activities as well as for hosting wine- and dance-fueled parties. It was during one of these that he was murdered by the members of his Turkish guard, the perpetrators spreading the news that he had choked on his wine.[25] One of Mutawakkil's sons, who reigned under the name al-Mu'tazz between 866 and 869, had memorized the Koran at a young age, yet would often start his benders before noon.[26] Al-Muhtadi (r. 869–70), by contrast, was an austere ruler who—taking 'Umar, the second Umayyad caliph, as his role model—prayed in a woolen garment and broke his fast on nothing more than bread, salt, oil, and vinegar. He was also actively involved in 'combating wrong', banishing liquor, dancing girls, and musical instruments from his palace.[27] Like some of his forebears, Caliph al-Mu'tadid (r. 892–902) apparently only drank on Sundays and Tuesdays, attending the remainder of the week to state affairs.[28]

Elite drinking in this period extended well beyond the caliph. Even some Muslim judges (*qādis*) are known to have imbibed. Surely the most colorful one of these is Abu'l-Qasim al-Tanukhi (d. 952), a man of refined taste and adherent of the Mu'tazilite doctrine. He belonged to a coterie around Abu Muhammad al-Muhallabi, grand vizier to the Buyid ruler Mu'izz al-Dawla, and was a regular guest of the parties that the latter threw twice a week. Attended by colleague judges and jurists, these were rowdy events that reportedly involved a golden cup weighing one thousand *mithqals* (around 4¼ kg), filled with 'delicious liquor, into which the attendees dipped their beards, sprinkling each other by "shaking off the drops"'.[29]

The antithesis of Harun al-Rashid and al-Muhtadi was al-Muqtadir (r. 908–32). A wastrel, al-Muqtadir was, at thirteen, the youngest Abbasid ruler ever to assume the office of caliph. He gave up on his responsibilities soon thereafter, leaving the affairs of state to 'women and servants, while he was busy satisfying his pleasure'.[30] With his successor, al-Qahir (r. 932–34), the Abbasids became figureheads of the Turkish slave soldier regiments. Regarding alcohol, the pendulum at this point swung again, at least in terms of outward appearances. Al-Qahir cultivated an image of austerity at his court, banning song, dance, and wine, and having singers expelled from Baghdad. This, though, was apparently merely a front designed to dispel the reputation of indulgence and immorality that had helped bring down his predecessor. Drinking, at times to the point of incapacity, was his wont. In fact, al-Qahir met his violent end—captured, blinded, and deposed by conspirators—while besotted.[31] By the time the last of the effectively ruling caliphs, Abu'l-'Abbas Ahmad ibn al-Muqtadir, commonly known as al-Radi (r. 934–40), assumed the position, little was left of a unified Abbasid realm. Al-Radi's successors were mere puppets of the Buyids, who took Baghdad in 945, and later of the Hamdanids, a Shi'i dynasty which ruled between 868 and 1014 in a region encompassing northern Mesopotamia and Syria.

This period, the mid- to late ninth century, paradoxically saw the rise of religious orthodoxy in the Abbasid realm. Under al-Ma'mun (r. 813-33) and his direct successors, al-Mu'tasim and al-Wathiq, Mu'tazilism and the Murji'i interpretation of the faith were popular, sanctioned, and indeed given a monopoly status at the court, in part because their refusal to judge man's behavior in the here and now provided perfect cover for the caliphs' unholy lifestyle. But, beginning with al-Mutawakkil, Mu'tazilism lost its status as the court's in-house philosophy, to be replaced by the far less flexible Hanbali school. Instead of speculative philosophy as practiced by the Mu'tazila, traditionalism now came to dominate at the Abbasid court. All this was a matter of process. Hanbalism would not become a discernable school until the late tenth century. Its founder, Abu Bakr al-Khallal (c. 848–923), who received his education from Ibn Hanbal's own students, still recommended private reproof in favor of active interference regarding commanding good and combating wrong.[32] Later, matters changed. The chief protagonist of the new line, a preacher and demagogue named Hasan b. 'Ali al-Barbahari (d. 941), led a series of campaigns against Shi'is and Mu'tazilites as well as practices such as the visitation of tombs. He and his men went around Baghdad ransacking shops and raiding private homes in search of liquor, musical instruments, and female singers. Reports of Hanbalites seeking to 'combat evil' by vandalizing homes and smashing wine barrels are common during later periods as well.[33]

This is also the time of the emergence of Sunni Islam as an identifiable interpretation of the faith imbued with proper legal norms, coinciding with the rise and consolidation of the ulama as its exegetes. The first reference to the office of *qādi* goes back to the last decade of Umayyad rule, but the practice of judges appointed by the caliph rather than by local governors only began in early Abbasid times. It was not until later that a judiciary autonomous from caliphal power evolved.[34] The *muhtasib*, the officer tasked to oversee the orderly and fair working of the market, checking weights and measures and the soundness of coins, comes into focus as well at this point.[35] As spelled out in treatises by al-Mawardi and al-Ghazali, by now the responsibilities of the *muhtasib* included control over public morality and extended to various aspects of public life well beyond the market, such as public baths and mosques. The *muhtasib* was also supposed to oversee the rights of and restrictions on religious minorities, the so-called *ahl al-dhimma*, mainly Jews and Christians.

The office was further institutionalized under the Buyids and their successors, the Seljuqs.[36] Under the latter, religious learning became part of the job description. Yet theory did not necessarily reflect practice. The actual *muhtasib* may have been a religiously sanctioned official, but his reputation did not always match his title. *Muhtasib*s were often feared by the general populace. Mocking verse from the Seljuq period portrays several as men of questionable morals, vainglorious characters, or sodomites who violated their own mandates.[37]

Despite this legal evolution, then as later, rulers paid little attention to the bans that they themselves might proclaim. Anti-alcohol measures also tended to target public consumption, seeking to avoid public scandal in the form of disturbances and brawls, rather than private drinking. Violators were typically fined or, less frequently, flogged or paraded in public.[38]

Alcohol in the Western Islamic World: Spain and North Africa

In a process that remains poorly understood, Islam managed to erase virtually all traces of Christianity from North Africa within a few centuries of its arrival in the region. Yet the new faith proved unable to eradicate North Africa's long-standing tradition of viticulture going back to Roman times. Medieval Arab authors describing the region mention wine made of dates, honey, and dried raisins. Wine was sold in Tunisia in the 1220s. As elsewhere, Jews were often the ones engaged in the production and trade of fermented drinks.[39]

Spain, with a climate and soil that allow the grape to grow almost everywhere, had a viticulture going back to the sixth century BCE.[40] When the Arabs invaded the peninsula in 712, they quickly adapted to its lifestyle. In keeping with their past predilections, the Umayyad rulers of Andalusia—including the most famous ones, 'Abd Al-Rahman III (r. 912–61) and al-Mansur (r. 981–1002)—were known for their fondness for wine. The latter is said to have consumed it all his life except for his final two years. His successors, 'Abd al-Malik al-Muzaffar (r. 1002–8) and 'Abd al-Rahman Sanchuelo (r. 1008–9), were serious boozers as well.[41] Many ordinary people imbibed too, mostly grape wine, while for those who wished to drink relatively guiltlessly *nabidh* was also available. Towns with strong populations of Mozarabs—Christians who did not convert—had taverns (*khammāras*) which were frequented by Muslims as well.[42]

As elsewhere, in Islamic Spain the pendulum swung quite frequently between indulgence and (officially proclaimed) abstemiousness. 'Abd al-Rahman III's son and successor, the bibliophile Hakam II (961–76), was known for his observance in the faith. Seeing that the use of wine and other alcoholic beverages had become quite common in Spain, he ordered the uprooting of all vines throughout his realm—although only at the end of his life. Hakam also proved to be well attuned to reality in other ways, as, when told by one of his counselors that this measure would spell the ruin of many poor people and that those who wished to drink would either bring wine from Christian lands or make it themselves from fruit, he revoked the order. He still ordered his officials to inflict summary punishment on all those found to be dealing in spirituous liquors, or consuming them at weddings and other festive events.[43]

The Spanish Umayyads descended into turmoil following Hakam's exceptionally peaceful rule, giving way to the so-called *muluk al-tawā'if*—Party Kings (in reference to their divisiveness, not their lifestyle)—rulers of more than thirty independent principalities, among them Toledo, Seville, and Granada. Most were lusty drinkers. Yahya b. 'Ali, who ruled the domain of Malaga between 1026 and 1035, was said to be perpetually drunk.[44] The tyrannical Badis b. Habus (r. 1038–73), a member of the Berber Zirid dynasty which held sway over Granada, remained ensconced in his palace, engaged in drinking, for such a long time that people came to believe that he had died.[45] 'Abbad II al-Mu'tadid, the ruler of Seville between 1042 and 1069, is said to have believed in only two things: astrology and wine.[46] His son and successor, Muhammad b. 'Abbad al-Mu'tamid (r. 1069–91), a well-regarded poet, sought oblivion in alcohol as the invading Murabitun—'fortress dwellers', a.k.a. the Almoravids—stood at the gates of his city.[47]

The Almoravids, followers of the Maliki school, originated as a confederation of Berber tribes in northwest Africa. Their founder, the jurisprudent 'Abdallah b. Yasin (r. 1040–59), was determined to impose a 'correct' Maliki version of Islam on his unruly constituents, a conglomerate of tribes living hardscrabble lives in the Sahara, and he proclaimed a ban on alcohol and music when he took Sijilmassa in southern Morocco. Marrakesh, founded in 1062, became the Almoravids' capital and home base after they had taken the High Atlas. In the 1060s and 1070s, they extended their control to the other urban centers of Morocco as well, at which point Yusuf b. Tashfin (r. 1061–1106) proclaimed himself *amir al-Muslimin*, commander of the Muslims, pledging allegiance to the Abbasid caliph of Baghdad.[48] In 1086, the Almoravids entered the Iberian Peninsula, after Yusuf b. Tashfin, who had been invited to assist the Party Kings of Andalusia, defeated Alfonso VI, the ruler of Leon and Castile.

The Almoravids derived their legitimacy from their efforts to purify Spain from the fiscally lax and religiously loose Party Kings.

They failed in these efforts[49] and proved in any case to be a short-lived dynasty. Barely a hundred years after taking power in North Africa, they fell under the onslaught of the Muwahhidun (Unifiers), otherwise known as the Almohads, an even more puritanical tribal dynasty that came out of the Mauritanian desert to conquer Morocco and then southern Spain in the early twelfth century. Drinking was strictly forbidden under Almohad jurisdiction, which followed the teachings of the literalist Zahiriyya school of jurisprudence (after its founder Dawud al-Zahiri [r. 815–83/4]). The dynasty's founder and spiritual leader, Ibn Tumart (c. 1080–1128/30), was a fierce critic of the practices that had gradually crept into life under Almoravid rule, including the sale of pork and wine in the markets of the Maghreb. Indeed, he abhorred drinking so much that he wrote an entire chapter on the prophetic *hadith* that proscribes it. In 1117, returning from Mecca, from which he had been expelled after wearing out the locals with his puritanical homilies, he set sail on a ship that took him from Alexandria to Mahdia in Tunisia. In a hagiographic story reminiscent of the tale of Jonah that is as famous as it is (most likely) apocryphal, Ibn Tumart is said to have harangued the sailors on board about their drinking, annoying them to the point where they threw him overboard, in part to calm a raging sea. When, half a day later, they found that he was still alive, bobbing along beside the ship, they reeled him back in.[50]

Despite these puritanical interventions, Spain under Islamic rule largely remained a land in which wine 'was in many ways part of a shared culinary culture that transcended exaggerated boundaries of difference'.[51] This remained the case as the Catholic Reconquista gathered momentum, turning ever larger parts of Andalusia into Christian-ruled principalities, until in 1492 the last of these Muslim states, Granada, fell to King Ferdinand of Aragon and his wife, Queen Isabella of Castile.

With the Reconquista, wine drinking became socially acceptable again in the Iberian Peninsula. The Moriscos, erstwhile Muslims who had been forcibly converted to Christianity but were suspected to be merely crypto-Muslims, are known to have imbibed even before they went over to the newly dominant faith. After conversion, many acquired vineyards, and consumption increased. At the turn of the sixteenth century, excessive wine bibbing and the disorderly conduct it often entailed had become so common among Moriscos that it prompted the newly acceding Christian authorities to act. Like their Muslim predecessors, they issued bans on the opening of taverns and the sale and consumption of alcoholic beverages.[52]

Egypt Under the Fatimids and the Ayyubids (996–1250)

Ibn Tumart would have been shocked to learn about the lax enforcement of Islam's strictures on drinking in Egypt. Indeed, travelers from the Maghreb at the time expressed their amazement at the relaxed attitude vis-à-vis intoxicants along the Nile.[53] Much of the information on conditions comes from European visitors, travelers, and pilgrims. One of the earliest of these is the Flemish merchant-traveler Anselm Adornes (1424–83) who visited North Africa and Egypt en route to Jerusalem in 1470. His observations about drinking in Islamic lands are as stereotypical as they ring true: Muslims, he noted, forbidden from making wine by their religion, procured it from their Christian compatriots and hypocritically consumed it under the darkness of night. Worse, he intoned, when Christians drank in their presence, Muslims rebuked them for doing so; yet, come the nightly hour, they themselves started indulging, almost always to the point of inebriation.[54] The German pilgrim Arnold von Harff, who visited Egypt two decades later, struck a similar note. He, too, told his readers that, although consuming wine was forbidden for Muslims on pain of death, many nonetheless indulged in secret.[55]

Egyptians had enjoyed alcohol since Pharaonic times. Under Islamic rule they continued to do so, albeit on a limited scale in the case of wine, in part because wine had to be imported clandestinely, mainly from Crete, and thus was expensive.[56] To the extent that they drank, ordinary people consumed *mizr*, a barley-based concoction going back to Pharaonic times. It was usually prepared at home, making prohibition virtually impossible. In due time, *mizr* seems to have been replaced by *buza*, a millet-based or malt-like beverage of low alcohol content. The elite, meanwhile, were given to drinking fermented mare's milk (*qummis*) a drink that had been introduced from the steppes of Central Asia by the Mamluks, slave soldiers who came to rule Egypt between 1250 and 1517.[57]

In Cairo, drinking and prostitution tended to be concentrated some distance away from the city, in squalid encampments on the banks of the Nile and its two islands, al-Rawda and al-Jazira, and along the canals connecting the city with the river. In time, the Bab al-Luq quarter, too, became a center of illicit activities, teeming with prostitutes who lived in miserable hovels amid rubbish heaps. As elsewhere in the Islamic world, non-Muslims—in this case Jews and Copts—were the main manufacturers and purveyors of spirits, and taverns tended to be concentrated in their quarters.[58]

In the late tenth century, Egypt fell under the rule of the Fatimids, a Shi'i dynasty with origins in modern-day Tunisia. Their most infamous ruler, the notoriously erratic al-Hakim bi-Amr-Allah (r. 996–1021) banned the consumption of wine as well as *mizr* in 1002, destroying the winemakers' shops, only to reauthorize the use of alcohol, then to ban it again. After his death in 1021, the prohibition was lifted and the atmosphere became generally one of pragmatic tolerance, except for the customary proscription during Ramadan.[59] The origin of Cairo's Wine Sellers' Street (*Darb al-Nabbādhin*) may go back to this period. The enormously large sales of grapes suggest that their output was not just for internal Jewish and Christian consumption but destined for Muslim home production. In the late summer and fall, it was often hard to find grapes in the market since most were used to produce wine.[60]

The Fatimids were succeeded by the Ayyubids, a short-lived dynasty founded in 1147 by the famous Saladin (Salah al-Din) (r. 1174–93), who was to earn his stripes as the main adversary of Richard the Lionheart during the Second Crusade. Hailing from the Iraqi Kurdish town of Tikrit, Saladin must have been thoroughly familiar with alcohol from a young age. Yet he repented and banned wine upon coming to power in Egypt, clearly with the intent of establishing his credentials as a good Islamic ruler. The ban enjoyed little popular support, though. It also soon fell into abeyance, for in 1171, with Saladin campaigning in Syria and his father, Najm al-Din 'Ayyub, administering Egypt in his name, bars and brothels reopened in Alexandria, most likely on account of the growing presence of Italian merchants in the city. These establishments must have flourished, for ten years later, with the authority undergoing another bout of religious orthodoxy, 120 of them were demolished. Conditions fluctuated for the remainder of Saladin's reign. His nephew, Taqi 'Umar, owned several venues where *mizr* was sold. Yet crackdowns on dens of iniquity are reported for 1178 and 1184, years when Saladin was again waging war in Syria and Egypt's administration was left to his relatives. In 1193, Saladin's son, 'Abd al-Malik al-'Aziz 'Uthman (r. 1193–98), succeeded him and, hard up for revenue—and given to the bottle himself—rescinded what was left of the ban, to popular relief. Two years later, when the money yielded by the newly imposed taxes fell short of the requisite royal revenue, the ruler doubled the impost and expanded the trade in wine, allowing the production to continue even during Ramadan.[61]

Mamluk Egypt (1250–1517)

The Ayyubids were succeeded by the Mamluks, descendants of Kipchaq-Turkish and Circassian slave soldiers, who began their ascent to prominence in the service of the Ayyubids and who would rule Egypt until the Ottomans conquered the country in 1517. The early Mamluks were *ghāzi*s, self-styled warriors for the faith, waging jihad against both the retreating Christian Crusaders and the infidel Mongols who at this point threatened to overwhelm the Islamic world.[62] The rise of the Mamluks in 1250 hardly betokened any significant change in Egypt's social structure, at least not immediately. Like the Ayyubids, the Mamluks were outsiders. In their case, this status was self-reinforcing, as new Mamluks were imported all the time, and many never learned Arabic, all of which perpetuated an affinity with the rough-and-tumble ways of the mountains of the Caucasus and the Eurasian steppes.

Unsurprisingly, heavy drinking was part of these ways. Taxes on vice were reintroduced under the dynasty's founder, 'Izz al-Din Aybak (r. 1250–57), the first of the Kipchaq-Turkish so-called Bahri (River) branch of the Mamluks, signaling his recognition and, effectively, toleration of formally forbidden behavior in the interest of fiscal exigencies.[63] Under the short-lived reign of Sultan al-Malik al-Muzaffar Sayf al-Din Qutuz (1259–60) this routine seems to have persisted. Drinking indeed remained quite common during the entire Mamluk period, most notably during festivals such as the (Persian) New Year (*nawruz*); the name days of local saints, or *mawlids*; weddings; and celebrations of sultanic military victories. Popular festivals were occasionally canceled because of excessive drinking.[64]

Beyond the perpetual need for tax revenue, the incidence of drinking in Mamluk Egypt depended above all on the personality and proclivities of individual rulers. The Egyptians generally seem to have put up with the unruly drunkenness of the Mamluks as the price to be paid for the measure of protection their overlords provided. The rulers, in turn, reacted differently to drinking in society. Even if they had wanted to, they would never have been able to eradicate alcohol consumption by Muslims while religious minorities were allowed to manufacture and use it for their own purposes. In practice, they only targeted public drunkenness if they had specific reasons to move against the offenders.[65] Tense relations with Christian Europe was one such reason. The second half of the thirteenth century, the height of the Crusade of Saint Louis, was rife with anti-Christian sentiment and the promotion of Islamic 'values'. It was less the rulers than preachers at the grassroots level who prepared the ground for a stricter policy on drinking in the following century. The later Mamluk period also may have witnessed a hardening of attitudes against drinking as a result of growing inter-communal conflict. The issuance of a series of decrees banning the production and consumption of wine, in a clear attempt to weaken Christian and Jewish communities, suggests as much.[66]

Information about the drinking habits of successive Mamluk rulers is uneven. The best-documented case is that of the fourth and the most consequential one, Sultan al-Zahir Baybars (r. 1260–77). Of Kipchaq-Turkish origin, Baybars started his career in 1250 as army commander in Ayyubid service, fighting the Crusaders at Mansura in Egypt. A decade later, he took advantage of the prevailing turmoil in the ranks of the Ayyubids following Saladin's death to gain power by assassinating al-Malik al-Mu'azzam Turanshah, son and heir of the reigning monarch, Salih Najm al-Din Ayyub, Baybars's formal master. In the 1260s, he led the forces that defeated the Mongols at

'Ayn Jalut in Palestine, halting their advance into Egypt, and next engaged in his second regicide by killing Sultan Qutuz during a hunting trip.

Baybars's two regicides were not the only reason for his deficit in legitimacy. Originally purchased as a slave, he was of lowly origins. To compensate for this handicap, he took the name al-Malik al-Zahir Rukn al-Din Baybars b. 'Abd Allah al-Salihi Bunduqdari, with the epithet 'Abd Allah, or 'slave of God', forging a connection with Islam and the patronymic 'al-Salihi' suggesting continuity with the Ayyubids whom he replaced. With the assistance of his official biographer-cum private secretary Ibn 'Abd al-Zahir, Baybars managed to burnish his Islamic credentials. His renown as *ghāzi*, both against the Crusaders and the Mongols, definitively established him as a ruler of impeccable moral credentials: just ('*ādil*), learned ('*ālim*), and respectful of the *shari'a*. In practice, this meant brutalizing heretical Muslims and persecuting Christians, pillaging their churches.[67] Otherwise, Baybars proved to be an effective ruler who solidified the union between Egypt and Syria. In time, he came to be likened to Solomon and Joseph, and was even called the 'Alexander of the Age' (*Iskandar al-zamān*).[68] Such was his fame that well into the nineteenth century his life's story was recounted in Cairo's coffeehouses.[69]

Baybars's stance regarding alcohol reflects his status as a self-styled Muslim champion.[70] He ordered the closing of places selling wine at various times during his reign.[71] He also launched an anti-vice campaign in Syria while he was battling the invading Franks in those parts. He is known to have destroyed winehouses and brothels, and put drunken soldiers to death. Alcohol went underground as a result. Yet Baybars did not practice what he preached: he is known to have died from an overdose of (possibly poisoned) *qummis* while watching a polo match in Damascus in 1277.[72]

Baybars was succeeded by a series of rulers whose stance vis-à-vis vice was informed more by their Central Asian background—which was constantly reinforced with the ongoing purchase of fresh slaves from the region—and their own personal predilections than by the tenets of Islam. The most illustrious of these rulers was Mansur al-Qalawun (r. 1279–90), a Kipchaq Turk called al-Alfi ('One Thousand'), in reference to the fact that he had been bought for the unusually high price of 1,000 dinars by an *amir* in the service of the Ayyubids. Sultan al-Qalawun initially allowed drinking in his orbit, but in 1280 he suddenly ordered any wine found in his realm to be poured out as part of an overall ban on the sale of intoxicating substances. Al-Qalawun was initially succeeded by his son Malik Khalil, the sultan who struck a decisive blow to the Crusaders by ejecting them from Palestine in 1291. He allowed alcohol to be sold and consumed again, and he drank wine himself, even during Ramadan.

After Malik's assassination in 1293, Al-Qalawun's younger son, Nasir Muhammad (r. 1293–94; 1299–1310, 1310–40), took over as sultan of Egypt. He stood out as a patron of the arts, yet his was a turbulent reign. He was first installed as sultan at age eight, but remained a puppet of various warlords until he finally consolidated his power in 1310. At first, Nasir Muhammad shunned alcohol as much as Baybars had, and for the same religiously inspired reasons. An earthquake that struck Cairo in 1302–3, retroactively attributed by the historian al-Maqrizi (d. 1442) to the whoring and boozing that was rife (by his reckoning) in the city at the time, must have strengthened Nasir Muhammad's aversion to sinful conduct. He kicked off his third and final accession in 1310 by issuing an edict against the fermentation of wine and the sale of alcohol. The taverns of Cairo were torched and their owners beaten. Fantastic amounts of wine, at one point reportedly numbering 1,202 vessels, were periodically discovered. Offenders could potentially have their noses cut off and their eyes gouged out. Christian and Jewish shops were included in the sweep as well, with even those who only served their co-religionists seeing their stocks destroyed. Mobs also ransacked Coptic churches, getting drunk on the sacramental wine found in the cellars. Domestic viticulture largely disappeared as a result.

As al-Maqrizi tells the story, the campaign—led by a zealous prosecutor named Al-Malik—ferreted out many violators and uncovered a huge storehouse which served as a 'den of iniquity frequented by drunkards and fornicators', with the Mamluk soldiers stationed in Cairo being its best customers. What is more, it seems that the sultan himself had used the enterprise as a revenue-raising scheme by sanctioning the activities of alcohol-purveying Armenians while taking a cut of the profits. So long as Nasir Muhammad ruled, Al-Malik was told to stay quiet about these corrupt practices. But, after rising to the position of viceroy under Nasir's ephemeral successor, Salih Isma'il, Al-Malik had the tavern-cum-brothel demolished and the Armenians dispersed. He followed up with a general anti-vice campaign that included the banning of illegal ram and cockfighting, fortune-telling, wrestling, and swordplay. Scofflaw soldiers were put to death.[73]

The four decades following the reign of Nasir Muhammad were marked by great instability. Mainly to blame for this was the Black Death of 1349–65, which may have carried off some one-third of Egypt's population.[74] The 1380s also saw a monetary crisis and a cratering economy. Two decades later, a new Central Asian warlord, Timur Lang (Tamerlane), invaded Syria. Throughout, Egypt was poorly governed. Nasir Muhammad's son and successor, Al-Malik al-Mansur Abu Bakr (r. 1341), was a forgettable figurehead operating in a vortex of competing forces. Barely three months after his enthronement, he was arrested and sent to prison, accused of debauchery. His successor, Nasir Ahmad, ruled mostly from his desert castle at Karak, where he engaged in frivolous pastimes, for the brief months that he was in power in the first half of 1342. Later that year, with the accession of the adolescent Sultan al-Salih Isma'il (r. 1342–5), the political climate momentarily changed and a brief period of stability followed. Salih Isma'il—or, rather, his deputy, Al-Malik—did everything in his power to make Egyptians abide by the law of Islam, which meant cracking down on 'corrupt' activities such as drinking and prostitution. This included destroying the encampments on al-Rawda Island, traditionally rife with drugs, booze, and prostitution. He also sought to prevent the Franks from importing wine into Egypt via Alexandria.[75] Kamil Sha'ban (r. 1345–6), another of Nasir Muhammad's sons, succeeded Salih Isma'il in 1345. Given to revelry, he proved to be another ephemeral dynast.[76] The last effective Bahri ruler, Malik al-Ashraf Nasir al-Din Sha'ban (r. 1363–77), was different. Firuzabadi, whom we encountered as the lexicographer who catalogued 357 terms for wine, praised him for having 'raised aloft the lamp of the faith and commanded the wine-jars to be smashed'.[77]

The Circassian Burji Mamluks, who in 1382 officially took over from their Bahri rivals, were no less colorful than their predecessors. As before, instances of open drinking alternated with clampdowns, depending on the character of the ruler and the political temper of the times. The first Burji Mamluk ruler, Sultan al-Malik al-Zahir Barquq (r. 1382–9; 1390–9), became notorious for his banquets, one of which degenerated into scenes of public drunkenness. During the *mawlid*—the festival of the Prophet's birthday—of 1588, 150 empty jugs were reportedly left near the lodge (*zāwiya*) of the Sufi Shaykh Isma'il, bearing testimony to the quantity of wine consumed.[78] Sultan Barquq also oversaw a ritual whereby he and his grandees would gather once a week in the hippodrome beneath Cairo's citadel to drink *qummis* from china bowls. This custom, together with the officially sanctioned celebration of *nawruz*, seems to have ceased with the ruler's death in 1399.[79] The sources are silent about the consumption of *qummis* among the Mamluks after Barquq's reign, suggesting they had become acculturated to a degree to a Muslim environment by that time.[80]

Barquq's son and successor, Sultan al-Nasir Faraj (r. 1399–1405; 1405–12), outdid his father in his dissolute lifestyle, gaining notoriety for the cruelty he inflicted on his entourage during drunken rampages. In 1405, during one of his regular drinking bouts, he jumped into a pool with some of his fellow revelers and almost drowned, causing a brief interruption in his rule. At the same time, his reign saw much violence directed against the wine business of Cairo's Copts, whose stocks and production facilities in Shubra, a suburb of Cairo, were destroyed at his orders in 1401.[81]

The ninth Burji Mamluk ruler, Ashraf Barsbay (r. 1422–38), was pious and sober. His reign also brought some stability in Egypt, even if the period was punctuated by several outbreaks of the plague, which resulted in great loss in agricultural output and severe demographic decline. The search for scapegoats this prompted helps to explain the surge in violence against non-Muslims that occurred in this period.[82] Five years into his reign, Barsbay proscribed the use of wine and hashish. Faced with a resurgence of the vice, he reaffirmed the ban, and had transgressors flogged and wine stores and hashish dens destroyed. In 1437, with the plague raging again, the sultan ordered his troops to break into the houses of Cairo's Christians and Jews and smash all the amphorae they could find.[83] The reign of Barsbay's successor (after a three-month reign by his son), the pious al-Zahir Jaqmaq (r. 1438–53), too, saw attacks by thirsty Mamluk soldiers on Christian houses and their cellars.[84]

The reign of al-Ashraf Qaytbay (1468–96) counts as the Indian summer of the Mamluks, a period of stability and relative prosperity. Sultan Qaytbay became known for his piety and charity. In 1472, while performing the Hajj, he was struck by the poverty of the people of Medina and moved to spend part of his own fortune to alleviate their plight. Ibn Iyas, the period's principal historiographer, insists in his obituary of Qaytbay that the sultan 'never drank wine, nor indeed any inebriating substance'.[85] Obituaries, of course, are never the place to look for the unvarnished truth about someone's life, and, even if true for the most part, at least one exception to the sultan's rectitude is on record. In 1477, he undertook a journey to Syria. Upon arrival in Damascus, seeking to ingratiate himself with the local population, he organized a shindig that included wine.[86]

Bilād al-Shām, the Land of Syria

Heavily contested territory, Syria suffered much turmoil between the twelfth and sixteenth century. From 1127 to 1183, Aleppo and its environs were ruled by the Turkic Zangid dynasty. In 1183, Saladin captured Syria. The region remained under Ayyubid control until the Mongols invaded and briefly seized Damascus in 1260. After four decades of Mamluk-Mongol warfare, Syria reverted to Mamluk control in 1303. Aside from the destructive interlude of Timur Lang's occupation of Damascus in 1400, it would remain in Mamluk hands until the Ottomans seized the land in 1516.

The Zangids resembled the various Egyptian regimes in their see-saw relationship with alcohol. Their founder, 'Imad al-Din Zangi (r. 1127–46), enjoyed his wine. His son, Nur al-Din Mahmud (r. 1147–74), by contrast, was known for his piety; he upheld a strict Islamic code and did not allow alcohol and music in his army camp. His son, Malik al-Sultan, continued to uphold this regime. As the story goes, at one point Malik al-Sultan was ill and his doctors advised him to drink alcohol, a prescription countenanced by the religious leaders in his entourage. But he rejected the advice with the argument that he would not attain heaven if he engaged in drinking. After his death, Sayf al-Din Gazi b. Mawdud, Nur al-Din's nephew, took over the town and region of Mosul. He got rid of the ban and again allowed the sale of alcoholic drinks. This tolerance did not last long, though. In 1179–80, a serious drought brought the people of Mosul out praying for rain and pleading with their ruler to reaffirm the proscription. Sayf al-Din acceded to this request, allowing people to plunder venues where booze was sold and served.[87]

Like Egypt, Mamluk-controlled Syria witnessed various instances of violence that targeted drinking but were in fact directed against non-Muslims themselves rather than just alcohol. Small wonder then that the Christian population of Damascus, apparently relieved to be freed from Muslim oppression, celebrated the arrival of the Mongols in March 1260 by ostentatiously holding a procession and sprinkling wine on Muslims and their mosques, knowing themselves protected by their new overlords. When the Mongols withdrew six months later, the Muslims took their revenge by destroying churches, ransacking Christian homes, and killing their inhabitants.[88]

Information on the state of alcohol in Syria in the last two centuries before the Ottomans took over is sparse. In the 1300s, the country, now again under Mamluk control, was subjected to the religious zeal of Ibn Taymiyya (1263–1328), who had wine cellars in Damascus and Tripoli vandalized.[89] Success was limited and certainly temporary, however. A century later, soldiers stationed in Damascus, known for their love of alcohol, were allowed to drink without too many problems. They were also in the habit of protecting the city's wine merchants while operating at least 100 wine presses. At one (unspecified) point, this provoked the ire of Damascus's pious denizens, prompting a fanatical local Sufi leader named Shaykh Mubarak al-Qabuni to launch a campaign against hashish as well as alcohol, with the aim of having taverns serving at prohibited hours shuttered. Christians and Jews caught drinking were targeted as well. When Mubarak was arrested, serious disturbances erupted between his Sufi followers and Mamluk soldiers irate at the curtailment of a prerogative they had typically enjoyed in exchange for providing a modicum of security for the locals.[90]

The Eastern Half of the Islamic Empire

The rulers of medieval Syria and Egypt were mostly descendants of slave soldiers hailing from the Caucasus and the steppes of Eurasia, their drinking habits naturally influenced by those of their ancestors. The popularity of *buza* in Egypt attests to this. Matters were little different in the eastern half of the Islamic empire, encompassing Central Asia, modern Iran, and Afghanistan. The successive dynasties holding sway in that vast region all had non-Arab roots. The Samanids and the Saffarids were Persian; the Ghaznavids originated as Turkic slave soldiers; and the Seljuqs were fully Turkic in origin. If anything, all drank at least as exuberantly as the rulers of Spain, Egypt, and the Levant.

The rulers of the ninth- and tenth-century Samanid and Saffarid dynasties, the first to achieve autonomy from their Abbasid overlords, are known for the gusto with which they and their entourage indulged in wine drinking at convivial gatherings known as *majālis-i sharāb* (wine sessions) and *majālis-i uns* (friendship sessions). The Saffarid ruler Abu Ja'far (r. 922–63), for instance, is said to have been drinking day and night.[91] Modern Persian poetry, which originated at their courts in mostly panegyric form, is replete with scenes of royal wine bibbing. This includes the lyrics of Rudaki and Manuchihri, who are today celebrated as the pioneering masters of Persian poetry. The former served the Samanids; the latter was employed at the court of the Ghaznavid Sultan Mas'ud (r. 1030–40).

The dynasty that took over from the Samanids, the Ghaznavids, stand out for the heavy drinking of its elites as well. Its founder, Sultan Mahmud of Ghazna (r. 998–1030), managed to combine serious carousing with sound statecraft, although just barely, as is evident from this famous anecdote. One day, in a drunken haze, Mahmud ordered his favorite (Georgian) slave, Malik Ayaz, to cut off his locks—the emblem of the boy's youthful beauty. Ayaz perforce complied. Mahmud went to sleep and woke up the next morning realizing the irredeemable harm he had done. This left the ruler in such a foul mood that no one dared approach him. The poet laureate 'Unsuri (d. 1039/40) thereupon was asked to compose something appropriate to the occasion. He wrote the following poem, encouraging his master to drink more wine to cheer himself up:

> Though shame it be a fair one's curls to shear
> Why rise in wrath or sit in sorrow here?
> Rather rejoice, make merry, call for wine
> When clipped the cypress doth most trim appear.

Mahmud was so pleased with the result that he regaled 'Unsuri with three mouths filled with jewelry, after which he summoned dancers and singers for a wine-soaked party that lasted into the night. [92]

Sultan Mahmud died in the spring of 1030, to be succeeded by his son Muhammad. Whereas the father had kept his drinking from interfering with state management, Amir Muhammad spent most of his time engaged in frivolous pastimes. His alcoholic insouciance contributed to the brevity of his rule—barely five months—as it quickly exposed his realm to foreign attack. When Muhammad finally acted on his retainers' advice to get ready to march, he found out that he had lost power and popularity with both the military and the people, and he was soon replaced by his brother Mas'ud. [93]

Mas'ud was hardly an improvement over his brother. As told by Abu'l-Fazl Bayhaqi, the main Ghaznavid historiographer, Mas'ud quaffed copiously, day and night, capable of drinking all of his boon companions under the table and still leading prayers in the morning. Competitive drinking sessions lasting multiple days and filled with song and dance are described in great detail by Bayhaqi, who portrays these without censure, clearly perceiving royal wine bibbing in the context of *adab*, living in sophisticated style, rather than with an eye to religion. [94] In one such scene, the Turkish army general Ayaruq held a drinking session lasting four days that put him out of commission, only to be summoned to a drinking banquet by Amir Mas'ud. Ayaruq tried to excuse himself by referring to his drunken state, but, unable to shirk the princely 'invitation', he set out for Mas'ud's court with an entourage consisting of 200 foot soldiers. Still fuddled, as he sat in the waiting room and contemplated returning home on account of his state, he scooped ice out of a water pitcher held out for him, completely oblivious to his impending fate, for the invitation had been a pretext to have him arrested and executed for sedition and massive embezzlement.[95]

Even more vivid is Bayhaqi's description of the fate of Hasanak, the former vizier of Mahmud and erstwhile governor of Khorasan, who had fallen out of favor and was accused of disloyalty. (He had shown allegiance to the Shi'i Fatimids of Egypt, and had supported Amir Muhammad in the succession struggle from which Mas'ud emerged the winner.) In early 1032, Hasanak was executed, stoned, and strangled at the orders of the caliph. Bayhaqi relates in gruesome detail how during a banquet his severed head, covered by a dome, was brought in on a platter garnished with fresh fruit and presented to the wine-bibbing guests among the sequence of dishes.[96]

Mas'ud kept up his reputation as one of history's champion boozers until the very end. On 22 September 1040, shortly before his defeat in battle, imprisonment, and death, he is said to have bested all his boon companions by downing (a clearly exaggerated) twenty-seven bumpers of wine, each containing about a quart, after which he went on to perform his noon prayers.[97]

The Ghaznavids in time gave way to the next Turkic dynasty—and the first to arrive from Central Asia not as slave soldiers but of their own volition—the Great Seljuqs. They took Baghdad in 1055, overthrowing the Buyids, and ruled until the early thirteenth century. Like other Turkic invaders, the Seljuqs had to earn their Islamic credentials. They thus had their chroniclers portray them as God-fearing, submissive to the caliph, generous to the poor, and, above all, defenders of the true (Sunni) faith against internal heresy. Recent scholarship has cast doubt on this pious image. If the Seljuqs acknowledged the Abbasids, this was mainly a form of political expediency. They appear to have been anything but religiously orthodox and were hardly concerned about restoring (Sunni) Islam. The record also shows that they engaged in much destruction when Tughril Bey and his troops entered Baghdad in 1055.[98]

Seljuq narratives portray the first rulers of the dynasty in particular as upstanding without necessarily hiding their flaws, their greed, unbridled sexuality, and alcoholic excess. Tughril and Alp Arslan in particular come across as fervently religious. With the later ones—Mahmud, Mas'ud, Sulaymanshah, and Muhammad II—debauchery gains momentum in the chronicles.[99] The *Jāmi'a al-tavārikh* thus describes wine-fueled banquets at the court of Alp Arslan (r. 1063–72).[100] Abu Sa'id Taj al-Dawla Tutush I (r. 1078–94), the Seljuq *amir* of Damascus, regularly drank himself into oblivion. The main ruler of the dynasty, Malikshah (r. 1072–92), who is remembered as a just king, was rather bibulous as well, spending his days in frivolous entertainment and dubious company. Malikshah's uncle, Qara Arslan Ahmad Qavurt, who contested the sultan's authority and was executed by him in 1073, ruined his reputation by indulging day and night.[101] Sultan Sanjar, one of Malikshah's sons, began his reign as a toper but repented and ended up outlawing booze in his realm.[102] Another son, Muhammad Tapar (r. 1105–18), who held sway in Baghdad at the same time that Sanjar ruled Khorasan, is by contrast remembered as an upstanding ruler: pious, chaste, and truthful.[103]

The last Seljuqs resembled most of their predecessors in their love of drinking. Sultan Malikshah III (r. 1152–53) was generous and good-natured but also 'adored drinking, hunting and sexual intercourse', and was deposed for spending all his time in such frivolous pursuits. His brother Muhammad, on the other hand, was known as a pious ruler with great regard for the ulama. The brief reign of his nephew, Sulaymanshah (r. 1160–1), ended with his forcible removal due to his 'unremitting inebriation'.[104]

About a century after the Seljuqs splintered into a series of successor dynasties, a new force emerged from Inner Asia and overwhelmed the eastern half of the Islamic world. The Mongols, who came to rule under the name Ilkhanids, had a well-earned reputation for binge drinking. *Qummis* was integral to their society, bound up with the very idea of what it meant to be a Mongol.[105] Visiting Christian missionaries recounted how the Mongols considered drunkenness an honorable state. So obsessive was their boozing that the young age at which most Mongol leaders died has been attributed in part to their alcoholic habits.[106]

Once the Mongols adopted Islam under Ghazan Khan (r. 1295–1304), they were bound to patronize the faith.[107] Ghazan Khan's efforts to tamp down on drinking must be seen in this light. His approach to alcohol was not devoid of realism, though: 'Even if we forbid [intoxication] absolutely', he is said to have observed, 'it will not go away'. Instead of the customary eighty lashes, he thus ordered anyone found drunk to be 'arrested, stripped naked and tied to a tree'.[108] His successor, Öljeitü (r. 1304–16), portrayed as a religious reformer by his grand vizier and chief propagandist, Rashid al-Din, followed suit by refraining from drinking alcohol, including *qummis*.[109] Following severe hailstorms in 1320, Abu Sa'id (r. 1316–35), the last effective Ilkhanid ruler, heeded his religious advisors' advice and had taverns and brothels closed in his realm.[110]

3

WINE IN ISLAMIC PAINTING, POETRY, AND *ADAB* LITERATURE

Introduction

Islam from the outset manifested itself in multiple ways. There was, of course, the 'formal' faith and its tenets. But, as in any society and culture, strict rules did not preclude good living, humor, lightness, and deviance. Indeed, the stricter the rules, the greater the need for relaxation. Piety for most Muslims did not stand in the way of the enjoyment of life, and bigotry generally met with little approval. Nor did faith necessarily obviate reason, doubt, and disputation. So next—and at times in opposition to— 'official', orthodox Islam, a set of beliefs and practices emerged that reflected urges and inclinations that fell outside the scriptural corpus contained in the Koran and the *hadith*. These included the realm of song and dance, as well as the domain of rational inquiry and skepticism. They also involved inner life, contemplation, and experiencing the divine in different, more intimate ways than provided for in the formal faith. Those operating in this alternative universe paid serious attention to the human element in the world, stemming from a belief that God has created everything for a purpose, that all humans share the same features as well as a common origin and destiny, and that diversity and tolerance of it are thus natural and proper.

All this is visible in the arts of Islam, in painting as well as in literature, and above all in poetry. The artistic realm also left room for the female voice, marginal to the 'official' manifestations of the faith, and gave free rein to the contemplative element in Islam. Moreover, it allowed contrarians—those who found reason to criticize or even poke fun at outward religion, its dogmas, and its hypocrisies—to express themselves. Even *mujun*—ribaldry, libertinism, and debauchery—was a mode widely practiced and accepted, following the notion that if God has created the universe in its entirety, this of course includes doubt and skepticism, and even the vulgar and the obscene.[1] The representatives of these strands of Islam come in different varieties, from philosophical rationalists to humoristic polemicists, those who played with ambiguity, pointed out the contradictions in religious revelation, and declared organized religion to be stilted and even superfluous; mocking the ulama and their pretensions; even branding prophets as magicians or charlatans.[2]

Wine is integral to this world, both as a substance and as a metaphor celebrating the beauty of creation and sublimated love, or representing contrariness and transgression. Since alcohol was formally outlawed, its link to reality was tenuous and strained. Wine (there is no *qummis*, raki or vodka in Islamic art) thus became a metaphor for the ardent feelings of the lover for the beloved in the imaginary world of painting and (mystical) poetry. Especially in the eastern half of the Islamic universe, in what today is called the Persianate world, art exuberantly celebrates wine as an object of pleasure and beauty, as well as a symbol of love, including divine love. Wine became 'a muse, a lifeblood sustaining an entire intellectual, social, and moral worldview'.[3] In classical Persian poetry, wine— whether presented literally or metaphorically—stands for worldly pleasure and often represents the tension between the religion that celebrates it (Zoroastrianism) and the faith that condemns it (Islam). In this, it associates the former with the good life while rebuking the dogmatism of the latter with 'flippant contempt'.[4] Wine in the Persian mystical universe became associated with Zoroastrianism through the *kharabāt-i Mughān* (the Magian taverns of ruin).[5]

The visual arts of especially the eastern Islamic world abound in drinking, portrayed in ways that are alternatively imaginative and realistic. There is often an element of 'disassociation', a reticence about displaying untoward behavior in the way alcohol is presented in Islamic art. For one, images of drunkenness seldom appear in royal frontispieces. It is usually also a courtier, not the ruler himself, who is depicted inebriated. This often adds a humorous element to the image, that of the wasted, semi-conscious official who is dragged away from the scene of royal revelry.[6] Yet paintings—especially from the Mongol and post-Mongol Persianate world, most of which appear in the form of illustrated manuscripts—are anything but furtive in the way they portray rulers, courtiers, or mystics engaged in carousing. Drinking is shown as a natural pastime, in the same way that it is described in many texts. Rulers and members of the upper classes, courtiers, and high-level bureaucrats all had their own wine cellar (*sharāb-khāna*), as well as a private sommelier (*sharābdār*).[7]

The pictorial repertoire of the post-classical period abounds in images of wine and wine-fueled banquets. The way it represents drinking varies. Some scholars see a mystical element in men and women dallying with cups and carafes of wine. But in scenes where women appear in seductive, sensual poses or where a man and woman embrace in amorous ways, a half-empty bottle by their side, wine seems to signal the intoxication of worldly love, infatuation, and eroticism.[8] Many paintings show ornately dressed cupbearers or elegant, finely attired women in dreamy poses offering wine in small chinaware cups on gold trays, typically to an invisible recipient—the shah, who is rarely shown in such compromising scenarios. These may appear as imaginary and idealized figures; yet, given what we know about the important role alcohol played at the Safavid court, it is more plausible to assume that they are the visualization of a wine-soaked palace culture, reflecting a measure of realism and possibly even portraying living models.[9]

Uniquely in early modern Islamic (and wider Asian) art, seventeenth-century Iranian painting evinces a remarkable receptivity to contemporary European art. Many Safavid paintings reflect a fascination with Europeans and European patterns and motives that expresses itself in a hybrid, so-called *farangi-sāzi* ('Europeanizing')

65

style of painting, the result of Iran's encounter with the output of a small number of Dutch painters who worked for the royal court in the early seventeenth century. Some of these depict Europeans in multiple poses, in which they are associated with various symbols beyond the headgear that throughout Asia was considered typical of Westerners. The most striking of these is the European man hovering over a voluptuous nude or semi-nude woman in a provocatively reclining pose. Another one is the lapdog at the side of the European. A third is alcohol, either in the form of a cup in the European's hands or a decanter by his side. At times, the two are depicted together, and some paintings show dogs drinking from a wine cup held by a European in a hat—suggesting a long-standing association of Westerners with alcohol.[10] In all cases, the tone is lighthearted or even humorous, the artist apparently making fun of Europeans for what must have seemed a silly attachment to their pets, or pitying them for their avowed monogamy or—in the case of Catholic missionaries—their incomprehensible celibacy. Yet such paintings lack any overt disapproval.[11]

Oenophilia permeates Persian(ate) visual culture. There is no better illustration of this than a wonderful miniature from Herat dating from the 1520s Worldly and otherworldly drunkenness (Fig. 2) accompanied by a verse from Iran's most beloved poet, Hafez of Shiraz (1325–90): 'The angels of mercy raised the cup of the pleasures of intimate company.' To Ahmed, this painting 'represents the denizens of both the seen and unseen worlds engaged in the same activity: wine-drinking'. Wine is, in his words, diffused through the entire canvas of existence as depicted in the painting. In Ahmed's interpretation, the activity of drinking wine operates on various levels. At the lowest, terrestrial level, wine serves as a medium of social intimacy. At the second level, that of the spatial hierarchy of existence, wine is raised up via a knotted rope to become a source of meaningful conversation and contemplation. Finally, on the most ethereal level, wine is transmogrified into the drink that links the world of the seen to that of the unseen, representing the two sides of Revelation of Truth.[12]

Another 'mutually-constitutive relationship between wine and Islam in history' can be found in the celebratory inscriptions on various wine vessels made for or acquired by the Mughal Emperor Jahangir (r.

1605–27), which proclaim this wine-bibbing ruler not just a defender of Islam, a 'world-seizing' Muslim warrior (the meaning of 'Jahangir'), but an illuminated 'knower of the signs, real and metaphorical'. A (rare) gold coin that depicts the same ruler with a wine cup conveys the same message, connecting him to Alexander and the Prophet Khizr, two powerful symbols of fame and immortality.[13]

Such ambivalence persisted above all in the Iranian tradition. The boundaries between private and public remain unclear in the intriguing paintings that survive from the eighteenth-century Zand period. But the romantic ambiance, depicting both male and female lovers in daring, provocative poses, with diaphanous blouses, wine glass in hand, breathe just enough verisimilitude into the images to rise above the mere ornamental or metaphysical level of traditional Persian art.[14]

It is in Islam's literary corpus that wine plays the most conspicuous role. This is especially true for its poetic repertoire. Poetry written in Arabic continued a pre-Islamic Arabian tradition. Persian poetry originated in the ninth century and was first declaimed at the courts of the Samanids and the Ghaznavids in the form of panegyrics praising the ruler, his valor, and his generosity. Typically written upon sultanic command or invitation, it presents and describes wine rather factually, as the natural accompaniment of the sophisticated court life. Some poets hint at a sense of unease toward endorsing a practice repugnant to Islam, but their works hardly portray wine as intrinsically sinful.[15] Indeed, much lyrical Persian poetry would possess little vigor and spirit without wine. Whenever the poet speaks of joy and happiness, wine is usually one of the key elements; conversely, whenever there is a murmur of sorrow, its only cure is wine. An excellent example is *Vis and Ramin*, an eleventh-century Persian-language romance by Fakhr al-Din Gurgani, which harkens back to pre-Islamic Iranian court culture in its treatment of wine— as an integral aspect of the ruler's enjoyment.[16]

Wine in Poetry: The Khamriyya

More than any art form, poetry written by Muslims has always used an endless array of ways to evade the strictures of Islam in its depictions of wine. One is that of the traveler who is exempt from the obligation to fast during Ramadan. The thirteenth-century poet Safi al-Din al-Hilli equates drink with the food that the wayfarer is allowed to consume during the month of fasting:

> Come with me if you're wise,
> Let's drink wine with young and old.
> For fasting's not for one like me travelling
> Fast from the table, jug in hand in July.
> This is the ruling of Muslim sages
> And the Prophet's words, on whom be peace,
> Some even say the fast is wrong at times:
> If one who fast will die, then he must eat.[17]

Another one is the time-honored tradition of praising alcohol for its invigorating and restorative qualities. This 'excuse' found many adherents among poets, who hailed wine as a balm on the tongue that increases the passions, chases away bad thoughts, brings opposites together, softens hard hearts, gives the coward courage, and opens the pockets of misers.[18]

Many poets, ignoring the faith—indeed, building on wine's forbidden-fruit status—unapologetically associated wine with a man's joy and pleasure. As Abu Nuwas (*c.* 757/8–*c.* 814) says:

> I see no pleasure, nor enjoyment
> Nor success, till the glass is in sight
> What a weapon wine is for a man
> Assailing woe, and forcing its flight
> Such wonders has wine that it could
> Rid the miser of his spite
> There's no life save that of drinking
> From the morning till the night
> Never shall I leave a glass, nor
> Accept in love, those who indict.[19]

There is a self-consciously subversive element in this poem by Manuchihri (1000–*c.* 1040):

> I like my slave-boy and my wine glass
> This is no place for blame or contempt

I know that both are forbidden.

It's this very 'forbidden' that makes them so pleasurable. [20]

The celebration of wine culminates in the wine poem, *khamriyya*, a term coined in the twentieth century to denote a genre of Bacchic poetry that goes back to pre-Islamic times. As was seen in Chapter 1, various pre-Islamic poets drew their inspiration from wine, and their way of expressing themselves, surviving the Islamic proscription, thrived in the eighth-century Umayyad state, to culminate at the court of the Abbasids. [21] Several themes developed by later poets, such as those of the boon companion (*nadim*) and the cupbearer (*sāqi*), were already present in the famous pre-Islamic collection of poems known as the *mu'allaqāt* ('suspended odes').

Pre-Islamic poets provided a model for a balanced life by recklessly flouting 'norms of caution and reasonable self-interest'. In the Islamic period, the poet remained a marginal figure whose work evoked the type of disorder and normlessness that confirmed the prevailing structure. Indeed, his license to engage in irreverent talk was validated by the Koran itself (26:226), which states that poets say one thing and do something else. [22] The transition from pre-Islamic to Islamic poetry is represented by someone like Abu Mihjan al-Thaqafi (d. 638), a *jāhili* poet—and a companion of the Prophet, no less—who was flogged and banished several times for drinking wine during the caliphate of 'Umar. Disregarding the ban on wine while reminding his audience of its life-imbuing quality, he wrote:

> When I die, bury me beneath the vine, that its roots may give drink to my bones (do not bury me in the desert, for I fear lest I never taste wine after death), that my flesh may be refreshed by saffron wine, and I'll be its captive who once used to lead it captive. [23]

If it remains unclear if the *khamriyya* genre is originally Arabic, it did associate wine with Persia's pre-Islamic kings, especially the Sasanians. [24] Persian poets practicing the genre, in turn, borrowed from Arabic motifs. Some of the celebrated Bacchic poets writing in Arabic were Iranian by origin and proud of their Persian ancestry. The most famous of these is Abu Nuwas, who is said to have liberally appropriated al-Walid II's wine poetry for his own work.[25] It is tempting to ascribe his disdain for Bedouins and their lifestyle to anti-Arab sentiments harbored by someone convinced of his own 'Iranian' superiority. But the categories 'Arab' and 'Persian' at this time should not be likened to modern identities. Even if Abu Nuwas, who was born in Ahvaz in Khuzistan—today an Iranian province with a large Arabic-speaking population—boasted about his Persian ancestry, he likely still saw himself as an Arab poet, writing in Arabic and in the Arab tradition.[26]

The *khamriyya* has its share of stock images and metaphors, such as the breeze-like coolness of wine in the throat and its fiery heat in the veins and, more dangerously, alighting at the wine shop, drinking until the crack of dawn, the 'call to prayer', and 'one more for the road', all of which lampoon formal religion. In the *khamriyya*, the day is reserved for sermons, the night for relaxation and liquid pleasure. On a darker note, wine and blood are often closely associated, both in terms of the coloration and, with the neck of the wine jug used as a simile for the neck of the drinker, of the ultimate punishment that awaits the latter.[27] The *khamriyya* knows an elaborate vocabulary for describing colors, the taste and quality of wine, its effects on the drinker, and its suitability for specific times of the day.

The *sāqi* is an indispensable companion of the host who organizes the drinking session in the *khamriyya*. The origins of summoning the *sāqi*—from which *sāqi-nāma*, the Persian term for wine poem, is derived—are unclear but surely go back to the beginnings of Arabic and Persian poetry.[28] The official's importance is seen in the multitude of other Persian terms that convey the same meaning.[29] The *sāqi* livens up the party, serves as a source of inspiration, but also reminds the drinker of the fickleness of fate and the fleeting nature of life and its pleasures. He constantly hovers over the drinker, handing him his nightcap as well as the *sabuh*, the morning wine in a chalice that resembles a rose or a tulip. The *sabuh*, in turn, is one of the tropes of the wine poem: it conveys the notion of the 'hair of the dog' that combats the hangover from the previous night, as much as the idea of the unconventional lifestyle of those who do not have to get up and go to a job in the morning.[30] The *sāqi* also comes with homoerotic connotations. Like the handsome Ganymede, who attracted the eye of Zeus in Greek mythology, he is the object of erotic attention.[31] He often stands for the beloved, who, as visualized by the (male) poet, is usually a male as well. The Persian canon especially is rife with ambiguity in this regard: the language does not differentiate between male and female in its unisex pronoun, *u*.[32] All in all, the *khamriyya* evokes an atmosphere beyond 'normal social restrictions and inhibitions'.[33]

Disassociation does occur in wine poetry, sometimes in a playful way. Poets often excused themselves for using wine in their poetry by introducing their work with the phrase, 'I had too much to say, and therefore spoke as poets do.'[34] But the obverse, a lack of obfuscation, exists as well. Outright dismissive of any kind of diffidence, especially when it involves hypocrisy, is Haritha b. Badr al-Ghudani (d. 684), who declares:

> If you are my drinking partner, take wine and give me some; pay no heed to him who sees you quaffing deep. I'm no man to drink under the cover of darkness; I sip my *nabidh* in all submissiveness to God—he knows what we are about whether in secret or openly.[35]

Two centuries later, the Abbasid poet Ibn al-Rumi (836–96) self-servingly mocks the different legal interpretations with this verse:

> The Iraqi holds *nabidh* to be permitted, and the drinking of it, but say that grape-wine and intoxication are both forbidden; the Hijazi says both drinks are alike. The two dicta together license wine—I'll take one half from each and drink wine—let the burden of guilt rest on him who imposes it.[36]

And the paradox between pleasure and religious ordinance, implied in the Koran itself, is given full expression in this verse by Ibrahim b. 'Ali ibn Harma (709–68):

> The Prophet's descendant forbids me wine, and gives me noble teaching; he says, 'Abstain from it and leave it alone, for fear of God, not for fear of man'. Yet how can I abstain from it, when my love for it is a love which has gained control over my frame? For me, the comfort of what is lawful is an evil, and my soul's comfort lies in the evil of what is forbidden.[37]

The high Abbasid court of Baghdad forms the backdrop to the wine poem at its height, conjuring an image of sophistication, as epitomized in the poetry of Abu Nuwas, who in his works paired (homoerotic) sexuality to wine in ways that are as impertinent as they are witty. Abu Nuwas lived and worked under the early Abbasid rulers. The nature of his poetry—which skirted blasphemy and thus made them risky at the best of times—inevitably created tension with his patrons. He never managed to get close to Harun al-Rashid, the celebrated caliph whose reign has come to be considered the acme of Abbasid power and splendor. Rather temperate in his drinking habits, Harun al-Rashid did not necessarily appreciate Abu Nuwas's daring verse. The poet found a far more kindred spirit in Harun al-Rashid's son and successor, al-Amin. He became a welcome guest at that ruler's saturnalian gatherings, which served as inspiration for the voluminous wine poetry he composed during this period. The fun ended when al-Amin lost power and ultimately his life following a conflict with his brother and successor, al-Ma'mun. With his patron's death, Abu Nuwas lost a boon companion as well as an employer. He died himself a few years later.[38]

Defiance of Islamic strictures is common in Abu Nuwas's wine poetry. He says:

> Reproacher, obey me now
> And reduce your censure
> And drink wine, and spare me
> From the daily prayer
> If the time for praying
> Or fasting should occur
> Banish the fast while drinking
> And swap prayer for slumber.[39]

And, even more pithily:

> Someone asked, 'Would you do the Hajj?' I said:
> Yes, were there no pleasure left in Baghdad.[40]

Yet it would be erroneous to conclude from such impious verse that Abu Nuwas was just a cynic or, worse, an unbeliever. He celebrated the *carpe diem* and *ergo bibamus* aspects of wine, but he also linked it to loftier themes, such as character, involving generosity, sincerity, forbearance, and good humor—all byproducts of (moderate) bibbing. He lived and wrote at a time before Islam had crystalized, before the lines between belief and unbelief had become sharply drawn, a period when the literalism of the Hanbali school still competed with the beliefs of the Murji'ites, advocates of the notion that judgment would be up to God, who 'forgives all sins' (Koran 39:53); a time, in sum, when the permissibility of alcohol other than grape wine could still be debated. Abu Nuwas was a libertine but not an apostate; it is entirely possible to argue that he was a 'perfectly sincere Muslim'.[41] He was, after all, careful not to cross the line of heresy by questioning the Oneness of God, engaging in the mortal sin of polytheism, explicitly forbidden in the Koran.

Various modern authors have made similar arguments regarding other poets, and some have pushed the point even further. Philip Kennedy, for instance, goes beyond the notion that the wine song 'is never quite free of the shadow of Islam' by stating that it actually 'invites the shadow of Islam', meaning that the poet acknowledges Islam facetiously as much as he refuses to bow to it, to accommodate it.[42] Thomas Bauer, citing a wine poem composed by a *hadith* scholar by the name of 'Asim ibn al-Hasan al-'Attar (d. 1090), argues that it does not matter whether or not the poet himself drank: poetry, including wine poetry, reflects an ideal—that of a life filled with alcoholic and sexual enjoyment—that is perfectly in accordance with the prescriptions of a society that follows God's rules.[43] Paul Losensky, analyzing the poetry of the Persian poet Baba Fighani (d. 1516 or 1519), makes a similar point. Fighani, he argues, fully aware of the fact that wine is prohibited, nevertheless pulls it in the direction of the permissible—into a value-neutral realm, so to speak—with the argument that, for the discerning, it opens a universe beyond good and evil, unlocking the treasure box of eternal wisdom and truth. Ordinary people, even those who seek the truth, have no idea about this level of truth, which makes it as exciting as it is dangerous.[44]

Sufism and Wine in Mystical Poetry

Many of the urges and sentiments ill-fitted to formal Islam found a home in Sufism (Islamic mysticism). Sufism—*tasawwuf* in Arabic, or *'irfān*, also an Arabic term denoting (gnostic) knowledge, and more often used in Iran—was influenced by mystical elements in existing traditions: Christianity, Manichaeism, Buddhism, and Neo-Platonism. It also draws on elements within Islam, including the Koran, that lend themselves to mystical interpretation. Sufism is difficult to define. Neither inherently conservative nor intrinsically rebellious, Sufism runs the gamut from the stoic and ascetic to the epicurean, from a focus on subliminal love to open celebration of scandalous behavior, to, occasionally, militancy. It stands for a vast countercultural spectrum ranging from a concentration on inner faith to a type of 'freethinking' that nowadays is rarely associated with Islam. It revolves around a different, more intimate understanding of the world in relationship to the creator than formal religion does. It posits an immanent God, as opposed to a transcendent one, an intimate friend rather than a stern father. The idea of love, the metaphysical *prima materia* of any culture, is central to its later development. Sufism has always expressed itself in song and dance, the irrepressible human urges that formal Islam tends to frown upon as distractions from the true focus of worship. It also makes room for the miraculous, which in formal Islam is the purview of the Prophet alone.

Like Islam's non-conformist aspects in general, Sufism did not decline in vigor and popularity with the passing of the so-called classical age, in part because it offered an alternative to 'orthodox' Islam and in part because it provided shelter through inwardness in troubled times. Indeed, it found its most vibrant expression precisely following Islam's formative period, with the coming of the Mongols, at which point it began to organize itself into orders (*turuq*; sing. *tariqa*), with lodges and meeting houses—known as *zāwiyas* (Ar.), *khānaqās* (Pers.), and *tekkes* (Turk.). Its most eloquent and profound poetry dates from this later period as well.

In its original eighth-century manifestation, Sufism focused on austerity, asceticism (*zuhd*), the renunciation of the world, and indifference to its temptations, induced by fear of the judgment to come and buttressed by an utter reliance on God (*tawakkul*), in preparation for the end. Adepts of this 'austere' variant chose reason and self-control over passion and desire in their attempt to ascend to the divine. The opposite side of the spectrum is represented by what modern scholars have dubbed the 'ecstatic' or 'drunken' School of Khorasan, referring to a variant that celebrated not asceticism but exuberance, transgression, even outrageousness and scandal.

That does not mean that members of the latter school consumed wine. Sufism and alcohol are not intrinsically linked. Most Sufis rejected wine as categorically as 'formal' Islam does. The distinction between 'sober' and 'drunken' played out mostly on the metaphorical level, denoting intoxicated unconsciousness, ecstatic unity, the removal of duality through the annihilation of the self. Yet in mystical poetry it is not always easy to distinguish between the metaphorical use of wine and references to the real thing. As Dick Davis puts it, often 'the literal meaning seems to be the only plausible one'.[45] The hallucinatory images of swaying rocks and undulating landscapes in Persian miniatures depicting Sufis certainly point in that direction.[46] Indeed, we have many reports of Sufis who actually drank, in particular members of the antinomian Sufi movement known as the Qalandariyya, who spurned life in this world as well as the afterlife and claimed to 'be above the law in the name of a superior comprehension of the law'.[47] Qalandars could be found anywhere in the eastern Islamic world, from Central Asia—where they seem to have originated—and the Indian subcontinent to Iran and Anatolia, wandering and begging, engaged in transgressive behavior, taking psychotropic drugs, free from the rules of man and God, indeed, actively soliciting societal disapproval. With their tattered clothing and bizarre, repulsive appearance, they were hard to distinguish from 'ordinary' marginalized people—vagabonds, drug addicts, the insane, the disabled, and the homeless—who lived miserable lives in the shadows, huddling in ruins, cemeteries, and caves, drinking or, more often, it seems, using hashish.[48] The late fifteenth-century poet 'Ali Shir Nava'i describes the itinerant dervishes of Herat as dissolute habitués of the squalid *kharābāt* (the ruins on the edge of town) downing the dregs of other customers' drinks.[49]

Mystical poetry overlaps with the *khamriyya* in that wine is important in it, although in mystical poetry, unlike the *khamriyya*, wine is not necessarily a central motif. Wine-related metaphors in Sufi poetry are most powerfully expressed by Hafez:

> That bitter elixir that the Sufi called Mother of All Evil,
> Is sweeter to us than a virgin's kiss.[50]

Wine stands for many things in Sufi poetry. The ruby-red liquid refracted in the sunlit goblet symbolizes the beauty of the world as gifted to us by God, but it also stands for divine radiance, love of and for the divine. Wine is of this world, yet it helps one go beyond it. The intoxication it produces represents one's rapturous love for God and the ardent desire for physical annihilation in His essence. It can also represent unrequited love, a surfeit of ardor unanswered, and thus bring about a plangent nostalgia.[51] It stands for the notion that life is short and evanescent, and that living it up is the only way to find momentary solace from this terrifying awareness. Ultimately, wine symbolizes the secret that is only accessible to the mystic, an initiated member of a select group capable of understanding the inner truth of religion, outside of the convention that holds ordinary folk, common Muslims, whose limited mental faculties and base urges necessitate the formal strictures and obligations of the faith: abstinence, prayer, and fasting. The notion of being one of the *khawāss*, the elite, mirrors the hierarchy of society at large, with its ideas of the ruling classes enjoying certain privileges and being exempted from societal conventions and religious strictures. And it is a way of thumbing one's nose at these.

On this deepest level, wine elevates the drinker to the domain of 'primordial desire to which the inner self belongs'.[52] The dissolution of the self it produces connects him to the realm of transcendence, resolving contradiction, paradox, the aporia of selfhood. The very transgression of the act of drinking transports the drinker to a space beyond good and evil, in which he attains true authenticity and proximity to divine essence: hence the metaphor of the maternal vine.[53] The *sāqi*, the handsome cupbearer, is part of this. He is an object of (sexual) desire, but far from standing in opposition to religion, he is a figure of deep religious significance, representing the transformation of identity, the longing to break out of and transcend the finiteness and futility of human existence, to connect with the celestial world. The *sāqi* is a terrestrial Ganymede, connected to Islam via the biblical avatar of Joseph, who dreamed about 'serving wine to his Lord', and incorporated into the Islamic poetic tradition as the emblem of beauty, the homoerotic bearer of immortality. The *sāqi* thus becomes the cupbearer of the two worlds, representing love by way of intoxication, both through wine as substance and the wine pourer as a comely, attractive lad.[54]

Finding truth through love is not for the fainthearted. As Hafez puts it, likening the dangers of exploring the Truth to jumping into a whirlpool:

> On this dark night, amidst these waves,
> The whirlpool's fearsome roar,
> What can they know of our distress
> Who watch us from the shore?[55]

And:

> The pampered are not fit to travel on love's road
> Only an outcast's heart can bear the lover's load.[56]

Those who do not know of 'our distress' include the ulama, who cannot conceive of true authenticity, cannot fathom that God is limitless in His transcendent essence. As Fighani proclaimed: 'What is not in the treasury of both worlds is in the tavern.'[57]

The tavern thus becomes the alternative mosque, the true prayerhouse, devoid of artifice and hypocrisy, a temple for the truly faithful, the 'realm of angels'.

In the words of Hafez:

> In love, the Sufi meeting house
> and wine-shop are one place;
> As are all places where we find
> the loved one's radiant face.[58]

Hafez is the free-spirited vagabond-drunk (*rend*) who stains his dervish cloak and prayer mat with wine to show how deeply wine is integrated into his way of experiencing religion, and to demonstrate his contempt for clerical bigotry and hypocrisy, which to him is the true mother of all evil. His poetry is filled with references to wine as a metaphor for defiance and dissent against the rigidity of orthodoxy and in particular the cant of the clerics, the self-appointed guardians of the faith:

> Go mind your own business, preacher! What's all this hullaballoo?
> My heart has left the road you travel, but what's that to you.[59]

Yes, we drink and live dissolute lives; we have tried a hundred times to repent. Repentance is fragile, though. It 'shatters as easily as a wine glass', and those who preach repentance 'rarely repent themselves'.[60] This includes the morality police:

> We drink our wine, we flirt, and we're licentious—yes,
> but who is in this city where we live of whom this isn't true?
> And don't go to the morals officers to make a fuss—He's on
> the constant lookout too for pleasure, just like us.[61]

Not all Sufis were poets, just as not all poets were Sufis. The famous Omar Khayyam (1048–1131) is a good example of this truism. Once thought to be the unique work of one individual, Khayyam's poetry is now seen as the outcome of a collective process, of poems written over a long period of time by various authors who may have sought shelter in anonymity. To the extent that his poetry is not an anthology of verse written over time, Khayyam was not a practicing Sufi even though his poetry contains Sufi elements.[62] Rather than an 'agnostic hedonist who prescribes worldly pleasure as a remedy for the meaninglessness of life', as the Victorians (and most modern interpreters) made him out to be, Khayyam was an epicurean as well as a stoic, detached from the temptations of the world.[63] Wine, for him, brings joy and happiness, but also demands a price:

> To drink good wine down and be happy—that's my way;
> Ignoring faith and blasphemy—that's how I pray.
> I asked the world to name her price, I'd marry her;
> She said, 'Your happy heart is what you'll have to pay'.[64]

As with Abu Nuwas, the pessimism, the cynicism, even the nihilism contained in Khayyam's poetry do not necessarily point to irreligion. They rather reflect a desperate attempt to explain the inexplicable, the existence of evil and injustice in a world created by God, who cannot be held accountable for this sorry state of affairs. Khayyam's poetry may be seen as one long *cri de coeur* against the lack of congruence between the perfect world created by God and the world as it is. The mystery is too deep; the solution to one's inability to live with the uncertainty of the meaning of life is to become intoxicated, to drink the wine of wisdom.[65]

Khayyam echoes this, with this verse:

When I am dead, wash me with wine,
Say my funeral service with pure wine;
If thou wouldst see me on the resurrection day
Thou must seek in the dust of the tavern door.[66]

Like Abu Nuwas and many of their peers, Khayyam eludes dichotomies: he was no orthodox Muslim, but neither was he simply an agnostic, let alone an atheist. In his search for truth and his rebellion against injustice, he transcended both faith and reason.[67]

Prose Works

Prose works that can be labeled *khamriyyāt* are rare. An early example of an author holding forth on wine in prose without any reticence is 'Abd Allah ibn al-Mu'tazz (861–908), the son of the thirteenth Abbasid caliph al-Mu'tazz (r. 866–69,) who himself ruled as caliph for only one day and night before he fell victim to a palace intrigue and was strangled. Ibn al-Mu'tazz was above all a celebrated poet. He authored the *Kitāb al-badi'*, a study of Arabic poetics, and a well-known poetic *diwān*. Less well known is his *Fusul al-tamāthil fi tabāshir al-surur* ('Chapters on the Representation of the Omens of Joy'). The many poems this work contains are embedded in a discourse on the merits and demerits of wine. The author discusses the four types of wine (black, red, white, and yellow); the properties of these; the scent of wine; the kind of glasses to be used; the evening drink (*al-ghabuq*); the morning drink (*al-sabuh*); drunkenness; and, finally, hangovers—which result more often from drinking blended wine than pure wine—and how to treat them.[68]

Yet another example is the *Qutb al-surur* ('The Pole of Pleasure'), an anthology written by Ibrahim Ibn al-Raqiq al-Qayrawani, a native of Kairouan in Tunisia who lived in the late tenth and early eleventh century. Al-Qayrawani served as the head of the chancellery of the Berber Zirid dynasty, which ruled the central Maghreb between 972 and 1148. He held the position of private secretary of three successive *amir*s: Mansur b. Buluggin (r. 984–96), Badis b. Mansur (r. 996–1016), and Mu'izz b. Badis (r. 1016–62). In that capacity, he also functioned as the main *nadim* of his masters, earning him the name *al-kātib al-nadim* (secretary-cum-boon companion). As shown in the previous chapter, his anthology provides us with a wealth of information about the drinking habits of successive Umayyad and Abbasid rulers. He also depicts for us a sovereign surrounded by a court composed of a vizier and other high officials engaged in learned discourse expressed in prose and verse as they enjoy sweet melodies and ample wine.[69] The *Qutb al-surur* frequently invokes Galen and Hippocrates as well as Abu Bakr al-Razi, and treats wine as a therapeutic agent, provided it is taken in moderation: it helps digestion, warms the blood, facilitates sleep, and mitigates stomachaches. The author gets around the Islamic interdiction by attributing a divinely imparted complex quality to wine: banned by Islam, to be sure, but also excellent, fortifying, mirroring youth and vivaciousness. He also plays with the casuistry surrounding *nabidh*.

A final prose work celebrating wine worth mentioning is the *Halbat al-kumayt*, from the hand of the Egyptian Shams al-Din Muhammad b. 'Ali al-Nawaji (1386–1455), a poet, grammarian, and Sufi. The title, translated as 'The Racetrack of the Bay', is a pun, since the adjective 'maroon' or 'bay-colored', can refer to both horses and wine. Nawaji's manual on wine is wholly 'secular' in that it barely refers to religion. Instead, it focuses on the virtues of wine and the delights of the banquet. Life's pleasures, the author submits, consist of three things: entertaining dear friends, the trade in wine, and the study of *belles lettres*. The *Halbat al-kumayt* accordingly is divided into chapters that address issues such as the origins of wine, its qualities, the accoutrements of the banquets organized around it, wine poetry, and the etiquette of drinking sessions.[70]

Adab

Adab—today the Islamic term for literature but originally, and literally, meaning manner, habit, condition—is the collective term for a literary corpus that was designed to educate, elevate, and acculturate the upper classes, with its ultimate aim being to maintain a well-balanced social order. The art of good living, part of the cultivation of the self, was an integral part of court culture from the Abbasid period onward. It contains uniquely Persian elements, articulated by the Iranian secretaries in the service of the newly created caliphate who drew upon their institutional knowledge of Sasanian models to express their views.[71] Its quintessence is that of practical wisdom accumulated over the generations: the opposite, in a way, of knowledge and practice originating in revelation. Its non-prophetic origin did not prevent *adab* from harmonizing with the *hadith* tradition, though.[72] Indeed, combinations of the two traditions do exist, the best example being the *Kitāb al-ashriba* ('The Book of (Alcoholic) Beverages') by the polymath Ibn Qutayba (828– 89), which is both a work of *fiqh*, in which *khamr* and *nabidh* are judged on their religious merits and demerits, and a work of *adab* celebrating wine and its poetic expression as a source of pleasure and accompaniment to sophisticated living.[73]

Etiquette: The Mirror for Princes Literature

The *bon viveur* image of the cultured courtier included not just the actual quaffing of wine but presupposed knowledge about when and how to serve and consume it, and, of course, how to come to terms with the fact that it is formally forbidden in Islam. All this is reflected in the medieval Persianate *nasihat* (Mirror for Princes), literature, which continued the pre-Islamic *andarz* genre of practical wisdom and prudential advice.[74] It represents what may be called the Iranian contribution to Islamic wisdom, the inclusion of kingship as parallel to prophecy, a complementary constituent element in a balanced spiritual and temporal order. Advice literature in the Islamic period was mostly designed to wean the new Central Asian, Turkic rulers from their coarse habits, and acculturate them to the norms and practices of Islamicate civilization, both urban and urbane. It includes advice with respect to hospitality and etiquette for royal drinking parties in its guidelines for proper conduct.[75] It uses the principle of a ruler who is autonomous, 'above and apart from society', operating at the center of a retinue consisting of his wives, eunuchs, and boon companions, but also the 'men of the regime': the administrators and military commanders, society's notables, advisors, and assistants, who act as instruments and intermediaries for good governance and organization of the society of the 'āmma (commoners).[76]

The andarz genre ranges from treatises composed specifically to educate rulers on the moralizing folk wisdom proffered by the likes of Sa'di Shirazi (1210–91/2), one of Iran's most popular poets. These works offer political advice, teaching the ruler how to maintain control after conquest with a divide-and-rule approach, but also contain tips and instructions for proper conduct, from table manners to how to deal with women and slaves. The underlying theme is to see the natural balance of the universe replicated in an equilibrium between the secular and religious domains of power, between the spiritual and practical elements of governance. The ultimate purpose of this is the maintenance of power by way of promoting stability and thus preventing internal revolt.[77]

Wine and wine drinking invariably is a topic in the andarz-nāma. Arabic works such as the Rāhat al-sudur and the Kitāb al-ashriba clearly attempt to strike a balance between morality and pragmatism. Persian-language examples tend to present palace drinking as natural and self-evident. Grand Vizier Nizam al-Mulk in his well-known Siyasatnāma, written for the Seljuq Sultan Malikshah (r. 1072–92), devotes a brief chapter to the rules and rituals of royal drinking parties. He calls good-quality wine a token of the king's lavishness in hospitality and advises him to choose his boon companions wisely, arguing that drinking parties must be conducted in a relaxed mood, for it is 'only through his boon companions that the king's spirit is set free'.[78]

No less relaxed is the Qābusnāma, an eleventh-century work written by Kay Ka'us b. Iskandar b. Qabus b. Vushmgir, a vassal of the Ghaznavids, for his son, Gilan Shah. Kay Ka'us is exemplary in his humanistic approach to the issue. Youth and drinking, in his account, are natural twins. 'I will not tell you to drink,' he admonishes his son, 'but I cannot tell you not to drink either'; the author then proceeds to give his offspring advice about the proper way to drink. It is best, he says, to start drinking three hours after consuming food so maximum benefit can be had from both. And start drinking after your afternoon prayers so that by the time you are drunk night will have set in and no one will notice.[79] Riding horses, hunting, and playing polo are proper pastimes of powerful men, Kay Ka'us concludes, especially when young. But 'everything should have a limit, measure, and method'. One should not go hunting every day. The same holds for drinking. The week has seven days: go hunting two days; two or three days occupy yourself with drinking, and one day tend to the affairs of state.[80]

Not all works of advice are positive or even neutral about alcohol. Some *Adab* literature argues that drinking wine leads to a loss of reason and thus equals stupidity and folly.[81] This is exemplified in the *Bahr al-fawā'id* ('The Sea of Virtues'), written in Syria in the twelfth century, which reflects a court seeking to restore Sunni orthodoxy amid discord and disunity. The anonymous author is adamant in his insistence that, by Muslim consensus, drinking wine is unlawful and wine is impure. Anyone who says otherwise is ignorant. Yet he acknowledges that doctors vary in their opinion of whether wine can legitimately be used as medicine if it helps to cure illness, and whether one is allowed to quench one's thirst with it if no other liquid is available. He also gives the obvious drunkard the benefit of the doubt, stating that the *muhtasib* identifying him should not automatically mete out punishment since the culprit may have been forced to drink against his will.[82]

All this unapologetic merrymaking notwithstanding, the notion of repentance for the sin of having imbibed is not absent from poetry. As Hafez says:

We'd better wash away the wine stains from
Our cloaks with tears of penitence—
Now is the season for sobriety,
For days of pious abstinence.[83]

Abu Nuwas refers to repentance, too, in his poetry. Indeed, he seems to count on it, and the reward it will bring from a forgiving

God, when he says, 'commit as many sins as you can/for you shall meet a forgiving Lord'.[84]

Yet not all sinners repented, at least not during their literary life. In fact, it was something of a convention to spurn and even mock the idea of *istighfār* (asking for divine mercy) for its connotation of 'caving in', of engaging in false contrition. Thus Abu Nuwas, associating sobriety with the primitive life of the desert and contrasting it to sophisticated urbanity, writes:

> Censurer, will you not relent awhile? Whoever hopes for my repentance will be let down. For this life [of pleasure] I have described is the one for me, not desert tents; this is the life, not [camels' milk]! How can one compare the bedu with Kisra's [Khosrow Parviz, a Sasanian monarch] palace and its surrounding expanses? You are beguiled if you insist on the repentance; tear your garment [of all I care]! I will not repent![85]

Another great example of the genre is the *Akhlāq-i Nāsiri* ('Nasirian Ethics') by Nasir al-Din Tusi (1201–74), a polymath from Khorasan who served the Isma'ili rulers of Alamut in northern Iran, was taken captive by the Mongols when they captured the fortress, and ended up serving them as head of the newly founded observatory in Maragha, in Azerbaijan. The *Nasirian Ethics* is Tusi's famous compendium on ethics, economics, and politics. First published in 1235, the treatise remains popular as a moral guidebook throughout the Islamic world today. Its section on the manners of wine drinking stresses the ingredients of conviviality which does not degenerate into brawling; conversation filled with 'witty anecdotes and attractive poems'; drinking short of drunkenness, for 'nothing is more harmful than drunkenness to one's concerns in this world and the next'; and proper decorum, consideration for one's boon companions, all of which is presented as commonsensical behavior.[86]

A final example of advice literature is the *Rāhat al-sudur wa-āyāt al-surur* ('Comfort of High Officials and the Sign of Enjoyment') written in 1205 by Muhammad b. 'Ali al-Rawandi (d. after 1207), a chronicler and propagandist of the Rum Seljuq ruler Ghiyath al-Din Kaykhusraw (r. 1192–6 and 1205–11). The work offers instructions about such important pastimes as chess and backgammon. In his chapter on wine, the author follows a typical formula of trying to find ways around the official ban on the consumption of alcohol by advancing arguments legitimizing elite drinking. Wine is clearly prohibited in Islam, al-Rawandi argues. Yet it just as clearly has many advantages. These range from medical benefits, involving the many ailments it helps alleviate, to social merits, seen in the wonderful effect it has on sociability in the form of the convivial gathering (*majlis*). All these virtues counteract the official ban, suggesting—indeed, demonstrating—that it can never have been God's will to ban wine altogether. Drinking, al-Rawandi concludes, is thus only unlawful if it leads to inebriation; otherwise, flexibility and accommodation are in order. He advises rulers to follow the moral example set by past leaders of Iraq and Khorasan, whose revels included proper feasting and fighting, and declares the ruler's wine cellar, the *sharāb-khāna*, a legitimate institution for the purpose.[87]

4

ALCOHOL IN THE EARLY MODERN
ISLAMIC EMPIRES
THE OTTOMANS AND THE MUGHALS

Introduction

In Chapter 2 we saw how existing drinking patterns among premodern Muslim elites were reinforced with the arrival of large numbers of Turco-Mongol elements from the steppes of Central Asia around the turn of the second millennium. The dynasties they brought forth all began as mobile, nomadic, or semi-nomadic dispensations and, over time, evolved into sedentary states. The rulers and their retainers invariably were heavy drinkers. For tribal folk, who saw life as virtually synonymous with campaigning, rousing drinking parties both served as a measure of a man's worth as a warrior and had a commensal, ceremonial function in establishing trust and reinforcing social solidarity.[1]

These patterns, combined with customs and habits already in place in Islamic lands, spread to the Indian subcontinent, where the Turkic Mughals took control in the sixteenth century, and the Iranian plateau, ruled first by Timur Lang and his successors and subsequently by the Safavid dynasty between 1501 and 1722. To a lesser extent, they also spread to Anatolia, the hearth and home of the Ottomans, who expanded from their fourteenth-century origins in the region to become the world's most powerful and longest-lasting Muslim state.

The states created by these dynasties over time became emphatically Muslim. Their rulers may not have been sincere believers, but they all used Islam as an instrument to reinforce their legitimacy and stay in power. And staying in power was the paramount objective of each individual sovereign. The sultan or shah reigned supreme but had enormous leeway; while he always professed Islam to be the ultimate pillar of his God-given legitimacy, he often behaved in radically un-Islamic ways, barely restrained by the clerical classes. Islam's lack of institutional, church-like qualities gave its functionaries, the ulama and the *qādis* few tools other than exhortation to compete with the *raison d'état*, let alone control the state—in ways that in premodern southern Europe the Catholic church often managed to dominate or strongly influence state and society. Inveterate elite drinkers thus found few obstacles in their way other than sermonizing preachers with scant political power.

Ottoman Sultans, 1400–1800

The Ottomans were the most successful of the myriad Turkic tribes that settled in Anatolia in the eleventh century. Their initial adherence to orthodox Islam was tenuous at best. Much about their early rulers remains unclear due to being unrecorded or poorly documented. As in the case of early Islam, the available information is by definition anachronistic and should thus be approached with caution. This is certainly true of anonymous fifteenth-century chronicles that nostalgically paint the first three Ottoman sultans, Osman (r. *c.* 1280–1324), Orhan Ghazi (r. 1323/4–62), and Murad I (r. 1362–89) as being unaffected by the vice of drinking. According to these narratives, Osman, Orhan Gazi, and Murad did not consume wine, as they were ashamed to do so in front of the ulama. Rather, the culpability belonged to courtiers and in particular the viziers of the Çandarlı family—who concluded a treaty with the Christian powers of Europe after the Ottomans had been crushed by Timur Lang in 1402—as well as a new type of cleric who seduced the clean-living early rulers with the bottle. Foreign influence was at work as well, according to the same accounts. Once the Ottomans began to consort with Iranians (who were notorious drinkers) and the house of Karaman, a rival dynasty ruling in south-central Anatolia, various forms of sin began to spread among the elite. Christian influence especially made itself felt in the form of a Serbian princess, a concubine of Sultan Bayezid I (r. 1389–1402), who had introduced him to alcohol.[2]

The reality is likely to have been different. The Ottomans did not need Iranians or Christians to become acquainted with alcohol. In Turkic Inner Asia, alcohol was common and plentiful. The semi-mythical tales that make up the fifteenth-century *Book of Dede Korkut*, set in northeastern Anatolia, associate the Oghuz Turks with wine.[3] Indeed, in the *Oğuz Destanı*, Oğuz Khan—the half-mythical founder of the Turks—is said to have demanded raw meat, various other types of food, and wine.[4] On the opposite side of Anatolia, in the southwest around Aydın, Umur Aydınoğlu (d. 1348), a local Turkoman warlord whose principality would soon be absorbed into the expanding Ottoman realm, managed to combine a façade of public piety with copious wine consumption.[5]

Some hard evidence that the early Ottoman sultans were enthusiastic drinkers is available as well. Judging by the inclusion of a large contingent of wine in the gifts offered to Orhan Ghazi, Ottoman rulers had a long-standing fondness for alcohol.[6] And not just rulers, or so it seems: Italian, Genoese, and Venetian merchants traded in wine all over Anatolia in the fifteenth century. The Genoese of Galata and Pera (suburbs of Constantinople north of the Golden Horn) also furnished it to the Ottoman court in the early 1400s.[7] Bayezid I may have become corrupted by a Serbian princess, but once acquainted with alcohol he earned a reputation as a heavy drinker (as well as an avid pederast).[8] His dipsomania over time became the stuff of legend: more than half a millennium after his death, people still saw the defeat he suffered in 1402 at the hands of Timur Lang near Ankara as divine punishment for his dissolute behavior.[9] Bayezid subsequently vowed to abstain and at least ended up tempering his intake, shamed into repentance by his son-in-law Emir Seyyid, who when asked to assess a newly built mosque in Bursa—still the

89

Ottoman capital at the time—replied: 'Nothing matches the beauty and grandeur of this edifice; the only thing missing is a tavern on each of its four corners'. These, he continued, when prodded to explicate, would enhance the building's magnificence and entice the sultan to go there often and enjoy himself with his friends. Upbraided by Bayezid for his lack of respect for both the sultan and the faith, Emir Seyyid explained that his words were less scandalous than they appeared; for, he said, 'if a man sullies his heart—God's altar—with wine and other sins, what could be against building taverns adjacent to a mosque, a mere brick and mortar structure'?[10]

Bayezid's offspring took after him. Byzantine sources present one of his sons, Süleyman, who controlled much of the Balkans following Bayezid's death, as a drunkard who, rather than earning his stripes on the battlefield, preferred to luxuriate in his bath, surrounded by poets and courtiers.[11] His grandson Murad II (r. 1421–44 and 1446–51) inherited the family's fondness for alcohol. Known for his ability to consume enormous quantities of wine, Murad apparently threw an (Arab) preacher who reminded him of the strictures of Islam summarily into prison and afterwards sent him into exile.[12] In 1451 he died, forty-seven years old, struck down by apoplexy during a drinking bout.[13]

In 1453, the Ottomans took center stage in the Islamic world by conquering Constantinople, which they renamed Istanbul and turned into their capital. They further burnished their Islamic credentials by capturing Syria, Egypt, and the Hijaz in 1516–17. The sultan, doubling as caliph, henceforth was the protector of Islam's two holiest shrines, Mecca and Medina. Although Ottoman rulers would continue to lead their troops into war for at least another century, they now came to preside over an urban-based, largely stationary court. If he did not reside in Edirne, the empire's military gateway to the Balkans, the sultan mostly reigned from the privacy of the Topkapı Palace, and his drinking, to the extent that it occurred, remained hidden from view.

The exalted, religiously underpinned status of the ruler did not automatically entail sobriety. Some sultans are known to have been teetotalers whereas others were notorious tipplers. Most proscribed alcohol, often with other controversial consumables such as coffee and tobacco, at one point or another during their reign—be that upon taking power, during natural disaster, urban unrest, or on the eve of military campaigns, motivated by religious fervor, pressured by the ulama, mindful of the approach of old age and the reckoning in the hereafter, or simply determined to maintain public order. In many cases, the impulse to ban coincided with private sultanic indulgence, and it almost always ran up against fiscal exigencies.

Mehmed II, the conqueror of Constantinople (r. 1444–6 and 1451–81), consumed wine during campaigns but apparently was not given to it.[14] His son Bayezid II (r. 1481–1512), by contrast, was a real boozer. Toward the end of his life, he gave up the habit, though. The reasons for doing so remain unknown but the reward was real, for the austerity of his final years earned him the epithet *veli* (saint).[15] Selim I (r. 1512–20), on campaign in Egypt, almost drowned in the Nile while drunk when his boat capsized.[16] His successor, Süleyman Kanuni, the Lawgiver, called the Magnificent by Westerners (r. 1520–66), seems not to have been averse to wine in his younger years.[17] Yet, as he grew older, he regularly attended public Friday prayers, stopped listening to music, and stayed away from alcohol.[18] In 1555 he acted on his convictions by becoming the first Ottoman ruler to outlaw the public sale of alcohol, making it difficult even for non-Muslims to obtain any. At the behest of *şeyhülislam* Mehmed Ebüssuûd Efendi (in office 1545–74), he ordered all taverns in his realm sealed or destroyed. He also sought to stem the importation of wine into the capital, and to that effect had wine-laden ships arriving in Istanbul set on fire. Unsurprisingly, the decree just drove drinking underground, so that the order had to be repeated. In 1564, for instance, the governor of Damascus was ordered to close all *buzahanes* (coffeehouses) and taverns in the city. The following year, an ordinance went out prohibiting the sultan's Greek subjects from selling wine and even keeping any in their own homes.[19]

Süleyman's son and successor Selim II (r. 1566-74) was different. No one could have accused him of religious zealotry. In the three months that the French diplomat Philippe du Fresne-Canay spent in Istanbul in 1573, Selim II went to the mosque all of two times.[20] Not surprisingly, he commenced his reign with an edict that rescinded the strictures on drinking issued by his father. Trade restrictions were lifted, too. This mainly benefited the Portuguese Sephardi Jew Joseph Nasi (1524–79), Selim's banker and confidant. Nasi, who had held the rights to the shipping of wine between Crete and Moldavia via the Bosporus since the late 1550s, under Selim acquired a monopoly on the empire's entire wine trade.[21] Apparently introduced to alcohol by Nasi, Selim soon turned into a *fainéant* alcoholic, leaving the affairs of state (including the decision to take anti-alcohol measures) to grand vizier Sokollu Mehmed Pasha (in office 1565–79). Nicknamed *mest* (the Sot), he is said to have taken as his motto, 'I think only of the pleasures of today; for the morrow I care nothing'.[22] He preferred wine yet would also down a half carafe of distilled liquor every morning. Popular Italian songs at the time portrayed him as the 'drunk in crimson cloth'. Selim's premature demise at age twenty-eight, in his bathtub, reportedly followed a days-long binge, during Ramadan no less.[23]

Selim's successor, the reclusive Murad III (r. 1574–95), started out as a teetotaler, possibly in reaction to his father's excesses, for which he is said to have cursed him. In early 1575, confronted by partying soldiers who drank to his health, he reinstated the edicts issued by Sultan Süleyman, banning winehouses in Muslim neighborhoods and in the vicinity of mosques and bathhouses.[24] Yet Murad's initial sobriety did not last: he is said to have imbibed in excess in the privacy of his palace in his later years.[25]

Official attitudes and policies vis-à-vis alcohol in the next half century must be seen in the context of a series of interlocking disasters that mark the period as an Ottoman 'Time of Troubles'. Upon acceding to the throne, Mehmed III (r. 1595–1603) removed all his rivals by having his nineteen brothers killed. Provincial revolts known as the Celali Rebellions raged amidst episodes of drought and famine. An increasingly debased coinage and rampant inflation eroded the pay of soldiers and brought large numbers of impoverished rural migrants to the capital. A new round of war against the Habsburgs was followed by the resumption of hostilities with Iran. The *sipahis* (the traditional cavalry) at times revolted in the heart of Istanbul, demanding to be paid in sound money. Their competitors, the janissaries ('new soldiers'), entered the fray as well. Originally created as the sultan's household troops, these infantry troops over time lost their exclusively military character and became noisily and at times destructively involved in urban affairs. The resulting violence, fuelled by serious rifts among the political elite, included the first two regicides in the House of Osman: first of Osman II (r. 1618–22), and then of Ibrahim (r. 1640–48). Adding to the misery were the huge fires that raged in Istanbul in 1633 and 1660, killing tens of thousands and laying large parts of the city in ashes.

These calamities and the need for scapegoats they created were partly responsible for the growing prominence of religion in politics, a process that culminated in the rise of the pietistic Kadızadeli movement, named after Kadızade Mehmed (1582–1635), a provincial preacher who in 1631 rose to the rank of Istanbul's *şeyhülislam*, the highest religious state official of the realm. After his death, his followers retained positions of influence in court circles. Most effective in this regard was Vani Mehmed Efendi (d. 1685), an Anatolian preacher who became the sultan's spiritual counselor after moving to Istanbul in the 1660s. The *shari'a*-minded Kadızadelis targeted smoking and drinking in particular, two activities that brought in substantial tax revenue.[26] Their war on vice resulted in frequent bans on the sale of liquor and the closure of taverns, yet also had to reckon with economic reality. Falling revenue due to rural banditry and drought combined with escalating military expenditure necessitated more rather than less state income. Fiscal urgency tended to trump piety. The lucrative wine trade between the Aegean islands and Istanbul thus was hardly ever outlawed.[27] Taxes on alcohol, now typically tied to a tax concession (*iltizam*) run by a non-Muslim, went up in 1573 and 1592. The proceeds might even serve religious purposes. The construction of Istanbul's 'New Mosque', Yeni Camii, begun in 1597 and only finished in 1665, for instance, was partly financed with money generated by the alcohol trade.[28]

Political unrest, natural disaster and, after 1631, Kadızadeli fervor are often difficult to disentangle from sultanic idiosyncrasy as animating forces behind policies vis-à-vis liquor. In the case of Mehmed III, urban strife and pressure from religious leaders rather than courtly piety played a dominant role. In 1595 and again in 1601, *sipahi* disturbances caused all taverns in the capital to be closed. Venetian sources identify grand vizier Damad İbrahim Pasha and the mufti of Istanbul as the driving force in the latter year. In their zeal to ban wine they even sought to prohibit foreign ambassadors from keeping any for their own use. The tremendous loss suffered by those engaged in the business may have played a role in the ban's reversal after a year and a half.[29] The sultan himself does not seem to have had a hand in these measures. Initially abstinent, he died at the age of thirty-seven, felled by a diet of fatty foods and copious drinking.[30]

Sultanic abstemiousness demonstrably informed official policy under Ahmed I, Mehmed III's son and successor (r. 1603–17). This devout ruler in 1613 ordered all wine shops in Ottoman territory closed and every wine press and vessel found in his realm destroyed, a measure that cost the state an estimated 100,000 *akçes* per annum.[31] The ban seems to have persisted under Osman II (r. 1618–22), who is known to have gone on nocturnal expeditions in the capital, in disguise and accompanied by the *bostancıbaşı* (the head of the imperial guards), in search of wayward janissaries enjoying themselves in taverns. Those found drunk were killed on the spot, their bodies ending up in the Bosporus. Osman himself would be removed from office and killed by rebellious janissaries preemptively acting against plans to have them disbanded.[32]

Murad IV (r. 1623–40), who mounted the throne at the tender age of eleven, represents a welter of contradictions in his stance vis-à-vis mind-altering substances. The first decade of his reign, when his mother, Kösem Sultan, and various grand viziers acted as regents, saw multiple Janissary rebellions, as well as a war with Iran that cost the Ottomans control over Iraq. The streets of Istanbul, meanwhile, were teeming with drunks and lined with taverns and coffeehouses filled with the dregs of society. Giorgio Giustinian, Venice's ambassador in Istanbul at the time, spoke of a society unmoored from its moral foundations, in which people drank openly and without inhibition.[33] All this changed in 1632, when Murad, now of age and ready to rule, became actively involved in state affairs. The conflagration of 1633, which reportedly destroyed 20,000 houses, prompted him to order the closing of coffeehouses throughout the empire as well as to outlaw smoking on pain of death. The measure, inspired by Kadızade Mehmed, was justified with reference to the fire hazard, but was really grounded in the sultan's view of coffeehouses as dens of Janissary sedition.[34] Alcohol's turn came a year later. Returning with great fanfare from a temporary residence in Edirne, Murad outlawed drinking, ordered taverns closed, and abolished the office of *şarab emini* (wine controller). He also had ships arriving in Istanbul with wine onboard set on fire. Murad rarely saw the inside of a mosque and never fasted, but went after drinking with the same zeal that he had brought to his war on coffee and tobacco, going around town and executing those found drinking on the spot, at times with his own hands.[35] Yet at some point, no later than 1637, he himself succumbed to alcohol, allegedly introduced to it by a commoner named Bekri Mustafa, who became his boon companion and who was to gain legendary status in the popular mind.[36] Murad remained a raging alcoholic until the end of his life, exceeding, in the words of Demetrius Cantemir, all his predecessors in drunkenness. He also allowed taverns to operate again, enabling their owners to purchase licenses from the *yeniçeri ağası* (the head of the janissaries). The sultan spent the last years of his life engaged in revelry, until liver cirrhosis got the better of him in early 1640.[37]

Murad IV's mentally disturbed and incompetent brother and successor, İbrahim, was more given to 'lust' than to wine.[38] Following his removal and strangling, his seven-year-old son Mehmed IV (r. 1648–87) was put on the throne. The new ruler naturally at first 'governed' under the watchful eye of courtiers, the two most important of whom were his mother, the powerful Hatice Sultan, and Vani Mehmed Efendi. The latter's influence is visible in the various measures that were taken following the terrible fire of 1660, which may have killed 40,000 people. Blaming the blaze and the subsequent outbreak of the plague on unislamic practices, Janissary debauchery, and the presence of minorities in Muslim quarters, the ulama succeeded in forcing the Jews of Eminönü to move to Hasköy across the Golden Horn. Wine could no longer be sold in Muslim neighborhoods. The ban was extended in the summer of 1670, first to any part of the capital that housed a mosque, next to private use, even by non-Muslims, and eventually to any town with a mosque throughout the empire. Smuggling and clandestine drinking went up and taxes plummeted as a result. Vani Efendi himself, meanwhile, indulged in secret; and grand vizier Köprülü

Fazıl Ahmed Pasha (in office 1661–76) may have followed the advice of his personal physician to continue the drinking that would kill him at age forty-one.[39] The last quarter of the century saw more instances of piety and profit vying for priority. Cantemir called Süleyman II (r. 1687–91) a sultan of 'great application and sobriety', and 'very devout in his religion'.[40] His successor Ahmed II (r. 1691–5), by contrast, apparently enjoyed wine.[41] Yet even as the former took power, the need to finance the ongoing wars in the Balkans prompted the state to allow drinking and smoking again. For alcohol, a şarab emini was (re-)appointed, and tobacco came under the supervision of an emin-i resm-i duhan. Yet less than two years later, the former position was abolished again in recognition of the illegality of wine drinking.[42] At the same time, grand vizier Köprülü Fazıl Mustafa Pasha (in office 1689–91) made the imposition of an official tax on spirits (müskirat resmi) on non-Muslims part of an overall tax reform. This impost was soon replaced by a doubling of the poll tax for dhimmis.[43]

These conditions of fiscally driven connivance at drinking punctuated by periodic bans continued in the eighteenth century and well into the nineteenth. Bans in later years just tended to be less frequent and of shorter duration than in earlier times. Instances when they were proclaimed are the 1703 Janissary rebellion that resulted in the deposition of Sultan Mustafa II and the accession of his brother, Ahmed III (r. 1703–30), the so called Patrona Halil uprising of 1730, and the Greek revolt in the 1820s.[44] No restrictions seem to have been imposed during the so-called Tulip Era, a period of relative peace, stability, and artistic flowering during Ahmed's reign. Grand vizier Nevşehirli Damad İbrahim Pasha, whose incumbency from 1718 to 1730 bookends the Tulip Era, may be seen as the ultimate symbol of the period's openness to European influence. His shopping list for Yirmisekiz Mehmed Efendi, who in 1720 was sent to Paris as the first Ottoman ambassador to France, included 1,000 bottles of champagne and 500 or 900 bottles of Burgundy. Mehmed Efendi may have been the first Ottoman to have tasted the newly invented type of wine that was champagne. He kept up appearances, though, for he never touched alcohol in public during his stay in the French capital.[45]

Ahmed's death in 1730 did not immediately end this spirit of relative freedom. Under his successor Mahmud I (r. 1730–54), a 'mild, affable and humane ruler' who savored 'his goblet of good wine in the afternoon or evening for the benefit of his weak stomach', there were reportedly 200 taverns in the Christian parts of the capital.[46] With the exception of a ban on the sale of wine in Galata and Pera imposed upon the appointment of the irascible Seyyid Abdüllah as grand vizier in 1747, Mahmud's reign seems to have been free from restrictions.[47] Subsequent rulers, faced with a proliferating number of taverns and attendant problems with impoverished migrants involving theft and prostitution, targeted alcohol again, typically upon taking power. Osman III (r. 1754–57) thus began his reign with an order to close all the taverns in Galata and Pera. Injurious to the financial interests of the *yeniçeri ağası*, the *bostançibaşi*, and the *voivode* (governor) of Galata, the rescript was widely violated and had little impact.[48] In fact, the sultan himself died under surgery from an illness caused by his intemperance.[49] His successor Mustafa III (r. 1757-74) reaffirmed the ban on alcohol sales.[50] Tavern owners had their licenses revoked as well by Sultan Abdülhamid I (r. 1774–89), who, nicknamed *veli*, strictly observed the Islamic law.[51] The next sovereign, Selim III (r. 1789–1808), kept up a tradition by banning booze upon acceding to power. Reissued several times in the next few years, the interdiction ran up against creative circumvention— Muslim males disguised as non-Muslim women would sneak drinks into their homes—but failed above all for economic reasons.[52] The people of the Aegean islands, deprived of their main source of income, filed petitions protesting the loss of their livelihood. Most importantly, for a state faced with a ballooning deficit due to war and reform, drinking proved to be too lucrative a source of income to forego. Within two years, Istanbul's wine shops and taverns were allowed to open again, and alcohol, burdened with a new tax (the *zecriye resmi*) once more became a significant source of state revenue. Pragmatism thus prevailed: people, and certainly *dhimmis*, were left alone in their drinking so long as the public order was not disturbed, and the authorities often effectively stimulated consumption for the revenue it generated, even if they would never advertise this as official policy.[53] Selim's partiality to French wines, meanwhile, was

97

no secret to anyone in the know, with his own seraglio rumored to be 'more accessible to bottles than to grandees'.[54]

Drinking Beyond the Court: Istanbul

Beyond the sultanic court, the level of alcohol consumption in Ottoman lands varied a great deal. As always, official censure hardly reflected reality. And official censure was unambiguous: the Ottoman mufti, Bahçe Abdüllah Efendi, declared that the mere act of looking at a carafe of wine was to commit a grave sin.[55] According to English diplomat Paul Rycaut, the Ottoman ulama had determined that if wine was spilled on the ground and a patch of grass should grow over it, and that grass was subsequently eaten by a sheep or an ox, their meat would be as harām as that of hogs. Rycaut also claimed that pious individuals fully abstained. Despite this prohibition, he added, wine was commonly drunk 'without caution or fear' by officials who were puzzled by the Western habit of diluting it with water, since only pure wine taken to the point of vomiting would satisfy their search for blissful besottedness (keyf). The Englishman echoed other observers by stating that people saw drinking as a natural extravagance of youth, yet a grave sin in old age.[56] The time-tested argument that wine counted as medicine was invoked as well by those intent on evading the Muslim taboo on drinking.[57]

One Italian traveler in the late fifteenth century claimed that, unlike Iranians, Turks did not drink wine.[58] Ample evidence gainsays this assertion, at least with respect to the elite. According to François Pouqueville, a French diplomat, only dervishes, soldiers, sailors and certain bourgeois types, as well as the lower classes, imbibed.[59] Lady Montagu—whose letters, written during her husband's tenure as British representative to the Porte in 1717–18, provide valuable information about Ottoman society—may have had these 'bourgeois types' in mind when she referred to Ahmed Bey, an official she met in Belgrade, who drank wine with total freedom. When asked how he squared this with his Muslim faith, he told her—alluding to the age-old elite-commoner distinction—that all of God's creation was there for man's enjoyment but that the ban on wine was a 'wise maxim' insofar as it targeted commoners, and that the 'Prophet never designed to confine those that knew how to use it with moderation'. He thus drank (albeit not in public, to avoid scandal).[60] According to James Porter, British ambassador to the Porte from 1747 to 1762, the Turks generally detested wine. Yet, echoing Lady Montagu, he recounted incidents where men of high rank engaged in alcoholic parties that might last days. They usually obtained their wine from trusted Christians. Porter even knew of officials who used leather boxes to carry wine home without the knowledge of their servants, or even smuggled alcohol into the palace in leather pipes 'pliant round their bodies'.[61]

These reports, as well as others, bring several features of 'Muslim' drinking into closer relief. One is the tendency to drink to excess. The sin lay in the act, not the quantity, and the volume of intake therefore did not matter. Reinhold Lubenau, a pharmacist who in 1587 spent time in Istanbul as a member of an Austrian mission, reports how Muslim Turks that he invited to his house would burst into loud shrieking before putting the glass to their lips, in hopes that their souls might move elsewhere while they engaged in drinking, lest they become tainted by this sin. Since the transgression was thought to be punishable regardless of volume, Lubenau added, people would keep quaffing until they 'collapsed on the floor'.[62] The French traveler Jean de Thévenot nearly a century later spoke in similar terms, insisting that many 'Turks' drank, often to the point of passing out, with the argument that, religiously speaking, consuming one cup was no different from downing ten pints. He added that they thought the 'Christian' habit of cutting wine with water absurd and incomprehensible.[63] The Flemish Ogier Ghiselin de Busbecq, Austrian envoy to the Ottoman court in the mid-sixteenth century, echoed these observations but also alluded to the belief in the redemptive power of repentance in old age:

> The drinking of wine is regarded by the Turks as a serious crime, especially by the older men; the younger men can commit the sin with greater hope of pardon and excuse. They think, however, that the punishment which they will suffer in future life will be just as heavy whether they drink much or little, and so, if they taste wine, they drink deep.[64]

99

Most people, Muslims and *dhimmi*s alike, drank (if they drank at all) in the privacy of their homes. Muslims would only frequent the alcohol-purveying Christian- and Jewish-run establishments stealthily, fearful of the punishment awaiting those who were caught. Following *shari'a* rules, the Ottoman law stipulated that in order to prove drunkenness, two witnesses must be willing to testify that alcohol had been imbibed voluntarily, in addition to the culprit himself confessing, or being in an active state of intoxication when brought before a judge. In all cases the breath of the offender must still retain the smell of alcohol. Punishment was eighty lashes or the bastinado. Drinking openly during Ramadan was a capital offence.[65] In a humanitarian twist, repeat offenders received the prescribed punishment two more times; but if caught again they would be considered incorrigible and labeled 'imperial drunkard' or 'privileged drunkard'. Once apprehended, such individuals would only have to announce their status to be sent home or taken to sleep on the warm ashes of a bathhouse.[66]

Contemporary observers have differing views on the prevalence of drinking in the Ottoman army. They praise the discipline of the sultan's military, attributing its success against the European armies in part to the relative sobriety of its soldiers and the absence of brawls among them, both of which were the result of strict measures taken by the authorities, including the closure of taverns and a ban on the sale of wine two or three days before the army's arrival at the site of a prospective battle.[67] None of this kept soldiers from drinking, though. The troops of Selim II, for instance, could not be 'compelled to abstain from wine'.[68] Drinking in the ranks of the Ottoman army indeed may have gone up with time. Writing in the late seventeenth century, Rycaut noted that the former military discipline had broken down, making drunkenness common among Ottoman soldiers. The unruly janissaries became notorious for their drunken brawls.[69] Later observers confirmed that the janissaries drank a lot—and often defiantly—and caused disturbances wherever they operated, and that the authorities at times sought to prevent this but as often allowed them to indulge in exchange for bribes.[70] The champion here was Bekri (drunkard) Mustafa Pasha (d. 1690), who started his career as an ordinary Janissary, became the head of the corps in 1679, and ended up serving as grand vizier between 1681 and 1689.

In Istanbul, drinking extended to the walled 'Muslim' parts of the city with their hidden taverns, semi-clandestine watering holes that operated in the shadows during the day and came to life after sunset. Two reports from the 1790s suggest the existence of hundreds of these, mostly unauthorized *meyhanes*.[71] Yet most of the drinking took part in the 'Christian' part of the city: the quarters lying north of the Golden Horn, Galata, and, further up the hill, Pera (modern Beyoğlu).[72] Galata, and in particular Hasköy, the lower part along the waterfront of the Golden Horn, abounded with drink shops run by Christians and Jews and frequented by locals as much as by foreign sailors. With tiled floors, a fountain in the middle, and wooden gallery seating for the guests along the walls, these were noisy places where entertainment was provided by crossdressing dancing boys (*köçekler*), mimicry, and musicians. The clientele consisted of 'hot-blooded young men, the potent youths fond of drinking and fornicating with women and boys', as well as 'chronically addicted scoundrels', Africans, and Russians 'of bad stock'.[73] Most of the customers were foreigners or local minorities, but Muslims would go there as well, entering in the morning and only reemerging under the cover of darkness. Every day, Muslims could be seen hammered on the streets, and not just in the capital.[74] For the truly down and out, those who only wanted to drink, there were also the *buzahanes*, which only served light-colored *buza* made from fermented millet, barley, or rice.[75] All this is confirmed by Evliya Efendi, who quoted the following as one of the typical local drinking songs:

> My foot goes to the tavern, nowhere else
> My hand grasps tight the cup and nothing else
> Cut short your sermon, for no ears have I
> But for the bottle's murmur, nothing else[76]

The sixteenth-century Ottoman poet Lâtifi called Galata the pleasure-house of the world, a quarter filled with drunkenness.[77] As the French botanist Pitton de Tournefort put it more than a century later, in Galata one sensed a kind of liberty hardly found anywhere else in Ottoman lands. It felt like a Christian town in the middle of Turkey, an enclave where cabarets were allowed and where the 'Turks' themselves came to taste alcohol.[78] All this lent Istanbul's Christian quarters an image of 'otherness', eliciting a reaction that was part abhorrence and part fascination-cum-envy on the part of Ottoman chroniclers.[79]

The Hungarian Baron de Tott, who spent eight years in the Ottoman Empire in the mid-eighteenth century, provides some more detail. Taverns in Istanbul, he insisted, were as public and numerous as the ones at home. Protected by the government, they were a source of tax revenue collected by the *şarab emini*, whose lucrative position was farmed out. During religious holidays, taverns were forced to close to 'prevent the fateful effects of the habitual debauchery of the people'. The police at such times would place a seal on their doors. Yet a wicket down below, intentionally overlooked by the authorities, would allow anyone to enter anyway.[80] Even when they were officially closed, such as during *bayram* ('*id al-adhā*, the sacrifice feast concluding the Hajj), they would still serve cautious and quiet customers through small side doors.[81]

Drinking in the Provinces

The use of alcohol in the Ottoman Empire was concentrated in the cities. And, even there, the incidence of drinking was not always obvious. Horatio Southgate, an American Episcopalian missionary who lived in the Ottoman Empire for much of the 1830s, claimed that, aside from in Istanbul, wine shops were rare to nonexistent in Ottoman territory. Having visited 'four-fifths of the cities of the Empire', he had 'never seen one', although he strongly suspected that many were hidden away in the Christian parts of towns.[82] East of Istanbul, the use of alcohol indeed seems to have been rather limited. We hear about fourteenth-century peasants settling in for the harsh Anatolian winter by stockpiling wines (*khumur*), in addition to jerked meat, oil, and butter. Near Denizli, in Asia Minor, pomegranate wine was produced during the same period.[83] Various strands of unorthodox Islam also allowed their members to imbibe without compunction. The Nizaris, Isma'ili adherents to a syncretistic form of Shi'ism that venerates 'Ali, are a case in point. The English clergyman Maundrell, traveling from Aleppo to Jerusalem in 1697, characterized them as follows:

> For 'tis their principle to adhere to no certain Religion; but chameleon like, they put on the colour of that Religion, whatever it be, which is reflected upon them from the Persons with whom they happen to converse. With Christians they profess themselves Christians. With Turks they are good Musselmans. With Jews they pass for Jews, being such proteuses in Religion, that nobody was ever able to discover what shape or standard their Conferences are really of. All that is certain concerning them is, that they make very much and good Wine, and are great Drinkers.[84]

The same holds for the Druze—descendants of a heterodox Shi'i movement with roots in eleventh-century Egypt who abided by few of Islam's injunctions and proscriptions, including the ban on the consumption of alcohol—as well as for many Sufi communities, most notably the members of the Bektashi order, to which many of the janissaries belonged and who were commonly associated with public drunkenness.[85]

Elsewhere in Ottoman lands, a strong Christian presence tended to coincide with Muslim drinking. Good examples are the Balkans and regions with a strong Greek presence. In 1675, the English clergyman-physician John Covel had this to say about Karağaç, a majority-Greek village located about a mile west of Adrianople (Edirne) to which he took refuge from the plague that was raging in the city at the time:

> This whole town lives by selling of wine, and every day come hundreds of people from Adrianople to be drunk, so that it was impossible but the plague should be brought thither. The Janizary Aga [head of the local Janissaries] eats at least 10000 dollars a year out of them for selling their wine; and yet he came there many times in shew of severity, but notice was always given at least an hour before he came, so that he always found the coast clear. By the by, I must tell you the Turkes love wine, and drink as much as other people. I am assur'd not one person in five

(through all this part that I have travelled) refuseth it; at court (excepting the Grand Signor himself, the Mosaíp [*musahib*, boon companion of the sultan] and Kaimmachám [*kaymakam*, deputy of the grand vizier] not a man but will take his kéiph [*keyif*, pleasure] profoundly. I have seen the Viziér himself mamúr [*mahmur*, drunk], that is crop-sick, several times. All the Greeks and Armenians (not daring to be merry in Adrianople in companies), come here to feast, and I have been several times by when 200 or 300 persons have all been setting together feasting and drinking like fishes; and the Turkes observe the same freedome, or rather take much more. My landlord (the parson) was the greatest vintner in town, and to secure his wine he put the greatest part of it into a place in the church, and in the yard by us the chief Turkes of the city would come and be merry publickly.... The common Turkes never drink but to stark drunkennesse.[86]

In the Balkans, age-old drinking traditions, introduced by Slavic tribes and indigenized as Christianity took hold, continued with no noticeable abatement. Officially, only non-Muslims were allowed to manufacture and consume alcohol. But, as elsewhere, Muslims indulged as well, at the risk of censure. In Albania, Muslims enjoyed their liquor as much as Christians did.[87] Bosnian Muslims generally obeyed the ban on wine prescribed by the *shari'a*, yet considered raki, an anise-flavored spirit distilled from grapes, to be permitted by Islam.[88] Eighteenth-century Sarajevo was home to twenty-one taverns.[89] In Ottoman Greece, conditions were no different. In Crete in the 1830s, Muslims were said to consume their wine 'as unscrupulously as any Christian'.[90] The majority Greek population of the Morea drank wine while the few Turks living in the region rather enjoyed *buza*. They also consumed an eau-de-vie of reportedly poor quality, in addition to a fierce concoction made with mint and hot peppers.[91] The Levant, with its age-old vinous tradition, remained a land of viniculture as well, and European travelers hailed the wines of Lebanon and Syria.[92] On the Aegean islands lining the coast of Asia Minor, which supplied most of the wine consumed in Ottoman lands, drinking was common and unproblematic.[93]

Izmir—or Smyrna, as Europeans called it—was the ultimate Levantine city. A small market town until *c.* 1660, Izmir in the late seventeenth century grew into a major, internationally connected port with a population of perhaps 40,000, some 20 percent of whom were Jewish or Christian. As the city grew into a hub for Middle Eastern commodities, principally silk carried by the Levant Companies, there came an influx of European merchants. By the 1670s, these may have numbered between 400 and 500, concentrating in a quarter around the 'Street of the Franks'. All this is reflected in the growth in the number of taverns from solely one to twelve or thirteen in the early 1600s.[94] In the process, the city became known among Muslims as *Gâvur İzmir* ('infidel Izmir').[95] To European visitors, by contrast, Izmir—endowed with a balmy climate and with its minorities protected by the ever-present European ships in its harbor—seemed much more relaxed than other Ottoman cities.[96] In the early eighteenth-century, Izmir's non-Muslim community kept its taverns 'open all hours, day and night'.[97] Those on the Street of the Franks appeared to be coffeehouses during the day, drawing Christians and Muslims alike, but at night turned into boisterous enclaves where wine flowed freely and drunken brawls occasionally resulted in death, leaving the Ottoman state and foreign consuls scrambling to establish order.[98] At times, ships from North Africa would dock at Izmir, bringing Muslim sailors who, only familiar with Christians as slaves, would roam around causing great drunken disturbances in the Frankish quarter.[99]

Greater restrictions applied in Aleppo, a caravan center located inland in Syria and distinctly less cosmopolitan than Izmir. With relatively few foreign residents, Aleppo had nothing like a Galata quarter or a Street of the Franks.[100] Wine in Aleppo was brought in from Kilis, the center of a thriving viticulture located some 70km to the north, by local Christians and Jews who, for a fee, were allowed to transport a limited amount of grapes into the city so as to make wine or brandy for their own use.[101] At times, this practice prompted the Ottoman government to intervene and threaten Jews and Christians with punishment.[102] Turkish officials and the local janissaries were known as unruly tipplers, and drinking by Sufis seeking ecstasy was generally tolerated. But semi-public consumption of alcohol was confined to the *Han al-gümrük*, the customs hostel where (foreign) merchants were lodged.[103] During Muslim holidays, Christian-run wine taverns closed their doors, or at least conducted their business as inconspicuously as possible. Syria's other main city, Damascus, felt the reach of the Ottoman law in a 1564 sultanic order to close cafés and taverns.[104] In the mid-eighteenth century, we hear of instances of wine being sold by Christians and Jews, which was ordinarily permitted but occasionally turned controversial, leading to vendors being fined and even expelled from the Jewish quarter.[105] It remains unclear to what extent such measures were influenced by the Istanbul-centered Kadızadeli movement or acted as harbingers of the imminent Wahhabi movement coming out of the interior of the Arabian Peninsula.[106]

Even the Arabian Peninsula was not alcohol-free. In Yemen, the Jewish community traditionally produced and (illegally) sold palm wine.[107] The risks involved are illustrated by an incident in 1725, when an inebriated Muslim who had purchased his wine from the Jews of Sanaa sexually assaulted a boy in the latrine of a mosque. The scandal that erupted almost led to the destruction of the synagogues in town and the expulsion of the local Jewish community.[108]

On the opposite side of the peninsula, in Oman, wine was especially common in the interior, where adherents to the Ibadi branch of Shi'ism formed the majority. The inhabitants of the verdant *wadi*s of Jabal Akhdar manufactured a blend of pomegranate juice and white grape wine. The people of the Banu Riyam tribe openly consumed large quantities of wine produced by their women; the same wine was sold on the coast as well. Much of the brandy smuggled into the country also made its way to the interior.[109]

In the port city of Jeddah, too, the center of the relatively open region of Hijaz, alcohol was to be had without too much trouble. In 1770, the Danish explorer Carsten Niebuhr noted that resident Greeks manufactured a poor-quality brandy.[110] The Swiss Johann Ludwig Burckhardt half a century later claimed that the Indian fleet brought raki in barrels to Jeddah and that, mixed in with sugar and extract of cinnamon, this was sold as cinnamon water.[111] The foreign consuls in town at times received limited permission to import booze for their own use as well as that of the tiny European community. But the illegal sale of local *arak* to Muslim residents was quite common.[112] The Indian Sikander Begum, performing the Hajj in 1863–4, noted that the Arabs of Jeddah lived chiefly on camels' milk but that the local Turks commonly drank wine and liquor.[113] Heinrich von Maltzan, a German traveler who visited Jeddah in 1860, tells us that raki was very popular in town but that, given its cost, only the (Turkish) pasha, his officials, Ottoman military officers, and some pilgrims consumed it. That still added up, as drunkenness in Jeddah, von Maltzan claimed, was on par with its incidence in England and the United States. He insisted that almost all Turks, and even some 'pious' clerics, excepting the 'traditional' ones, were given to drinking. Most indulged in secret, but some imbibed quite openly. Von Maltzan even reported seeing servants of 'rich Turks' on the streets carrying raki. Pilgrims, too, enjoyed their alcohol, And poor people would drink *buza* to forget about their misery for a while.[114]

Even the holy cities of Islam, Mecca and Medina were not immune to alcohol. *Nabidh* had been available to pilgrims in ninth-century Mecca.[115] According to Burckhardt, 'Neither the sanctity of the holy city, nor the solemn injunctions of the Qur'an are able to deter the inhabitants of Mekka from the using of spirituous liquors, and the indulging in all the excesses which are the usual consequences of drunkenness'. The religious and secular leaders of Mecca and Jeddah—the ulama, the merchants, and the notables—he added, were all in the habit of drinking sweetened raki imported from India, 'which they persuade themselves is neither wine nor brandy, and therefore not prohibited by the law'. The less wealthy made do with fermented liquor made from raisins brought in from Ta'if, in the 'Asir, while the lower classes consumed *buza*. While in Ta'if, Burckhardt had met a Turk, a member of the suite of the Egyptian ruler Muhammad 'Ali, who openly sold privately distilled brandy.[116] Von Maltzan, who also visited Mecca, confirms this, observing that there was no lack of raki shops in Islam's holiest city. However, pilgrims would only frequent these under the darkness of night.[117] The English poet-traveler Charles M. Doughty (1843–1926) half a century later spoke of the incidence of 'drunkenness and harlotry' in Medina, adding that there was 'much tippling in arrak, hemp smoking and excess of ribald living'.[118]

Egypt and North Africa

Information about alcohol consumption in Ottoman-controlled Egypt is spotty. When the Ottomans conquered the country in 1517, the local population was shocked to see the Turkish soldiers drink openly.[119] The Ottomans initially left the Egyptians in charge of their own affairs. The first governor who served under them (after the brief tenure of grand vizier Yunus Pasha), Hayir Bey, was an Egyptian (of Abkhazian background), a 'bad-tempered, often drunk and cruel' man, as historiographer Ibn Iyas characterized him.[120] After Hayir Bey's death in 1522, the Ottomans established more direct control by appointing their own pashas to govern Egypt. These imposed a regime that narrowed the legitimacy of Islamic jurisdiction to that of the Hanafi school, resulting in the dismissal of Egyptian judges. Naturally the local population resented this policy, and civil unrest followed. Claiming to represent a renewal of the faith, some of the newly installed judges doubled down on stamping out vice, meting out severe punishment for the slightest infractions. A good example is chief Ottoman judge Husayn b. Muhammad Husam al-Din Qarachli Zada, appointed in 1579, under whose regime 'no scent of intoxicant was smelled in Cairo'.[121] Measures against drinking typically went hand in hand with attempts to suppress prostitution, and were often undertaken with the aim of propitiating the divine whenever the Nile did not rise to its required height fast enough. Here, too, enforcement remained erratic, running up against the need for the tax revenue yielded by alcohol.[122]

Under the Ottomans, wine continued to come from abroad. In Alexandria, a port city more or less autonomous from central control in the late eighteenth century, the local authorities levied a tax on its importation and sale.[123] In nineteenth-century Egypt, the Coptic population distilled *arak* from dates, while local Greeks produced *tafia*, a sweet beverage of reportedly poor quality made with molasses and sugar cane.[124] *Buza* was consumed in Egypt, too, as it was elsewhere in the Ottoman Empire, mostly by members of the lower classes as they whiled away their time in disreputable *buzahanes*. *Buza*, which spoiled after a day in Egypt's hot weather, came in an alcohol-free version—so-called 'sweet' *buza*—which was legal, and a 'bitter' alcoholic one, which was not.[125]

A few rare references to the period of Ottoman rule in Egypt occur in a local text known as the *Damurdashi Chronicle*. One, from 1702–3, refers to an official who organized a wine-fueled party in a different house each night. The chronicle also mentions the head of the janissaries, who acted as *muhtasib* in eighteenth-century Ottoman Egypt, launching an attack with his military escort on *buza* houses throughout Cairo and, more particularly, on wine shops in the city's Jewish quarter.[126] Yet, most of the available information about drinking in early modern Egypt comes from foreign sources. These tell us that for all practical purposes Muslims might imbibe, except during Ramadan, when those caught would be put to death.[127] One observer in 1589 insisted that the country's vineyards had all been ruined by Muslims, but that wine imported from Crete, Cyprus, and Lebanon was nevertheless available in the country, albeit at a hefty fee.[128] Johann Wild, a German who spent years in Ottoman captivity at the turn of the seventeenth century, claims that drinking had been banned by the pasha to prevent abuse by the local janissaries. Anyone found violating the ban might receive lashes on the soles of his feet and subsequently be shamed in public by being bound to the back of a donkey, facing backwards, with sheep entrails coiled around his neck and the stinking lining of its stomach draped on his head. He would then have to suffer children throwing mud at him as he was paraded around town.[129]

Another eyewitness offering information on the use of alcohol in Egypt is Johann Michael Vansleb (Wansleben). Having arrived in Damietta in early 1672, this German discovered that the bark that had carried him was laden with wine destined for the French men in town, including the consul. Onward transportation toward Cairo required a special permit from the capital's pasha, though, since the Ottoman sultan had banned all alcohol imports. Vansleb called Damietta a city of a great many taverns serving *acqua vitae*, the tax on which was pocketed by the corrupt local governor, who also confiscated six barrels of Cyprus wine from the ship that had transported Vansleb.[130] Anthonius Gonsales, a Flemish friar, insisted during the same period that pious Muslims, especially those who had performed the Hajj, would not only not drink but get out of the way when they saw Christians consume wine. Those who imbibed often used a separate room where they would also sleep, or they indulged in Christian homes. Janissary soldiers in Cairo at times got so hammered they had to be brought home on donkeys.[131]

Further west in North Africa, Jews invariably were the ones who manufactured wine as well as brandy, and many Muslims enjoyed these in private.[132] Alcohol was widely available in the coastal areas but harder to find further inland.[133]

Early modern Tunisia, nominally under Ottoman control, comes across as relatively relaxed. One visitor called it a land of liberty where no one bothered people about their religious beliefs, where one prayed and fasted when one felt like it, and where anyone drank who could afford it.[134] That included Muslims, who preferred French wine and also consumed wine from Sardinia, Spain, and Sicily, but mostly stayed away from brandy and rum.[135] A local tipple called *lagmi*, or *lakmi*, extracted from the date palm, was popular as well. Taverns were mostly situated outside the city walls, as was common throughout North Africa. The ones in the old city, the medina, were generally close to the *baños*, the prisons where Christian slaves were housed. Tavern keepers were often Christian slaves as well; indeed, for many of them, running a tavern was potentially a ticket to freedom.[136]

As elsewhere, official policy in Tunisia varied from ruler to ruler. The members of the short-lived Muradid dynasty (1613–1702) are all said to have celebrated their ascent to power with wine-fueled banquets.[137] The next ruling house, that of the Husaynids, were far less taken with alcohol. Husayn 'Ali Bey (1705–35), the founder of the dynasty, gained his religious credentials by having taverns adjacent to mosques demolished and moved to the outskirts of the city. His son and successor, Abu Hasan 'Ali I (r. 1735–56), fearing riots after his sons rebelled against him, forbade the sale and purchase of grapes for the purpose of making wine, threatening to have offenders burned alive.[138] The fourth Muradid dynast, 'Ali II b. Husayn (r. 1759–82), continued this ban and destroyed any remaining taverns in the city.[139] Still, imports of wine, legal or otherwise, are recorded throughout the seventeenth and eighteenth centuries.[140] At all times, importing wine, even by resident Europeans, required a permit (*tadhkira*) from the bey. The facility of obtaining such a permit fluctuated. While Louis Frank was the personal physician of Hammuda Basha Bey (r. 1782–1814), it was difficult to get, and nothing made the bey angrier than those who managed to smuggle in alcohol without one.[141] Yet MacGill relates that the same magistrate had been a great lover of Bacchus in his early years, until, in a drunken stupor, he ordered some people strangled to death for making too much noise. Relieved to discover the following day that his grand vizier had disobeyed his order and merely incarcerated the culprits, he never touched alcohol again. Still, 'thirsty for gain', Hammuda Basha Bey freely allowed wine to be imported under the pretense that it was vinegar.[142]

Morocco, in the far west of North Africa, lay beyond Ottoman control, yet its drinking patterns resembled those of Algeria and Tunisia. Jews and Christians manufactured wine and other alcoholic drinks for themselves as well as for Muslims who dared to break the law of the faith, except during Ramadan, when everyone abstained.[143] As elsewhere, the country's rulers varied in their inclinations. The Sa'dian dynasty (1554–1659) had its fair share of alcoholic chieftains. Indeed, all the later ones, except for Moulay Zidan (r. 1603–18), seem to have been topers. This is true for Moulay Muhammad b. 'Abdallah al-Mutawakkil (r. 1574–76) and Muhammad al-Shaykh al-Ma'mun (r. 1603–8), as well as for 'Abd al-Malik (r. 1618–36), who was assassinated by his boon companions while sozzled. His brother al-Walid resembled him, both in his being devoted to the bottle and in his being murdered—soon after mounting the throne—by members of his own retinue, whom he had treated with great cruelty.[144]

The Sa'dians fell into paralyzing decadence and lost control over their country in the course of the seventeenth century. The first ruler of the succeeding 'Alawite dynasty, Moulay Rashid (r. 1666–72), died young during an alcohol-fueled party, struck by the branch of an orange tree while galloping his horse.[145] His son Moulay Isma'il (r. 1672–1727), who would be the longest-reigning ruler in Moroccan history, was a model of temperance in terms of food and drink. He scrupulously observed all religious duties and had the Koran carried in front of him by a religious scholar whenever he went out riding. In 1693, he received the French envoy Pidou de Saint Olon with his face covered up to his eyes, presumably so that he would not have to smell the alcoholic breath of an infidel. According to the Frenchman, Moulay Isma'il achieved his highs with opium, although his compatriot Busnot suspected that Moulay Isma'il did in fact imbibe, but in secret, making sure that the effects never showed.[146] Unlike Moulay Isma'il, several of his many sons did nothing to hide their dissolute behavior. One was Moulay Zidan, the heir presumptive until he was executed by his father in 1707. No less cruel than his father, he drank to excess, impervious to the latter's admonitions to desist.[147] Moulay Isma'il's oldest son, Moulay Ahmad al-Dhahabi, who ruled between 1727 and 1729, was a 'great lover of drink and very lavish and expensive in his cups, but parsimonious when sober'.[148] The father nevertheless appointed him as his successor, perhaps, as John Braithwaite surmised, to lend his own reign greater glory by contrast. Ahmad al-Dhahabi was quickly overthrown by his half-brother, 'Abd al-Malik, but reinstated in 1728/9 by the black slaves who supported him, allowing him to rule for another year.[149]

The Moroccan upper classes were not exactly teetotalers either. Joseph de Léon, an eighteenth-century captive-observer, writes that the elite would host evenings in private homes enlivened by music and dance as well as wine and eau-de-vie.[150] Other well-informed observers write of similar occasions. According to James Grey Jackson, a British merchant who lived in Morocco for sixteen years, many Moroccans considered any food or drink deemed medicinally beneficial to be 'lawful to indulge'.[151] The Dutchman Hendrik Haringman, who accompanied his father on a diplomatic mission in 1788, reports how during a reception in the garden of the Swedish ambassador in Tangier, the local basha and his entourage enjoyed the alcoholic offerings—Malaga, Bordeaux, and various liqueurs—like the best Christians.[152]

Alcohol in Mughal India

Since in most parts of India the grape does not thrive, wine was not readily available in those climes. François Bernier (1620–88), a French physician who resided in the subcontinent between 1658 and

1669, informs us that the region was essentially dry.[153] Wine, if it was to be had at all, was imported from Shiraz in Iran and consequently very expensive. Those who drank consumed *arak* (*arack*), an acrid, vodka-like brew made of sugar cane, which was also the main ingredient in a cocktail called *bouleponge*, most likely a bastardization of 'bowl of punch'. *Toddy*, a beverage made from the unfermented sap of the palm tree, was most popular among the lower classes.

Pace Bernier, alcohol had become a staple in India with the arrival of the Timurids. Ruy Gonzáles de Clavijo, who visited Timur Lang's court in Samarqand in 1403–4 as envoy of the Spanish king Henry II, described the banquets organized and overseen by the chieftain as endless pre-meal alcoholic affairs, where guests' cups were filled continuously, and whoever was able to hold his liquor the longest earned the epithet *bahādur*, or hero. Women fully participated in these bacchanals and, indeed, held their own drinking parties.[154] Indigenous sources bear witness to the centrality of alcohol in Timurid society. The *Zafarnāma* ('Book of Victories') describes an outdoor gathering near Samarqand in 1404, a year before Timur's death, as follows:

> From end to end were goblets of jade and crystal filled with wine, koumiss, honey, *muthallath*, liquor, and sherbet. The pages of time that glittered with night and day were inscribed with myriad designs of gaiety and glad tidings … When the princes and *noyas*, in accordance with the custom and ritual, drained one after another their goblets filled with ruby-red wine, and the ritual of toasting was completed, trays laden with more food and multitudes of more various edibles were set than can be described.[155]

Timur's successors were hardly different. Two of his sons, Jahangir and 'Umar Shaykh, died prematurely from excessive drinking. Another one, Miran Shah, 'large, corpulent and gouty', had mental problems. He was a heavy drinker, as was his wife, as Clavijo found out when he attended a boozy banquet that she was hosting.[156] Faced with deceased or incapacitated offspring, Timur chose his grandson, Pir Muhammad ibn Jahangir, as his successor. However, Pir Muhammad shared the family vice in that he spent most of his time 'quaffing fire-colored liquid and listening to the sound of the lyre and the harp'. Lacking the necessary support of his relatives, he failed to take over. After he was murdered by his own vizier in 1407, the throne fell to Shahrukh, the son Timur had passed over for being too meek and pacific.[157]

Shahrukh (r. 1405–47), who presided over a brilliant court in Herat, was different, at least outwardly. An observant Muslim, he moved away from the Chingizid law and in 1411 reinstated the *shari'a*, marking the occasion by destroying taverns. His zeal in preventing untoward behavior was apparently such that he allowed his *muhtasibs* to violate the Muslim code of privacy and enter people's homes, even those of high-ranking officials. Apprized that the palaces of his own son and grandson contained wine-cellars, he personally made sure that their contents were ostentatiously poured out on the street. The success of these campaigns was limited, though. Various courtiers and some of Shahrukh's own family members are on record as avid drinkers. His favorite son, the artistically inclined Baysunghur, died of alcoholism.[158]

At any rate, the official austerity ended with Shahrukh's death. His oldest son and successor, Ulugh Beg (r. 1447–9), was at least as cultured as his father (a polyglot, he became famous as a mathematician and astronomer, and he even has a lunar crater named after him), but he was less inclined to emulate his austere lifestyle. Starting out as the governor of Samarqand, the dynasty's ancestral capital, in 1409, Ulugh Beg only ruled the empire for a brief two years after his father's death. In that period, Samarqand became known for being the site of royal feasts, with the guests treated to singing, dancing, and copious amounts of wine, earning the ruler ample rebuke from dervish shaykhs and religious officials.[159]

The last of Timur's descendants, Husayn Mirza b. Mansur b. Bayqara (r. 1469–1506), who ruled Khorasan before it fell to the Uzbek Shaybanids in the early 1500s, followed a time-honored tradition of issuing bans on the consumption of alcohol (and the shaving of beards) on the grounds of it being contrary to the law of Islam. Mostly enacted to propitiate the religious classes, this interdiction remained a dead letter, certainly within court circles. Sultan-Husayn Bayqara himself abided by the strictures of Islam by remaining sober during the first six or seven years of his reign.

After that, there was not a day in which he did not imbibe, although never before midday. His sons and the members of his military were alcoholics as well.[160] In 1500, one of his sons, Abu'l-Husayn Mirza (d. 1507), governor of Marv, reconciled with his father after having launched a rebellion against him. He demonstrated his repentance by publicly pledging to give up drinking. Yet, in good Timurid tradition, he remained an inveterate toper. Indeed, his defeat-cum-demise on the battlefield against the Uzbeks was due in part to after effects of the revelry he had engaged in the night before.[161]

In early modern Muslim India, as elsewhere, drinking alcohol mostly seems to have been the province of the privileged, who consumed it in the privacy of their own homes.[162] The Mughals, who ruled much of the Indian subcontinent from the early sixteenth until the mid-eighteenth century, offer us countless examples of excessive and, in some cases, obsessive drinking. No one exemplifies this more than the founder of the dynasty, Sultan Zahir al-Din Babur (r. 1526–30), whose father, 'Umar Shaykh Mirza II (r. 1456–94), may have died from alcoholic excess.[163]

Abundant firsthand information about Babur's boozing can be found in his tell-all autobiography, the *Baburnāma*. The *Baburnāma* can be read as one long drinking confessional, with its vivid portrayal of the author carousing with his companions until they become tanked-up and stagger away on horseback.[164] Babur seems to have been particularly fond of taking the 'hair of the dog' the morning after.[165] Indeed, he just stopped short of Peter the Great's adage that one should never go to sleep sober by declaring 'only' Saturdays, Sundays, Tuesdays and Wednesdays to be drinking days. The other two days Babur reserved for the enjoyment of *ma'jun*, a paste of opium with various additives.[166]

Babur and his warband used alcohol as a social lubricant, as a way of bonding with one another, relaxing between battles, and coping with the physical and psychological stress of military life. Babur's Islam, leavened by the relative toleration of the Hanafi strand, seems fully compatible with these wild ways of the steppe, alternating drugs, drink, and women with religious piety and fervor, and considering all of it of a piece with the righteous path.[167] As he says in one of his poems:

Ramadan came and I a pious wine-sot.
'Id arrived and with it the remembrance of wine.
Neither fasting nor prayer [but] years, months,
Nights and days with wine and *ma'jun*, crazy and drunk.[168]

Yet Islam's strictures did not leave Babur unaffected. In his own words, he did not drink for the first thirty-seven years of his life, taking up the cup in the city of Herat, which at the time was known for its freewheeling lifestyle.[169] Nor was he free from guilt. When he was thirty-nine, Babur stated that, although he drank wine 'most copiously', he fully intended to keep with the convention that saw Muslim men reconsidering their wayward behavior when they turned forty.[170] However, forty came and went and there was no sign of abstinence. (It is not clear whether he did repent later on, as his memoir is interrupted between 1519 and 1525.) Babur seems to have continued in his intemperate ways until 1527, when he was again overtaken by remorse. He used his victory against the Rajputs in the Battle of Khanwa that year to declare his determination to turn his back on wine. Many of his retainers followed him in this, and soon a sultanic decree backed up by a fatwa declared the use of wine forbidden on religious grounds. Babur seems to have abstained for the remainder of his life, although his craving never ceased, and he continued to indulge in the use of opium as an obvious substitute.[171]

The next two Mughal rulers—Babur's son, Humayun (r. 1530–40 and 1555–6), and Sultan Akbar (r. 1556–1605)—were opium addicts rather than boozers. Akbar occasionally drank a glass of wine, but he preached moderation and believed that 'indulging in intoxicants and being reckless is not the habit of emperors'.[172] He did, however, allow the Europeans in his realm to cultivate the grape and drink wine with the argument that their relationship with wine was like that of fish with water and that depriving them of it was like killing them.[173] Yet two of Akbar's sons and potential successors, Shah Murad (1570–99) and Danyal (1572–1605), were real topers. The first died prematurely from alcohol poisoning; the latter was passed over for promotion to a high rank in the Mughal military due to his alcoholism. Eventually, he too succumbed to excessive drinking, leaving (Salim) Nur al-Din Jahangir the only viable candidate for the throne.[174]

Jahangir (r. 1605–27) was little different from his brothers. Contemporary sources—both the Persian-language record as well as European eyewitness reports—agree that he, too, was a heavy drinker, taking up the cup at age eighteen and gravitating to hard liquor once wine lost its kick, at which point he added opium and electuaries made with opium 'for greater stimulation'.[175] Mughal chroniclers all agree that Jahangir had a drinking problem, yet they vary in the extent of their criticism of his lifestyle, depending on whether their sympathies lie with the ruler or with his rebellious son, who came to power in 1628 under the name Shah Jahan. European observers offer details: the Englishman Thomas Roe, who visited Jahangir's court in 1615 as the first representative of the English East India Company (EIC), 'never saw a man soe enamord of drincke as both the King and Prince [Khorram] are of redd wyne'. On one occasion, Roe found the ruler 'so neere druncke … that I had not the oportunitye to moue business to him'.[176] Roe's need to justify his failure to obtain free trade for the EIC may have played a role in his negative portrayal of Jahangir as a stereotypical Oriental despot.[177] Yet his words are echoed by other eyewitness visitors. For instance, William Hawkins, an EIC official who spent nearly three years in Agra between 1609 and 1612, recounts how in the afternoon Jahangir would first pray, next eat a bite, and then drink a glass of ardent liquor. He would then retire to a private room and stay there in the presence of those he had invited—Hawkins claims he was regularly among Jahangir's guests for two years—and quaff five more 'cupfuls', which, the Englishman adds, was 'the portion that the physicians alot him'.[178]

Another informant is the Venetian physician-traveler Nicolao Manucci, who arrived in India in the mid-1650s, and would remain until his death more than sixty years later. Manucci's account about Jahangir's penchant for alcohol is thus based on hearsay, but it aligns with the other evidence we have, including the sultan's own writings. Manucci called the Mughal ruler a 'man with no desire to undertake the labour of further conquest and one who contented himself with enjoying the fruit of his father's labours'. Jahangir, he claimed, had initially tasted wine (and pork) out of curiosity and, confronted with the fact that both are proscribed in Islam, had used his royal power to cow the clerics, threatening to become a Christian, until they proclaimed that the 'King might eat and drink whatever he liked'. Thereafter the sultan 'seized every occasion to aggravate the ulama, ordering the casting of pigs in gold and refusing to fast and even eating and drinking—wine—while holding audiences during Ramazan'.[179]

The Dutchman Francisco Pelsaert wrote in 1628 that, a handsome man in his youth, Jahangir was at first a severe ruler who meted out strict justice to evildoers. Yet, once he married Nur Jahan, his favorite wife, in 1611, he fell under her spell and ended up engaging in little more than hunting and other pastimes. Routinely swilling three jugs of wine after a day of chasing animals, he would fall asleep after Nur Jahan undressed him.[180] According to Manucci, it was Nur Jahan who made him temper his ways, prevailing upon him to quaff no more than 'nine cupfuls' each time he drank, which she herself handed him. The Venetian presents the relationship, in Orientalist fashion, as a romantic tale involving a strong-willed, scheming woman and a henpecked husband who at first revolts against the limitations set by his spouse but ultimately submits to her demands.[181]

It is hard to tell what to make of these stories, some of which may be apocryphal, picked up as part of bazaar gossip or spread by the sultan's detractors after his death, and written down almost a century after the events. However, like his great-grandfather Babur, Jahangir wrote an autobiography in which he freely talks about his boozing. Also like Babur, the reason he gives both for drinking and for reducing his intake is almost entirely devoid of references to religion, or to Nur Jahan. In his own words, he was an incorrigible toper, often consuming 'twenty phials of double-distilled spirits' every twenty-four hours—fourteen during the day and the rest at night—and eating but one meal a day. But then, in 1600, five years before ascending the throne, Jahangir found himself weakened by excessive boozing and suffering terrible hangovers. He resorted to following his doctors' advice and began to reduce his intake by two-thirds, and thus ended up drinking only at night. In 1615, he declared that he had stuck to this regime for the past fifteen years. But, as Roe's eyewitness account reveals, Nur Jahan's assistance failed to wean him off the bottle. At the onset of his reign, the Mughal sultan declared a ban on the manufacturing and sale of 'wine, spirits or any sort of intoxicant or forbidden liquor', clearly a move to conform to what was expected of a new ruler upon his accession. However, again in his own words, he kept drinking himself. In 1627, his condition deteriorated. Unable to walk, he now had to be carried in a palanquin. In his last months, Jahangir was no longer able to take opium, and thus was forced to break a four-decade habit, although he still managed a few bowls of wine each day.[182]

Jahangir's second son, Parviz Mirza (1589–1626), who was initially slated to succeed him, took after his father. The Dutch said that he was sloshed every day of the week, drinking at night and sleeping during the day, which inevitably was detrimental to the effectiveness of the army he commanded on his father's behalf. After suffering a bad bout of *delirium tremens* followed by a coma, he died at age thirty-eight, his body ravaged by excessive drinking.[183]

Jahangir's third son and successor, Khurram (1592–1666), who took the name Shah Jahan after mounting the Mughal throne in 1628, represents a radical departure from his immediate forebears in that he remained a teetotaler well into his twenties. On 5 January 1616, his twenty-fourth birthday and 'weigh' day (when the emperor was literally weighed against valuable commodities and foodstuff, which were then distributed among the poor throughout the year), Jahangir allowed him to drink on *nawruz* (festival days) and other special occasions, alluding to alcohol's presumed health benefits. Yet he cautioned him to imbibe in moderation so that he might enjoy the benefits of alcohol rather than suffering its harmful consequences.[184]

In 1621, years before coming to power, Shah Jahan was on his way to the Deccan to give battle when he officially proclaimed his abstinence as well as a ban on alcohol throughout his realm. He ostentatiously collected all the cases of wine and spirits his staff could find and had the contents poured into the Chambal River. He next had all the gathered gold- and silver-ornamented drinking vessels smashed and their mangled remains distributed to poor villagers. His drastic repudiation may have been inspired by watching the debilitating effects alcohol had had on his father's health. Yet it remained an act of repentance, a gesture all the more remarkable since it was made by a ruler in the bloom of his life, at an age for which drinking counted as a natural pastime. The temperance anyhow did not last, for in 1657—a year before he was forced to abdicate and then imprisoned by his son, Aurangzeb—Shah Jahan had a beautiful wine cup made from white jade carved out for himself.[185]

Shah Jahan's sons, too, knew their way around alcohol. One, Shah Shuja', took after his father, being a 'lover of songs, dances and women, among whom he spent days without giving audience, drinking wine to excess'.[186] The predilections of Dara Shikuh, Shah Jahan's eldest son and heir apparent, are less clear. His brother Aurangzeb accused him of 'brazenly drinking alcohol in public' with his shameless and apostate companions. But this was in 1558, a time when Aurangzeb had reason to delegitimate his brother, as he was ready to usurp power after imprisoning their father.[187] The case of Muhammad Murad Bakhsh (1624–61), the sultan's youngest son, is far less ambiguous. If we are to believe François Bernier, who served as court physician to Dara Shikuh and Aurangzeb, Murad Bakhsh was very fond of drinking, and he was frequently plied with booze by his brother Aurangzeb.[188]

Sultan Aurangzeb (r. 1658–1707)—the last of the strong-willed Mughal rulers as well as the longest-reigning one—is celebrated (or loathed, depending on one's viewpoint) for his *shari'a*-mindedness and his attendant puritanism.[189] Ending the nonsectarian religious regime that had prevailed among his forebears, he sought to reimpose the strictures of Hanafi Islamic law on the society he came to rule.[190] This followed his own cathartic experience with alcohol, in which he fell madly in love with a girl named Hira Bai in 1653. As the story goes, Aurangzeb pursued Hira Bai, and one day she put him to the test by offering him a cup of wine, despite his protests, and insisting that he empty it. As soon as he succumbed, she took the cup from him and drank it herself, informing him that this had been a test of his love and 'not to make your palate bitter with this liquor full of evil'.[191]

Aurangzeb's purity campaign targeted 'heretical' practices, Shi'ism, and the celebration of *nawruz*, as well as intoxicants of any kind. He thus kicked off his reign with a ban on the use of drugs and stimulants. Manucci, now speaking from experience, claims that it was Akbar who had first given his subjects license to drink by allowing Christians of his realm to indulge. The situation then worsened, with Muslims taking up the bottle under Jahangir who, as we saw, was a great tippler himself. During the reign of Shah Jahan, they drank with full liberty, Manucci insists, and the shah—tolerant of diverse lifestyles, though not a drinker himself—had done nothing to curtail the habit. When Aurangzeb mounted the throne, the Venetian quipped, he had observed that in his entire realm only two people did not drink: Aurangzeb and his chief judge, Shaykh 'Abd al-Wahhab (d. 1675), who (at least outwardly) was a 'stickler for religion'. And even that was not true, according to Manucci, who personally sent the magistrate a bottle of wine every day, which the latter savored in secret.[192]

Aurangzeb went about his ban rather methodically, if we are to believe Manucci, who was partisan to Dara Shikuh, a rival and ultimately a victim of his brother.[193] He first forced all resident Europeans except physicians to leave the port city of Surat and settle beyond its suburbs, where they were free to consume—but not sell—alcohol. He next sent the police inspector (kotwal) to search out both Muslims and Hindus who sold spirits. Punishment for violators was severe, involving the loss of a hand and a foot and, not infrequently, death. Manucci himself claims to have seen six scofflaws left to die on a dung heap. Christians who were caught selling alcohol faced incarceration and might see their shops plundered by soldiers. At first, the new regime was strictly enforced, emptying Delhi's shops of wine.[194] Yet in time the rules were relaxed. As always, the ingrained habits of the elite prevailed: withdrawing into the privacy of their homes, they continued to imbibe.[195]

India After the Mughals

Muslim India in the eighteenth century, and really until the formal dissolution of Mughal rule in 1858, shows great continuity with respect to the place of alcohol in high society. The 'dry' days of Aurangzeb came to an end with his death in 1707, judging by the seventy-five chests of distilled liquor brought and successfully distributed by the Dutch Ketelaar embassy of 1711–13 among various

Mughal magistrates in Agra, Delhi, and Lahore.[196] It is not clear how much each of the last fourteen Mughal rulers imbibed. Bahadur Shah (r. 1707–12), Aurangzeb's immediate successor, indulged, at least before he mounted the throne in 1707.[197] His ephemeral successor, Jahandar Shah (r. 1712–13), oversaw a court filled with frivolous entertainment.[198] Muhammad Shah (r. 1719–48) is said to have been a 'besotted drunkard and a debauch', although his main biographer calls these aspersions into question.[199] John Henry Grose, who in the mid-eighteenth century served as an agent of the English EIC, described conditions at the time as follows:

> Few of the Moors abstain from wine or spirituous liquors but are fonder of cordials and drams than of wine, which they do not think strong enough for them, no not even the arrac, unless treble-distilled: and, what is more unaccountable, they pretend that brandy, for example, better known on the Indian coast by the Portuguese name of Aguardiente, is cooling, when moderately taken in the very midst of any faintness, brought on by fatigue, or excessive heat of the day. They manage, however, with so much discretion and reserve in this article, that even those who have the character of the greatest drinkers among them, are never seen, in public, in the indecent disorder caused by that vice, which is not only fatal to their reputation, but sometimes precipitates their governors and great men into a dangerous abuse of their power.[200]

5

ALCOHOL IN THE EARLY MODERN ISLAMIC EMPIRES

THE SAFAVIDS

Introduction

Following the death of Timur Lang in 1405, his empire, to the extent that it was ever unified, fragmented into separate pieces covering large parts of the eastern Islamic world, from Afghanistan to Anatolia. Beginning with his son Shahrukh (r. 1405–47), Timur's direct successors ruled from Herat in western Afghanistan, presiding over an artistically brilliant court. Already before Timur embarked on his conquests, a Turkic tribal confederation known as the Qaraquyunlu (Black Sheep') had come to power in the west, and more specifically in northern Iraq. Holding out against Timur's depredations, they would rule over Azerbaijan, the southern Caucasus, Iraq, and eastern Anatolia until 1468, when their main rivals, the Aqquyunlu ('White Sheep') dynasty engulfed them and ended up ruling not just their territory but the entire Iranian plateau until they, in turn, were absorbed into the Safavid state in the early 1500s.

Sultan Uzun Hasan (r. 1453–78), the best-known and most prominent Aqquyunlu ruler, reportedly 'always drank wine with his meals', and thus conformed to a well-established pattern.[1] Like

123

many Muslim rulers before and after him, he also proclaimed a ban on drinking. The edict in question, issued in 1470–1, possibly in anticipation of a planned campaign against the Ottomans, was engraved in stone placards, which were affixed to the entrance portals of mosques.[2]

The integral role alcohol played in the lifestyle of the Turkmen elite applies in equal measure to the rulers who defeated and took over from the Aqquyunlu, the Safavids. Originating in thirteenth-century eastern Anatolia as a mystical order of presumably Kurdish stock, the Safavids at first espoused a blend of ill-defined Sunni beliefs and pre-Islamic rites and customs. Over time, in a switch that remains poorly understood, they came to champion Twelver Shi'ism, the branch of Islam that reveres 'Ali, the Prophet's cousin and son-in-law, and his eleven descendants. Together, they are known as the Twelve Imams, the last of whom is believed to have disappeared and is anticipated to return at the end of time to reestablish justice on earth. By taking Tabriz in 1501 and proclaiming Twelver Shi'ism the faith of his realm, Isma'il (r. 1501–24), the dynasty's first political leader, marked his family's transition away from leadership of a Sufi dispensation to rule over an incipient territorial state. Assisted by fierce Turkmen warriors known as Qizilbash, or 'red-heads' (in reference to their red headgear), the Safavids next expanded their dominion across the Iranian plateau and proceeded to rule well into the eighteenth century.

Safavid Shahs and Alcohol

Wedded to the open spaces of the mountains and steppes of Azerbaijan, the Safavids and their Turkic retainers held on to their tribal ways longer than the Mughals and much longer than the Ottomans. High-volume outdoor consumption of alcohol was part of this, recalling the *razm-u-bazm* tradition of hard fighting and hard drinking as the expected pursuit of warriors. Safavid society would eventually evolve into a direction similar to that of the Ottoman Empire—from a band of freebooting, hard-drinking warriors to an urban-based, bureaucratic order professing a more scriptural version of Islam and susceptible to (clerically inspired) censure—but the path was circuitous and the pace much slower.

Shah Isma'il especially lived up to traditional tribal customs and expectations. Indeed, with Babur, Isma'il must count as one of the great boozehounds of all time. The head of a wild tribal warrior band, revered by his followers as an incarnation of the divine and espousing a form of Islam suffused with pre-Islamic, semi-pagan customs and rituals, Shah Isma'il threw lavish banquets at which he drank copiously, surrounded by the Qizilbash, who, having brought the Safavids to power, continued to form the mainstay of their military. Paradoxically, the shah's marathon drinking did nothing to detract from his aura, and indeed augmented it. Drinking among the early Safavids was a physical contest, a sign of masculine strength and virility.[3] But royal binge drinking also had an ideological, and even sacral, dimension, for it projected the image of a ruler who inhabits his own moral universe, beyond the strictures of religion. The Safavid shah was thought to possess supernatural as well as healing powers, conferring holiness on anything he touched, and his body was considered incapable of being 'sullied by the use of wine and other impurities forbidden by religion'. Thus, it was believed that he was committing no sin by consuming alcohol; indeed, all those he forced or allowed to drink with him were equally absolved.[4] Beyond the ruler's warrior masculinity and his supralegal stature, drinking was inherently part of the fun and merriment to which he was entitled.[5] The shah had the right to engage with unbounded pleasure so long as he did not neglect his realm and his subjects.

Shah Isma'il's fondness for alcohol is well documented. Some of the earliest European reports about the Safavids self-servingly present him as hostile to the Prophet of Islam and favorably inclined to Christianity, even (falsely) claiming that he had let himself be baptized. Portuguese eyewitness accounts confirm the image, reporting how the Safavids drank alcohol with abandon and ate pork with gusto. Hailing from a culture in which public drunkenness was frowned upon, (southern) European guests were shocked to witness raucous scenes of ritualized drinking interspersed with hunting trips amounting to a permanent party at the shah's gatherings.[6] Islamic sources, including Turkish ones, convey the same image. The Ottoman poet Fuzûlî is said to have dedicated his *khamriyya* collection *Beng ü bâde* to Isma'il.[7] Propagandistic tracts circulating in Ottoman lands associated drinking with Shi'i excess, insisting that the Qizilbash felt no need to abide by Islam in their conduct and considered sodomy as well as alcohol to be lawful and legitimate.[8]

The Persian-language sources, too, refer to Isma'il's excessive drinking. According to chronicler Mirza Bayg Junabadi, the shah moved seamlessly from morning drink (sabuh) to evening drink (ghabuq).[9] Qazi Mir Husayn Maybudi, a judge in early sixteenth-century Yazd, no doubt spoke metaphorically when he claimed that, during the rule of Isma'il, local mosques and madrasas were turned into stables and taverns.[10] But the unapologetic way in which contemporary sources describe Isma'il's carousing leaves little to the imagination. They mention parties filled with riotous drinking, music-making, and dancing performed by young boys who were also sexually available to the attendees.[11] Isma'il's dipsomania could be gruesomely vindictive and performative. In 1510, following the defeat and killing two of his enemies—the Uzbek ruler Muhammad Khan Shaybani and the Tatar ruler Azbak—he had their skulls turned into gold-plated drinking vessels, humiliating his foes posthumously by making them part of his incessant boozing.[12]

Isma'il's warrior career came to a premature end in 1514, when he suffered a terrible defeat at the hands of the Ottomans on the plain of Chaldiran, near the current Turkish-Iranian border. The Iranians famously lost this decisive confrontation in part because, the night before the battle, the Qizilbash had organized a drinking party that went on until dawn. Beyond the actual defeat, it remains unclear whether the shah's subsequent intemperance was encouraged by his courtiers, who were keen to bamboozle a fuddled ruler for their own interests, or whether it resulted from grief over the loss of his favored wife, Bihruza Khanum, who had been taken captive by Sultan Selim at the battle.[13] Following the debacle, a depressed Isma'il, his drinking worsening, is said to have given up on making war. Withdrawing into isolation, he spent much of his time carousing until 1524 when, barely thirty years old, he succumbed to his dipsomania. Isma'il's Ottoman counterpart and rival, Sultan Selim I (r. 1512–20), said of him that the wine cup illuminated his gatherings day and night, dispelling the sadness of his realm, which he was unable to govern with the same strength and energy as his forebear, Uzun Hasan.[14]

All Safavid rulers after Shah Isma'il drank at one point or another. Even Isma'il's son and successor, Shah Tahmasb (r. 1524–76), indulged in his early years—indeed, in early 1524 the Portuguese traveler Tenreiro witnessed Tahmasb at barely ten years old participate in one of his father's drinking gatherings[15]—before he had a change of heart and issued a ban on drinking as part of his so-called Sincere Repentance (to be discussed below). His successor, the ephemeral Isma'il II (r. 1576–7), was known as much for his cruelty as for his dissolute lifestyle. The next shah, Muhammad Khudabanda (r. 1577–87), upon ascending to the throne, issued a ban on drinking and other 'un-Islamic' activities. There are no records of its effect on society, but compliance certainly did not include the ruler himself, who soon 'turned day into night', spending all his hours engaged in *lahv-u-la'ib* ('lust and play'), which consisted of sexual activity, music-making, and consumption of large amounts of wine.[16] Hamza Mirza, Muhammad Khudabanda's eldest son and the heir apparent until he was murdered in 1586, followed in his father's footsteps by being a toper as well.

The most celebrated of Safavid rulers, Shah 'Abbas I (r. 1587–1629), consumed alcohol at all hours of the day, but never allowed its effect to get in the way of cool-headed decision-making. His grandson and successor Shah Safi (r. 1629–42) reverted to the immoderate drinking habits of his forebears and died, thirty years old, in a drunken stupor. Safi's son and successor, 'Abbas II (r. 1642–66), also indulged, resembling his great-grandfather in that he routinely invited guests, including foreigners, to his drinking parties. That inclusiveness ended with Shah Sulayman (r. 1666–94) and Shah Sultan Husayn (r. 1694–1722), the last two effective Safavid rulers. Both drank, although mostly in a secluded court setting. Shah Sulayman kept at it until the very end. He died at age forty-six, and his last words were reportedly, 'Bring me some wine.'[17] At the onset of Sultan Husayn's reign, the 6,000 bottles of wine found in the royal cellars were ostentatiously poured out on Isfahan's *maydān*. Yet soon thereafter, persuaded to take up the cup by his alcoholic great-aunt, Sultan Husayn too succumbed to the lure of alcohol, even though a ban on drinking in his realm remained in place.

Alcohol in Safavid Society

In addition to the pre-Islamic legacy and the customs of the Central Asian steppes, drinking in Safavid Iran was also influenced by the rites and rituals of the Christians of the Caucasus. Georgians especially were known as lusty drinkers.[18] Shah Isma'il is said to have had some 10,000 Christians in his service.[19] Over time, thousands more were brought to Iran as so-called *ghulāms*, or royal 'slaves', where they were given high military and administrative positions with the aim of sidelining the unruly Qizilbash. By the seventeenth century, the upper echelons of the Safavid army were dominated by Georgians, while Armenians were prominently present in the ranks of the bureaucracy. Georgian women, in turn, infiltrated the harems of the shah and his grandees by becoming their favorite consorts. Indeed, the mothers of most Safavid rulers were Georgian (or Circassian) concubines. One late Safavid chronicler refers to the *ghulāms* as people who ate pork, drank wine, and 'indulge[d] in other depravities characteristic of drunkards' inside mosques.[20]

All this helps to explain the acceptance of alcohol as an integral part of life among the Safavid elite. The royal palace in Isfahan contained a winehouse (*shira-khāna*) so elaborate that it would have been the envy of any European ruler.[21] The famous French taveler Jean Chardin describes it as a beautiful and pleasant building set in the middle of a garden, filled with an infinitude of long-necked wine bottles made of cornelian, jade, crystal, onyx, agate, gold, and silver, some of them inlaid with precious stones. The shah naturally had his own sommelier, known as the *shirachi-bāshi*.[22] Moreover, wine was unapologetically included in *mihmāndāri*, the daily allowance of victuals to which foreign representatives (even Muslim ones) visiting the country were entitled.[23]

Wine was also integrated into the Safavid tax regime. After Georgia fell under Safavid control in the mid-sixteenth century, the region's fiscal obligation to the central state came to include a biannual supply of twenty cases of wine to the royal wine cellar.[24] Georgia outstripped other regions in the perceived quality of its wine, but it was not the only purveyor to the court.[25] The Jesuit missionary Villotte in 1689 passed a vineyard near Sava, about 100km southwest of Tehran, which supplied wine to the shah's palace.[26] No region furnished as much as Shiraz, traditionally the capital of Iranian viticulture. In the seventeenth century, 1,200 liters of top-quality Shiraz wine were set aside each year to be sent to Isfahan.[27]

The Safavid elite was not just given to wine. Vodka or aquavit was routinely included in the presents Russian envoys brought for Iran's rulers.[28] Nor was drinking limited to the royal court. Many Safavid high officials were tipplers. These included, just for the late seventeenth century, provincial governors such as Biktash Khan Afshar of Kerman, who was supplied with booze by the local Zoroastrian community; Safi Quli Khan Yazdi, who drank himself to death; and Nasir 'Ali Khan, who, shortly after arriving in Bandar 'Abbas to take up his post, often stayed indoors engaged in drinking for eight to ten days at a time.[29] Clerics were not necessarily abstemious either. During his stay in Kerman, the French merchant-traveler Jean-Baptiste Tavernier was invited by a mullah who served him a rather good wine.[30] And the Armenian chronicler Zak'aria of Agulis called the *shaykh al-islām* of the northwestern town of Ordubad, who was notorious for oppressing the local Christian population, a 'drunk and a debaucher'.[31]

Drinking clearly was widespread in Safavid Iran, even if most ordinary people and certainly Muslims never consumed anything but water and fruit juice. Alcohol was not associated in any way with sociability, and consuming it usually had only one purpose. To get drunk fast, Chardin insisted, was what Iranians sought from alcohol, which is also why they preferred strong, undiluted wines, ones with *damāgh* (a kick).[32] Wine grapes were cultivated all over, from Georgia and Armenia to Fars and Yazd. Tavernier tells us that the people living near Lake Van in eastern Anatolia did a brisk trade catching fish from the lake and exporting them to Armenia and Iran, since Armenians and Muslim Iranians liked to drink wine and eat fish on festive occasions.[33] The people of Shiraz especially lived up to a long-held stereotype: they 'revel[ed] all the night and drink the round/till wine and sleep their giddy brains confound'.[34] This mostly involved wine, but other forms of booze were consumed as well. Arak made from dates thus was the typical tipple on the Persian Gulf coast.[35]

As elsewhere in the Islamic world, the manufacturing and sale of wine in Safavid Iran was mostly the bailiwick of non-Muslims. In Isfahan, the local Armenian community was engaged in this. The Jews of Shiraz, numbering between 600 and 1,000 families, produced more than half a million liters per year in the 1660s.[36] In both cities, European missionaries were involved in viticulture as well. In 1616, the Carmelite fathers planted 25,000 vines on a plot of land that Shah 'Abbas I had given to them. Since the annual yield of several thousand liters exceeded their private consumption, their employees ended up selling wine and brandy, earning the men of the cloth the sobriquet of tavern owners. In Shiraz, too, the Carmelites engaged in vintnery, although it is not clear if they sold what they produced to anyone other than to European residents.[37] The local European residents—the Portuguese, the English, the Dutch, and the French—had a license to produce wine, too, all for export purposes, with India being the main destination.[38]

Courtly Drinking and Its Purposes

Royal drinking had various practical purposes. In an Iranian tradition that goes back to antiquity, wine allowed Safavid rulers to pry secrets from the lips of their courtiers. For this, the shah used an oversized gold ladle studded with precious stones, called *hazār-pisha* (a 'thousand crafts'—after the remarkable feats those who drank its contents were said to be able to perform). Depending on who was telling the story, this vessel could hold anywhere between a pint and four liters.[39] It would be brought out to heighten the festivities during drinking sessions, but more often the shah would use it to hear out or test his officials, at times to fatal effect.[40] In 1691, Shah Sulayman presented his newly appointed grand vizier, Muhammad Tahir Qazvini, with a full *hazār-pisha*, asking him to explain what he thought were the most pressing needs of the country.[41] In late 1691, during a court gathering, the same ruler offered all courtiers in attendance the royal wine cup, except for Saru Khan Sahandlu, the *qurchibāshi* (head of the tribal guards), who had displeased him. This proved to be an ominous sign, for the official was beheaded following the meeting.[42]

Royal drinking, as these examples show, was in part about the power of the dynast to assert his authority by forcing his underlings to drink. 'Abbas I especially employed alcohol to show his entourage who was in control. The awesomeness of royal power comes through most dramatically in an incident that took place in December of 1608, coinciding with Ramadan. During a meeting attended by Portuguese missionaries as well as some Iranian clerics—including the *sadr*, the state's highest religious official—Shah 'Abbas ordered wine to be brought for the Christian guests. He then invited everyone to drink a small amount. According to António de Gouveia, the Portuguese envoy and narrator who sat next to the shah, 'Abbas then turned to him and whispered: 'When you leave here and meet the pope, tell him how, during Ramadan, I ordered wine in the presence of all my judges and their chief, and made them all drink it. Tell him that, although I am not a Christian, I am worthy of his esteem.'[43]

The Drinking Parties of Shah 'Abbas II

Safavid shahs drank above all to celebrate—victory in battle, diplomatic alliances, friendship—and 'Abbas I and 'Abbas II routinely invited foreigners to partake in these events. 'Abbas I shared his gold drinking cup with the Polish envoy Muratowicz as part of the latter's farewell audience in 1600. The Safavid ruler first drank half of its contents to the health of the 'great and famous king' (of Poland), had it filled again, and invited his guest to do the same.[44] Shah 'Abbas II ordered the royal goblet to be brought out to toast to the victory of the Austrians against the Turks at the Battle of St. Gotthard (Mogersdorf) on 1 August 1664. The same ruler, having been told that Europeans drank with their heads uncovered, from crystal glasses which they subsequently would throw down, did the same. In an act that was highly unusual and would otherwise be considered an outrage, he even removed his turban, ordering his boon companions to do the same in honor of his 'very close friend, the emperor of the Romans'. The custom, it is said, subsequently became known as *'abbāsiyāna*.[45]

That Western visitors were not just included but were in some cases even allowed to share the shah's own cup betrays the secular make-up of rulers who not only transgressed the general Muslim ban on drinking but were willing to flout the more specifically Shi'i proscription on mingling with non-Shi'is as well. The Safavids were exceptional in the Muslim world in their openness to interacting with Europeans and their receptivity to outside influence. The ease with which especially 'Abbas I and 'Abbas II sat and conversed with Christians is attributable in part to their familiarity with Christianity, but it also owes something to a certain convergence between Shi'ism and Catholicism with respect to narrativity and iconography. Fascinated by rituals and images involving martyrdom and resurrection that must have seemed close to those of their own faith, Iran's rulers showed a genuine interest in Christianity and its stories. Shah 'Abbas I regularly engaged in discussions about matters of faith and philosophy with official visitors, diplomats, merchants, and missionaries.[46] Whenever he was in a good mood, Shah 'Abbas II invited the European goldsmiths living in Isfahan to sit and drink with him.[47] The same ruler in 1652 invited the Dutch envoy Joan Cuneaus to a session during which the two men discussed varieties of wine. Cuneaus thereupon ordered his men to bring six or seven bottles from the lodge of the Dutch East India Company.[48]

We have several eyewitness accounts of parties organized by 'Abbas II which had Europeans in attendance. One conspicuous instance occurred in late 1665, a mere six months before the shah died. The occasion was a reception for members of the first official French delegation to Iran, representing Louis XIV, who were hosted at one of Shah 'Abbas II's palaces for an evening of entertainment and hijinks, including the watching of fireworks. The French missionary in attendance claimed that the libations included 'excellent Shiraz wine', of which the guests were offered several rounds in gold cups. The shah then promised that henceforth he would send some to the great monarch of France, on French ships, each year.[49]

We have a particularly detailed description of a party held earlier that same year, on 3 February 1665, in honor of the foreign residents of Isfahan, Dutch and French merchants and missionaries. The guests included Reinier Casembroot, the resident director of the Dutch East India Company (VOC); Tavernier and his companion, André Daulier-Deslandes; and Raphaël du Mans, the Capuchin friar who resided in Iran for nearly fifty years, serving as the shah's main interpreter.[50] The party started at 9am, with food and—in Daulier-Deslandes's words—'world-famous Shiraz wine', served from long-necked bottles of sculpted Venetian crystal. The palace staff, aware that Europeans liked to have food with their drink, had prepared meat as well as trout from the Caspian Sea region. The atmosphere was relaxed, the conversation alternating between light topics and serious matters involving the present military strength of the Ottomans, geopolitical conditions in Europe, and the difference between the monarchical and republican forms of government, which the Dutch in attendance were asked to elaborate on. Turning to more intimate topics of conversation, the shah, assisted by du Mans as his interpreter, asked Tavernier if he had visited India. 'Abbas showed his French guest various paintings of rulers, which Tavernier recognized as Shah Jahan and the sultans of Golconda and Bishapur. The shah next made Tavernier bring out the portrait of his wife, which the latter had shown him a few days earlier, and asked if he had any images that revealed European ladies' dress. 'Abbas was also offered two oil paintings of courtesans brought from Venice or Livorno by Armenian merchants. All this prompted the ruler to ask Tavernier about his taste in women and his ideas about female beauty, to which the Frenchman diplomatically responded by pointing out that beauty is in the eye of the beholder and that different cultures have different aesthetic standards. Père du Mans, meanwhile, who never touched wine other than during the Eucharist, was persuaded to drink before being allowed to leave at 11pm.

Throughout its course, the party was enlivened by the dancing and singing of more than a dozen dancing girls. There was also a Georgian playing the harp and an Armenian performing on an organ that the Russian tsar, Alexis Mikhailovich, had presented to the shah as a gift. A certain Mr. Sein, a Frenchman who served the shah as a goldsmith, was invited to play the flute. One of the Armenians in attendance presented 'Abbas II with a spinet which he had brought from Holland. With the shah's approval, the attendees soon started singing drinking songs, such as 'Enfants du mardi gras, voici la fête aux bons ivrognes'. 'Abbas, having made each of the attendees finish a *hazār-pisha* in one gulp, ended up in a jolly mood, to the point of doling out money to his guests and allowing them the exceptional honor of drinking from the royal goblet. He jokingly asked Tavernier which one of the dancing girls he preferred, suggesting that he choose one of them for himself. The Frenchman, in his own words, managed to extricate himself from this dilemma by insisting that married Frankish men remained faithful to their wives even while traveling abroad.

Not everyone was happy. During the almost sixteen hours that the party lasted, the eunuchs on guard remained in their erect positions without eating or drinking anything. Several courtiers stood by as well, watching from a downstairs porch and afraid to enter the hall, frowning disapprovingly at their sovereign behaving with such familiarity with foreigners. All this went on until after midnight when the shah, alerted to that fact that his guests' attention was flagging, gave them permission to leave.[51]

After the party, Shah 'Abbas II stayed in his harem for four or five days. Then he once again invited several Frenchmen to join him in a party, confirming what Daulier-Deslandes had said of him: that the shah liked to drink with Europeans since they were able to hold their liquor better than Iranians. Daulier-Deslandes was again summoned to play the spinet. Another Frenchman played the violin, and again the wine flowed freely—until someone ruined the spinet by breaking a bottle over it. Tavernier tells us that this time matters turned grim, as one of the guests, deep in his cups, made a buffoon of himself by dancing wildly and knocking the turban off the head of another guest, who had recently come back from the hajj and had thus chosen not to drink. The shah became so irritated with this behavior that he ordered the inebriated fellow thrown to the dogs. Four or five guards jumped on him and dragged him out of the hall. However, instead of being fed to the dogs, the most ignominious death possible, he was kept alive until the next morning and then beaten to death.[52]

As this cruel ending suggests, drinking at the Safavid court might turn from raucous fun, with rulers amusing themselves as fuddled courtiers were carried out horizontally, to murder and mayhem in a flash.[53] Excessive wine consumption indeed routinely resulted in rowdiness and, occasionally, in real violence. Drunken officials are said to have argued and hurled insults at each other in front of the newly acceded Shah Safi in 1629.[54] A few years later the same ruler, keen to assert his legitimacy, got rid of the ruler of southern Iran, Imam Quli Khan, who was Safi's main general and also his main competitor. In a grisly scene reminiscent of the story of John the Baptist and Salomé, he had the heads of Imam Quli Khan and his two children served up as a surprise dish during a drunken banquet.[55] Nor is the story of the guest who was supposed to be fed to the dogs the only instance of cruelty displayed by 'Abbas II in an alcoholic haze. Tavernier offers several examples of the shah ordering the killing of those who declined his invitation to drink.[56] The Dutch refer to Haydar Beg, a courtier forced to drink until he expired.[57]

Shah 'Abbas II's successor, Shah Sulayman, engaged in similarly unpleasant behavior. At one point, he is said to have ordered the blinding of one of his brothers in a drunken stupor.[58] His reign also offers the most vivid examples of the burlesque element in Safavid royal drinking, a watered-down version of Peter the Great's 'Drunken Synod', as exemplified in his treatment of his long-serving grand vizier, Shaykh 'Ali Khan (in office 1669–89). The shah had an especially complicated relationship with Shaykh 'Ali Khan, who was known for his moral rectitude, which included principled abstinence. Relying on his competence, the shah left the grand vizier in charge of state affairs while he himself spent most of his time engaged in pleasure in the seclusion of his harem. We have disturbing reports about the ruler humiliating Shaykh 'Ali Khan by forcing him to drink in his presence or, the height of degradation, by cutting off his beard. After sobering up, he would show great remorse, apologizing profusely and bestowing robes of honor on his vizier. Sulayman seems to have admired his grand vizier's abstemiousness as much as he resented it, for during Ramadan he abstained himself, suggesting a guilt-ridden effort to emulate his grand vizier's probity.[59]

Guilt, Inhibition and Bans

As much as alcohol permeated early modern Iranian society, consuming it remained a custom at variance with religious prescriptions. In Safavid court culture, alcohol enlivened banquets

135

and acted as a social lubricant, but it could never go beyond furtive embrace and public disavowal. Commoners who disturbed the public order while intoxicated might be severely punished. Nicolao Manucci, writing from Isfahan in 1654, reports having seen two men paraded around town, 'bound, each on a camel, their bowels protruding', for causing a disturbance after drinking wine in public.[60] And since the Safavid state from its inception presented itself as a faith-based enterprise, no shah could simply disregard the strictures of Islam. Indeed, the impulse to ban goes back to the very beginning of the Safavid experiment. The founder of the Safavid order, Shaykh Safi al-Din (1252/3–1334), issued various ordinances against loose living—including the consumption of alcohol—which were reiterated in Ardabil, the ancestral town and original center of the movement, after his death.[61]

The first well-documented Safavid ban occurred under Shah Tahmasb I, who, as said, is known to have indulged as a young boy. In 1526, less than two years after taking power, he issued his first *farman* outlawing drinking as well as gambling and prostitution, clearly with the intent to establish his legitimacy. In 1532–33, this was followed by a more comprehensive anti-vice campaign known as the Sincere Repentance. In his autobiography, Tahmasb alleges that this change of heart was inspired by a dream he had during a pilgrimage to the shrine of the Eighth Imam in Mashhad. The shah refers to a pending campaign against the Ottomans, who were threatening Iraq at the time, and mentions the alcoholic excesses of the Qizilbash that had contributed to his father's terrible defeat at Chaldiran.[62] In addition to striking a blow at the Qizilbash, Tahmasb's new policy may also have been a rebuke to Sufi practices prevalent among court-connected clerics.[63] Most importantly, the Sincere Repentance marked a phase in the loss of the shah's divine pretensions that had begun with the defeat of Shah Isma'il in 1514, symbolizing a switch in the ruler's image from incarnation of the divine to that of trustee of the Hidden Imam, from a force capable of defying norms and laws to guarantor and enforcer of orthopraxis.

That Tahmasb's Sincere Repentance came in several installments stretching over three decades suggests that there were problems with compliance and enforcement, but it also reflects changes in the

Safavid state's political and religious make-up. Its second iteration, proclaimed in Herat in 1534, proscribed not just alcohol, gambling, and prostitution but also frivolous pastimes such as pigeon flying, which was deemed dangerous since it was done from rooftops, allowing the practitioner to peer into adjacent private courtyards.[64] The timing is significant in more than one way. After a decade of civil war that almost brought him down, by 1534 Tahmasb had finally managed to gain the upper hand against the unruly Qizilbash.

As important is an evolving religious climate. Largely unfamiliar with scriptural Islam, both Shah Isma'il and Tahmasb invited a number of clerics from Jabal 'Amil in Lebanon, Bahrain, and Iraq—all traditional strongholds of Twelver Shi'ism—to teach them the actual tenets of their faith. The first to heed the call and the most prominent of these migrants was Shaykh 'Ali al-Karaki. In 1532–3, al-Karaki was given a mandate over religious and moral issues by being appointed *nā'ib al-Imām*, the representative of the (Hidden) Imam. He contributed to a more *shari'a*-minded society by writing tracts and issuing fatwas that targeted public singing and storytelling, activities associated with Sufis and the Qizilbash.[65] The sources also refer to the highest religious official of the realm—the *sadr*—Mu'izz al-Din Isfahani (in office 1537–42), as being particularly active in targeting taverns, brothels, and gambling houses.[66]

Tahmasb's second ban was not without effect. In 1534–5, all taverns, gambling parlors, and brothels in Herat were reportedly closed, striking 12,000 *tumāns* from the tax rolls. Several high-ranking violators were caught and punished by having their beards cut off and then being pilloried and hanged.[67] Inuka Ughli was suspended with a wine bottle around his neck. Muhammad Salih, the governor of Astarabad, was punished by being put in a barrel and thrown to his death from the top of a minaret.[68]

Yet the enforcement of the new law was less than fully successful, least of all among the ruling elite. The shah's own brother, Bahram Mirza, a notorious toper, continued to drink 'aqua vita, spirits of spices and as well as of cinnamon and spices', and he ultimately died from it.[69] Tahmasb seems to have indulged him in this. An album with illustrated manuscripts known as the Bahram Mirza Album, completed in 1544–5, opens with a painting of Bahram

Mirza, signed by Shah Tahmasb himself and dedicated to his 'beloved brother' Bahram. The setting is a *suhbat*, a learned discussion as part of a convivial gathering fueled by dance and drink. The painting is humorous in the way it shows corpulent figures in awkward poses.[70] The shah also tolerated at the drinking habits of the famous painter Kamal al-Din Bihzad, who 'could not live for a moment without ruby-red wine'.[71] And when the Mughal Emperor Humayun and his entourage visited Iran in 1544, Tahmasb treated his guests to 'various wines and liquors' in Qazvin.[72]

The years 1555–6 saw an even more comprehensive iteration of the Sincere Repentance. This time, the ban did not just target drinking and prostitution but extended to the arts.[73] This third installment caused many Iranian artists to move to India, to the Mughal court and the various princely courts in the Deccan, or to provincial cities with a less oppressive cultural climate.

Little is known about conditions in the following decade other than that Shah Muhammad Khudabanda issued a ban on drinking during his reign. We are better informed about Shah 'Abbas I, who, plied with wine by servants carrying gold carafes and cups, drank throughout the day, yet never to the point of losing control in public.[74] The Roman nobleman Pietro Della Valle, an eyewitness, claimed that the shah would retire to his harem whenever he felt that his drink was about to overwhelm him. According to Della Valle, he did not even abstain during Ramadan.[75] The fact that, at times, he did, shows that 'Abbas little consistent in his stance toward alcohol. He is not known to have imposed any restrictions during the first fifteen years of his reign, when he was busy reorganizing his government and military. In 1603, having completed the project and ready to take on the Ottomans, 'Abbas issued his first ban on drinking.[76] The remainder of his reign saw several more such bans. The impetus behind these varied from case to case. In 1606, when Imam Quli Khan, the governor of Fars, outlawed alcohol as well as prostitution, the king's displeasure with the fact that soldiers spent all their money on wine and women was reportedly the cause.[77] It is less clear why, in August 1620, coinciding with Ramadan, 'Abbas 'repented' and issued a ban on drinking, threatening vendors with disembowelment and consumers with having molten lead poured down their throats. Della Valle attributed the measure to an unspecified illness from which the shah had been suffering for some months. [78] Yet clerical exhortation may have been the more important factor in this case, with Baha al-Din al-'Amili (Shaykh Baha'i; 1547–1621), the influential *shaykh al-islām* of Isfahan at the time—who also had a hand in the persecution of Iran's Armenian population a year later—being a likely instigator. [79] Similar pressure may have caused 'Abbas in 1626 to appoint another cleric—Sayyid Mirza Bayg, *muhtasib* of Iran—with the task of combating all forms of un-Islamic behavior. [80]

The shah, however, remained the ultimate arbiter of royal behavior, forcing his religious leaders to accommodate his own drinking. Muhammad Amin Astarabadi (d. 1623–4 or 1626–7), the founder of the so-called Akhbari school—which focused on the traditions of the Shi'i Imams as the most important source of religious knowledge—wrote a treatise under the self-explanatory title, *Risāla fi tahārat al-khamr* ('Treatise on the Purity of Wine'), in which he argued that, contrary to the opinion of the Sunnis, wine was a pure beverage. This work, which may originally have been designed to justify 'Abbas's drinking, later served to 'solve' the legal conundrum of how to legitimize Shah Safi's bibulous lifestyle. [81] Moreover, king and clergy clearly colluded when, at the end of his reign, 'Abbas commissioned the Friday preacher of Isfahan, Qazi b. Kashif al-Din Muhammad, to write an essay on wine and its benefits. The author obliged, and in the resulting *Jām-i jahān-nāma* prides himself on having consulted the writings of physicians and scholars from Greece, India, Iraq, and Europe in gathering his findings. He gives a detailed description of both the virtues and drawbacks of wine, the etiquette of consuming it, when to enjoy and when to avoid it, and how to deal with hangovers. Having legitimized wine as a substance of medicinal value, he discusses the properties of different types— white and red—according to the principles of humoral pathology, the effects of drinking wine with different foods, and its relationship with tobacco and opium, all with frequent references to the famous Abu Bakr al-Razi. [82]

The last four Safavid shahs all declared bans on drinking at one point or another during their tenure. Shah Safi I did so upon coming to power in 1629.[83] This inaugural resolution did not last very long, however. Advised by his physicians to treat a cold resulting from his frequent opium use with alcohol, Safi soon succumbed to hard drinking.[84] A few months after his accession, the Dutch attended a royal banquet where the shah showed up three hours late, deep in his cups and accompanied by an equally inebriated Imam Quli Khan.[85] According to Tavernier, Safi would often visit the residence of the Armenian mayor (kalantar) of New Julfa to get soused. If we are to believe the same author, he killed one of his spouses following one of these nocturnal outings, after which he issued a short-lived ban on alcohol.[86] As mentioned, Safi prematurely died from his dipsomania in 1642.[87]

Safi's successor, Shah 'Abbas II, also proclaimed a ban on drinking upon acceding to the throne at the tender age of nine. Indeed, the first order he issued was for the closing of taverns and the smashing of wine vessels, a measure that extended to the Shiraz wine customarily sent to the court. In a move that may have been a reaction to the wine-soaked legacy of their shah's father, several high-ranking inveterate drinkers sent letters of repentance to the new shah, pledging to abstain from frivolous activities as part of their fealty to him.[88] In 1645, following the appointment of the cleric Sultan al-'Ulama (a.k.a. Khalifa Sultan) as grand vizier, a more extensive anti-vice campaign involving the closing of taverns and brothels got underway.[89]

This campaign did not last either. Four years later, still in his teens, 'Abbas II took up the cup while celebrating nawruz on the banks of the Helmand River during his triumphant return from an expedition that had resulted in the capture of Qandahar from the Mughals. Vala Qazvini Isfahani, the chronicler who narrates the events, justifies the shah's change of heart by referring to the adage which states that God and the law both permit happiness and pleasure, especially in youth. For good measure, he absolves 'Abbas II from any personal responsibility for drinking by blaming his courtiers for setting the tone with their own alcoholic excesses.[90]

The relaxed mood that came to characterize 'Abbas II's court from c. 1650 onward is amply reflected in the annalistic chronicles of the time with their lengthy descriptions of wine-fueled nawruz festivities. The carousing was temporarily interrupted when in 1653 the *shaykh al-islām* of Isfahan urged the shah to foreswear wine, possibly in connection with a Mughal threat to retake Qandahar. However, in customary fashion, the ban became moot within a year. Life returned to its normal state of ambiguity and the shah resumed his previous lifestyle, indulging until his untimely death in 1666, reportedly from excessive drinking.[91]

Most bans issued under the last three shahs bear a clerical imprint, reflecting a growing self-confidence among the increasingly prominent ulama—a development that bears some resemblance to the simultaneous surge in piety in Ottoman lands. Foreigners report hearing them grouse about boozing shahs, and the censorious looks of the staff at Shah 'Abbas II's party described above suggest that they were not alone.[92] However, openly criticizing the sovereign remained risky, as demonstrated when Mullah Muhammad-Tahir Qummi (d. 1689), long-time leader of the Friday prayer in Qom, upbraided Shah Sulayman for his drinking. The ruler responded to this insolence by ordering Qummi's execution, and only the intercession of the cleric's influential allies persuaded the shah to summon him to Isfahan to be reprimanded rather than killed.[93] A much safer option was veiled criticism, such as practiced by Mullah Muhammad Baqir Sabzavari—*shaykh al-islām* under Shah 'Abbas II— in his *Rawzat al-anvār-i 'Abbasi*, a treatise on political philosophy and its moral foundations. In a chapter on *tawba*, the author enumerates the sins for which good Muslims should repent, giving historical examples. A section on Shah Tahmasb's Sincere Repentance discusses the importance of atoning for one's sins, with Koranic references linking nobility with piety. Nowhere is 'Abbas II mentioned by name, but there can be little doubt that he was the real target of Sabzavari's rebuke and exhortation.[94]

Exemplifying the shift that the Safavid state had undergone since its inception, from tribal dispensation to agrarian-based urban-centered polity, the last two effective shahs, Sulayman and Sultan Husayn, no longer ruled as warrior kings on horseback. Instead, they lived ensconced in their palaces, engaged in 'lust and play'. Yet they, too, are known to have targeted alcohol. Sulayman's erratic track record suggests a sickly ruler with a drinking problem. Poor health was by all accounts the main reason why he gave up alcohol prior to his second coronation in 1668, when he changed his name from Safi II to Sulayman.[95] It is also clear that this abstemiousness did not last, given the shah's undignified drunken behavior referred to above.[96]

Iran's urban centers were reportedly dry at the time, but this soon changed: in the spring of 1675, restrictions on the sale and consumption of alcohol were lifted and, given pent-up demand, wine became expensive.[97] In 1678, Sulayman, now hidden from public view for long stretches of time, is said to have abjured the bottle around 'Ashura (10 Muharram, the day when Shi'is commemorate the death of Imam Husayn on the battlefield of Karbala in 680), so that he could administer justice 'in a proper fashion'.[98] Six years later, Engelbert Kaempfer attended an official dinner for foreign envoys where wine—together with song and dance—was conspicuously absent, presumably because the shah, recovering from an illness, had been advised by his physicians not to drink. Alcohol had again been banned throughout the land.[99] Then, no later than early 1691, the shah fell off the wagon again.[100]

The long-term trend toward 'privatized' royal tippling culminated under Shah Sultan Husayn. Upon his accession, this famously pious ruler granted the request from his tutor, the doctrinaire Muhammad Baqir Majlisi (d. 1699), to outlaw all drinking in his realm, as well as other forms of behavior considered to be at variance with the *shari'a*, such as kite flying, coffee consumption, and women going out unaccompanied. The 6,000 bottles of wine found in the royal cellar were demonstratively poured out on Isfahan's royal square.[101] Since the ban applied to all and included the possession of alcohol at home, even Christians had their wine urns smashed. The measure also affected French missionaries residing in Yerevan. They saw their convents raided by officials and only managed to save their stock by insisting that the prohibition only applied to the shah's subjects, not to his guests. This resulted in their cave being sealed, but in such a way that it was possible to enter and leave without breaking the seal.[102]

In this case, too, the ban did not last, and the first to violate it was the shah himself. In the fall of 1694, mere months after it had gone into effect, Sultan Husayn resumed drinking upon the medically grounded recommendation of his great-aunt Maryam Bigum, a noted tippler herself.[103] Wine again became a staple at court. In 1696, the Portuguese envoy Pereira Fidalgo, invited to an afternoon audience with the shah, happened upon a scene enlivened by music, wine, and waterpipes. Three years later, Don Ferrante Palma d'Artois, a.k.a. Bishop of Ancyre, who was in Isfahan to negotiate favorable conditions for resident European missionaries, was offered wine during a similar royal audience. The same prelate witnessed Sultan Husayn drinking with his grandees in the newly built Sa'adabad palace on an elevated platform overlooking the Zayanda Rud, the river that separates Isfahan from the Armenian suburb of New Julfa, to celebrate the recent victory of the Safavid army over the Kurds.[104] Ultimately, it was the court eunuchs who derived the greatest benefit from it all; their ability to bamboozle a bibulous shah helped them gain and maintain dominance at the court.[105]

Public drinking remained illegal throughout Iran until at least 1703. In the fall of that year the Dutch traveler-painter Cornelis de Bruyn, traveling between Qazvin and Qom, got hold of wine for the first time since arriving in the country. Alcohol, he explained, was hard to find since its sale was illegal. Four years later, during his return journey, the same author reports that the governor of Shamakhi (the capital of Shirvan, currently in the country of Azerbaijan) and his men were given to excessive drinking, with the argument that Sultan Husayn had legalized the consumption of alcohol.[106] Matters remained unchanged until the fall of the Safavids in 1722. In 1716, the Armenians of Rasht in the Caspian region were said to produce an excellent wine.[107] A year later, Shah Sultan Husayn regaled Russian envoy Artemii Pertrovich Volynski with fifty bottles of expensive Georgian wine.[108]

6

CHANGING DRINKING HABITS IN THE
NINETEENTH CENTURY
PART ONE
THE OTTOMAN EMPIRE AND NORTH AFRICA

Introduction

The previous two chapters showed that drinking in Ottoman lands and on the Iranian plateau was quite common in court circles and among the elite, but less so among ordinary people. Some rulers abstained, but most sultans and shahs along with their entourages were serious boozers. To the extent that commoners drank, it was part of a subculture of subterfuge and furtiveness, with men sneaking off—usually under the cover of night—to back-alley taverns in the non-Muslim quarters of town, run by Armenians, Jews, or Greeks. Such venues were dark haunts associated with the seamy side of life, their owners occupying 'roughly the same place on the social scale as the prostitute, the overt homosexual, and the itinerant entertainer'.[1] Drinking thus remained 'invisible', even though in some ways it took place in full view. Control and regulation varied with the ruler and his disposition. Restrictions in the form of bans failed to eradicate the practice of consuming alcohol, in no small part because the ever-insolvent state desperately needed the tax revenue it generated.

145

Many of these patterns endured, some of them until today. Change nevertheless set in at the turn of the nineteenth century, mostly because of a marked increase in European influence on the lifestyle of, first, the elite classes and after them society's middling segments. The effects were felt in the Ottoman Empire, in North Africa, as well as in Qajar Iran, albeit in different ways and under variable circumstances. In some cases, the intrusion was abrupt and radical, as in Napoleon's occupation of Egypt, the French invasion of Algeria in 1830, and the British intervention in Egypt in 1882. Elsewhere, such as in the Ottoman Empire and Iran, the intervention was more gradual and insidious, taking the form of indirect control and a creeping influence of Western ways rather than 'imposed' habits and customs.

With military defeat came political and economic pressure, forcing Middle Eastern rulers to open their domestic markets to European manufactured goods at reduced toll tariffs and giving foreign powers far-reaching economic and legal rights and privileges. This allowed their resident nationals and protégés to become heavily involved in the alcohol business in ways that eluded Ottoman authority, creating conditions akin to what Schrad calls alco-imperialism.[2]

All this instilled a sense of crisis among rulers and elites and an urge to catch up, militarily as well as administratively. The ensuing reforms built on previous initiatives were more sustained and consequential, aided by great infrastructural improvements: the telegraph, railways, steam navigation. Students returning from Europe and emerging print capitalism contributed to a new openness to the world as well. Egypt's Muhammad (Turk. Mehmed) 'Ali (r. 1805–48) was the first Middle Eastern ruler to engage in far-reaching military, educational, and infrastructural reform. Sultan Mahmud II (r. 1808–39) embarked on similar reforms, beginning with the abolition of the Janissary corps in 1826. He and his successors set the tone for an increasingly mobile and better-informed society by emerging from their seclusion, showing themselves in public, visiting different parts of their realm, and eventually even making the journey to Europe. Developments in Qajar Iran were similar, albeit more haphazard and intermittent.

The period between 1839 and 1876 saw an acceleration and systematization of this process in the Ottoman Empire, with the so-called Tanzimat (reorganization) reforms. The Tanzimat were mainly a 'movement in legislation' enacted as a series of decrees.[3] Their objective was not openness for its own sake, much less the secularization of society or the leveling of differences, least of all of religious differences. The ultimate rationale behind the reforms was rather the need to prop up a weakening state through centralization as well as enhancing revenue for a treasury facing bankruptcy. The advocates of the Tanzimat also sought to gain international recognition for the Ottoman Empire by satisfying European demands for reform. However, the new ideas that came with such reform had unintended consequences: they undermined the traditional Islamic order of divinely appointed sultans governing subservient subjects differentially according to creed. These ideas included popular representation and man-made laws applying to all regardless of faith, as well as their corollary: religious freedom and civic equality, the emblems of modernity as perceived and propagated by Western powers. *Dhimmi*s, who had always held a subordinate place in society, became European-supported religious *millet*s (nations) claiming equal rights with Muslims. This change was reflected in the abolition of the poll tax for Christians in 1856 (replaced by the *bedel*, a tax to be paid by those who wished to be exempted from military service) and the striking of the popular Turkish term for infidel, *gâvur*, from official documents. In this way, non-Muslims were allowed to gain in prominence in a society that was fast becoming integrated into the world economy.[4]

Alcohol, the types available, who consumed it, how it was consumed, who took advantage of the new trends, and how society reacted to these trends was entwined with all these processes. War brought hard-drinking Western soldiers to Muslim capitals: the French to Cairo in 1798 and to Algiers in 1830; the French, the British, and the Italians to Istanbul during the Crimean War of 1853–6 and again in 1919, in the dying days of the Ottoman Empire; the French again in Lebanon in the 1860s; and the British once more to Cairo in 1882. Alcoholic drinks, including new varieties such as cognac and champagne, were among surging imports following the commercial Treaty of Balta Limanı that Britain concluded with the Porte in 1838. Growing numbers of Europeans, diplomatic envoys, entrepreneurs, and carpetbaggers followed, further influencing Ottoman lifestyles. The new 'openness' this represented weakened inhibitions with respect to public drinking in official circles. The sultan and his courtiers began to mingle with Western diplomats, attending dinners and receptions where alcohol was served. The non-governmental elite followed suit, many adopting alcohol and Western ways of consuming it as a token of modernity.

The growing visibility of alcohol naturally provoked reactions; some old, such as renewed calls for interdiction, and some new, such as a growing anxiety about its negative effects on the physical and mental health of consumers. At the behest of European-trained physicians and journalists, modernizing governments increasingly came to see alcohol as dangerous and addictive, contributing to the rack and ruin of society. The new calls for restrictions that followed did not involve Islamic strictures so much as concerns about the health of the body politic.

These gathering anxieties went hand in hand with suspicions about the growing prominence of Christian minorities in the Ottoman economy. *Dhimmi*s, who had always played a major role in economic life—and a preponderant one in the production and sale of alcohol—developed a mutually beneficial relationship with the increasingly influential foreign powers, involving useful brokerage in return for protection and economic opportunity. As the empire weakened, this resentment grew, causing a coalition of traditional Islamic elements and progressive, secular nationalist forces to target Greeks and Armenians for aiding and abetting foreign interests.

The (late) nineteenth century was, in sum, the moment when Muslim culture became self-aware, keen to imitate and adopt 'modern' ways but also defensive and increasingly resentful, torn between attraction and revulsion vis-à-vis the 'West'. In some ways, the modern understanding of the Islamic world—both as part of a global community of nations and as a distinct civilization, 'backward' and in need of reform—came into being precisely in this period. What used to be a clear understanding of a world unto

Fig. 1: Farrukh Beg. Emperor Babur returning late to
camp drunk after a boating party in celebration of
the end of Ramadan in 1519 (dated 1589).

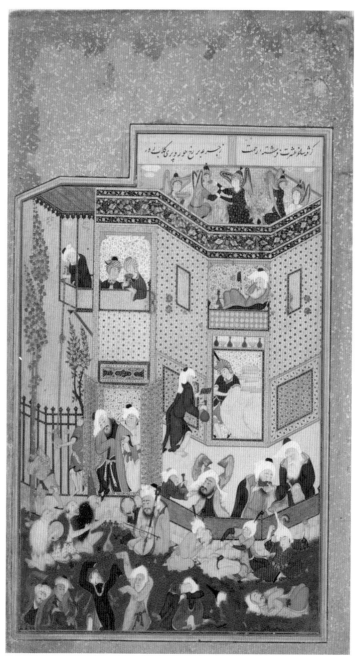

Fig. 2: Sultan Muhammad, worldly and otherworldly
drunkenness (*c.* 1520).

Fig. 3: Les yvrognes, the drunkards, in Nicolas de Nicolay, *Les quatre premiers livres des Navigations et Pérégrinations Orientales* (1586).

Fig. 4: Gold coin: Jahangir
and winecup.

Fig. 5: Meeting of Shah 'Abbas I and Wali Muhammad Khan Uzbek,
wall painting in the Chehel Sotun Palace, Isfahan, c. 1647.

Fig. 6: Muhammad Qasim Musavvir. Shah 'Abbas I and
a page boy (1627).

Fig. 7: Riza Abbasi, European giving a dog a drink (1634).

Fig. 8: Courtier refusing to accept wine from Indian courtesans (1650-1700).

Fig. 9: A couple in front of a tavern, Ottoman Empire.

Fig. 10: Destruction of an Ottoman tavern, seventeenth century.

Fig. 11: Seated woman holding a glass of wine, Iran,
early nineteenth century.

Fig. 12: Ottoman tavern, early nineteenth century.

S. A. Brasserie Bomonti.

Fig 13: Bomonti brewery, Istanbul, postcard.

Fig. 14: Late Ottoman *meyhane* (tavern), *Diken* magazine, 1918.

Fig. 15: Late Ottoman *meyhane* (tavern) with Russian waitress,
Ayine magazine, 1922.

its own, divided by religion in self-evident ways, in this period was reconfigured into a newly dichotomous universe, divided between religious and traditional elements and secular and modern ones.[5]

Drinking at the Ottoman Court

Beginning with Sultan Mahmud II, nineteenth-century Ottoman sultans broke out of their traditional insularity by moving from the inward-looking Topkapı Palace in the 'Muslim' part of Istanbul to the other, 'Christian' side of town, across the Golden Horn, where they built new, opulent, more 'extrovert' palaces along the Bosporus, first Çırağan Sarayı, then Dolmabahçe Sarayı, and, finally, up the hill, Yıldız Sarayı (Palace of the Stars).[6] This greater visibility manifested itself in royal outings and receptions, as well as an unprecedented use of the sultan's image in the form of honorary medals, commemorative medallions, official portraits, and, eventually, stamps.

In 1826, inspired by the example set by Egypt's Muhammad 'Ali and having secured the support of the country's ulama, Mahmud II initiated drastic societal change by eliminating the unruly janissaries. He simultaneously banned the Bektashis, a Sufi order with close ties to the janissaries. Three years later, a clothing law abolishing the turban and mandating the fez for all religious and civil officials ended the traditional sartorial distinction between Muslims and non-Muslims. In 1831, the first government-controlled newspaper, Takvîm-i Vekâyi, was launched. Two years later, a postal service was instituted. Nonreligious education made great strides, too, beginning with the creation of a medical school in 1827. The first kıraathane (literary coffeehouse) carrying foreign newspapers opened its doors in Istanbul in 1861. Book publishing took off in the same period. The railway connecting Turkey to Europe came to Istanbul in the 1880s, as did gas lighting, which soon gave way to electricity.

Change was evident early on. The well-informed British ambassador Stratford Canning noticed a new atmosphere in the Ottoman capital when he returned to Istanbul in 1832 after an absence of five years, during which time the elimination of the janissaries had taken place. There were 'fewer turbans and more hats', he observed, and in the seraglio the 'old humiliating etiquette' had been abolished.[7] Whereas earlier sultans had been mostly ensconced in the Topkapı Palace, Mahmud II, following the example set by his European peers, showed himself in public, went riding through town, gave receptions, and attended concerts. Mahmud II's son and successor, Abdülmecid (r. 1839–61), increased the frequency and nature of such public appearances: not only did he take walks in Istanbul's public gardens, he would also visit the theater and inspect schools and factories. During the Crimean War, he even participated in the diplomatic life of the capital, honoring foreign embassies with his presence. Abdülmecid also continued his predecessor's habit of visiting various parts of his realm with some regularity. Sultan Abdülaziz (r. 1861–76) raised the sultan's visibility to the next level by touring around Istanbul almost daily. He even took the unprecedented step of traveling to Europe, visiting Paris during the Exposition Universelle, and London and Vienna in 1867.[8]

Alcohol played an unmistakable role in this new 'openness'. Robert Walsh, Irish chaplain to the British embassy in Istanbul from 1820 to 1827, observed how under Mahmud II the former curtailing practices had become 'restrained', with the sultan himself giving up his temperance and becoming an avid wine drinker. Mahmud, he said, was 'particularly fond of champagne'. A bottle was 'set beside him every day at dinner', and he was 'greatly amused' watching the cork explode out of the bottle and the wine fly up to the ceiling.[9] Southgate echoed these observations. The sultan, he claimed, celebrated his birthdays and the anniversaries of his accession with 'powerful potations of champagne', which as rumor would have it was his favorite wine. Southgate cautioned that, given the secrecy surrounding the Turkish court and the fact that the ruler never showed any outward signs of having imbibed, he could not vouch for the accuracy of the story.[10] Yet the description of the party given on 4 November 1829 by Sir Robert Gordon, the British representative, in honor of the sultan on the warship *Blonde* leaves little doubt about the sovereign's taste. Decked out with Ottoman banners and the flags of various European nations, the ship carried, beside the sultan himself, some 200 dignitaries, Ottoman grandees, and European diplomats. The guests drank considerable amounts of champagne, played cards, and danced the polka with the European women in attendance. The captain is said to have offered the dignitaries 'his best port'. The sultan liked it very much and ordered the purchase of a few dozen bottles.[11]

Mehmed Husrev Pasha, the Ottoman *serasker*, commander in chief, was among the tipsy guests at the floating soirée. A French report about a dinner organized on 5 October 1833 by the same magistrate provides more evidence for Mahmud II's interest in alcohol but also reveals that the topic remained a taboo. Three types of French wine were served with the meal, which was held in the name of the sultan for the representatives of the major European powers. According to a French diplomat present, Baron Charles-Joseph-Edmond Sain de Boislecomte—who also authored the report—the sultan savored all three 'in moderation'. Grand vizier Mehmed Emin Rauf Pasha awkwardly accepted the wine he was served yet only pretended to consume it. The other Ottoman invitees freely indulged, though, including the sultan's chief physician (the *hekimbaşi*), Behcet Mustafa Efendi, a member of the ulama. The French envoy's account remained unpublished; the *Takvim-i Vekâyi* did report on the event, although it remained silent on this aspect (and, for that matter, on the presence of foreign women at the dinner).[12]

Later in life, Mahmud is said to have taken to ever more potent tipple, until his final two years, when regular fare did not excite him anymore, he ended up drinking 'pure alcohol'. Army officer turned journalist Charles White, the source of this information, had the imperial wine merchant—a Belgian named M. Le Moine—state that he was forced to falsify all wines by adding brandy, since 'the sultan found even the strongest unadulterated ones too insipid'. Citing 'well informed' sources, White called this indulgence mainly responsible for the *delirium tremens* that ended Mahmud's life on 1 July 1839. After the sultan's death, many hundreds of bottles were found in his cellar.[13]

Abdülmecid initially followed the advice of his mother, the *valide sultan*, who, eager to set a good example for her adolescent son, persuaded him to dump all the booze found in the palace at Mahmud's death into the Bosporus. White called the new sultan 'extremely temperate and abstemious', ill-disposed to drinking as well as to smoking.[14] Abdülmecid indeed kept up his reputation as a pious ruler until his last breath, though he did not heed his mother's advice for long. Said to have taken to alcohol as consolation for the loss of a favorite concubine, in his later years this 'gentle sybarite' spent most of his time in his harem as intrigue and corruption flourished around him.[15]

Great hopes for reform accompanied the enthronement of the next sultan, Abdülmecid's brother, Abdülaziz, in 1861. Before acceding to power, Abdülaziz had been kept secluded in the harem, surrounded by clerics and dervishes.[16] His initial reign was promising. Once enthroned, he put away the diamonds that had been his predecessors' pride, trimmed down the royal harem, and whittled away at the bureaucracy, all to regain power for the crown, and all to great popular acclaim. Pious to a fault—he never warmed to Western culture, and his strong faith initially even made him shun all contact with Europeans—he is not known to have consumed any alcohol whatsoever.[17] Even after Abdülaziz turned into a spendthrift, possibly following his journey to Egypt in 1863 and the magnificent reception he enjoyed there, alcohol does not seem to have been on his list of indulgences. However, his extravagance did contribute to a financial crisis that in the 1870s made the empire teeter toward bankruptcy. Simultaneous revolts in Bosnia-Herzegovina prompted the European powers to intervene with demands for tax reform and free worship for members of all faiths. Rather than complying, the Ottoman authorities responded with repression, inviting more foreign pressure accompanied by threats. The sultan, caught between European calls for tolerance and a populace clamoring to see the Muslims of the Balkans protected, refused to yield to a demand for a written constitution. The members of the Young Ottoman reform party, led by former grand vizier Midhat Pasha, thus had Abdülaziz deposed in May 1876 and put Murad, his eldest son, on the throne.[18]

Murad, mentally unstable and notoriously addicted to cognac and champagne—a condition that should have disqualified him as heir apparent—proved to be a poor choice. However, his younger brother Abdülhamid initially enjoyed little favor as an alternative candidate. But as Murad's condition grew worse and the palace fell into disarray following the suicide of the ousted Abdülaziz, support for Abdülhamid grew among the Young Ottoman reformists, especially since he declared himself in favor of a proposed constitution that promised full equality for religious minorities. After just three months on the throne, Murad was thus deposed in favor of Abdülhamid.[19]

Abdülhamid II's reign (1876–1909) in some ways represented a return to old ways. At first, the new sultan continued the practice of his three predecessors by (selectively) showing himself in public. But after the Russian army came within miles of Istanbul in 1877, he withdrew into seclusion. There were no more excursions, hunting parties, or overnight stays in villages along the Bosporus. Increasingly paranoid, Abdülhamid instead took refuge in the newly built Yıldız Palace, better protected due to its location in the hills above Beşiktaş. For the remainder of his reign, the sultan's outings were restricted to selamlıks (ceremonial meetings) with members of the ulama on Fridays, and appearances at religious holidays. Indeed, religion became a tool in the sultan's attempt to buttress his legitimacy by restoring the mystique of the sultanate-cum-caliphate.[20] Naturally, drinking did not fit into the image of a pious sultan-caliph, and Abdülhamid neither drank nor gambled, at least not habitually and certainly not in public. He did not spurn punch in private, though, and it seems that he occasionally even savored a glass of cognac at his doctors' orders.[21]

Abdülhamid's reign saw continued modernization in the form of improved communications, the development of steam and rail, the building of roads and ports, and the introduction of conscription, all of which increased (social) mobility. Such mobility appeared in the form of newly created venues for interaction—public spaces, cafés, theaters, and reading salons—where communities that had formerly lived side by side now began to rub shoulders.[22] The Young Turk Revolution of 1908 gave a further boost to the process of creeping secularization (at least in Istanbul), as seen in the more frequent public transgression of the rules of fasting and diminishing disapproval of drinking among the educated classes.[23] In these conditions, outlawing alcohol was no longer possible, not even for Abdülhamid. All a pious sultan could do was try and ban the consumption of spirits in Muslim quarters and by Muslims, or at least limit the opening hours of taverns, by way of irades (decrees).[24] Yet

153

the very fact that there were so many of these decrees betrays their ineffectiveness. The 'believing' sultan thus failed to turn his capital into a virtuous city.[25] As the Italian traveler Edmondo de Amicis put it in his customary purple prose, the 'father of abomination' was 'every day gaining converts among the Turks … If someday a thick darkness should descend over Constantinople, and after an hour, the sun should suddenly shine out, fifty thousand Turks would be found with the bottle at their lips'.[26]

Increased Elite Drinking

Alcohol indeed was widely available in late Ottoman times, domestically produced and, increasingly, imported. As before, wine mainly came from the Aegean islands, most notably Samos (Turk. Sisam), Lesbos (Turk. Midilli Adası), and Tenedos (Turk. Bozcaada), as well as from Cyprus and Crete.[27] Domestic viticulture measurably expanded once the state realized that restrictions hampered economic activity and harmed the treasury. The people of Bursa thus had learned to produce a 'rather good' wine in the 1820s. The man behind the initiative was a Swiss national named Falkeisen.[28] Other foreigners involved in export-oriented cultivation included French vintners from Perpignan who, escaping a wave of the Phylloxera pest at home, in the 1880s, set up a (short-lived) wine industry in the area around the city of Lüleburgaz, in what is now the European part of Turkey.[29] Around 1900, annual domestic production was estimated at *c*. 1 million hectoliters.[30]

For much of the nineteenth century, foreign spirits were mainly consumed by European residents.[31] Turks reportedly liked champagne but were not enamored of claret, madeira, or sherry, and they abhorred port.[32] Cider, beer, punch, and European liqueurs were still barely known in the 1830s. The only exception was rum, the annual import of which shot up from 8,530 to 97,108 gallons between 1827 and 1834.[33] By mid-century, annual French imports of wine and spirits were valued at FF. 292,000 and FF. 164,000, respectively.[34] At the turn of the twentieth century, the French had a near monopoly on the sale of fine wines, cognac, and liqueurs. Ordinary wine, meanwhile, came from Italy, Greece, Cyprus,

Palestine, and Syria.[35] Istanbul alone at that time imported wines, mostly Bordeaux and champagne, worth some FF. 2 million.[36]

Since the vast majority of Ottoman Muslims continued to abstain, the domestic customer base for these spirits was limited. So strong was the dislike of spirituous liquors among high-ranking Turks, James de Kay claimed in 1831, that their European employees would abstain from drinking while dealing with government officials, 'lest their breath should reveal the fact'.[37] This did not apply to all top officials, some of whom seemed suspended between tradition and modernity. Helmuth Graf von Moltke, a Prussian officer who helped modernize the Ottoman army in the 1880s, refers to Mehmed Husrev Pasha, the commander of the armed forces, calling him both 'the second most powerful man of the realm' and the 'most moderate, sober person in the world'. Political calculation made this official drink champagne with any passing European of standing, just to show how enlightened he was and in the full knowledge that a positive article in the Western press would follow. However, Husrev Pasha vastly preferred a sip of mineral water from Istanbul's famous spring of Çamlıca.[38]

Others seemed eager to embrace and even flaunt new norms. Such 'free thinkers and free livers', as de Kay called them, were not exactly a new phenomenon, as we saw in Chapter 4.[39] In the nineteenth century there were just more of such 'deists', as Lady Montagu had labeled them. They replaced, at least symbolically, the janissaries. Indeed, the elimination of these undisciplined forces in 1826— officially referred to as the 'Auspicious Event'—may have helped diminish the consumption of alcohol, at least temporarily.[40] The number of taverns in Istanbul, many of the owned by janissaries, fell from 554 before 1826 to 215 the following year.[41] But the number of (semi-clandestine) alcohol-purveying establishments is but one measure of the incidence of drinking. A broader perspective on the matter is offered by Southgate, who signaled an alarming rise in alcohol consumption in the metropolitan Ottoman Empire. He linked this development to an 'increased intercourse with Europeans' following the obliteration of the janissaries, who had always been hostile to Franks and their 'innovations'.[42] Their place had been taken by a new, corrupt administrative class known as the Istanbul effendis.[43] All the intemperate Turks Southgate knew in Istanbul were men who had acquainted themselves with Europeans or had lived in Europe. Priding themselves on their knowledge of Western manners, they drank, often in excess and at times 'for no other reason than to show their superiority to prejudice', ridiculing those who did not indulge. The Europeans they mostly dealt with were the 'unprincipled and profligate, fugitives from justice and reckless adventurers', carpetbaggers who introduced Western vices.[44]

References to this 'new' Ottoman class abound in the sources. In 1829, R. C. Mellish, an attaché to the British embassy, referred to Ottoman officers who 'dine[d] their European counterparts and conduct[ed] themselves quite like Christians, particularly in drinking'.[45] Charles MacFarlane, a Scottish writer who spent sixteen months in the Ottoman Empire in the late 1820s, spoke of a small and hesitant group of high-ranking Osmanlis who 'affected Frank society', going so far as to 'invite jovial parties of them to their houses'. He singled out Katiboğlu, a former governor of Izmir who had 'so completely contracted European habits that he seemed never happy but when he was with them'. This official played cards without guilt and had even fewer scruples about accepting a glass of wine from a non-Muslim. There was also Süleiman Agha, the former mayor of Athens—in which capacity Lord Byron met him—and the receiver of tolls in Izmir until he was appointed governor of a *pashalik* in Crete. He, too, loved Westerners and their ways, and would visit their houses as well as casinos. He only drank champagne, which, in his estimation, did not resemble wine at all and would never be recognized by the Turks as such.[46] Walsh, too, noted that many Ottoman officials 'drank as freely as any of the company' during receptions given by European ambassadors, always preferring a large goblet and never mixing their drinks with water.[47] And White spoke of boat excursions on the Bosporus where, after dark, the wine would come out. Many men of rank, he added, were known to drink freely, at times swallowing a 'pint, or even a bottle, of the strongest raki … as a foundation for the evening meal'. At foreign embassy receptions, they might 'be seen pouring down glass after glass of champagne'.[48] David Porter, America's chargé d'affaires in Istanbul, in 1832 describes a party attended by high government officials who 'drank champagne like water'. Russia's resident minister, too, gave parties where Turkish invitees enamored of Western society amused themselves mightily.[49]

The fact that the Ottoman authorities, followers of the Hanafi rite, distinguished between wine and other alcoholic beverages, and that Ottoman jurists saw the use of ardent spirits as less sinful than that of wine, no doubt facilitated the increased levels of alcohol consumption. The Ottoman code accordingly favored those who drank brandy or rum over those who indulged in wine. Turks, who were said to be more strictly observant of Islam than the Iranians, thus paradoxically developed a much greater taste for hard liquor than their neighbors. Two American missionaries in 1830 saw this phenomenon in action while passing through Gerede, a town 145km north of Ankara. To their amazement their hosts drank brandy openly but were circumspect about wine, which was passed to the guests 'carefully concealed under a cloak'.[50] However, rather than wine or brandy, by far the most popular drink for those pretending to be good Muslims became *mastik* (distilled with anis), and especially raki (*mastik* without the resin), which was mostly imported from Chios. In majority-Christian neighborhoods, the distillation of *mastik* might take place in the open and Muslims would consume it in plain sight, arguing that its fire had eliminated the impure aspect of the wine.[51] By the late nineteenth century, raki had become a common drink, especially among bureaucrats, who saw it as a symbol of modernity, much like wearing a fez or a raincoat, or reading a newspaper. A first raki factory was established in the 1880s.[52] In 1903, its annual consumption in Istanbul alone was estimated at 37,000 hectoliters.[53]

Taverns in Istanbul

Unsurprisingly, the Ottoman capital remained the epicenter of traditional drinking and became the fulcrum of the newly developing 'free living' phenomenon. Separated from the 'traditional' Muslim part of the city by the Golden Horn, Galata and Pera were filled with *meyhane*s and brothels.[54] By the late 1860s, the number of such venues in the Ottoman capital, now with a population of at least a half a million people, had gone up to an astonishing 1,152. In keeping with an old rule that taverns could not operate in majority-Muslim districts or near mosques, schools, or Muslim cemeteries, most were located near the city walls and on the city's outskirts.[55] But, following the Treaty of Balta Limanı, more and more taverns sprang up in the Muslim quarters of the city as well.

Most drinking in Istanbul remained 'traditional'. Southgate described conditions in the taverns of Pera as follows:

> They are under the supervision of an officer, without whose permission no wine can legally be made. They pay a small fee for license, and are as public as shops of any other description. They are large and dark, opening upon the street, and having a bar much in the fashion of shops of the same description in this country. Wine and strong drinks are retailed in them by the glass, and the stranger is always made aware when he is passing them, by the noxious fumes which fill the narrow street. At sundown, as the population are retiring to their homes, the bloated keepers may be seen standing at the doors, and crying in Greek and Turkish, Oriste and Bouyouroun, which are equivalent to our Yankee phrase, Walk in. The Mussulmans who resort to them are only of the lower class, and both they and the keepers are liable to be seized and punished for their transgression. The Christians, on the contrary, simply because they are Christians, have the privilege of drinking as openly and as much as they please, provided always that they get peaceably and safe home after it.[56]

We have some detailed indigenous descriptions of the tavern scene in Istanbul in the late nineteenth century as well, courtesy of journalist and litterateur Mehmed Tefvik (1843–1912). Additional information about the topic can be found in a work on Istanbul's traditional *meyhane*s by Reşad Ekrem Koçu (1905–75), who borrowed from Mehmed Tevfik's work. Both echo Southgate's portrayal of Istanbul's drinking culture.

Ottoman grandees, Tefvik stated, drank in the privacy of their homes with trusted friends.[57] Taverns—*meyhane*s or *humhane*s, so named after the *hum* (wine) jar—served the common man, soldiers, sailors, artisans, porters, and palace guards. They came in two forms: unauthorized ones, called *koltuk*, and the ones licensed by the state, termed *gedikli*. The former typically were part of shops whose owners, come evening, rolled down their shutters to serve men on their way home with a few quick glasses of raki. A bribe would secure complicity on the part of the authorities. *Gedikli* taverns, also known from the time of Sultan Abdülaziz as *selatin meyhaneler*, or 'sultanic' winehouses carrying the sultan's stamp of approval, came in different types. There were the dank ones filled with dirty tables where forlorn men (*harabati*s) would come to get hammered. Regular customers, typically shopkeepers who could not afford to drink during the day and thus indulged after hours, were known as *akşamcı*s (night owls). There were also the more elaborate venues with straw-matted chairs and raised platforms, fish tanks, and often extra rooms for special guests, where drinking was enlivened by music and storytelling. Patrons were served by *saki*s—young, handsome men between the ages of eighteen and twenty-three, mainly from the island of Chios—wearing a red, black-tasseled fez and dressed in baggy, black trousers and a white shirt, over which they wore a silver-embroidered silk waistcoat. *Köcek*s, cross-dressed boy dancers with shoulder-length hair—originally Roma and Greeks, later often Armenians and Jews—might be found in these establishments as well. Wearing transparent pants and shirts, these would entertain the guests, their gyrations adding to the homosocial atmosphere.[58] *Köcek* performances had always been controversial, with various sultans outlawing the practice in earlier times. It came again under fire and was banned during the Crimean War of 1853–6, with the excuse being that the phenomenon would look 'very ugly' to the foreign (French and British) soldiers stationed in the capital at that time. Still, *köcek* dancing persisted until the early twentieth century.[59]

There was also the 'ambulant tavern' (*ayaklı meyhane*), in the form of a vendor, invariably an Armenian dressed in a kaftan with a towel over his shoulder—a sign that he served booze—accompanied by a chest on wheels containing various alcoholic beverages, a ladle, and glasses. He could be found at dusk at all the city's landing places (*iskele*s) at the waterfronts of the Bosporus and the Golden Horn, ready to serve the city's fishermen, oarsmen, porters, and firefighters. Or he might carry his wine in a sheepskin wrapped around his waist, to be poured out via a spout.[60]

Taverns in the capital were supposed to close at sundown. The *bostancıbaşı* and his men would go around to give notice, but if paid a bribe the police would look the other way, allowing the taverns to stay open and the *akşamcıs* to keep quenching their thirst. A large bell was attached to the door post, and a watchman boy would pull the cord as soon as a *zabit* (policeman) came in sight, whereupon the tavern would quickly close. As soon as the danger had passed, the boy would pull the cord again, signaling that the place could reopen. This was a 'don't ask, don't tell' affair, Tevfik explains, with the police being fully aware of the practice.[61]

Toward the end of century, traditional *akşamcı* drinking was joined by more 'modern' types of alcohol and ways of consuming it. One was beer, which made its appearance in the metropolitan Ottoman Empire in this period, via Western channels.[62] The first beerhouse, Kavkas (Caucasus), in the city appeared in the 1860s, in the wake of the Crimean War, which brought European soldiers to Istanbul as well as thousands of Muslim refugees from Circassia, Abkhazia, Mingrelia, and Georgia. Located in Sirkeci, in Eminönü, near the waterfront of the Golden Horn, Kavkas quickly became one of the city's most popular drinking venues. Its popularity only grew in 1890 when Istanbul's train station was built nearby, after which it became the Brasserie du Caucase, a name it carried until 1955.[63] The Proksch Beer House opened its doors following the great fire of 1870. Another well-known beerhouse was Dimitri's Gambrinos, across from the Concordia theater in Pera. In 1888 or 1890, the Swiss Bomonti brothers, Walter and Curt, set up the first brewery— named Bomonti—in Istanbul.[64] Beer became firmly associated with Germany following the 1898 visit of the German Kaiser to Istanbul, at which point the city housed at least thirty beerhouses.[65] Mostly small, unregulated, and ephemeral, these mainly catered to (foreign) travelers, expatriates, and sailors.

In Istanbul and other major cities, Izmir and Salonica above all, patterns of alcohol consumption were in flux in the late nineteenth century. As the grip of Islam loosened and a growing sense of individualism set in among the elite, intellectuals and educated folk began to take liberty with its strictures, openly breaching the rules around fasting and public drinking. As described by French diplomat

Henri Mylès, two of the Young Turks who came to power in 1909, Cemal Pasha and Talat Pasha, drank lustily during a reception given by the French ambassador in late 1913. Also in attendance was an unnamed high-level bureaucrat who had studied in Paris before he became attached to the Ottoman legation in Vienna. Representing an American automobile company, this quintessentially 'modern Turk' kept a residence in Pera, since returning home from nocturnal receptions and balls would be too inconvenient if he lived south of the Golden Horn.[66]

Indeed, a whole new world of leisure and entertainment sprang up in Pera, today's Beyoğlu, during the late nineteenth century. The quarter assumed an increasingly Western, Paris-inspired appearance following various fires that ravaged much of the area in 1820, 1831, 1848, and again in 1853 and 1870, the latter being especially destructive. The Grand'rue or Rue de Péra—currently İstiklāl Caddesi, the mile-long artery that runs through Beyoğlu—became the center of entertainment once it was paved in the 1880s.[67] As part of the rebuilding, the city's mostly wooden houses gave way to brick structures, roads were paved, and gas light exposed its appearance. This last innovation, soon replaced by electricity, imbued the city's modernity with light, creating a phantasmagoric atmosphere around the various new hotels that sprang up in the last decade of the nineteenth century: the Pera Palace and the Grand Hôtel de Londres (1892), the Bristol (1893), and the Tokatlian (1895).[68] Modern drinking establishments known as *gazino*s (from the Italian *casino*) also appeared in this period. Furnished with tables and chairs and open to men and women, a venue like Arkadi Gazinosu Beyoğlu offered 'modern', European-style entertainment which included singing and orchestral music.[69]

In Western eyes, by the century's end Levantine Pera had become a 'second-rate European wannabe', a pale imitation of the West, inhabited by swarthy, unreliable people. But among the Ottoman elite and, increasingly, the middle classes, a different image of the quarter took hold. As Eldem puts it: 'what had previously been perceived as a vague notion of exoticism was now being transformed into an image of modernity tainted with envy'.[70] In the 1890s, drinking moved further north, toward Taksim Square, which became the center of a newly developing middle-class leisure culture, with brasseries, cafés chantants, and casinos run by Greeks crowding out the traditional *meyhane*s and *şaraphane*s.[71] By the early twentieth century, alcohol was rapidly emerging from the shadows and moving into the respectable public sphere, to the point where it was even being advertised in newspapers.[72] All this prefigured developments usually ascribed to the period of the Turkish Republic.

Drinking in Izmir

The onset of commercial capitalism in the 1830s radically transformed the coastal cities of the Ottoman Empire, turning sleepy ports into thriving maritime *entrepôts*. The quintessential example of this process is Izmir. Always more open and free-spirited than other Ottoman cities, Izmir became the 'cosmopolitan' Levantine city par excellence. In 1840, Izmir had a population of some 140,000, 40 percent of whom were Muslim.[73] By the early 1900s, the number had more than doubled to 300,000, only 90,000 of them Muslims.[74]

Beer, first introduced into Ottoman lands in the 1830s by German immigrants, made its appearance in Izmir even before it came to Istanbul.[75] In 1839, following the Treaty of Balta Limanı, 247 barrels of beer and 400 gallons of brandy were imported into Izmir from England.[76] The first beerhouse opened its doors in 1846. Twenty years later, the town was home to at least one brewery. Besides brewing its own, Izmir also imported beer in barrels from Austria and Alsace, and bottled beer from Munich, Trieste, and Strasbourg.[77] By the 1880s, Izmir counted dozens of alcohol-serving establishments, none of them in Muslim hands. Yet Muslims frequented these as well.[78] Customers were entertained by Eastern-European musicians and female dancers, impoverished women from Bohemia and Galicia.[79] In 1921, with Izmir under Greek control, the number of saloons grew to 266. At that time, the city was home to forty-three beerhouses. Most of its 495 coffeehouses served alcohol as well.[80]

The *beau monde* of Smyrna would assemble on the waterfront each day at 7pm, the hour of the 'aperitif', either at Café-Brasserie Kramer, to the sound of Romanian Roma music, or at Brasserie

Klonaridès (until 1907 known as Café-Théatre Loucas), with live music by Maestro Adinolfi, or at Café de Paris, for political discourse. By 1920, a growing Anglo-Saxon influence was reflected in the opening of establishments with names such as Café de Boston and Café John Bull.[81] When electricity came to Smyrna in 1907 — surreptitiously, since Abdülhamid would not hear of such diabolical novelties—cinema was introduced at these various cafés as well. People would also visit the suburb of Kokaryali (Güzelyalı), by boat, by *calèche*, or by horse-drawn—and, later, electrified—tram, to enjoy themselves in the many brasseries along the waterfront.[82]

All this liveliness ended abruptly at the end of the Greco-Turkish War with the great fire of September 1922, which destroyed much of the non-Muslim part of the city.

Drinking in the Provinces

Among the potentates who ruled the Ottoman provinces in the name of the sultan, drinking remained common. Good examples are 'Ali Pasha (r. 1788–1822), who for decades held sway in Ioannina in Epirus; Ahmed Pasha al-Jazzar (the butcher), the brutal warlord of Bosnian origin who held multiple positions of authority in Syria, Lebanon, and Palestine between 1776 and 1805; and 'Ali Rida Pasha, the governor of the *pashalik* of Baghdad from 1834 to 1842.[83] Many lesser provincial officials, some of them stationed in remote places, were given to the bottle, too. As in Qajar Iran, most were of the traditional type, not modernizing, French-speaking ones. Although formally punishable, such behavior tended to be countenanced and—unless it created a public spectacle or otherwise jeopardized state interests—rarely led to irreversible disciplinary measures, let alone outright dismissal.[84]

As before, commoners, and especially the inhabitants of the heartland, were mostly sober. Wine never caught on in Anatolia, despite the fact that at the turn of the twentieth century the Ottoman *şeyhülislam* declared it legal for Muslims to consume if they thought it beneficial for their health.[85] Indeed, beyond Izmir, public drinking simply disappeared, with water and coffee taking the place of wine and spirits.[86] The Muslim town of Aydın, located a mere

90km inland from Izmir, in the 1880s does not seen to have had any (official) venues where alcohol was served.[87] This was not the case everywhere, though, especially not on the Black Sea littoral, home to many Christians. The majority-Greek city of Trabzon counted fifty-one *meyhanes* in 1876.[88] The Laz, a Muslim people who inhabit the southeastern littoral of the Black Sea, converts from Christianity and related to the Georgians, were avid consumers of wine as well as brandy manufactured by local Greeks.[89] The young people of Amasya, near the Black Sea coast, apparently preferred the locally produced eau-de-vie because it brought about the desired state of intoxication much faster than wine.[90] In a multi-denominational place like Mosul, in today's northern Iraq, members of all faiths at the turn of the nineteenth century are said to have been 'much addicted to wine'.[91] The Turkmen inhabiting the area where the Euphrates originates drank wine just as freely as they ate pork. Ottoman-dominated Baghdad, finally, had its winehouses and watering holes.[92]

A great deal of drinking, most of it unseen, also occurred among the Alevis, members of an eclectic branch of Shi'i Islam, as well as among the Bektashis, followers of a Sufi-like, commensal tradition closely connected to the Alevis. Their beliefs and practices—they neither pray in mosques nor keep Ramadan, and they permit the consumption of alcohol—barely qualify them as Muslim in most eyes. Rabbi David d'Beth Hillel, visiting Gaziantep in the late 1820s, no doubt referred to the Alevis or Bektashis when he wrote:

> I witnessed there a curious custom, the Mahometans in their circumcising, festivals, or in their weddings, bring large copper pots filled up with wine and liquor, and in them great copper cups called in Arabic Tassa; these they place in the midst of the congregation, and everybody drinks according to his desire[93]

This suggests he was witnessing the *cem*, a religious ceremonial session organized in private Alevi homes or in the *cem evi*—the *cem* house—which includes the sacrificial consumption of alcohol.[94]

Lebanon and Palestine, too, were influenced by Western ways. Henry Harris Jessup, an American missionary who spent most of his life in the region, claimed that intemperance had greatly increased since 1861, when the French landed 6,000 troops in Syria to end

164

the communal violence that had cost thousands of lives earlier that year. When Jessup first visited the area in the mid-1850s, the pasha of Beirut had the only grog shop in town closed. Half a century later, Beirut was home to 120 licensed saloons, and both 'Turkish civil and military officers and the lowest class of boatmen and artisans' drank as much as any Christians.[95]

Syria produced its own wine in late Ottoman times. In Lebanon, the Bekaa Valley was (and still is) the main center of viticulture, with wine produced according to French methods. The origins of the region's modern viticulture go back to the efforts of French Jesuits in the mid-nineteenth century. Although they initially used the wines they produced for personal and liturgical purposes, their enterprise, facilitated by the French intervention of 1860, is at the basis of Château Ksara, which remains the largest winery of Lebanon. The commercial application of wine goes back to the initiative of a French military engineer named François Eugène Brun, who in 1868 created Domaine des Tourelles, still a prominent winery in the Bekaa Valley. And the Carmel operation, founded in 1886 by Edmond James Rothschild, is still Israel's largest winery.[96]

State Regulation and Reaction: Resistance and Calls for Boycotts

Ottoman state intervention in the alcohol business became more sustained and systemic in the nineteenth century. It also shifted from proscription to surveillance. Whereas in earlier times the authorities had periodically banned drinking and ordered the closure of taverns, as of the 1830s they took a less punitive approach and began to monitor drinking establishments in different ways. The penal codes enacted in 1840, 1851, and 1858 thus no longer focused on alcohol-related infractions.[97]

Money was, as always, the crucial issue. The state had always been complicit with the operation of taverns because of the revenue they yielded, only forcing them to close during Ramadan.[98] The need for fiscal income was clearly behind the imposition of a new tax on wine in Ottoman Crete in 1834, as well as the decision to turn the sale of alcohol into a state monopoly two years later (a monopoly that was invalidated in 1838 with the Treaty of Balta Limanı).[99] In time, taxes were streamlined, with a 20 percent tax replacing the myriad imposts levied previously. In 1860, a department of spirits was established within the Ministry of Finance. A year later, the 20 percent tax was cut by half, and tavern owners were required to purchase annual permits, with venues located within 200 meters of religious sites unable to apply. In subsequent years, rates and regulations were changed several more times. In 1881, alcohol-related revenue became part of the newly created Ottoman Public Debt Administration.[100]

Resistance to drinking took various forms, involving different interests and motives. When Sultan Mahmud II ordered the closure of Istanbul's *meyhanes* in 1826 as part of his move against the janissaries, angry owners appealed to the government and offered large sums of money to keep the alcohol flowing.[101] As said, Sultan Abdülhamid sought to restrict the sale of alcohol, but failed in the face of subterfuge as well as resistance by tavern owners who petitioned for the right to keep their establishments open until five hours after sunset. The fact that the government eventually struck a compromise—differentiating between licensed taverns and unauthorized ones in that the former were allowed to stay open two and a half hours after dark—illustrates the growing power of private interests.[102]

The ulama unsurprisingly opposed any relaxation of the strictures on drinking in public. Religiously motivated resistance seems to have subsided in the latter part of the century, though, especially with the onset of the Public Debt Administration, which made taxes—including the excise on alcohol—a matter of paying debt, lending alcohol an aura of legitimacy. Still, the secular authorities continued to navigate an ambivalent course between wariness and countenance through licensing.[103]

Opposition to alcohol increasingly came in the form of resistance to outside intrusion of a perceived collusion between non-Muslims and foreigners. The official policy of lifting restrictions on *dhimmis*, identifiable as early as 1809 and increasingly manifest under Mahmud II, bred resentment among Muslims whose worldview was built on the natural superiority of Islam.[104] The Greek war of independence of the 1820s and growing unrest in the mainly Christian Balkans fueled those flames, and the Treaty of Balta Limanı created an institutional link between foreign-protected non-Muslims and the production and sale of alcohol. It opened Ottoman markets to British products, and gave British subjects and protégés the freedom to engage in commerce throughout Ottoman territory. Claiming that trade included retail trade, the British against Ottoman objections licensed taverns and spirit shops to their Maltese and Ionian Greek subjects living in Istanbul under the extraterritorial privileges of the Capitulation regime. The resulting spread of taverns beyond the traditional 'Christian' parts of town, and a rise in crime and prostitution bred growing resentment against heavy-handed foreigners and their non-Muslim protégés. Following protests, attempts were made to regulate this business, but these remained halfhearted and ineffective.[105] The Crimean War and the thirsty foreign soldiers it brought to Istanbul fascinated as much as repelled Turks, convincing Muslims already wary of imperious Westerners that their civilization equaled 'wine, women and the roulette table'.[106] When, as part of the Tanzimat reforms, non-Muslims formally received equal rights, the mutually beneficial relationship between foreign powers and *dhimmi*s grew even stronger. Muslim resentment grew accordingly, culminating in the early 1900s.

The nineteenth century also saw the medicalization of alcohol, as part of growing attention to matters of public health and hygiene. First seen in Muhammad 'Ali's Egypt, this is reflected in the creation in 1888 of an Ottoman General Public Hygiene Commission. Whereas traditionally religious leaders had been the main opponents of drinking in Muslim societies, from the 1880s onward journalists and physicians who had studied in Europe (or at least were familiar with European, mostly French, ideas) increasingly raised the alarm about alcohol and the toll it took on the human body and mind. The period accordingly saw the emergence of a scientific discourse about alcohol in the form of treatises warning of its debilitating effect on the body and soul. These views were shared at a series of conferences held in various European capitals between 1885 and 1912.[107] A prominent Ottoman participant was Besim Ömer (1862–1940), the founder of modern Turkish obstetrics and gynecology who received his medical education in Paris in the 1880s. His booklet, *Mükeyyefat*

167

ve Müskirat ('Narcotics and Alcoholic Drinks'), warned about the dangers of drugs and alcohol. In 1891, another pamphlet about alcohol's social perils written by one Halid Vanizade saw the light.[108] In 1904, Osman Nuri Eralp (1876–1940), a French-educated veterinarian and microbiologist, came out with a tract about the physical ailments and the mental and moral problems caused by drinking.[109] Ali Kemal, an exiled intellectual who in the late 1890s served as Paris correspondent for the magazine *İkdam*, wrote about the ruinous effects of alcohol he witnessed in the French capital. Drawing attention to private initiatives as well as to measures taken by the French state to curb the use of alcohol by monopolizing its production and sale, he exhorted the Ottoman state to follow suit.[110]

Alcohol in Nineteenth-Century Egypt

In nineteenth-century Egypt, too, change was afoot. Indeed, the Nile valley was the first part of the Ottoman Empire to be enduringly affected by Europe and its ways. Various French liqueurs are listed as import items as early as the 1780s.[111] Napoleon's soldiers shamelessly guzzled wine in Cairo's venerable al-Azhar Mosque, and the Greek grocers of Alexandria and Cairo took advantage of the French presence by opening grog shops.[112]

Napoleon's occupation of Egypt, though brief, was enormously consequential in the way it prepared the ground for the first great modernizing ruler of the Middle East, Muhammad (Mehmed) 'Ali, a warlord of Albanian descent who took power in 1804 and ruled Egypt for the next forty-four years, effectively ending Ottoman control over the country.

While most of Egypt's Muslims continued to shun alcohol, drinking is said to have increased among upper-class Muslims during and after the French occupation.[113] Edward Lane, an Englishman who lived in Cairo almost uninterruptedly between 1825 and 1849, insisted that, the Koranic proscription notwithstanding, 'many of the Muslims ... in the present day, drink wine, brandy &., in secret; and some, thinking it no sin to indulge thus in moderation, scruple not to do so openly'.[114] Among those who drank, members of the 'Turkish' elite seem to have prevailed.[115] Of the originally Albanian

Muhammad 'Ali, it remains unclear if and to what extent he imbibed, and what happened to the hundreds of bottles of Tokaji Hungarian wine he received from the Austrians as a present in 1828.[116] His son Ibrahim Pasha drank in moderation and is said to have given up alcohol altogether, albeit temporarily, during his stay in Mecca while waging war against the puritanical Wahhabis in 1816.[117] Ahmed Pasha Yeğen, Muhammad 'Ali's nephew, did drink while he served as governor of Mecca—and even organized banquets in the holy city—until he gave up, exhausted by illness and the rigors of war, and adopted a pious lifestyle.[118]

Like Istanbul, mid-nineteenth-century Cairo and Alexandria had their share of licensed *khammāras* frequented by the lower classes. These operated not directly under government supervision but as 'franchises' overseen by contractors, who acquired their concession by auction and paid a licensing fee to the state. To be found drunk on the street after visiting these establishments was apparently no major crime; the person in question would just be hauled off to the nearest police station. Otherwise, drinking was linked to public entertainment involving music, dance, and prostitution, all of which was mainly the business of non-Muslims.[119]

There were yet more signs of modernizing reform in nineteenth-century Egypt. One was a change in the role of the *muhtasib*, the market inspector-cum-tax collector responsible for maintaining fair price levels as well as preventing untoward behavior, including drinking. In 1837, the entire office had been abolished. Four years later, a decree was issued that effectively 'medicalized' public health by having the duties of the *muhtasib* taken over by a range of new officials, who made the rounds accompanied by a physician. The *muhtasib* became a local informant who just assisted the police in checking the quality of food being traded in the market.[120] All this was part of a shift from official concerns about public morality to a preoccupation with public health and hygiene, a step in the bureaucratization process. In 1883, the rules of *hisba* were included in a newly drafted penal code, marking the next phase in the state-led concerns about public morality.[121]

A similar influence of European ideas is visible in the changing perception of alcohol as part of the transition from traditional Galenic medicine based on humoral pathology to modern medicine. The new manuals that were used for Cairo's Qasr al-'Ayni medical school, founded in 1827 and led by the famous French doctor Antoine Clot (Bey), describe alcohol not in traditional Islamic terms but in the context of public hygiene. Rather than focusing on morality, the new approach was one of clinical attention to its effects on the human body and the mind, cautioning about consumption in hot climates and pointing out its usefulness in cold climes.[122]

Irreversible change would come with Egypt's next major reformer, the Khedive Isma'il (r. 1863–79), whose famous words, 'My country is no longer in Africa, it is now in Europe', reflected aspiration more than reality, yet gave voice to the fact that Egypt was opening up to the world at an accelerating rate. Benefiting from a cotton boom caused by a temporary slump in American exports due to the Civil War, Isma'il had the means to engage in major infrastructural projects. Egypt's first railways were built under his auspices. So was his crowning achievement, the Suez Canal, finished in 1869. With this came an influx of Europeans, many of whom became long-term residents. The result was a phenomenon termed 'effendification', an emerging class of locals keen to 'perform' modernity by imitating a Western lifestyle, thus separating themselves from both the traditional elite and the religious masses.

Cairo especially underwent dramatic change in this period. Its remaking centered on the Azbakiyya Gardens, located in a district outside the original city walls known for its many ponds. Under Napoleon's brief occupation, the area was connected to the city and became the site of the first modern restaurants and cafés. The Azbakiyya area underwent further transformation under Muhammad 'Ali, who had it cleaned up and turned into a European-style park in the 1830s. The 'French' Muski quarter, which grew around the newly built Muski Street, is where the city's first modern hotels were constructed, including the Shepheard's Hotel in 1849. Yet its proximity to Was'a Square, a center of vice and crime filled with coffeehouses, taverns, and brothels, and teeming with prostitutes, peddlers, and hustlers, initially made the area less than welcoming to Europeans.[123]

Khedive Isma'il's visit to Paris on the occasion of the Exposition Universelle in 1867 brought more drastic reform. Impressed by the radical changes Baron Haussmann had wrought in the French capital, the khedive resolved to remake Cairo. The area between the old city and the Nile was totally redesigned; new, straight streets were laid out; a railway station was constructed; and an opera house rose up around Azbakiyya. Between 1869 and 1872, the actual gardens were radically transformed at the hands of Jean-Pierre Barillet-Deschamps, the landscape architect who had designed the Bois de Boulogne in Paris and who used the same city's Parc Monceau with its waterways and pavilions as his inspiration. More hotels and cafés opened their doors, and a French theater, a circus, and a hippodrome were built. Modern bars and cafés followed, adding to a burgeoning entertainment quarter, so that by the 1890s establishments such as the Splendid Bar and the New Bar attracted a (male) clientele of foreigners, Levantines, and country dwellers visiting the city. Located near the Shepheard's Hotel, where champagne, Bordeaux, and Rhine wine were served, the park became a favorite strolling ground for European residents and visitors. Before long, these began to lament that Azbakiyya was losing its romantic, Oriental allure and had become 'too European'.[124]

Despite the radical transformation of the Azbakiyya Gardens, the neighboring Was'a remained a center of vice, prompting Cairo's municipality to take disciplinary measures. A Police Act enacted in 1880 mandated police involvement in segregating brothels, taverns, and coffeehouses from respectable neighborhoods. Article 8 instructed shaykhs and police commissioners not to allow prostitutes to dwell among upstanding residents. Article 13 singled out major thoroughfares such as Clot Bey and Muhammad 'Ali streets, where Christian and Jewish women had recently opened many brothels. It instructed the police to close these establishments for the sake of public security. No new coffeehouses and taverns could be opened near mosques and religious shrines, and those already operating in such locales were to be shuttered.[125]

A contrary impulse came with the British occupation of Egypt in 1882 and the wave of soldiers and administrators it unleashed, especially to Cairo and Alexandria. Missionary and temperance advocate Samuel M. Zwemer claimed in 1919 that Egyptians had taken to hard liquor since the days of Napoleon and the British occupation. 'Everywhere on walls and fences and billboards and in every newspaper of the polyglot city of Cairo,' he wrote at the end of the First World War, 'you may see advertisements of English and Scotch whiskey, French cognac, German beer and Greek wine'. Whisky advertisements also adorned all train stations from Alexandria to Khartoum, and liquor was sold at 'every railway restaurant'. Brandy and whisky imports had doubled between 1914 and 1918, now exceeding one million dollars. Egypt even exported locally manufactured brandy, with whisky, rum, and gin being manufactured in the country as well. All this without any tax or government control![126] Harry Johnston, a colonial administrator with long experience in Africa, concurred: Muslim Egyptians, he intoned, had been abstainers until the arrival of the British, but the young men in the towns had picked up the 'whisky habit' from their soldiers, and now a 'good deal of masculine "young Egypt" was whiskified and drunken'.[127]

These developments spawned a domestic nationalist and abolitionist reaction which identified the West as the source of debauchery and decadence. Its representatives decried those who spent their time in bars and cafés drinking, smoking hashish, and frequenting (licensed) brothels, and urged the state to take its role as regulator of the moral order seriously. In response, officials in 1895 adopted an interventionist policy at the behest of the ulama, seeking to impose new restrictions on prostitution such as a ban on Muslim women singing and dancing in cafés.[128]

Yet such reactions were no match for imperialist laws and customs. The British occupation left the alcohol business unregulated for a long time, thus creating opportunities for the same foreign nationals—Ionian Greeks, Italians, Maltese—who operated under the Capitulation laws in Istanbul. Combining alcohol sales with moneylending, they set up drink shops in Muslim villages located in the Delta, alongside newly laid railway tracks.[129] In 1899, it was estimated that there were over 4,000 such establishments. From the licenses issued in Cairo between 1891 and 1896, we get a sense of the dynamics of the business. Greeks, and to a lesser extent Italians, descendants of those who had settled in Egypt in the 1860s, played an especially significant role in this proliferation, receiving three-quarters of the licenses given out in 1893. Jews, Copts, and even Muslims owned some as well, receiving 10 percent of the issued licenses by 1904.

Despite local opposition and British concerns about the spread of alcohol among Egypt's rural Muslims, the Capitulation regime and the bribes Greeks doled out to maintain their position meant that little could be done about these activities.[130] The rules regarding alcohol were rather lax in general. All that was needed to open a drink shop was a permit, and requests were only denied in cases where it would be used to sell alcohol in villages. Drinking venues were also banned in the vicinity of houses of worship, schools, and cemeteries. And there were mandatory closing times. Yet none of these applied to the 'European' quarters of Egyptian cities, which remained free of any restrictions. Only in 1915 and 1916, following the arrival of yet more British soldiers, did a new law bring alcohol under stricter control, preventing the sale of adulterated liquor, banning absinthe, and tightening closing times. Yet alcohol remained untaxed.[131] No wonder that Johnston scolded the British for doing little to stem the flow of alcohol in Egypt (and Sudan).[132]

The British occupation of 1882 did not just bring thirsty soldiers to Egypt, but teetotaling temperance advocates as well. Indeed, the first Egyptian temperance movement dates from 1884 with the creation of an Egyptian branch of the American Woman's Christian Temperance Union (WCTU), led by the Boston-based Mary Clement Leavitt, who in the three months she spent in Egypt spoke fifteen times on the theme of 'spreading the white ribbon'. Rather than responding to an Egyptian desire to mitigate the abuse of alcohol (and of intoxicants in general), this Western, Anglo-American initiative, spearheaded by the American Presbyterian Church, was an outgrowth of a campaign to spread the Protestant gospel around the world. The organization's success remained limited, though, and the membership never exceeded more than a few dozen. However, this initiative did set the stage for later, more indigenous temperance movements, to be discussed in Chapter 8.[133]

North Africa and Alcohol

North Africa evinces some of the same patterns as other parts of the Ottoman Empire, which until 1830 loosely controlled the eastern half of the region. As elsewhere in the Islamic world, the region's Muslims tended not to touch liquor. In Morocco, the sale of brandy and wine was strictly forbidden in the mid-nineteenth century, even though both could be bought by those with the means.[134]

Moroccan Muslims typically went to the Jewish quarter, the *mellah*, to purchase and consume alcohol. *Mellah*s of note were those of Marrakesh, Fez, and, above all, Tetouan, a city known as Pequeña Jerusalén on account of the many Jews who had been living there since their expulsion from Granada at the turn of the sixteenth century, and who 250 years later made up roughly a third of the town's total population of *c.* 15,000.[135] It was predominantly members of the well-to-do classes that availed themselves of the opportunity of getting hold of alcohol in this manner, and so long as matters were handled discreetly, problems rarely ensued.

Wine had been around in North Africa since Roman times, but, at least in the Muslim period, most of the grapes cultivated ended up as raisins. The French settlement of Algeria changed all that, although not immediately; aside from an initiative undertaken by French Trappists in 1843, wine cultivation took decades to take off. Algeria was supposed to assimilate with France, but initially the plan was for it to provide products lacking in the metropole, and that did not include wine. Following legislation in 1863 that overrode tribal authority and ceded large tracts of land to settlers from France and other southern European countries, wine cultivation was at last given a chance to flourish.[136] The Phylloxera epidemic of the 1870s, which devasted France's wine industry, brought more settlers (*colons*), who were given the green light to plant vines on a wide scale without being accused of undercutting France's domestic wine production. Using the latest technology and transportation techniques, these settlers brought 70,000 hectares under cultivation by 1885, yielding 960,000 hectoliters of wine. By 1907, these numbers had gone up to 7.8 million hectoliters produced on 186,000 hectares.[137] While ownership by indigenous growers dropped by almost half between

1864 and 1878, the acreage owned by *colon*s more than doubled in the same period.[138] From the 1890s onward, the vineyards came to employ many Arab Algerians squeezed by economic hardship and colonial restrictions.[139]

Drinking patterns followed on a par with the increased cultivation of the grape. Indeed, viticulture and French settlement had a mutually reinforcing effect in Algeria.[140] A decade after the occupation, wine and spirits, imported through the ports of Algiers and Bône (modern 'Annaba), were available throughout the land. Berbers (Imazighen), known to be less strict in their observance of Islamic rules, were said to drink more readily than Arabs.[141] One observer noted in 1889 that in Algeria's large cities the natives had begun to imitate foreigners by drinking wine and absinthe.[142] Champagne especially was enjoyed by those who could afford it. As the German Moritz Wagner put it, wherever the French tricolor fluttered, champagne bubbled with undiminished vigor, even in the farthest reaches of Bedouin territory. He added that the Arab sheikhs loved to see the stoppers pop and few of them spurned the drink, holy writ and local *marabout*s notwithstanding.[143] As with beer, Algerian Muslims often justified their taste for champagne by arguing that it resembled sparkling water (hence the name 'gazouze'—from (*eau*) *gazeuse*—for champagne in nineteenth-century Algeria) and was thus legitimate.[144] Those who imbibed might also be careful not to be seen doing so around fellow Muslims for fear of being censored by them.[145] All this gave the French a perfect double standard for branding abstinent Muslims as unsophisticated and calling those who did drink, under the pretext that their faith countenanced it, 'fake' Muslims, hypocritical, or ignorant of their own religion.[146] The French, after all, operated in North Africa by fostering the self-serving myth that they had revived a viticultural tradition going back to Roman times that had been interrupted by the Arab-Muslim invasion in the seventh century, thus casting France in the role of a civilizing force.[147]

In mid-nineteenth-century Tunisia, where most wine was imported from Italy, the government was mainly concerned about the taxes it derived from its sale.[148] Tunis saw a steady increase in the number of taverns even before the French takeover in 1881.

In 1861, the municipal registers counted thirty wine shops run by Jews, Sicilians, Greeks, and Maltese, and twenty-five with owners who operated under British protection. Tunisian Muslims, workers above all, more and more frequented these. With this came an increase in public intoxication and prostitution, leading to brawling and violence. Between 1861 and 1863, drunkenness came in as the second-most frequent infraction, after indebtedness. Since drinking was mostly an after-dark affair, nocturnal crime went up as well.[149] Yet overall, Tunisians remained moderate drinkers well into the era of the Protectorate.[150]

In Morocco, European influence intensified after 1856, when the country opened to the world by way of a British-Moroccan 'friendship treaty'. This did not immediately bring many Europeans to the country. In Casablanca, the country's largest city, resident Europeans never numbered much more than 500 for the next half-century. Yet their economic weight and cultural magnetism gave this expatriate community an outsize influence on the city and later the country, as is seen, for instance, in an increase in the consumption of alcohol by the local population.[151]

Tangier holds an exceptional place in this respect. As its population grew from 16,000 to 45,000 between 1866 and 1900, it became Morocco's first 'modern' city, a multicultural port open to the world and a gateway for European goods and consumerism. This naturally included alcohol, which became emblematic of the city's modernity. By 1884, Tangier boasted 110 alcohol-serving cafés, almost half of them catering to a 'Moorish' clientele. A decade later, the number exceeded 200. European imports included beer, wine, and spirits from Spain, France, Germany, and England, as well as domestically produced spirits, principally locally produced *mahia*.[152]

7

CHANGING DRINKING HABITS IN THE
NINETEENTH CENTURY
PART TWO
QAJAR IRAN

Introduction: Between the Safavids and the Qajars

Many aspects of life and society are poorly documented for the 75-year period between the fall of the Safavids in 1722 and the accession of the Qajars at the turn of the nineteenth century. Mainly responsible for this is that in the intervening period Iran suffered a great deal of instability, resulting in a degree of de-urbanization that some have equated with 'retribalization'. Whereas the Ottoman Empire experienced its first 'modernizing wave' in the early eighteenth-century, Iranian society, little affected by Western models until a full century later, retained its traditional ways for much longer.[1] From the little evidence available, it appears that the Afghans—that is, the Pashtun tribes that took Isfahan in 1722—were averse to alcohol. Nadir Shah, the warlord who controlled part of the country between 1736 and 1747, was a moderate drinker, especially toward the end of his life, when he is said to have given up brandy.[2] Otherwise, traditional drinking patterns appear to have persisted, reflecting a society that in many ways remained unregulated and 'undisciplined', where practices might flagrantly contravene (religious) 'norms' without leading to serious corrective measures by either the state or religious authorities.

In 1737, the Dutch allude to such Iranian traditions by referring to the habit among Iranians of all classes of organizing banquets, for which they would collect large amounts of grapes as well as raisins, which were needed for distilled drinks.[3] In the 1760s, the Frenchman Ferrières-Sauveboeuf similarly claimed that Iranians drank freely.[4] Indeed, in at least one instance, merrymaking was officially licensed, even actively encouraged. The place of action is Shiraz, and the enabler is Karim Khan Zand, the warlord who emerged from the chaos following the death of Nadir Shah in 1747 to take control of much of southern Iran. In the 1770s, Karim Khan turned his capital into an 'abode of pleasure' (dār al-'aysh), filled with brothels and taverns so as to accommodate the appetites of his soldiers, but also in an attempt to 'civilize' the tribal elements that had taken over Iran after the fall of Safavid Isfahan (and which probably included the forces Karim Khan had brought with him from Luristan).[5]

Rustam al-Hukama, a nineteenth-century man of letters, portrays Karim Khan as a ruler engaged in sexual and alcoholic debauchery, but claims that he nevertheless cared for his people, echoing the old adage that royal high living mattered little so long as it did not come at the expense of good governance.[6] Rustam al-Hukama may have had Karim Khan's eldest son, Abu'l-Fath Khan, in mind with his reference to the absence of good governance. Abu'l-Fath Khan, who briefly ruled Fars in a co-regency with his brother after their father's death, upon entering Shiraz is said to have succumbed to 'perpetual drinking' (shurb-i mudām), in the company of beautiful young lads, unconcerned about the management of the state and the army.[7] Other rulers in Karim Khan's orbit, men such as 'Ali Muhammad Khan, who briefly ruled Basra in 1775–7, and Ja'far Khan, a nephew of his, were known for their heavy drinking as well.[8]

The Qajar Period: Old Habits Die Hard

In many ways, the cultivation, production, and consumption of alcohol in Iran remained traditional throughout the nineteenth century, its manufacturing the bailiwick of non-Muslims, who were also its principal consumers. Approaching Qazvin on his way from Tabriz to Tehran in 1848, Horatio Southgate rode 'four miles through uninterrupted vineyards', which 'extended to an equal distance in the other direction'.[9] Half a century later, Qazvin was still a renowned center of viticulture.[10] In 1872, Henry Walter Bellew noticed the vineyards around Hamadan in western Iran, which, he said, produced a good deal of wine: a hock-like white and a red that resembled claret.[11] The Scotsman MacGregor, visiting Quchan in Khorasan in the late 1870s, referred to the surrounding area as 'one vast vineyard'.[12]

The quality of Iranian wines as described by foreigners varied a great deal. Bellew called the stuff from Hamadan of 'inferior quality and crude flavour'.[13] Charles James Wills, an English physician and long-time resident of Iran, went into some geographical detail. Wine from the Tehran region he called an 'abominable concoction made of watered grapes mixed with vine-leaves, and supposed to resemble claret'. Wine from Kerman was 'strong, rough, and carelessly made'. Isfahan, by contrast, produced 'fairly good' wine, which resembled a light port and improved with age. Wills disagreed with Bellew about Hamadan wine, which in his estimation was a 'delicious pale white wine, with a powerful natural bouquet resembling Moselle'. The queen of Persian wines, all agreed, was that of Shiraz: sweet when fresh but soon turning dry, of great potency, and with a delicate aroma and nutty flavor. Three-year-old good Shiraz wine, Wills averred, resembled nothing so much as the best virgin sherry.[14]

As elsewhere, the law in Qajar Iran allowed religious minorities to manufacture wine in private and for their own use. The Russian diplomat Baron Korf, passing through Tabriz in the mid-1830s, reported that the region's barely potable wine was produced by local Armenians.[15] Yet according to his compatriot Ilya Berezin, in Kashan wine was (also) manufactured by Muslims.[16] The Hungarian scholar-adventurer Vámbéry similarly claimed that in Shiraz both Armenians and Muslims were involved in viniculture.[17]

New Julfa, the Armenian suburb of Isfahan, naturally was a center of production as well as consumption. Few of its inhabitants were teetotalers, and each household had its own winepress for making wine and raki, some of it quite good, in Wills' estimation.[18] The process of winemaking suggests age-old practices. In Hamadan, people used 'large earthen jars which [were] sunk a yard deep in the ground', each of which held 600 to 800 bottles. The local wine was sold in 'glass bottles thinner and lighter than Florence flasks'. As was the case in Safavid times, the bottles were packed in loose straw, the cases sewn with string, and a 'piece of rag or cotton-wool [was] placed at the mouth of each carboy, and a handful of mud or plaster-o-Paris [was] dabbed on it'.[19]

In the 1790s, the French naturalist Antoine Guillaume Olivier echoed a common view by stating that Iranians had fewer scruples evading the law of their Prophet than Turks, convinced as they were that the Prophet was intent less on an absolute ban on wine than on preventing disorder and crime through excess.[20] As elsewhere in the Islamic world, in Iran most drinking took place in private, at nocturnal sessions behind the high walls of people's homes, and with trusted friends.[21] But the boundary between private and public was a fuzzy one. Many Sufis drank just as they smoked *bang* (hemp)—quite openly—'holding all things to be from God' and claiming a private moral sphere so powerfully articulated by Hafez and his fellow poets.[22] Also, as Southgate explained, officers charged with the enforcement of the religious law were often corrupt, and typically sales took place quite openly. 'Everyone bought, but nobody pretended to know of anyone's buying,' as he put it.[23] That is to say, everyone knew where to find the private dwellings of local Christians, Jews, or Zoroastrians. New Julfa thus was the scene of a 'barely concealed' traffic in liquor with Muslims, under the venal eyes of the authorities.[24] Matters were no different in Tabriz. Eugène Crampon, the French consul between 1867 and 1871, noted in one of his perceptive reports that the local Armenians had a monopoly on the sale of alcohol, which they manufactured for Muslims who 'consider[ed] it sacrilegious to produce yet very agreeable to drink'.[25] Wills adds some detail: 'The Mussulmans generally, save the most bigoted, have no objection to lend a hand. The grapes are trodden out in a tank, which exists in every rich man's cellar; or, failing that, in pans'. For his own winemaking, Wills had secured the service of an expert mullah, who 'used to enliven his labour by quotations from the Koran and songs from Hafiz'.[26] Nowhere was alcohol consumed as publicly as in Shiraz, Vámbéry claimed. Everyone in town, from day laborers to civil servants—indeed, even the ulama—liked to imbibe. Women too participated in these festivities, Vámbéry observed, which was unique to Shiraz.[27] Moreover, the absence of public drunkenness and brawling, and 'deserted homes and broken hearts' in private—hailed by Southgate as the effect of Iran's 'prevailing inebriety'—does not seem to have applied to Shiraz.[28] Upon arrival in 1854, the (originally Jewish) Anglican missionary Henry Aaron Stern was confronted with 'numbers of idle, drunken vagabonds, parading the streets and bawling forth the most obscene Bacchanalian songs'. The turmoil following the reign of Karim Khan Zand had destroyed the city, Stern claimed, and the 30,000 remaining inhabitants were notorious for their fondness of wine and arrack and lax morals overall.[29] The kharābāt continued to do a brisk business, attracting men from the lower orders, many of them ruffians known as lutis. Accounts from the late 1870s speak of drunken brawls causing injury and, at times, death.[30] Similar scenes are reported about New Julfa, where Muslims visiting Armenian homes in search of booze occasionally resulted in violence, and even stabbings.[31] Police reports for late nineteenth-century Tehran, too, frequently refer to instances of public drunkenness and disorderly conduct.[32]

Iranian drinkers indeed exhibited a widely reported lack of restraint. In the words of James Baillie Fraser, a British traveler-spy with intimate knowledge of the country, 'their maxim was that there is as much sin in a glass as in a flagon; and that if they incur the penalty, they will not forgo the pleasure'.[33] According to Berezin, since getting soused was the point, vodka was the most sought-after tipple.[34] In 1817, von Kotzbue saw the Iranian guests at a banquet in Yerevan quaff liqueur in 'immense quantities'. He had met men who 'drank off a bottle of rum at once without appearing to suffer any inconvenience of it'.[35] And the French artist-traveler Eugène Flandin vowed that he had never seen anyone who did not consume alcohol without getting blitzed. Many, he added, alluding to the 'repentance' ritual common among Muslim men, would indulge in this and other vices until about the age of fifty, at which point they would atone. Quite a few persisted in their alcoholic habits until the very end, though.[36]

There was plenty of alcohol to be had in Iran's urban centers, but it was not so easily found in rural parts, except in Armenia and parts of Khorasan.[37] Southgate claimed that there were even fewer shops that openly sold it in Iran than in Ottoman lands on account of the small number of Christians living in the country.[38] This points to the paradox that, even if public drinking venues were few and far between, creating the impression that Iran was a rather dry country, Muslim Iranians in fact tended to imbibe more than Turks, at least when it comes to wine. In Southgate's words:

> A traveller who goes over the country with the speed of a post-horse, or who does not seek to introduce himself to the interior of Eastern society, might imagine that there was not an intemperate Mussulman in Turkey or Persia. But if he could be with them in their private repasts, or in their clubs (for they have such, especially in Persia), where every man is known to be a true friend of the bottle, he might witness scenes worthy of the most desperate band of bacchanalians that ever consummated their orgies in the purlieus of an American dram-shop. The Persians carry the habit much farther than the Turks and practice it with much less reserve and secrecy. I feel safe in affirming that there are few Persians, out of the religious orders, who do not drink wine. Most of those about the court are notoriously addicted to it, though, at present, they are compelled to be more secret in their indulgence, because the Shah [Muhammad Shah] frowns upon it.[39]

Even the religious classes were 'not altogether free from the vice', with some having 'the reputation of being perfect adepts in the practice'. Here, too, Southgate posited how Iran differed from Ottoman lands, where religious leaders were 'almost uniformly rigid in their abstinence'.[40]

As always, alcohol involved stratagems. According to Ritter von Riederer, an Austrian advisor to the Qajar government in the 1870s, an Iranian would observe the religious rules so long as others watched him, but he would do whatever he deemed comfortable and pleasurable once he was in the privacy of his home. Drinking was one of these activities. The state, von Riederer added, followed a time-honored convention by punishing only those who caused a public nuisance and never bothered to intervene with indoor drinking parties, even if in the end 'all were lying about'.[41] Secrecy was key. Adolfo Rivadeneyra, the Spanish consul to Iran in the 1870s, experienced this when the governor of Hamadan invited him to his home for a dinner party, requesting that his guest keep the invitation a secret lest the people find out that their town's first magistrate had hosted a wine-fueled party for an infidel.[42]

One way of squaring theory and practice was the time-honored method of getting a physician to declare wine necessary for the preservation or restoration of one's health.[43] J. P. Ferrier, visiting Herat in 1845, claimed that no one was allowed to manufacture wine in the city. Consumption was a different matter; all one needed was a medical certificate, which was ordinarily obtained from physicians, for whom this was a source of income.[44]

Alcohol as medicine also figures in a story told about foreign minister Mirza Saʻid Khan Ansari Muʼtamin al-Mulk (1815–83), who on his deathbed was prescribed wine by court physicians seeking to help him recover. Ronald Thomson, British Minister in Tehran at the time, donated a crate of Bordeaux for the purpose, but the foreign minister did not allow this precious gift to enter his house. Instead, it was sent to the residence of Mirza Mihdi Khan Mumtahin al-Dawla, the narrator of the story, who proceeded to make Saʻid Khan Ansari drink a glass before lunch and dinner.[45]

A similar story involving the 'medical alibi' is told by Mirza Riza Khan Arfaʻ al-Dawla (1853–1902), who had to 'prove' to Amin al-Sultan, the minister of court, that his having drunk wine while abroad did not disqualify him as a Muslim. Arfaʻ al-Dawla acknowledged that, strictly speaking, he had violated Islamic law, but he justified the act by arguing that he had committed it at the orders of a 'skilled physician' who had given him a 'certifying' document based on the words of the Prophet who had declared that, when a man is ill, he is allowed to drink as long as it is prescribed by a 'skilled physician'.[46]

The medical excuse was only one ploy. Self-fashioning through shifting identities was another. The Russian engineer S. Lomnitskii offers an anecdote in his perceptive travelogue that is as amusing as it is informative in the way he describes a drinking party at the residence of a wealthy Iranian where clerics were in attendance. At some point during the event, the host ordered 'something and the hats' to be brought in. A servant entered carrying a tray with an array of hats; each of the clerics took one hat and put it on his head, declaring that he was now no longer a mullah but a private person. After this, the attendees set out to play Islamically forbidden games—checkers, chess, cards—while availing themselves of the 'something', which turned out to be an array of alcoholic drinks: vodka, cognac, wine, and liqueurs.[47]

A post-hoc scheme was to 'pay' one's way out of punishment. The British major Scott Waring noted that the position of *dārughā* (city constable) in early Qajar Shiraz was a lucrative one since anyone found drinking wine or keeping company with prostitutes would have to pay a hefty fee for the official to look the other way.[48] Corruption indeed was common. Berezin was asked for vodka as a *pishkish* (a bribe-like gift) at the Isfahan tax office.[49] When the aforementioned Stern alighted at a half-ruined caravan halfway between Shiraz and Qumisha in 1849, he was approached by the head of the *rāhdārs* (the officials in charge of road security), who instead of toll money demanded 'a bottle of arrack, to make some keif (pleasure)'. Disappointed to hear that the teetotalling Stern and his party did not carry such a beverage, the official said that if the foreigners had any, he would not have to break the Prophet's law, swearing 'by Ali and all the 124,000 Mahomedan prophets, that sherab [wine] and arrack were only interdicted to those who prayed; but, as he never prayed, he could not be included in the law'.[50]

None of these stratagems protected Iran's minorities from occasionally being targeted by religious leaders who blamed them for natural disasters such as bad harvests and epidemics. In the spring of 1815, a severe drought struck Tehran. The city's *shaykh al-islām* attributed the ensuing famine to the presence of Armenians who ran wine shops in town. A mob led by the *shaykh al-islām* set out in the direction of the city's Armenian quarter and proceeded to pull down a church as well as said wine shops. As was often the case, the secular authorities stepped in next. When Fath 'Ali Shah (r. 1797–1834) heard of the incident, he was incensed. Questioning the authority of the clerics to incite people against a community that had the right to live in security and peace, he imposed a 1,000-*tumān* penalty (some £500) on the culprits. The victims received the enormous sum of 3,000 *tumāns* in compensation, and the church was to be rebuilt at government expense.[51]

In the summer of 1892, we hear of another example of clerically incited mob violence against minorities. A virulent cholera outbreak that year prompted the religious leaders of Gorgan (modern Astarabad) to rile up the local rabble to storm Armenian shops with the argument that they violated Islamic law by selling alcohol, and that the epidemic was God's retribution. The incident prompted the town's Russian consul to send a contingent of Cossack troops to protect the local Russian community.[52]

Foreigners were occasionally targeted as well. In 1838, a mob in Bushehr, acting at the behest of a local judge, raided the city's Jewish quarter, under the pretext that the money changer of the British Residency was involved in the alcohol trade, but mostly in retaliation for the British attack on the isle of Kharq earlier that year.[53] In 1902, a mob in Tabriz, exhorted by the ulama to demand the removal of Armenians and foreigners from the city, ransacked an Armenian grog shop. Here, too, the local Russian consul, working with the Tehran government, intervened to calm tempers.[54] Similar types of violence in Tehran and Shiraz resulting in the destruction of homes and property are recorded in the first decade of the twentieth century.[55]

Elite Drinking in the Provinces

Iran's ruling classes clearly continued to imbibe, at times in enormous quantities. Southgate estimated that, among men of authority, at most one in ten abided by the religious ban on drinking.[56] As said, most of this went on in private, though there were certain outliers who clearly did not keep their habits private. One of these was Muhammad Husayn, governor of the western city of Kermanshah in the 1820s, who performed the wake preceding his father's funeral in 'true Irish fashion' by passing the night drinking and singing. He was joined in this by the local *mullābāshi* (the governor's erstwhile tutor), a cleric who had appeared sloshed during the funeral procession earlier in the day.[57]

The sources give us many other examples of elite drinking. Von Kotzbue reports that in 1817 Husayn Quli Khan, the *sardār* (military commander) of Yerevan, drank with gusto, 'made no secret of his love of spirituous liquors and openly declared that he could not live without them'. His personal physician, insisting 'that the Prophet had been a fool to forbid wine', boasted that he had found in spirits the panacea that he prescribed for all his patients.[58] Rabbi d'Beth Hillel, when he visited Tuyserkan in western Iran, claimed that all its inhabitants, most of whom were Muslim, 'drank wine and liquor in public, even the governor himself'.[59] Herat, until the 1830s part of Iran, was no different. In 1830, the British envoy Arthur Conolly arrived in Herat to find the city a dirty den of iniquity filled with wine taverns. The most important question the local potentate—Kamran Shah, a debauched man who normally quenched his thirst with 'vile arrack' or 'thin sour wine' made by the local Jewish community—had for Conolly was whether he could procure a 'liquor that would make his Majesty drunk at once'.[60] Fifteen years later, following an Iranian siege that had left the city in ruins, Ferrier called Lal Muhammad, Herat's *sartip* (brigade general), a man given to Bacchus. The regional governor, Yar Muhammad Khan, threw a farewell dinner for Ferrier where wine flowed freely and all attendees got hammered.[61]

Successive governors of Azerbaijan qualified as serious boozers as well. The American missionary Justin Perkins called Muhammad Khan Amir Nizam Zangana, who ruled the province in the 1830s, 'broken down by hard drinking'.[62] The same magistrate entertained Flandin and his men to a copious meal where all the attendees, irrespective of religion, freely indulged. By evening's end, the bottles on the Iranian side were all empty, and many of the guests were drunk.[63] The man who served as governor of Azerbaijan a decade later, Malik Qasim Mirza, an uncle of the shah and an adept of European ways, loved pork and wine.[64] Isma'il Khan, the governor of Tabriz in the 1840s, was known as a 'notorious drunkard'.[65]

Khorasan was another hot drinking spot. This did not apply to the nomadic Turcoman population, who knew about wine but consumed it 'sparingly and moderately'.[66] But especially in parts inhabited by Kurds—descendants of the ones Shah 'Abbas I had transplanted to the region two centuries earlier to defend the northeastern borderlands against Turcoman raids—drinking was rife. In 1873, G. C. Napier procured wine in the village of Nawkhandan without the usual assistance of Jews or Armenians.[67] James Fraser, traversing the vast region in 1821–2, met quite a few bibulous officials, most of them Kurds. Farrukh Khan, the officer in charge of the local artillery of Nishapur, proclaimed himself to be an observant Muslim, yet he 'indulged very freely in the use of wine' and openly boasted about it.[68] The Muslims of Sabzavar produced a 'low-quality wine' and manufactured and consumed arak from locally grown plums.[69] When British officer Valentine Baker alighted at the town of Bojnurd on his way to Mashhad in 1873, he was hosted by the mayor, Yar Muhammad Khan, a member of the Kurdish Shadlu clan that held sway in the district. A cultivated man, Yar Muhammad Khan served wine, although he told Baker in front of all his attendees that he himself preferred arak and brandy, thinking wine 'not strong enough'.[70]

Surely the most striking case of intemperance in Qajar times is the Kurdish elite of Quchan in northeastern Khorasan. For much of the nineteenth century, the town and environs were administered in hereditary fashion by members of the Za'faranlu tribe, bibulous men who indulged in the locally produced white wine.[71] Fraser visited Quchan in 1822 and spent the entire day fruitlessly trying to obtain the necessary permit for his onward journey, until he discovered that the local chieftain, Riza Quli Khan Za'faranlu, and his men were 'dead drunk and perfectly unable to transact business of any kind'.[72] Outright notorious was Riza Quli Khan's son and successor, Amir Husayn Khan (Shuja' al-Dawla), who ruled the town for decades. An array of Western diplomats and travelers passing through report on his prodigious drinking. When Baker visited Quchan, he found Amir Husayn Khan quite unprepared to receive him, as he was asleep after a night of revelry. (He made up for this mishap by providing chairs and a table for his guests and serving some good local wine the following day.)[73] The Russian general Nikolai Ivanovich Grodekoff, governor of 'Ishq-abad (today Ashkabat, the capital of Turkmenistan), who in 1880 visited Khorasan in disguise, offered this description of the magistrate's court:

> Knowing that he was fond of liquor, we placed several bottles of wine, liqueurs, and vodka before him; and in a very short time the Shuja had drunk several glasses of different wines, and then called in his singers and musicians. The men who came with him, his surgeon, and his favourites, Vali Khan and Ramzan Khan, drank themselves stupid, and a regular orgy began. Next day, I went to see the Amir, and presented my documents to him. Bottles were already standing before him, and he explained that he was recovering from his intoxication. During our conversation he repeatedly partook of brandy, opium, hashish, and wine, and by noon was quite drunk. In the evening of the same day he invited us to a European supper, and again got intoxicated to the last degree.[74]

In 1894, almost fifteen years later, the same official was still at it, quaffing large amounts of Russian brandy.[75] The eldest son, Abu'l Hasan Khan, meanwhile, had inherited his father's weakness.[76] Even the clerics of Quchan were not above alcoholic excess. I'timad al-Dawla, writing in the late nineteenth century, reports that the town's *shaykh al-islām* was known to drink until the wee hours of the morning, which meant that he was wont to sleep from mid-morning until dinnertime.[77]

Numerous other local magistrates with a reputation for overindulgence appear in the sources for the second half of the nineteenth century. Ernest Floyer, a British telegraph employee, recounts his meeting with Chiragh Khan, the bibulous governor of Kahnu in remote Baluchistan, who had his servant pour him a quart of brandy in the presence of Floyer without offering his guest any. Floyer later spent a good week in Kerman, passing his evenings at the residence of the local khan, Vakil al-Mulk, where he took part in a 'tremendous wine party, often prolonged into the small hours'.[78] Finally, Wills came upon quite a scene when he visited the southern town of Fasa in Fars to attend to the local governor, Mirza 'Ali Akbar, a huge and overweight man of about thirty-eight, 'a general debauchee, opium eater, wine- and spirit drinker, and bhang smoker', who, unsurprisingly, was suffering from gout. Having been informed about the magistrate's illness, Wills was offered a tumblerful of 'strong spirit'. Throughout that same afternoon, the governor drank copiously from a bottle that he produced from under his pillow, all while ingesting a bolus of opium every two hours. Wills left for dinner, and when he returned at about 10pm he found most everyone in the room engaged in drinking, while the patient was entertained by a chorus of dancing boys and singers.[79]

Changes at the Court

The first few decades of Qajar rule saw little change in the drinking habits at the royal court. Agha Muhammad Khan (r. 1789–97), the founder of the dynasty, imbibed the old-fashioned way. Alcohol flowed at this coronation ceremony.[80] Under the influence, 'he would forget tomorrow the orders which he had given today', as von Kotzbue put it. At one point, probably intoxicated, he took a pistol and shot at his octogenarian grand vizier, Mirza Jafi, just to torment him.[81]

It is unclear if Fath 'Ali Shah, the second Qajar ruler, consumed alcohol, but, given the frequent occurrence of wine metaphors in his poetry, he is likely to have indulged in private.[82] His entourage was most certainly not sober: Mullah 'Ali Asghar, the shah's chaplain (mullābāshi), was known for his bibulousness and was even bastinadoed for it by royal order.[83] On the other hand, the shah forced his grand vizier, Mirza Shafi', to drink in celebration of the wedding of his daughter, Asya Khanum (Mahd-i 'Ulya), or pay a hefty fine. The grand vizier refused and handed over the enormous sum of 5,000 tumāns. He followed up by writing a letter to Mirza Abu'l-Qasim Qummi, a mujtahid (high-level cleric), explaining his refusal. But instead of praising Mirza Shafi', the prelate rebuked him for having rejected a cup of wine made permissible (halāl) by royal order, adding that he should have donated the money to charity.[84]

'Abbas Mirza, Fath 'Ali Shah's oldest son, crown prince, and reformist governor of Azerbaijan, indulged as well, certainly after suffering military defeat against the Russians in 1813.[85] In 1825, the

French scholar Charles Bélanger attended a reception hosted by him during which everyone engaged in copious drinking.[86] In a policy reminiscent of Karim Khan Zand's, 'Abbas Mirza licensed a wine shop in Tabriz for the use of the battalion stationed in that city, which included many Russians. The Iranian soldiers apparently followed their Russian colleagues in their drinking habits, yet would get drunk much faster than the Russians and were frequently flogged for it.[87] 'Abbas Mirza died at age forty-one, probably from liver cirrhosis. His son, Firuz Mirza Nusrat al-Dawla (1818–86), who held a variety of gubernatorial posts, was also known as a *bon vivant*. He once fell off his horse in a state of intoxication during the month of Ramadan, and the shah made an attempt to quell the scandal by imposing a 10,000 *tumāns* fine on him.[88] This had little effect, though, and alcoholism hastened Nusrat al-Dawla's death.[89]

The persistence of traditional ways notwithstanding, nineteenth-century Iran did undergo various changes in its drinking culture. Some were similar to developments in Ottoman lands, even if they typically occurred later than the changes that took place in the urban centers of Iran's western neighbor. Others were unique to Iran, reflecting its peculiar societal and historical circumstances.

Like the Ottoman Empire, nineteenth-century Iran had its 'free thinkers', men of Western-inflected disposition who consciously flouted the laws of the Prophet. The British minister to the shah's court Justin Sheil noted that many of those who drank in excess 'pretended to laugh at the Prophet's prohibition'. He claimed to know one Iranian gentleman, 'a shocking drunkard but rather religious, who often bewailed to me his unfortunate propensity. "I know it is wrong", he used to exclaim; "I know I shall go to Jehennam [hell]; every day I make a towbeh, and every night that rascal, my appetite, gets the better of me"'.[90] Flaunting one's drinking in this way was an explicit political statement, by which one displayed one's 'modern' attitude by way of heaping scorn on obscurantist clerics and their cant, and as such is a variant on an old Iranian tradition. The German archaeologist Heinrich Brugsch connected the issue of wine-bibbing 'free thinkers' with the inner and outer: the tendency to treat the privacy of the indoors as a haven, a sanctuary for true enjoyment and delight, rigorously separated from the public sphere, where social decorum and religious norms must be upheld. It is worth quoting his observations in full:

> Those who somehow believe in Allah, Muhammad, Ali and the saints, join the teachings and the views of one of the many religious sects, or, by contrast, very quietly follow freethinking and free-spirited views, which often come close to atheism. They read banned books, such as the writing and mystical revelations of the founder of the sect of the much-persecuted Babis ... or become absorbed in the quatrains of the famous philosopher Omar the tentmaker [Khayyam] ... or eagerly read the wine and love songs of the immortal Hafez, laughing at the learned exegesis of the orthodox clergy, which distorts the clear and obvious meaning of the text, making it refer to the faith and the divine. They drink their wine and find in the utter enjoyment of life the real contentment in this earthly vale of tears.[91]

The context that enabled people to express such opinions was the remarkable freedom of speech Iranians enjoyed, a topic already noted by Chardin in Safavid times and on which Mary Sheil, Justin's spouse, had this to say:

> Freedom of speech is on an equality with freedom of religion. It is the Persian substitute for liberty of the press, and the safety-valve of popular indignation. Everyone may say what he likes. If needy, disappointed, or oppressed, the sufferer may seek consolation in reviling the Shah and his minister, and all their measures to the contentment of his heart.[92]

A particularly colorful example of someone who taunted the clergy with his 'libertine' lifestyle is the aforementioned Malik Qasim Mirza. Fluent in French and able to express himself in English and even some Russian, he wore European clothes and drank wine. After being appointed governor of Borujerd in Luristan, he was soon accosted by the ulama, who upbraided him for his scandalous infidel behavior. At first evasive, he eventually gave them the obligatory libertine response, namely that if he went to a hot place, they were under no obligation to join him. Finally, he invited them to see 'his'

priest. When they agreed, he ordered his servants to open the doors
of his residence, and out rushed the:

> ... greyhounds, spaniels, pointers, large dogs used for fighting
> wolves and wild boors, and curs of almost every description.
> Horrified, the mullahs tucked up their robes and began hopping
> about to avoid being contaminated by touching the dogs and
> went away spitting right and left and cursing the Prince in the
> most classic Arabic—they never troubled him again.[93]

A countervailing trend in drinking patterns was simultaneously
underway at the top. Successive Qajar rulers continued to imbibe,
but (an outward display of) royal abstemiousness more and more
became the norm. The most important reason for this is the fact
that the Qajars lacked the religious credentials of the Safavids.
They neither could boast a (fictitious) lineage going back to the
Shi'i Imams, nor did they introduce a new (variant of the) faith.
To project legitimacy, they thus cultivated an image of public piety,
and temperance was a conspicuous aspect of this image. A second,
related process was the rise to prominence of the Shi'i clergy, who
had emerged from the turmoil of the eighteenth century as the sole
guiding force for an impoverished, rudderless populace.

Outward religiosity indeed gained in prominence under the
Qajars, most conspicuously so under Muhammad Shah. Lieutenant-
Colonel Charles Stuart, writing from Tehran in 1835, reported that
the Iranians he met did not drink 'for fear of the eunuch, a sober
and strict Muslim'.[94] This is an obvious reference to Hajji Mirza
Aqasi, an idiosyncratic erstwhile dervish who held the position
of grand vizier and court counselor under Muhammad Shah and
was instrumental in his 'great temperance', as Southgate called
it. Muhammad Shah neither drank wine nor smoked the waterpipe
(qalyān), although he is said at times to have indulged in English
porter, a drink 'on which the laws of Muhammad were silent'.[95] Yet
the palace at large was hardly dry. At a royal dinner party held for
the French ambassador Comte de Sercey in 1840, Georgian wine
was served, and many of the Muslim guests reportedly could hardly
keep themselves upright by the time the ambassador raised a toast to
the shah's health.[96]

A final factor in the retreat of courtly public drinking was the definitive sedentarization of the shah and his entourage. From the reign of Fath 'Ali Shah onward, court life no longer revolved around the outdoors, the open steppe, but came to center on the royal palace, now located in what would be Iran's first fixed capital, Tehran. The shah ceased to be a warrior, and the *razm-u-bazm* tradition of royal fighting and feasting came to an end. In a reflection of how far Iranian kingship had moved away from the open-air bacchanals of the Safavids, Nasir al-Din Shah, the longest-ruling Qajar monarch (r. 1848–96), liked to drink a glass or two of Bordeaux or domestic wine for dinner. I'timad al-Saltana, the ruler's confidant and minister of publication, reports in his diary that the shah also drank to calm his nerves in anticipation of public executions.[97] By the end of his reign, the raucous drinking fests of the Safavids had been replaced by the distribution of stew (*āsh*) during public occasions.[98]

This new sobriety did not make alcohol disappear from the royal court. Indeed, only Nasir al-Din's successor, Muzaffar al-Din Shah (r. 1896–1907), is on record as a teetotaler.[99] His son Muhammad 'Ali Shah (r. 1907–9), by contrast, showed himself to be a cognac-loving wastrel even before mounting the throne. Yet, outwardly he also presented himself as scrupulously observant in religious matters.[100] Muhammad 'Ali Shah, in other words, exemplifies the fact that Qajar rulers did not necessarily give up alcohol but rather drank in more discreet settings. Since the Qajars were much less inclined than the Safavids to invite their (foreign) guests to private parties, it often remains unclear if and how much individual rulers imbibed. The English envoy Harford Jones Brydges offered a detailed description of Fath 'Ali Shah's daily activities, albeit admitting that he was not sure how he spent his evenings.[101]

Fortunately, we have I'timad al-Saltana's diary, which contains numerous references to private occasions where alcoholic beverages—mostly wine, but occasionally beer, champagne, or cognac—were consumed, usually with meals and typically in small quantities.[102] The same author reports how Iran's foreign minister, Amin al-Sultan, guzzled wine with great gusto at the French legation.[103] He also tells us that the shah's European doctors recommended wine as a cure for his hemorrhoids.[104] His diary remains silent on the fact, reported elsewhere, that royal harem women consumed wine as well.[105] I'timad al-Saltana further suggests that the dilemma between pleasure and guilt persisted. During their stay in Moscow in 1889, a stop on Nasir al-Din's third European journey, the shah's companions did not observe the annual Shi'i commemoration of the martyrdom of Imam Husayn (*ruz-i qatl*), but instead indulged in the wine offered to them by the mayor of the Russian capital. The next day, to expiate the sins committed the night before, they rolled out their prayer rugs and engaged in worship. Yet as soon as the prayer was over and lunch beckoned, they started drinking again, with the excuse that the water in Moscow was undrinkable.[106]

Different Types of Alcohol and New Forms of Resistance

European spirits in the late Qajar period gained popularity among the ruling classes in a process similar to that taking place in the Ottoman Empire at the time, by which Qajar Iran saw a growing entwinement with the outside world, and found itself being incorporated into the global market by way of trade, taste, and table manners. Until the end of Nasir al-Din's reign, alcohol remained largely hidden, even in Tehran. At the century's end, it was gaining in visibility, mainly on account of the more conspicuous presence of Armenians and a growing number of Europeans in the country.[107] As early as 1875, Dr Tholozan, Nasir al-Din Shah's personal physician, suggested setting up a wine export industry in Iran as a means to improve the country's dismal balance of payments.[108] I'timad al-Saltana refers to a growing entanglement with foreign powers when in 1890 he wrote in his diary that 'years ago, Iran was not yet caught in the clutches of the English, but now it is, with the grand vizier who used to be a pure and pious man, now drinking wine and playing backgammon'.[109] The year before, the shah had granted a concession to a Belgian company, Société Générale du commerce et industrie de la Perse, for the manufacture of alcohol throughout Iran, from which he was to receive an annual revenue of £7,000.[110]

The new ways, first visible during the reign of Muhammad Shah, filtered in through two channels. One was the growing trade with western Europe, with Tabriz—connected to the world via the so-called Trabzon Black Sea link—acting as its gateway. The other was Russian influence coming in from the north and affecting in particular Azerbaijan and the Caspian provinces. In the mid-1830s, Justin Perkins, an ardent abolitionist, intoned that 'European liquors are rolling in upon the country like a flood'.[111]

Tabriz was the center of this development. French diplomat Comte de Sercey, visiting Iran in 1840, witnessed the Iranian predilection for alcohol upon his arrival in Tabriz, where he attended a dinner party hosted by the Amir Nizam, the provincial governor-general.[112] At around the same time, the German natural scientist Moritz Wagner attended a dinner at the house of Mr. Morfopulo, the head of the local Greek community, which afforded him insight into the luxurious lifestyle adopted by resident Europeans. There were 'Asiatic delicacies': fish from the Caspian Sea, game from the forests of Gilan, grapes and mulberries from Azerbaijan, and the 'most delicate pasties, coloured jellies', while 'iced Cliquot champagne of the best quality, graced the board'.[113] Mary Sheil a decade later offers a vivid description of the new type of spirits available at the tables of the Muslim elite in Tabriz. Invited by the governor-general, she noted that the 'table (for there was one) was covered with a complete and very handsome European service in plate, glass, and china, and, to crown the whole, six bottles of champagne displayed their silver heads, accompanied by a dozen other bottles of the wines of France and Spain'.[114] By 1867, 6,000 bottles of French, English, and Russian wines and liqueurs had been imported into Iran via Tabriz. The consumers of such luxury items were, in the words of Crampon, a class of individuals unaffected by the general impoverishment of the nation.[115]

Russian influence was especially paramount in northern Iran, the result of a historically strong presence eventually turning into outright military occupation of parts of Azerbaijan and the Caspian littoral. Lomnitskii makes the following interesting observation with respect to the link between geography and drinking in Qajar Iran:

One of Tehran's old residents tried to convince me that all Persians drink alike. He is not exactly right. It seems to me that if we divide Persia into three belts, northern, central and southern, and calculate the approximate percentage of those who drink, it will turn out that in northern Persia among the Gilakis, Mazandaranis and residents of the Gaz shore those who drink compose 80 percent of the [area's] population, in the middle zone with Tehran—70 percent, and the southern part of Persia—40 percent.[116]

Russian aquavit had been a staple of diplomatic gifts from Russia since Safavid times, and hard liquor remained popular among Iranians, in part because it shortened the process of getting intoxicated.[117] Wills also linked high-octane spirits to portability. Drinking in Iran, he said, always culminated in drunkenness, and consequently arak, potent and portable, 'in a country where there are no wheeled vehicles, and where casks are unknown', was the favorite drink of many.[118]

As Russia's influence on Iran grew, its alcohol imports and tastes clearly affected the country's northern parts. In 1812, the governor of Mazandaran gifted the British diplomat Gore Ouseley with red wine brought by Armenian merchants trading with Astrakhan.[119] Like the Ottoman upper classes, Iranians also took to the habit of consuming vodka with *zakuska* (pl. *zakuski*), or hors d'oeuvres.[120] By the century's end, it was said that more arak was consumed in Tabriz than in Tbilisi.[121] In 1909, the French consul in Tabriz reported that the 'cabaretiers' of the lower orders had 'triumphed' by bringing about the free circulation and consumption of alcohol.[122] The German author Walther Kuss at that time claimed that Russia's influence had made vodka common in the Caspian region, adding that the stuff manufactured in Rasht often was not real Russian vodka but a concoction prepared with turpentine.[123] A report from the early 1920s, when Gilan was under Russian control, called alcoholism rampant among the region's Armenian and Russian inhabitants, adding that a predilection for the best wines and spirits prompted a search for good French wines, cognacs, and liqueurs among the well-to-do classes.[124] According to the French consul in Rasht at the time, much of the wine consumed in Gilan came from Russia, and alcohol was sold clandestinely in the region's coffeehouses.[125]

Foreign imports are recorded as early as 1740, when the Dutch noted that small quantities of French wine entered Iran via

Bushehr.[126] From the mid-nineteenth century onward, more figures are available. Far from 'rolling in like a flood', European wines were far from ubiquitous at that point. Justin Sheil called the Iranians 'extremely fond of European wines', though he cautioned that even the very rich, as yet unwilling to bear the cost of having it imported from Europe, contented themselves with less fancy domestic fare.[127] Still, in *c.* 1860, a Swiss company imported several hundred bottles of French wine and spirits—Bordeaux, cognac, champagne—which sold within days, even though the finest liqueurs among them carried the hefty price tag of one *tumān* per bottle.[128] An 1869 overview of imports into Tabriz lists wines and spirits from France, England, and Russia worth FF 56,000.[129] In 1896, the French consul in Tabriz noted that almost all wine imports came from France, but that consumption was modest since the number of resident Europeans was too low to make a real difference.[130] British sources convey the same message about Shiraz, where in 1893 the 'demand for European wines, beer, and spirits was very limited'.[131] Demand seems to have gone up in the next decade, for in 1902–3 imports amounted to 12,850 bottles of French wine, 19,834 bottles of Russian wine, and 3,944 bottles of wine coming from Great Britain. During the same period, 260,346 bottles of spirits, 85 percent of them imported from Russia, entered the country.[132]

Beer had made inroads at this point as well. Most of it was consumed by resident foreigners, but it also found a ready market among affluent Iranians. In 1902, a total of 134,634 bottles, 121,130 of Russian origin, were imported.[133] In the north, Russian brands were common, from Samara, Astrakhan, Riga, and Odesa. In the south, the great heat made strong brews popular. The German and English types that prevailed there even showed up in the small Gulf ports; yet they were relatively expensive and could not compete with American stuff, most notably Schlitz-Milwaukee, which toward the century's end found its way to Iran in relatively large quantities.[134]

Cognac, too, entered Iran at that time, from India as well as from France and Greece. However, the most popular alcoholic drink among the upper classes was champagne, and fantastic prices were paid for this luxury item. Regular wine was imported from France and Germany for the same clientele. Medicinal wine, so-called

China wine, Vin de Bugeaus, and Servallo (from Trieste) found a good market among the elite. Liqueurs mostly came from France, with the firm Potin offering various cheap, generic types.[135]

The aforementioned Prince Arfa' al-Dawla in his autobiography offers a glimpse of elite alcohol consumption in the late Qajar period. Serving as Iran's consul-general in Tbilisi between 1890 and 1895, he purchased a mansion (which survives today in a dilapidated state), and had it renovated by Italian craftsmen who constructed two pools in the garden, one in the 'shape of a round flat champagne glass'. He next organized a house-warming party for the *beau monde* of the Georgian capital. Scaffolding was put around the pool for the occasion, and a huge vat able to hold 3,000–4,000 bottles and filled with red Kakheti wine was raised onto a platform. The vat was connected to the fountain with a rubber hose 'in such a way that when the tap was turned on, wine shot upwards to the height of the platform and filled the pool'.

> Enlivened by music and fireworks, and the area around the pool 'decorated with colourful flowers and ornamental trees', the 'hundreds of Chinese and Japanese lanterns placed above and around the pool lit up the wine', making it look 'rosé-coloured rather than dark red'.[136]

Drinking, in sum, appears to have gone up in the late Qajar period. John Wishard, who served as hospital director in Tehran between 1889 and 1909, suggested as much, claiming that the incidence of alcohol consumption had been growing since his arrival in the country. But he also made it clear that traditional practices still prevailed. Liquor was sold in many shops and stores, yet there were no saloons in Persia. The common people drank ordinary arak, distilled from raisins and containing 30 to 50 percent alcohol, in addition to a 'good deal of native wine'.[137]

All this provoked the ire of traditional forces but also raised concern among modernizing elements. Anti-liquor campaigns, often following riots instigated by clerics and targeting minority property, would occur into the twentieth century. But a new discourse emerged as well, involving a growing medicalization and anxiety about alcohol's negative impact on individual health as well as on societal wellbeing, all of it inspired by American and European temperance movements. A good example is the creation of a Western-style society to combat alcohol among Armenians in Azerbaijan, which organized illustrated lectures about the hereditary nature of alcohol abuse and the physical harm it caused.[138] Publicists, too, began to present drinking as harmful, using arguments borrowed from European scientific research—itself a function of urgent contemporary concerns about working-class drinking. Opium received the bulk of the attention in this movement because it was rightfully seen as the greater problem. But alcohol, too, came under fire for its debilitating effects on both the body and the brain, leading to a loss of judgment and memory, quite aside from the lack of willpower it was thought to both reflect and produce.[139] An early manifestation of this new discourse appeared in the newspaper *Iran* in 1872, in the form of a serialized treatise on the 'decline of order in the world as a result of alcoholic beverages'. Its author, a physician from Kashan, voiced concerns about European influence in the form of Iran's ready acceptance of all kinds of new liquors.[140] The regulations issued in 1896 by the Ministry of Security that promised punishment for people engaged in obscene behavior, as well as for drunks and gamblers, also seemed more concerned about public order than the transgression of Islamic codes.[141] The new age heralded by all this would first manifest itself with the Constitutional Revolution of 1905–9, to appear in full force during the reign of the modernizing Riza Shah.

8

ALCOHOL IN THE MODERN AGE
NEW DRINKS AND DRINKING CUSTOMS
PART ONE
THE ARAB WORLD

Introduction

The year is 1914. We first meet the protagonist of Isabella Hammad's novel *The Parisian*—Midhat Kamal, the son of a wealthy textile merchant in Nablus in Ottoman Palestine—as a passenger on a boat between Alexandria and Marseille, on his way to medical school in Montpellier. In a first sign of 'modernity', Midhat is offered a glass of whisky—just before being introduced to the art of dealing with French women—by Faruq al-Zameh, his Arab fellow traveler, someone with previous experience in France. Until that moment, Midhat had only tasted alcohol once, 'when he was sixteen from an illicit bottle in his school dormitory'.[1]

The suggestion made in Hammad's novel is that in the Islamic world (fancy, modern, European) alcohol equals worldliness and the temptation of (forbidden) freedom. The previous two chapters showed how this liberating lure came into being in the 1800s. A century later, the association between alcohol and worldliness was publicly on display in the form of bars, casinos, and restaurants in

201

capital cities such as Istanbul and Cairo, which in the aftermath of the First World War experienced their version of the 'Roaring Twenties'. It was also firmly in place in port cities such as Izmir and Alexandria, 'cosmopolitan' centers inhabited by large numbers of so-called Levantines—Italians, Greeks, and Jews—with quarters where they conducted their own lifestyles along with foreigners, sailors, and soldiers. Cafés, bars, nightclubs, and brothels run by non-Muslims tended to concentrate in such quarters. Even Jeddah had at least two public saloons on the eve of the First World War.[2]

One gap that widened in this 'modernizing' process was that between classes and status groups. Whereas, in traditional drinking, rich and poor had shared the same alcoholic beverages of often questionable quality, the affluent now flaunted their worldliness by sipping imported champagne in expensive restaurants over a dîner dansant while the indigent continued to guzzle local rotgut in dark drinking dens. The distinction became even more marked in the second half of the twentieth century when the Middle East saw a mass migration toward the cities, resulting in a degree of ruralization accompanied by a persistent adherence to traditional norms. The newcomers, after all, did not necessarily walk a straight 'modernist' path toward 'development', but sought out their own 'authentic' identity by navigating the traditional and the modern. The result was an even greater demarcation between 'modern' drinking, which now often took place in nightclubs and international hotels—symbols of consumerist modernity—and 'traditional' drinking, which remained hidden, isolated in side streets or on the margins of spatially divided cities.[3] Conspicuously visible in cities from Cairo to Karachi, such juxtapositions turned into outright segregation in colonial North Africa, where the French-Mediterranean villes nouvelles—open, with straight boulevards lined with drinking establishments—arose at some physical distance from the traditional villes arabes, labyrinthic, grouped around the suq, concerned with preserving privacy (including the privacy of drinking). Modern tourist resorts serving alcohol in countries where it is otherwise taboo or hard to obtain are another form of such segregation.

Modernity had other effects as well. In the industrializing West, traditional, 'undisciplined' ways of consuming alcohol adapted to the new rhythms of life following mechanization and the 'rationalization' of time that came with the introduction of the clock. The Islamic world, where alcohol had never been integrated into social life, was far less affected by this process. Still, even in Muslim societies, the adage that the 'odd bender was less disruptive in traditional cultures with undisciplined pastimes and work settings' applied.[4] The bibulous Kurdish governors of Quchan we encountered in the previous chapter were a holdout from the past; they no longer fit the image of a modernizing Iran under the Pahlavi regime.

Modernity in the Islamic world manifested itself above all as colonial modernity. The consumption of new drinks in new venues took place under the eyes of Western authorities: the British in Egypt and Iraq, the French in North Africa and the Levant. Foreign companies purveying alcohol made inroads into Middle Eastern markets under their auspices. This represented a new phase in 'alco-imperialism', yet it fell far short of imposition. Indeed, even the colonial authorities, well attuned to cultural norms and sensibilities, fretted about the extent of Muslim drinking and sought to curtail and contain it. At the same time, the gusto with which many Muslims took to alcohol (and other vices) was and remained as much a matter of demand as of supply.

Regardless of agency, the intrusion of 'modern' ways inevitably elicited reactions: traditional ones in the form of protests by established religious leaders, and progressive ones articulated by those who evaluated alcohol not from a religious perspective but from concerns about its effects on the physical and mental health of users; by nationalists who accused Westerners of trying to undermine their countrymen with alcohol, and by the spokesmen of 'Islamic fundamentalism' who demanded a total ban on drinking. Health-related anxieties about alcohol grew in volume. Physicians and politicians speaking the language of European and American temperance movements exhorted their compatriots to follow their example and called on their governments to help them do so with restrictive measures. Nationalists softened their anti-alcohol tone once they became rulers of independent countries. The secular regimes that came to power in the Arab world in the 1950s and

1960s were largely indifferent to drinking, even if, at times, they opportunistically sought to appease religious forces by giving in (or at least paying lip service) to demands for proscription. These demands now mostly came from Islamist forces bolstered by war and revolution. The humiliating defeat Israel inflicted on the armies of the secular Arab regimes in the Six-Day War of 1967 exposed the hollowness of their boasts and promises, and made the alternative—a return to 'authentic' Islamic values—seem attractive to many. The Yom Kippur War of 1973 was as consequential. The oil boycott instituted in its aftermath and the resulting quadrupling of world oil prices marked a shift in the balance of power and wealth in the Arab world from Egypt and Syria to the oil-rich nations of the Arabian Peninsula and the Persian Gulf. Egyptian and Yemenite migrant workers may not have liked their Saudi and Emirati employers, but they did absorb elements of the Gulf States' austere brand of Islam, which they took back home along with their television sets and VCRs, as part of a new-found status.

The Iranian Revolution of 1978–9 was the other catalyst. Its outcome, a stern Islamic Republic, turned the tables on the lax, Western-oriented Pahlavi regime. Khomeini's urge to his followers to export their revolutionary fervor to the Arab world created the specter of an Iranian-style Islamic revolution that has haunted the rulers of the region ever since. The heightened sectarianism that resulted was fueled by a Saudi regime that, equally troubled by Iran's expansionism and the quasi-socialist regimes of the Arab world, resolved to preemptively spread its literalist interpretation of Islam beyond its borders. In the ensuing decades, the Saudis spent an estimated US$100 billion around the globe, putting pressure on regimes from Egypt to Pakistan to make their public sphere conform to Islamic strictures.

In recent times, all Muslim countries have seen an increase in recreational drinking, integral to global mobility, international travel, and youth culture. Foreign tourism today plays an important role in the economies of countries like Tunisia, Egypt, Turkey, and the United Arab Emirates. As elsewhere, holiday resorts in Middle Eastern countries are often little more than secluded enclaves. Yet they do not just cater to non-Muslims; the lifestyle they symbolize is part and parcel of an international culture of desire propagated via television and social media and consumed by almost everyone.

The result of all these conflicting trends and messages is an uneasy coexistence between the reality of grocery stores selling alcohol in inconspicuous ways, of bars keeping a low profile, hiding behind opaque windows, and an official morality of censure and denial; between alcohol promising freedom and alcohol as a metaphor for the dystopian, lonely, fallen world represented by the West as depicted in the modern Arabic novel. This final part of the book will trace these complex developments and processes, with this chapter focusing on the Arab world and the final chapter focusing on parts of the eastern half of the Islamic Middle East comprising Turkey, Iran, and Pakistan.

North Africa

The countries of the Maghreb (lit. the West)—Algeria, Tunisia, and Morocco—all fell under French control and influence in the nineteenth century, beginning with Algeria in 1830. Tunisia followed suit in 1881 when it became a French protectorate. Morocco came under French supervisory rule in 1912, when the country's last independent Alaouite ruler, Moulay 'Abd al-Hafiz, a traditional boozer who used water only for his ablutions, agreed to abdicate while under the influence.[5]

In Chapter 6 it was seen how in Algeria the arrival of the French drastically changed the role of alcohol in society. The same holds true, albeit to a lesser extent, for Tunisia and Morocco. In pre-colonial Tunisia, alcohol was little known outside Tunis and beyond European and the Jewish communities.[6] In Morocco, alcoholism was widespread only among Jews, who, besides boukha (bukha) made from figs, consumed mahia, a distillate of figs, dates, and various other fruits.[7]

In Algeria, viticulture—increasingly brought under a capitalist regime that favored economies of scale—continued to grow, from producing 7.8 million hectoliters in 1907 to 13.5 hectoliters in 1930, to 22 million hectoliters, an all-time record, in 1934.[8] Most of this was exported; at the peak of production, some 2 million hectoliters were consumed in Algeria itself.[9] Until the end of French rule, Algeria was the world's fourth-largest producer of wine, which accounted for more than half of the value of the country's exports.[10] Wine cultivation in Tunisia and Morocco took off as well in the late nineteenth century. At the time of the French arrival, Tunisia produced no wine. A little over ten years later, 95,000 hectoliters were produced by less than 6,000 hectares of soil, a figure that went up to 400,000 hectoliters produced on almost 40,000 hectares in 1911. By 1933, the surface dedicated to viticulture had gone up to 50,000 hectares, producing 1.7 million hectoliters, most of which was sent to France. By the time the French left in 1956, Tunisia produced 720,000 hectoliters on 25,000 hectares.[11] In Morocco, the acreage devoted to viticulture went up from a negligible 106 hectares in 1914 to 700 hectares in 1919. Twenty years later, wine grapes were cultivated on 23,000 hectares; in 1947, overproduction had reduced this to 16,425 hectares.[12]

Beer and hard liquor made their entry in French North Africa in the early 1900s. Beer was hardly consumed in Tunisia until the First World War. Seen as healthy and little offensive on account of its low alcohol content, it gained popularity after 1925, when domestic production commenced with the creation of the Société frigorifique des brasseries. The company, operating breweries in Tunis, Sfax, and Bizerte, soon produced some 50,000 hectoliters per year. The Moroccan Société des brasseries du Maroc annually put out a more modest 18,000 hectoliters.[13]

Consumption went up as well during the Tunisian Protectorate, increasing from c. one liter per person before the First World War to c. 2.8 liters in the 1950s. Beer accounted for much of this growth.[14] Early twentieth-century Tunis, a city of c. 90,000, was home to some fifty official alcohol-serving venues, a figure that went up to 217 in the mid-1930s, when the population had more than doubled. In 1956, this number rose to 237. In Casablanca, too, the number of such establishments rapidly increased, from 184 in 1936 to 289 in 1956. Since both cities grew substantially in this period, the proportion of drinking venues to population remained about the same. Cafés and bars were also heavily concentrated in both, mostly located in the European quarters and serving foreign residents, who now made up about half of all the inhabitants of Casablanca and Tunis.[15] Official sources for 1956 listed nine drinking places per 10,000 inhabitants for the ten largest cities in Algeria, and six and 3.5 per 10,000 inhabitants for Tunisia and Morocco respectively.[16]

Reservations and Restrictions: France's Politique des Égards

Regarding restrictions placed on the alcohol production and consumption in the French-controlled Maghreb, least affected was Algeria, which had been colonized much earlier and was far more assimilated into French administrative and economic structures than Tunisia and Morocco. The authorities followed the example set by those in France by banning absinthe at the onset of the First World War, but otherwise made few attempts to limit the consumption of spirits until the Second World War, when anxiety about the loyalty of the population to the metropole resulted in their taking restrictive measures. In Algeria, after all, the laws were supposed to apply equally to all citizens; and wine played a significant role in the economy.[17] Opposition to the country's viticulture was limited and mainly took the form of economic protests directed against agricultural capitalism, targeting colonial labor practices or mechanization.[18]

Alcohol use in the Maghreb remained sensitive above all from a religious perspective. In early twentieth-century Algeria and Tunisia, Muslims—some influenced by the pan-Islamic movement of the time—railed against the consumption of alcohol by their co-religionists. Some used the language of health and hygiene to call for American-style prohibitionist measures. Nationalists blamed France and its agents for eroding their countries' identity, and even accused the French of poisoning Muslims with their intoxicating beverages.[19] An article in *La Voix de Tunisie* in May 1932 lamented that, before 1881, alcoholism had been rare in Tunisia, except among foreigners and the local Jewish community. Since the French occupation, however, thousands of drinking establishments had infiltrated Muslim quarters and could even be found near mosques, spreading debauchery.[20] Habib Bourguiba, the father of the Tunisian nation, was among those who argued that the French had introduced wine to weaken the Tunisian society.[21]

In part to preempt such criticism, the French pursued a so-called *politique des égards*, based on 'respect' for the indigenous population. This type of 'respect', prefigured in Napoleon's policy vis-à-vis the Egyptians, involved a segregation of the indigenous population from European residents. This aspect of the *politique des égards* is still visible in the physical separation of the traditional cities of the Maghreb, with their walls and crowded souks, from the colonial towns with their wide sidewalks and spacious palm-lined avenues. The authorities also oversaw zones where prostitution and drinking were tolerated along racial lines. A fear of sexually transmitted disease led to the demarcation of one or more so-called *rues réservées* in small towns, lined with *maisons de tolérance*, with dance halls and booths selling cigarettes and beer. Later, entire *quartiers réservés* were set up, segregated red-light districts where North African prostitutes were allowed to work. In 1881, this system was institutionalized with the promulgation of a penal system known as the *code de l'indigénat*.[22]

The earliest manifestation of the *politique des égards* with respect to alcohol in Tunisia dates from 1898. In response to the rapid increase in the number of *débits* (alcohol-vending establishments), a decree was issued requiring authorization to open new ones.[23] A year later, an ordinance stipulated that none could be located near houses of worship, cemeteries, hospitals, and schools. The same period saw the creation of a Tunisian temperance movement, a branch of the Ligue française contre l'alcoolisme, which drew most of its modest membership from the medical profession. Its success remained limited. The onset of the First World War, when Muslim loyalty to France was at stake, brought new regulations. In September 1914, a law banned the manufacture and consumption of alcoholic beverages in Tunisia in areas with a limited European population. Anyone serving alcohol to Muslims risked a prison sentence of up to fifteen days.[24] Similar ordinances were issued in 1920 and again in 1937. Drinking establishments were also divided into three categories: non-alcoholic ones, so-called *cafés maures*, ones that only served wine and beer, and ones that sold hard liquor. The idea was to limit the number of permits for the second type of venue and to try and root out the third altogether.

In 1940, a decree finally outlawed the production, sale and consumption of aperitifs containing more than 16 percent alcohol, as well as the sale and use of alcoholic drinks—except for *boukha*— on Tuesdays, Thursdays, and Saturdays. The main result was a surge in *boukha* consumption beyond the Jewish community. In August 1940, a new law made it illegal to sell alcohol to Muslims. A year later, a rapport suggested tightening the existing laws, banning the sale of *boukha,* ensuring a limited number of third-class *débits*, extending existing dry zones, and forbidding alcohol sales in areas where Europeans made up less than 10 percent of the population. A final ordinance, issued in 1948, limited the number of *débits* to one per 750 non-Muslim inhabitants.[25] None of it had much effect.[26]

In Algeria, no restrictions on drinking were imposed until October 1941, when the Vichy regime prohibited the sale of alcohol to Muslims.[27] By contrast, Morocco resembled Tunisia in restricting drinking at the onset of the First World War. In 1916, Resident General Hubert Lyautey issued a decree that made alcohol imports illegal. The fact that it was reissued a year later suggests its ineffectiveness.[28] In 1924, a law criminalized public drunkenness while banning alcohol sales throughout the country, except in Casablanca. Restrictions instituted in the 1920s and 1930s and targeting individual Moroccan cities left the old city of Fez fully dry in 1934. In Meknes, Port-Lyautey (now Kenitra), and Salé, alcohol became illegal for natives to consume. In 1937, the 1924 law was amended; Muslims were no longer allowed to drink or to run *débits*. Between 1933 and 1939, the municipal council of Casablanca took similar measures. And in 1940, a law proscribed the sale of alcohol to minors and its consumption on Tuesdays, Thursdays, and Saturdays. As in Tunisia, these laws were routinely flouted, and clandestine drinking parlors continued to make good money selling to Muslims.[29]

Tangier remained outside this regime. Open to the world since the mid-nineteenth century, the city became even more cosmopolitan with the onset of the French protectorate and the international status conferred on it in 1912. This brought about a flood of moderately taxed imported alcohol, making a glass of absinthe in Tangier cheaper than in Paris. Until 1956, the city housed a profusion of cafés, bars, and cabarets. Tangier indeed became synonymous with alcohol in ways inscribed through film and literature. Attendant social problems such as crime and prostitution received little attention, and few heeded the accompanying anxiety about the practice of Muslims drinking to get soused and its negative effects on the mental and physical health of the population.[30]

After Independence

Independence in North Africa entailed the departure of the settler wine growers and the loss of viticulture. Vineyards were abandoned and production further suffered from European laws forbidding the cutting of European wines with inferior foreign ones.

In Algeria, wine came under threat with the outbreak of the war of independence in 1954. The National Liberation Front, though a secular movement, used the moral language of Islam to attack wineries.[31] In 1962, independence struck a further blow to the wine industry, although not a lethal one at first. Viticulture was brought under self-management and wine remained central to self-managed farms. Soon, Algeria lost its easy access to French and, later, European markets. The Boumédiène regime (1965–78) next adopted a policy designed to break ties with France and become self-sufficient in food. A program started in the 1960s of uprooting vines and replacing them with cereals sounded the death knell for Algeria's wine industry.[32] By 1975, a mere 210,000 hectares remained under cultivation, producing no more than 4 million hectoliters. Ten years later, the yield had dropped to less than one million hectoliters, the lowest volume in a century. The lip service the government paid to the Islamic opposition also limited the availability of retail alcohol. Imports were halted, and as early as 1963 cafés in many small towns were no longer allowed to serve alcohol and closed early. The civil war of the 1990s put the last nail in the coffin of Algeria's wine industry. Islamist groups began to intimidate wine growers, threatening to kill them if they continued tending to their vines. By 1997, output hit a new low at 357,000 hectoliters; it went up afterwards, but imports continued to exceed exports.[33]

However, drinking did not disappear. The Dutch journalist Harm Botje, reporting from Algeria in the early 1990s just before the civil war broke out, described a country awkwardly suspended between its French colonial legacy and the national pride that, since independence, is supposed to sprout from its primordial Arab and Berber identity. Tunisia-produced Celtia beer flows freely, according to Botje's narrative, as does Ricard Pastis, an anise- and licorice-flavored aperitif. Even in the quarter of Bab al-Oued, formerly a stronghold of the OAS (Organisation de l'armée secrète, the far-right French resistance organization active in Algeria during the war of independence) and now dominated by Islamists, Botje finds himself treated to a glass in a bar-cum-brothel that, careful to avoid a run-in with the neighborhood, only opens its doors at dusk.[34]

Since the 1990s, Algerian producers and consumers have been engaged in an ambiguous struggle with sectors of the state controlled by Islamists. During the civil war (1991–7), the government made sure to safeguard the right to drink, protecting points of sale and even encouraging venues to stay open late. Alcohol thus was never formally declared illegal. Indeed, consumption went up during the conflict. Yet, in the aftermath of the war, alcohol came under new scrutiny as part of President Abdelaziz Bouteflika's attempt at national reconciliation.[35] Salafists began to petition the authorities to close urban bars and alcohol-serving restaurants. Matters turned serious in 2006 with a memorandum from the trade ministry, which in that year came under Islamist directorship. It required bars to comply with safety regulations and update their details on the business register every year. Many lost their licenses in the process. Some bars took on a new life as clandestine vending points. Others opted to become snack bars or fast-food joints. The French press in 2012 saw Algeria, once renowned for its bars, sliding into prohibition, with watering holes harder and harder to find. Soon none were left in most major towns, and even in Algiers only fifteen struggled on. As imports dried up and official sales points diminished in number, clandestine imports and sales increased, as did alcohol-related crime.[36]

A decade later, an awkward juxtaposition of competing forces and impulses remains in place. Since 2013, the municipality of Algiers has sought to enliven the city's public life again, but this has not led to the reappearance of licensed public drinking. Fear continues to drive politics: an initiative by the Minister of the Economy in 2015 to liberalize the alcohol trade was struck down by Prime Minister Abdelmalek Sellal, under pressure from Salafists who accused him of waging war on God and demanded the full implementation of the *shari'a*.[37] Price hikes following tax increases in 2015 and 2016, meanwhile, made alcohol unaffordable for many. The result is the perpetuation of a general malaise. A superficial national reconciliation through pardoning has failed to alleviate the trauma caused by the horrors of the 1990s, leaving the country numb, with many turning to puritanical Islam as an analgesic. The Islamists, in other words, have lost the war but vanquished the country's spirit.

To be sure, Islamist pressure has not deterred entrepreneurial Algerians from finding ways to revive their country's traditional viticulture. A private wine company called Grands Crus de l'Ouest (GCO) was launched as early as 2001. Based in Oran and concentrating on the northwestern part of the country, GCO has since grown into Algeria's largest vintner.[38] Other, mostly export-oriented initiatives by local producers and purveyors have followed.[39] Yet in today's Algeria, children are taught to equate the vine with *la culture de Satan*.[40] In these conditions, public drinking, not to mention social drinking, does not thrive. Opening a bottle of wine means 'closing the door, the blinds, and the curtains'.[41] The alternative is to 'take refuge to a somber, smoky bar, behind protective metal bars with a sinister bouncer at the front door'.[42] Otherwise, people have taken to drinking out of their cars, on cliffs overlooking the Mediterranean, in parks, and in wooded areas.

Tunisia's independence had a profound effect on the sale and consumption of alcohol, too. On 2 March 1956, two days after the country gained independence, the authorities set out to craft a new national, teetotaling identity by imposing a new tax on alcohol-purveying establishments. A few months later, the ordinances of 1914 and 1920 forbidding sales to Muslims were reinstated. In 1960, a law restricted licenses to run *débits* to Tunisian citizens. In 1964, the French made the importation of Tunisian wines more difficult. Less than twenty years later, the acreage dedicated to viticulture had fallen by half and production by two-thirds.[43]

In modern Tunisia, competing forces are at work, too. The ascendance of the Muslim Brotherhood-inspired Ennahda Party and the substantial tax increases that followed its rise to power in 2011 have made alcohol both more contentious and less affordable. Sales are forbidden on Fridays and during Ramadan. Alcohol is totally banned in the religious stronghold of Kairouan and in Berges du Lac, a joint Saudi Arabian-Tunisian development project outside Tunis. Public drinking is concentrated in urban centers catering to foreigners and the country's 'Frenchified' bourgeoisie. In suburbs and the countryside, where alcohol is hard to come by, people drink to forget their misery and easily fall victim to tainted alcohol which can cause blindness and even death.[44]

Nevertheless, consumption has gone up. That of beer has increased dramatically in the last few decades, from c. 350,000 hectoliters in 1985 to more than 1.8 million in 2016. The tax hikes of 2013 and 2015 by the Ennahda-dominated government slowed this down but not by much. The dominant brand created in 1951, Celtia, used to be the only beer available. Of late, it has shed its fusty image to become associated with modern living, so that it is now the heavily promoted booze of choice during summer festivals. This success has also enabled it to stand its ground against the competition, most notably Heineken, which entered the Tunisian market in 2009. Alcohol invariably gives rise to local spats, with the opening of sale points prompting protestors to demand prohibition. Generally, though, the norm is thinly veiled invisibility, exemplified by beer served in plastic cups enveloped in paper napkins at events where drinkers mingle with non-drinkers.[45]

The latest development in Tunisia is the promotion of 'halal' or 'Islamic' tourism in the form of alcohol-free 'family' hotels in popular Mediterranean resort towns such as Hamamet, Monastir, and Mahdia. From one in 2014, opened by Ennahda leader Rachid Gannouchi, by 2018 their number had risen to a dozen. The 2015 attack on the beach of Hamamet by Islamic State, which left thirty-nine people dead and forty wounded, has affected this trend as well. Traditional tourism registered a precipitous drop as a result, and halal tourism came to be seen as a relatively safe alternative. Tunisian tourist agencies now include alcohol-free 'family' hotels in their holiday packages in response to the rise in demand by conservative Tunisian and Algerian families.[46]

As in Algeria, in post-independence Morocco much land dedicated to viticulture was initially abandoned and plowed under. Yet, at the same time, a new viticulture was allowed to develop with the blessing of the monarch, Hasan II (r. 1961–99). The main beneficiary of this royal support was Brahim Zniber, a businessman who after 1956, the year of independence, acquired thousands of hectares of land, much of it as part of a restitution from French colonists. In 1964, Zniber created Celliers de Meknès. Over the years, this company grew into the country's largest producer of wine and spirits; by 2014 it was good for 85 percent of the country's wine production, selling 35 million bottles of wine every year.[47]

Despite its state support for viniculture, Morocco, too, applies a double standard regarding alcohol. Following a law from 1967, only foreigners are allowed to purchase and consume it. Yet liquor is available in certain supermarkets, bars, and upscale restaurants, where it is kept hidden behind opaque glass or thick curtains. The country's Carrefour supermarkets sell spirits as well, but as a matter of prudence no receipts are provided at the check-out, guaranteeing anonymity. The domestic wine industry currently produces some 40 million bottles per annum, on par with Algeria, generating more than one billion dirhams (some US$100 million), bringing in more than $22 million in taxes and employing between 17,000 and 20,000 people. The country's vineyards now cover c. 37,000 hectares. This is down from the c. 100,000 hectares cultivated in 1955, but it still makes Morocco the largest producer and exporter of wine in the Arab world. In contrast to colonial times, when the country mainly produced cheap blended wines for export to Europe, domestic vintners—seeking to reach the global market with 'signature' wines—currently invest in higher-quality types and emphasize terroir. Morocco now even produces organic wine. According to a 2013 study, Moroccans (and foreign residents and tourists) annually consume 131 million liters of alcohol, 400 million bottles of beer, 38 million bottles of wine, 1.5 million bottles of whisky, and 140,000 bottles of champagne.[48]

Yet Morocco, too, has been under pressure from Islamists, even before they gained seats in parliament in 2011. They were enraged by a wine festival held in Meknes in 2007. In December 2009, hardline Islamic jurist Ahmed Raissouni issued a fatwa calling on Moroccans to boycott supermarkets that sell alcohol. The following year, the mayor of Fez, the country's premier religious center, suggested that, as in the 1930s, his city become the first dry one in all of Morocco. In 2012, the government raised taxes on alcoholic beverages. None of this seems to have had much effect, though.[49] Alcohol consumption is still on the rise, increasing by 7 percent in 2016–17. In 2019, imports went up by 19 percent, far outpacing a 6 percent increase in tourism.[50]

Egypt's Roaring Twenties

Zwemer's and Johnson's alarmist language about European spirits having seduced the Egyptians since Napoleonic times notwithstanding, alcohol in Egypt mostly remained an urban phenomenon. According to Thomas Wendworth Russell (Pasha), a British officer who served as the head of the Cairo police between 1902 and 1946, Egypt's peasants, the *fellahin*, were 'a sober race who did not touch alcohol'.[51] Yet the same official painted a grim picture of the red-light district of Cairo, the Was'a al-Birka, located next to the Azbakiyya quarter. From being a respectable area, in the late nineteenth century the Was'a became the European prostitution quarter, populated by 'third-class category' European women 'for whom Marseille had no further use'.[52] It continued to function as such until the Egyptian government cleaned up the area in 1924. The First World War, which brought large numbers of Commonwealth soldiers to Cairo, gave the Wazza (or Wozzeer, as they called it) a new lease on life. The number of brothels increased, and 'Imad al-Din Street became the center of a thriving night life with cabarets and dancing halls. Frequent drunken brawls and rioting in 1915 culminated in the partial destruction of the quarter by soldiers from New Zealand and Australia, leading to calls for more restrictions on vice in the city.[53]

Following the war, an Egyptian Roaring Twenties got underway, with bars and cabarets where female dancers and singers performed, such as the divas Shafiqa al-Qibtiyya, Mounira al-Mahdiyya and Tahia

Carioca. Champagne, the presence of which was justified in that it was considered mere mineral water, flowed freely at these venues.[54] Female entertainers were supposed to perform the *fath* (opening) of the bottle by approaching customers and asking if they would like to have a drink with them. In a competitive exhibition of wealth-cum-masculinity, the customer might order a dozen bottles and have them brought by a train of attendants to show off.[55] Popular culture followed suit. Films produced between 1930 and 1950 show upper-class men and women dressed in fine Western clothes, enjoying alcoholic beverages while listening to music and watching belly-dancing girls. Yet moralism was built into the portrayal of what remained a controversial topic. A common theme in pre-1960s Egyptian movies was that of the ordinary, lower-class Egyptian (the *ibn al-balad*) who drinks yet ultimately suffers for it.[56]

Beer made the greatest strides in this period. Its history in Egypt goes back to 1897, when a group of Belgian investors founded the Crown Brewery of Alexandria.[57] Its success and that of similar initiatives during and after the First World War invited other firms to invest in Egypt as well, so that by 1927 thirty-six breweries operated in the country. By far the most successful of these was the same Bomonti Company that had been active in the Ottoman Empire since the 1890s. Initially supplying beer to the British occupying forces, by 1928 the Bomontis had secured a monopoly over the Egyptian beer industry. A decade later, Egypt counted more than 300,000 beer drinkers. Over the next few decades, a campaign to 'Egyptianize' the country's economy got underway. This led to a search for a brand without foreign associations. They settled on the name Stella, Italian for 'Star', evocative of Italy's well-regarded culture as well as easily pronounced in Arabic, for what would become Egypt's quintessential beer.[58]

The Egyptian Temperance Movement and the Rise of Islamism

Resistance to drinking in twentieth-century Egypt was in part a function of the continued 'medicalization' of alcohol, a movement that, in an ironic return to Ibn Sina, evaluated alcohol on its medicinal qualities. Thus, when the modernist magazine *al-Muqtataf* in 1920 introduced a section where experts answered questions from readers, it assessed the merits and demerits of alcohol from a health perspective. The editors gave it a negative rating yet recommended a little red wine as beneficial for the body.[59]

Temperance movements followed the same approach, except that they saw no positive value in alcohol at all. The American Woman's Christian Temperance Union (WCTU) continued to limp along, with the Cairo branch having a mere twenty-five members. The organization received a boost in 1928 when Secretary Agnes Slack, on tour in Egypt and the Levant, established branches in Beirut, Alexandria, Fayyum, Beni Suef, Minya, and Asyut. Still, few Muslims rallied to what they saw as a Christian cause. Membership thus remained small, and activities were only organized during visits by foreign representatives.[60]

No foreign label or female association adhered to the indigenous (and male-dominated) Egyptian Temperance Association (ETA; Gami'at man' al-muskirāt li-'l-qutr al-Misri), founded in 1905. Headquartered in Alexandria, the ETA had branches in various Egyptian towns. It was inspired by the pseudoscientific approach of the WCTU, which it combined with traditional Islamic thinking. Ahmad Ghalwash, the organization's Western-educated founder and life-long president, proposed including contemporary English-language temperance literature in the Egyptian educational curriculum. Seeking to bridge the gap between Western argumentation and traditional Egyptian-Islamic rhetoric, he used America's Prohibition legislation at once to extoll the inherent virtue of Islam's aversion to alcohol and to argue that drinking had nothing to do with freedom— and indeed embodied 'slavery'—and that temperance was actually modern in its focus on physiological and mental health. Turning Western triumphalism on its head, Ghalwash admonished Muslims to follow the injunction of their faith by emulating the example set by the prohibitionist United States, the 'most advanced country in the world'.[61]

The most tenacious anti-alcohol crusaders in Egypt were the Muslim Brothers, Islam's first modern 'fundamentalist' movement. Hasan al-Banna (1906–49), who founded the association in 1928, made alcohol a priority in his struggle to turn Egypt into a true

Islamic society. In early 1942, the Brothers had some success: they pledged not to run candidates in that year's parliamentary elections, and in return Prime Minister Nahhas Pasha issued instructions to restrict the sale of liquor to certain times of the day and banned it during religious holidays, in particular Ramadan.[62] However, they failed to achieve much more than a ban on the issuing of new liquor licenses, and this did not even extend to the only sites where it would have mattered: Cairo, Alexandria, and the Canal zone cities. Still, the Brotherhood managed to have some of their anti-alcohol admonishments included in the national educational curriculum.[63]

Egypt's urban centers experienced a new surge in drinking following another influx of British soldiers during the Second World War. New bars sprang up in the center of Cairo, at Bab al-Hadid, along 'Imad al-Din Street, and especially in the 'Berka', the area north of Azbakiyya, where beer, whisky, arak, and the 'delights of the female flesh' were readily available. British soldiers, unfamiliar with Egyptian mores and flouting their own government's admonition to maintain good relations with the local population, caused scandal with their open drinking and brawling. In Alexandria, where the 'air was fresh and sparkling compared to dusty Cairo', their arrival just added more excitement to the city's cosmopolitanism.[64]

Growing resentment against the continued British presence in the country came to a head in the unrest that culminated in the violence of Black Saturday, 26 January 1952. It is hardly surprising that alcohol was a main target of the rioters. Beginning with an attack on Madam Badia's Opera Casino and an assault on the Turf Club, they targeted British and Jewish establishments, banks and travel agencies, the British Institute, and bars, cinemas, cabarets, and wine merchants in Cairo's modern center. They then proceeded to destroy the nightclub establishments along the road to the Pyramids, places like Auberge des Pyramides and the Club Royale de Chasse et de Pèche.

Gamal 'Abd al-Nasir (Nasser), who took power five months later, made Egypt fully independent but also set it on a course of xenophobic nationalism. This, as well as his socialist policies, which included the nationalization of industries and the expropriation of private property, hastened the demise of the country's Levantine culture. With the exodus of the resident Jews and Greeks, Cairo and especially Alexandria lost much of their diverse character. By 1970, the year Nasser died, Egypt's Roaring Twenties were a distant memory. Of course, drinking as such did not disappear. The elites who survived the Nasserite period continued to enjoy their gilded lifestyle in private clubs and exclusive beach redoubts.[65] In a way, this lifestyle was legitimized under Anwar Sadat, Nasser's successor. With his Open Door (*Infitāh*) policy, Sadat aimed to lift Egypt out of its socialist torpor by inviting foreign investment while reducing the overbearing role of the state. He also sought to exorcise Nasser's secular-leftist ghost by making concessions to conservative Islamic forces. Sadat thus helped create a society at once ruled by private capital while still beholden to modern Islamism.

The traffic of migrant workers between Egypt and the countries of the Arabian Peninsula reinforced this hybridity. It introduced a literalist 'Wahhabi' form of Islam into Egypt, although less in the poor neighborhoods than in new areas of 'air-conditioned luxury', filled with shopping malls that have sprung up all over Cairo in the new millennium. Popular preachers, most notably Yusuf al-Qaradhawi (1926–2022), the so-called global mufti living in exile in Qatar, proclaimed Islam compatible with entertainment provided it did not include alcohol and sex.[66] In this environment, the consumption of alcohol became largely confined to newly built hotels—the Hilton, the Marriott, and the Sheraton—that catered to international tourists and the local elite. By the 1980s, as the nightclubs along the Pyramid Road had returned to life, the former cabarets and dance halls downtown had become gloomy and forlorn spaces in crumbling buildings, passed by in the rush toward a neoliberal future. This process is nowhere better described than by novelist Alaa Al Aswany in *The Yacoubian Building*:

> Thus it was that, as the 1980s dawned, there remained in the whole of Downtown Cairo only a few, scattered, small bars, whose owners had been able to hang on in the face of the rising tide of religion and government persecution. This they had been able to do by one of two methods – concealment or bribery. There was not one bar downtown that advertised its presence.

Indeed the word 'Bar' on the signs was changed to 'Restaurant' or 'Coffee Shop', and the owners of bars and wine stores deliberately painted the windows of their establishments a dark color so that that what went on inside could not be seen, or would place in their display windows paper napkins or any other items that would not betray their actual business. It was no longer permitted for a customer to drink on the sidewalk in front of the bar or even in front of an open window that looked on to the street and stringent precautions had to be taken following the burning of a number of liquor store at the hands of youths belonging to the Islamist movement.

At the same time, the few remaining bar owners were forced to pay large regular bribes to the plainclothes police officers to whose districts they belonged and to governorate officials if they wanted to continue. Sometimes the sale of cheap locally produced alcohol would not realize them enough income to pay the fine, so that the bar owners found themselves obliged to find 'other' ways of adding to their income. Some of them turned to facilitating prostitution by using fallen women to serve the alcohol … Others turned to manufacturing alcohol in primitive laboratories instead of buying it, so as to increase profits … These disgusting industrially produced drinks led to a number of unfortunate accidents, the most celebrated of which befell a young artist who lost his sight after drinking bad brandy at the Halegian Bar. The public prosecutors' office ordered the bar closed but its owner as able to reopen later, using the usual methods.

Consequently, the small remaining downtown bars were no longer cheap, clean places for recreation as they had been before. Instead, they had turned into badly lit, poorly ventilated dens frequented mostly by hooligans and criminal types …[67]

The modern consumerism of the Sadat era did not just prefer new venues but also led to changes in taste. The newly affluent classes who supported Sadat's Open Door policy favored imported liquors—Johnnie Walker, champagne and the like—anything but Stella, which held some 90 percent of the Egyptian beer market at the time but appealed neither to the neoliberal nightclub scene nor to ordinary

Egyptians, who continued to prefer their waterpipes and coffee. In the Nasser period, the Egyptian beer industry had begun to advertise its product to those with modern aspirations as pure and refreshing and, invoking a traditional belief in alcohol's medicinal benefit, as restorative and curative. Companies pitched their product to the young, associating it with summer fun, freedom, and sociability.[68] Stella reached its sales peak in 1988 but soon thereafter went into steep decline, plagued by mismanagement, poor production standards, and fundamentalist pressure. By the 1990s, the brand's uneven quality had made it the butt of jokes.[69] In 1997, the government was forced to sell it off as a distressed asset to a consortium linked to the Danish Carlsberg Company at about one-third of its estimated value. The new owner restructured the Ahram Beverage Company (ABC) and introduced a line of nonalcoholic beverages to the company's portfolio. In 2002, Heineken International once again acquired ABC. Today Stella remains king in Egypt, but 'of a much smaller kingdom'.[70]

Alcohol in Modern Egypt

Today, Egypt, having gone through four decades of neoliberalism, only allows the sale and consumption of alcohol in restaurants, hotels, and tourist facilities approved by the Ministry of Tourism. Since 1986, Asyut province in Upper Egypt—a region of high Islamist membership but also home to a large Coptic population and the scene of frequent communal strife—has been alcohol-free.[71] The state continues to emphasize temperance and moderation, and effectively stymies the growth of the industry. Acquiring a new liquor license is nearly impossible for prospective owners of liquor shops, retail stores, bars, and three-star hotels. In 2014, the tax on beer went up by 200 percent; on local and imported wines it went up by 150 percent. The government also slapped an absurd 3,000 percent tariff on whisky, ostensibly for 'religious and cultural reasons', but more likely to fight off foreign imports.[72]

Egypt's conservative society provides support for such policies. In line with the growing influence of a new piety movement among the lower and lower- to upper-middle classes, there has been tendency to 'clean up' weddings. Regular popular ones still include beer, as well as hashish, but 'Islamic' weddings do not.[73] This trend also affects the minority Coptic community, whose members must deal with 'two Gods during their everyday lives'. Since the Muslim God is more powerful than the Christian one, both legally and societally, Copts must balance their interaction with God, with Muslims, and with other Christians. This forces them to be circumspect in their alcohol consumption, even within their own community.[74]

Egypt never became dry, to be sure, even under the brief reign of Muslim Brother President Morsi in 2011–12. Officially, alcohol at the time was only available in so-called tourist governorates, but these included the major cities—Cairo, including Giza, and Alexandria—and only left out regions where alcohol had never been available. In Cairo and Alexandria, one finds remnants of the bygone era in watering holes such as the Tout Va Bien in Cairo, the Cap d'Or—a bar by the same name in both cities—and the Spitfire in Alexandria. The first of these figures in Naguib Mahfouz's celebrated Cairo Trilogy as a sophisticated place symbolizing cosmopolitan modernity, a venue for secret dalliances. Today, they are melancholic dives, reminders of olden times with lots of tacky memorabilia on the walls, places where old men drink cheap Stella but which mostly cater to nostalgic Western tourists.[75]

The modern scene, meanwhile, has moved on. Cairo's upscale districts—Zamalek, Heliopolis, and Maʿadi—now sport air-conditioned liquor shops and British-style pubs with a cover charge of more than 200 EGP (US$26). In the new millennium, various upscale nightclubs have opened: Graffiti at the Four Seasons Hotel, O Bar at the Fairmont Hotel, Cavalini and The Roof at the Sunset Mall, and Level in Zamalek. Buying and consuming alcohol in affluent neighborhoods requires little effort, whereas in low- to middle-class quarters like Giza and Sayyida Zaynab the poor continue to drown their sorrow in a few remaining *buza* bars. Otherwise, getting hold of booze is like engaging in a drug deal. Since the failed Arab Spring of 2011, the demand for alcohol as a distraction from misery and relief from stress has only gone up.[76]

Egypt now also has its Drinkies, the retail chain of ABC which operates more than eighty premium stores across the country. Its website offers various beers, wines, and spirits such as rum and gin, both Egyptian and foreign, along with pairings of food. It also features tours to the Gianaclis winery in the Delta. Drinkies shops exist across major cities. Cairo has some thirty-five and Alexandria eighteen, mostly located in Coptic neighborhoods. Otherwise, the stores are concentrated on the Mediterranean and Red Sea coasts. The service includes deliveries, made by couriers on black scooters carrying boxes of the same color.[77]

Lebanon

Lebanon is part of a wider region where arak ('araq, raki) is indigenous. Long known to be the national drink, arak in modern times has lost some of its prestige. A representative of Heineken, researching the market in 1960, called Lebanon a 'market of snobs', explaining that any Lebanese who had attained some social status and could afford to purchase imported beer would dismissively choose whisky or brandy.[78] Yet arak, known as 'lion's milk' (halib al-asad), remains the drink of choice for most.[79]

Lebanon has long been a center of viticulture as well. The country is home to numerous wineries, the first of which go back to the mid-nineteenth century, when entrepreneurial French Jesuits initiated the production of the Cinsault variety in the Bekaa Valley. Château Ksara thus began life in 1857 in the region between Tanail and Zahleh. When in the later part of the century the Phylloxera disease threatened to end cultivation, it was saved by the planting of local vines. Yet it was not until the 1940s that new production got underway, with the rather low-quality Cinsault grape initially prevailing. The departure of the French—the main consumers of wine—in 1946 did not result in the expected collapse of the wine industry, for the Lebanese had embraced French ways, including a passion for wine. In the 1960s, when Beirut established its reputation as the Paris of the East, Lebanese wine, facing little foreign competition, took off. Brands like Château Ksara, Château Kefraya, and Château Musar became popular among the modernizing, mostly Christian classes. Still, a full-fledged, competitive wine production had to wait, since the market initially plummeted with the Lebanese civil war of 1975–90, the Israeli and Syrian invasions, and the rise of Hezbollah in the 1980s, which led to vandalism of alcohol-purveying shops and the closing of cafés in areas it controlled. The Shi'i *'Āshurā* commemoration in 1984 saw Muslim militants enforcing a ban on alcohol by ransacking bars and nightspots in West Beirut, which until then had been a center of cosmopolitan 'live and let live' culture. At one point more than 100 veiled Moslem women 'went on a two-hour night rampage, smashing liquor bottles and furniture in several boarded-up bars and bingo parlors on Phoenicia Street, once the hub of West Beirut nightlife'.[80]

Change only came with the return of a modicum of stability in the 1990s. Wine still faced competition from arak and whisky among the lower and upper classes, respectively. The growing clamor of Islamist voices emanating from West Beirut did not help either. But exports provided a way out. In 1997, a Lebanese consortium of wineries, the Union Vinicole du Liban, was established in the interest of pursuing a niche in the international market. They also successfully lobbied for a new wine law. Adopted in 2000, this law stipulates quality criteria regarding grape varieties and sugar content.[81]

In today's Lebanon, alcohol is part of a 'what will be will be' attitude, lubricating the 'hedonism of the present' while obliterating the 'turbulence of the past'.[82] The wine industry flourished, at least until the country descended into chaos in 2020, and domestic craft beers registered a 300 percent growth between 2016 and 2021. At first, Hezbollah elements attacked nightclubs and bars. But its leadership soon found this to be an impractical policy in a diverse, multi-denominational country where effective rule required some level of acquiescence from the non-Muslim community. Now, even in areas of Beirut controlled by the group, non-Muslims can purchase alcohol largely unmolested.[83] And thus the famous dance club B 018, located in a former Beirut slum and shaped like a coffin, has continued to be wildly popular, packing in hundreds of revelers every night until 7am (until the outbreak of COVID-19 in early 2020, that is). Since then, Beirut's rave and house scene has persisted, but otherwise the country's economic crisis, exacerbated by the lethal explosion at the Beirut port in August 2020 and the collapse of the national currency, has put a serious dent in its reputation as the nightlife capital of the Middle East.[84]

Iraq Under Baath Rule

The onslaught of modernity left few places in the Middle East untouched. The following description of the changes that took place in the early twentieth century in Baghdad, still under Ottoman control, far from the influence of oceans and ports, illustrates the point:

> Drinking has crept into the land, and this also is due to the Westerner. It has become very common. In the market are liquors of all kinds which were not there when we first came to Baghdad. Small hotels sprang up overnight like mushrooms, the proprietors depending almost solely upon the sale of liquor for their income. Muhammad had forbidden the use of these intoxicants, and wisely so for a people living in a hot and trying climate. Europeans have made drinking in Iraq to appear respectable and the proper thing to do; and many have imitated them with the idea that in order to be up to date in social etiquette and to entertain in the proper style, it is necessary to serve liquor. Even the poor people are spending their hard-earned money for the cheaper, yet very intoxicating 'arak, which is made from grapes or dates.[85]

Kermit Roosevelt Sr., son of President Theodore Roosevelt, who fought in the First World War for the British army in Mesopotamia, described the offerings at the residence of Asad Allah Khan, the Iranian consul in Baghdad at the time, as follows:

> Coffee and sweets of many devious kinds were served with arrack and Scotch whiskey for those who had no religious scruples. The Koran's injunction against strong drink was not very conscientiously observed by the majority, and even those who did not drink in public, rarely abstained in private. Only the very conservative—and these were more often to be found in the smaller towns—rigorously obeyed the Prophet's command.[86]

Little changed in the period 1919–30, when Iraq lived under British mandate rule. Faysal, handpicked by the British to be the country's first king, was rather abstemious even if, on occasion and in the company of Christians, he might savor some whisky. At times he also drank champagne with his meals, with the argument that it 'must be medicinally valuable, since it was given to invalids'.[87]

Newly independent Iraq adopted a law in 1932 prohibiting the manufacture, sale, and consumption of alcohol for all Muslims.[88] This law remains in place yet was never really enforced. Indeed, the availability of spirits only increased over time, so that by 1958, the year of the bloody coup that ended the Iraq monarchy, alcohol had become an integral part of (urban) leisure and entertainment.[89]

In the absence of a wine-growing tradition, beer and hard liquor have always been the booze of choice in Iraq. A wealthy Shi'i businessman named Madhaf Khedairi was the first to produce Western-style beer by buying a small brewery after the Second World War. This became the Iraq Brewery. A decade later, another (Christian) entrepreneur, Khaduri Khaduri, established the Eastern Brewery Co., near Baghdad. Later named the Eastern Beer Company, it produced the Farida brand, a lager which is still popular as of this writing. Both men did a brisk business catering to foreign expatriates as well as to a burgeoning Iraqi business class. The breweries continued to operate following the 1958 coup and the subsequent rule of the military, leading to the Baath coming to power in 1968. The regime nationalized the country's breweries five years later but did nothing to stem the flow of alcohol. In the mid-1970s, branch breweries were built in Mosul and, more problematically, in religiously sensitive 'Ammara, where Chinese workers had to be recruited to run the plant. Its operation briefly interrupted by the Gulf War in 1991, the Eastern Brewery remained in business through the sanctions imposed after the war ended, continuing to import hops and malt despite enormous obstacles.[90]

The Baath regime was ostensibly secular. However, it did take popular sensibilities into account. It never banned alcohol outright but fluctuated in its stance on religious traditions such as fasting and drinking according to its degree of self-confidence, imposing restrictions when it felt weak and vulnerable to Islamist pressure and relaxing these whenever it considered itself powerful enough to do so. Approaching its first Ramadan in November 1968, the Baath leadership thus ordered all coffeehouses, casinos, bars, and liquor stores—except for some fancy hotels and outlets at railways stations, ports, and airports—closed during the day for the duration of the month. At sensitive times, such as the day when Shi'is commemorate the assassination of Imam 'Ali in 661, and *Laylat al-qadr*, the night when the Koran is believed to have been first revealed, all bars and liquor stores were ordered shuttered at night as well. In the following years, the government gradually loosened these curbs, allowing 'restaurants deemed highly necessary' and ones located away from main streets or with entrances on side streets to remain open during Ramadan.[91]

With Syria and South Yemen, Iraq in the 1970s was the freest Arab country in terms of alcohol production and consumption, both of which peaked in the 1980s. In Basra, the discos closed at dawn and the available beer stocks were routinely depleted by Kuwaitis crossing the border to quench their thirst in ways that were impossible in their own 'dry' country.[92] The presence of sizeable religious minority communities clearly contributed to this state of affairs. The plain of Nineveh, home to an ethnically diverse population, including many Assyrian Christians and a large Yazidi community, is a case in point. Ground zero of this ethnic diversity is the town of Ba'shiqa, known as a 'Little Iraq', located some 20km northeast of Mosul. Throughout the 1960s and 1970s, this 'alcohol capital' of Iraq was home to nearly 400 arak-producing distilleries as well as countless liquor stores.[93]

These conditions remained in place during the 'good' years, when Johnnie Walker Black Label was practically Iraq's national drink. Things only changed in 1982, three years into the presidency of Saddam Hussein, whose palaces were well stocked with semi-sweet Portuguese Mateus Rosé, his favorite drink, and two years into the Iran-Iraq War, following a downturn in Iraq's fortunes.[94] As the casualties mounted, a fourth night—that of the commemoration of the Battle of Badr in 624, when the forces of the Prophet defeated the pagan army—was added to the ban on entertainment. Governors were also told to make sure that popular restaurants only remained open in case of 'extreme need' and in the 'smallest number possible'. As the war dragged on, further restrictions were imposed, including the full closure of all bars and liquor stores during Ramadan. Even so, top-tier restaurants in Iraq's main urban centers remained exempt.[95]

The Iran-Iraq War ended in the summer of 1988, to be followed two years later by Saddam's next reckless adventure, his invasion of Kuwait. He rhetorically justified this assault by presenting it as a jihad against the sybaritic, hypocritical Gulf Arabs—the 'Jews of the Gulf', as his in-house newspaper, *Babil*, called them—and a first step toward the liberation of Jerusalem and even Mecca itself. During the ensuing First Gulf War, Saddam assumed the role of religious savior, coming close to equating himself with the Prophet. To preempt the charge of blasphemy, this epithet necessitated a serious faith campaign. New mosques were built, an Islamic bank was created, the *takbir* (God is Great) formula was added to the Iraqi flag, community prayer was encouraged, and *shari'a* punishment was (partially) introduced. This 'wahhabization' of public life included the formal disappearance of liquor from the officers' mess, though not of drinking among the army and party elite.

Basra's boozy days ended in March 1991, when the American-incited Shi'a uprising against Saddam vaulted the Iranian-backed Badr Brigade into prominence. After taking control of the town and the province, they burned down the Sheraton Hotel as well as the city's bars and casinos, declaring a (short-lived) local Islamic Republic. Baghdad fared slightly better. In 1993, more than half of its nightclubs and all but five discotheques were closed, leaving the remaining ones concentrated in five areas. Alcohol was virtually banned from the Shi'i shrine cities, Najaf and Karbala, and everywhere else its sale became severely restricted in the vicinity of mosques, schools, and hospitals. In the summer of 1994, a total ban on public drinking was proclaimed, leaving hotels, bars, clubs, and restaurants dry. Only non-Muslims were now allowed to operate alcohol stores, provided these were located at least 200 meters from mosques. Only the very rich now could afford Scotch, which remained the drink of choice of the elite. Some speculated that this measure was designed not just to placate the society's religious elements but to 'appease an impoverished middle class resentful of the speculators and professional criminals who alone have the money to drink Johnnie Walker in Baghdad's nightclubs, restaurants, and bars'. Others more cynically ventured that this was a ploy to allow Saddam's son Uday to consolidate his presumed monopoly on Scotch imports. In 2001, Uday and his friends indeed assumed partial directorship of the company. Either way, Saddam acted pragmatically, from expediency rather than conviction. Cognizant of the interests and predilections of his base, the secular Baath cadres, he never totally banned the sale of spirits, just their public consumption. Alcohol thus continued to flow. Laws enacted in 2001 allowed regulated premises with an annual alcohol license to operate so long as they were not situated in Iraq's sacred cities or within proximity of mosques, hospitals, and schools.[96]

Iraq Since 2003

In post-Saddam Iraq, beset by sectarianism and Islamic radicalism, things have been in flux. The American invasion of 2003 resulted in a competitive market for imported liquor that catered to the foreign troops. But a year later, with a sectarian war brewing, Shi'i fundamentalists firebombed shops selling alcoholic beverages, attacking and, in some cases, killing their owners. Violence forced hotels and restaurants out of business, and people stayed at home rather than risk being bombed or kidnapped.[97]

By 2006, a nadir in the tumultuous post-invasion era, little remained of the vibrancy of Baghdad, now a city in the grip of fear and terror. All restaurants on Abu Nuwas Street, the traditional entertainment heart of town, had closed, and the police would habitually go around hotels to enforce a no-alcohol policy. The only site where foreign embassy personnel, war contractors and, occasionally, American soldiers flouting the US army ban on drinking could indulge was the Baghdad Country Club, a tiny enclave inside the Green Zone, a 'walled garden within a walled garden', located next to the party headquarters of the Supreme Council for the Islamic Revolution in Iraq. The Baghdad Country Club is supplied by local Christian merchants and enabled to persist by bribe-taking insurgents who turn a blind eye to its illicit activities.[98]

With the exodus of large numbers of Christians and the effective secession of Kurdistan with its secular traditions and its substantial non-Muslim population, Iraq has turned into a country where conservative Shi'is make up the majority of the population. Official policy reflects this trend. In October 2016, just as the offensive to dislodge Islamic State (ISIS) from Mosul was going into high gear, Baghdad's Shi'i-dominated parliament passed a law forbidding the importation, production, and sale of alcoholic beverages, with a fine of up to 10 million Iraqi dinars (US$10,000) for anyone violating the ban. This decree hit Iraq's minority purveyors of alcohol especially hard, and Christian lawmakers vowed to appeal it, arguing that little proper debate had preceded the legislation, that the ban was unconstitutional because it violated the rights of religious minorities, and that it was really designed to force them out of the country through harassment and exclusion.[99]

On 22 October 2017, Iraq's parliament voted to prohibit the sale, import, and production of alcohol, except in Iraqi Kurdistan. The supporters of the bill argued that the availability of alcohol contravened Islam as well as the constitution. Christians demurred, calling the move a violation of minority rights. To date, the ban remains in limbo, amid widespread objections. In the summer of 2018, the governor of the Salah al-Din governorate just north of Baghdad, which had been under ISIS control between 2014 and 2017, bowed to clerical pressure and closed all liquor shops amid concerns about the preservation of traditional values and 'problems caused by alcoholism, such as car accidents, family problems and youth drug addiction problems'.[100] Meanwhile, in late 2020 religious extremists began expressing their unhappiness with alcohol in the loudest possible way, by targeting liquor stores in Baghdad with explosive devices.[101] The result is that Baghdad has a muted, semi-clandestine bar scene, with barely a handful of restaurants that serve alcohol, all of them under perennial threat of vandalism and closure.[102]

Matters in the north further deteriorated in 2012 when many of those involved in the arak-producing industry in Ba'shiqa, Iraq's former booze capital, succumbed to Islamist pressure. Two years later, ISIS swept in and imposed its harsh rule, including a total ban on liquor. The ISIS men displaced the town's Yazidi and Christian population and ransacked the remaining liquor stores, driving the drinking culture underground as they were unable to eradicate it fully. When Kurdish troops dislodged ISIS from power in late 2016, a few dozen minority members and some businessmen returned to a depleted Ba'shiqa.[103] Several liquor stores reopened as well, which now keep a low profile, meaning they do not put up signs or advertise. Still, they do a brisk business, with one owner in late 2017 reporting that his store saw up to 1,000 customers daily, most of them Muslims. In the fall of 2018, Ba'shiqa—now in disputed territory, legally part of Iraq but controlled by Kurdish security forces—saw the opening of a new distillery producing a brand of arak called 'Araq Ba'shiqa. To date, the alcohol business remains fraught with danger, with purveyors forced to pay bribes to stay in business and at risk of having their wares confiscated.[104] Even semi-independent Kurdistan has not been spared harassment and violence. In late 2011, several liquor stores were torched in Zakho, and afterwards leaflets appeared threatening death to the owners if they reopened.[105]

The Arabian Peninsula

In Chapter 6 we saw how even the Arabian Peninsula was never alcohol-free. The British diplomat Bullard, writing from Jeddah between 1923 and 1939, stated that liquor was clandestinely distilled in the country, and that in Mecca, as well as in Riyadh, locally produced arak of bad quality was to be had. In Jeddah, he claimed, almost all the rich Muslims drank, and there was a great demand for contraband liquor. The first thing people would do upon boarding a foreign ship was 'to cadge a drink of spirits'. The same chief of police whose job it was to ferret out illegal sale and consumption, Bullard claimed, was constantly pestering foreign legations for whisky 'for his health'.[106] All this seems to have been limited to the urban environment. William Gifford Palgrave, traveling in the Arabian interior in the 1860s, noted that even the memory of how palm wine had once been quite common in the region had been lost among the locals.[107]

Ibn Saud, the founder of the modern country of Saudi Arabia in the 1920s, had his own drinking issues. Bullard had it on good authority that the monarch enjoyed, 'under the impression that it is a kind of tonic, a brand of invalid wine manufactured in England but disguised by a change of label in Egypt'.[108] The same ruler apparently was also very fond of Cointreau, which he 'consumed in large quantities'.[109] Always uncompromising on their stance against the sale and consumption of alcohol, Saudi Arabia became particularly strict following the dramatic events of 1979—the assault on the Holy Mosque of Mecca, the Iranian Revolution, and the Soviet invasion of Afghanistan—all of which shook the ruling regime to its foundations, prompting it to appease its hardline religious forces. Of course, for those who wished to quench their thirst and could afford it, there was always freewheeling Lebanon and lively Cairo, where 'furnished apartments' (sha'a mafrusha), garishly decorated in a Bordeaux-red brothel style, were widely available as summer rentals, frequented by Arabs from the peninsula in immaculate dishdashas. In modern times, Munich, Geneva, Paris, London, and Marbella have drawn the truly wealthy.

Yemen, in the southern part of the peninsula, has a long drinking tradition. Arak was brought to the port of Mocha from India in the eighteenth century. Elsewhere, it was hard to find any booze other than in Sanaa, the capital, where the Jewish community manufactured both (poor-quality) wine and brandy.[110] A traditional culture existed in the 'Asir and northern Yemen, lasting far into the twentieth century, in which taverns and coffeehouses run by women were deemed venues of 'tavern prostitution'.[111]

In the 1960s, Marxist South Yemen, emerging from decades of British rule and with a large population of Africans and Indians, was the only part of the peninsula where people drank openly in bars and nightclubs, most of their alcohol brought in from Djibouti across the Red Sea. Although not quite Hong Kong or Singapore, Aden's European districts of Tawahi and Khormaksar knew an active nightlife throughout the 1980s.[112] Vodka was the preferred drink of the many Russian expatriates living in South Yemen at the time, but otherwise the spirit did not find much demand. Yemenis drank beer to counteract the effects of qat, the mildly narcotic plant that is chewed by many.[113] Locally brewed beer was available as well. Indeed, South Yemen housed the only brewery in the Arabian Peninsula, the

Aden Sirra (Seera) Beer factory in al-Mansura. Founded in *c.* 1980 and run by Ekkehard Zitzmann, a West German who had managed a brewery in Tehran until the Islamic Revolution of 1979 put an end to his business, the National Brewing Company produced about 50,000 hectoliters a year. Steep taxes made the price of beer cripplingly high at about US$3 per bottle—the equivalent of more than US$15 today. The facility operated against all odds in other ways as well: its workers were shunned by the local community for producing alcohol, and the bottles were sold as discreetly as possible.[114]

These conditions lasted until the reunification of South Yemen with its far more puritanical northern neighbor in 1991. Of course, people in North Yemen drank too, most of the tipple—including the popular Johnnie Walker Black Label—being smuggled in from the south. When the border first opened in 1988, a steady stream of North Yemenis in their Toyota Land Cruisers descended upon Aden every weekend to take advantage of the city's readily available vices: booze, belly dancing, and affordable prostitutes.[115] But soon alcohol came under assault. Intolerance grew to the point where public drinking disappeared. Zitzmann's delivery trucks were pelted with rocks. Firebombs were thrown over the brewery walls. He and his workers received death threats, and only the presence of Soviet-trained army officers prevented a full-scale storming of the brewery. In 1990, a government-issued order forced the Aden Sirra Brewery to stop production during Ramadan. Zitzmann had to comply but always made sure to fill the storage vats before unplugging the machines at the start of the holy month. The following summer, Victoria, the country's main supermarket, stopped selling alcohol. In 1994, at the height of the civil war, northern troops burned the Sirra Brewery to the ground, forcing the 'last brewer in the Arabian Peninsula' to leave the country.[116]

In modern Yemen, it is relatively easy to obtain alcohol, even if it is officially unavailable. There is now even a locally brewed vodka, called Baladi. Vodka, whisky, beer, and gin are also smuggled in from Ethiopia and Djibouti. The popularity of whisky prompted President 'Ali 'Abdullah Salih to joke with US General David Petraeus that he loathed drugs and weapons coming from Djibouti, but that whisky was fine, so long as it was good whisky. There are even towns such as al-Hayma and 'Amran, some 80 kilometers west and 50 kilometers northwest of Sanaa respectively, where whole streets are lined with little shops that sell booze behind their metal doors. At first glance these appear to be your average Yemeni grocery store, with cans of beans, laundry detergent, and cigarettes lining the walls. But they often have a clandestine side room stocked with crates of Heineken beer and whisky of assorted brands. The law prohibits the consumption of alcohol in public and sanctions public drunkenness. If caught, violators are sent to prison. What happens in private homes, however, is another matter. Yemen does not have religious police, and the regular police do not as a rule search private dwellings for alcohol.[117]

9

ALCOHOL IN THE MODERN AGE
NEW DRINKS AND DRINKING CUSTOMS
PART TWO
TURKEY, IRAN, AND PAKISTAN

The Ottoman Empire 1908–23: Freedom Drowned in War and Occupation

Between 1908 and 1923, the Ottoman Empire careened toward its convulsive end, going from revolution and war to occupation and collapse. The revolution was that of the Young Turks who finally ended Abdülhamid's oppressive rule in 1908, first by forcing him to reinstate the constitution of 1876 and then—in 1909, following a conservative countercoup—by removing him from office. The Committee of Union and Progress (CUP) that came to power in the process promised to replace autocracy with the blessings of parliamentary rule.

Freedom was indeed in the air in 1908: people of all faiths and ethnicities celebrated in public. The proletariat, women, young people, and journalists all inhaled the fresh air of liberty. Drinking, too, increasingly freed from its traditional opprobrium, became common among members of the administrative class. The return of many exiled Turks who had tasted alcohol in Paris, Brussels, and

235

Geneva contributed to this sense of openness. The consumption of raki accordingly went up from 50 to 80 million liters between 1911 and 1914.[1]

But freedom also meant freedom for oppositional forces. The Young Turks themselves were moved by a desire to curb alcohol imports, albeit more from a nationalist perspective than from religious concerns. The year 1911 also saw a split in the CUP, with conservative forces demanding legislation against public drunkenness and proper zoning for taverns. Taking advantage of the new press freedom, they aired their views in journals and magazines such as *Sırat-ı Müstakim* (*The Straight Path*) and *Âfiyet* (*Health*), a magazine for families, warning about the dangers of alcohol, denouncing those who considered drinking integral to civilization, and warning that alcohol concealed a Western wish to destroy the Ottoman Empire and Islam. In 1910, a temperance movement, *Osmanlı Men'-i Müskirat Cemiyeti*, was founded in Istanbul.[2]

Nor did the freedom last. As the new regime consolidated power, its liberal agenda was lost, and in July 1913 the CUP—led by a triumvirate consisting of Talat Pasha, Cemal Pasha, and Enver Pasha—established a dictatorship. By that time, the Ottoman Empire was embroiled in the First Balkan War, a conflict that would blur into the Great War and then the Greco-Turkish War. In the intervening decade, freedom was quashed and replaced by an autocracy that fed on exclusionary nationalism and painted minorities as profiteers. One harbinger of things to come was the interethnic tension that erupted in Izmir following Greece's annexation of Crete in 1908.[3] The Balkan War of 1912–14 aggravated conditions, shredding what was left of the fragile fabric of Ottoman inter-communal relations. Muslim Turkish literati attributed the humiliating defeat their country had suffered in part to weakness caused by their co-religionists' indifference to commerce. Looking for culprits, they increasingly came to view non-Muslims—who considerably outperformed Muslims in education, entrepreneurship, and the accumulation of wealth—as handmaidens of foreign domination, traitors to the Turkish cause. In Thrace and Asia Minor, Greeks and Jews became the target of harassment, prompting many to seek security in the larger cities.[4]

The Armistice of Mudros of 30 November 1918 ended the Ottoman Empire's participation in the First World War, and five years later, the Republic of Turkey rose from its rubble. Its founder and first president, Mustafa Kemal, the later Atatürk, had briefly been a member of the CUP before earning his military stripes in the various wars the dying Ottoman Empire had fought. In the intervening period, from late 1918 to late 1923, the population of Anatolia continued to suffer war and humiliating foreign invasion. Mustafa Kemal's birthplace Salonica had been taken by the Greeks in 1912 and subsequently ceded to Greece. The Greeks also controlled Izmir following their invasion of Asia Minor in 1919, only to lose it to the Turkish nationalist forces three years later. Allied troops occupied Istanbul between late 1918 and 1923.

Both Salonica and Izmir suffered bitterly. Salonica, its cafés and cabarets catering to a motley crew of Allied forces, lived through one 'final cosmopolitan paroxysm' until, in August 1917, a gigantic fire reduced its old city to ashes. Once the Greeks invaded, Izmir saw its ethnic diversity destroyed in a welter of nationalist hatred. Its (mostly Greek) center, too, was annihilated in an inferno upon the arrival of Mustafa Kemal's army in September 1922.[5]

The occupation of Istanbul, the first time the city had been taken by foreigners since 1453, did not spell destruction; it just brought misery and deprivation, and thousands of hard-drinking French, British, Italian, and Greek soldiers. With them came a proliferation of alcohol-purveying establishments, mainly in Galata and Pera but reaching into the city's Muslim quarters as well. In Galata, Heptalophos, an elegant tavern with an outdoor terrace, became a favored meeting point for Allied officers.[6] Numerous other bars opened to cater to common sailors and soldiers, with telling names such as Anglo-Franco Bar, Bar de la Paix, and Brasserie Britannia.[7] In 1919, a stream of Russian refugees fleeing the Bolsheviks added to this influx of cultures. Numbering anywhere between 40,000 and 200,000, these *ayılar* (or bears, as the Turks called them) left their mark in the form of dozens of Russian restaurants and drinking establishments with names such as Le Grand Cercle Moscovite, Rose Noire, Splendide, Türkuaz, Kit Kat, and Stella—the latter run by a most unlikely refugee from Red Russia, an African American named Frederick Bruce Thomas.[8] They all offered a *dîner dansant* and floor shows; served *piroshki*, meringue, and borscht; and—a first—proudly advertised that '*dames russes*' (Russian ladies) did the serving. Illuminated by electricity, these establishments featured fountains of vodka, served with hors d'oeuvres (*zakuski*), to customers ranging from high-class Turks in tuxedos to Allied military officers.[9]

By 1921, Istanbul was home to 257 restaurants, thirty-one cafés, and 471 beerhalls; of the latter, 444 were Greek-run, and only four were under 'Turkish' ownership. Of the city's 654 wholesale places licensed to sell alcohol, 528 were in the hands of Greeks, while Muslims ran only twenty-eight. Most of these were rather disreputable *meyhane*s (taverns) or *birahane*s (beerhalls), where 'black-eyed Greek and Armenian girls who had been kind to "Fritz" were now lavish in their attention to the French and British soldiers'.[10] The Allied occupation was positively received by those who stood to gain from it, namely Greeks and Armenians, who had been living under increasingly discriminatory circumstances. Indeed, many welcomed the Allied troops as liberators.[11] For Muslims, by contrast, the scenes of public drunkenness and brawling which resulted in material damage, injury, and even death were an outrage, the more so because they involved misbehavior by foreign occupying forces who mostly acted with impunity. Even though the military authorities eventually increased patrols, imposed curfews, and closed bars, the indignity of it all fueled anti-Christian resentment, nationalist ire, and the potential of communal violence among Turks.[12] Religious and secular Turks, having lost a major source of employment with the fall of the Ottoman administration, took out their resentment on the Christian population, accusing them of disloyalty and profiteering.[13] The religious establishment, led by the *şeyhülislam* Mustafa Sabri Efendi, expressed its concerns in religious-medical terms. The conservative press joined in, likening the excessive drinking of the Allied soldiers to the behavior of animals. The loudest protests came from the newspaper *Sebilürreşad*, which, frequently censured and even closed down by the Unionist government, sprang back to life following its resignation.[14]

The institutional response to the arrival of the 'wet invaders', building on the initiative of 1910, was an indigenous temperance movement—*Yeşilay* (Green Moon), originally called *Hilâl-i Ahdar Cemiyeti* (Green Crescent Society)—founded in March 1920.[15] Its leader, a physician named Mazhar Osman (1884–1951), was influenced by the Swiss psychiatrist, eugenicist, and social reformer Auguste Forel (1848–1931), a man of ascetic-Calvinist disposition and a pioneer in Europe's scientific anti-alcoholic movement.[16] The *Yeşilay* movement was part of a transnational initiative led by temperance advocates in the United States, whose leaders communicated and converged with its American counterpart, the Anti-Saloon League of America (ASLA). Thinking globally, in 1918–19 the ASLA formed an international task force. Its leadership saw Turkey, presumably a dry nation until the First World War, as an ideal field of operation for its message, and it was convinced that Muslims would welcome a total ban as prescribed by their religion. And welcome they did: even the *şeyhülislam* hailed the American initiative as an ineluctable example for Islam. Turkish articles were translated in the American press, and even the soon-to-be-deposed Sultan Mehmed VI chimed in, trying to salvage his throne by currying favor with the Americans.[17]

The Turkish prohibitionists did not just react to American overtures. They initiated partnerships; they tried to influence the American administration through the press; they cultivated contacts with Admiral Mark Bristol, the US High Commissioner in Istanbul who was sympathetic to the Turkish cause and wary of Allied designs to partition the country. Not only were Ottoman temperance advocates their own agents, they also had their own agenda. They solicited support from the United States in part because they saw it as an up-and-coming world power that might become an ally against the Europeans, who, they argued, sought to rob Turkey of its sovereignty by partitioning it among themselves.[18]

The Allied occupation and Britain's full military control over Istanbul forced the abolitionist movement to move its operations to Ankara, then a provincial town in the Anatolian interior. In April 1920, following the dissolution of the Ottoman parliament, it was in Ankara that the provisional national government gathered under the leadership of Mustafa Kemal, determined to resist foreign occupation and lay the foundation for a national Turkish state. Heated debates pitted Westernizing modernists against a wide spectrum of populist traditionalists. Ali Şükrü Bey (1884–1923), the representative from Trabzon, proposed a ban on the manufacture as well as the consumption of alcoholic drinks. The rationale he adduced was not, as might be expected, primarily Islam but included the new American Prohibition regime and, to a lesser extent, Australian anti-alcohol initiatives as well as the ban on drinking just decreed by the Bolsheviks in Russia. Şükrü Bey's argument was that, with these non-Islamic countries combating alcohol, an emerging Muslim nation should surely follow suit. His goal was threefold: to save his country's population from the scourge of alcohol; to gain the respect of some of the world's most important nations; and to enhance Turkey's standing in the Islamic world.

The vote, which was tied until the very end, was not simply a matter of 'conservative' forces versus 'progressive' ones. Its proponents based their support less on religion than on health, morality, and economic sovereignty, arguing that it was unconscionable to indulge in a product associated with Christian powers while these very same powers were waging war on the homeland and holding part of it occupied. Considerations of foregone tax revenue lost out against the powerful argument that most income from alcohol went into the pockets of domestic Armenians and Greeks. Pleas to exempt non-Muslims had to cede to the notion that the new order would benefit the health and social wellbeing of the entire nation.[19]

The *Meni Müskirat Kanunu*—the law prohibiting the production, sale, and consumption of alcohol for all inhabitants of the realm controlled by the Kemalists—was approved, by the narrowest of margins, on 28 April 1920. It took effect in early 1921, promising fines and even *shari'a*-inspired corporal punishment for offenders. The ordinance had no teeth, though, in part because there was barely a government to enforce any laws, least of all in parts of the country not yet under the control of the nationalist forces. With the disappearance and murder of Ali Şükrü Bey in March 1923— by an associate of Mustafa Kemal—the movement also lost its main advocate and thereby its momentum.[20]

The initiative did have some effect, though. In October 1923, as the foreign troops were in retreat, the anti-liquor laws adopted in Ankara came to Istanbul, throwing the city's thriving liquor business into disarray. An untold number of taverns and beerhalls were forced to close. Istanbul's Bomonti Brewery was reduced to producing carbonated soft drinks. Owners of drinking establishments either diversified or, more often, went out of business, and all manner of subterfuge flourished, including the emergence of speakeasies. The nationalist press welcomed the blow to the livelihood of those engaged in the liquor business as a victory over religious minorities.[21]

These dry conditions lasted a mere six months. In April 1924, the *Meni Müskirat Kanunu*, widely flouted and injurious to state revenue, was replaced by a law that, while ending prohibition, still forbade drinking and otherwise contained a series of regulations that included licensing and new taxes. Initially, a tax of 10 *kuruş* (piasters) per liter was levied on wine; in 1931, this was reduced to 5 *kuruş*. The results were disastrous. The new regime, imposed as most foreigners and thousands of non-Muslim nationals were leaving, proved so onerous that Istanbul's alcohol industry went into a steep systemic decline. By late 1925, only eight bars remained in the entire city. *Gazinos* remained more numerous, with 227 staying open. On 22 March 1926, the new Turkish government officially repealed the ban on public alcohol consumption and put into effect a state monopoly. By then, the Russian waitresses and entertainers had moved on, mostly to Paris, and the venues where they had performed were closed or replaced by so-called *pavyons*—from the French *pavilion*, or bar-dancings—where piano and violin playing accompanied variété shows to replace female entertainment. For the remainder of the twentieth century, no legal restrictions were imposed on drinking, at least in the big cities.[22]

Alcohol in Twentieth-Century Turkey

In keeping with Atatürk's vision, the Turkish Republic became a secular state after the French model, a society in which religion was deliberately marginalized. Mustafa Kemal's own drinking habit, which he picked up during his second year of study at the War College in Istanbul, came to symbolize this. His initial taste for beer turned into a life-long passion for raki following a visit to Büyükada, one of Istanbul's Princes' Islands. The ban adopted by the Anatolian provisional government did not prevent him from obtaining his regular supply, although he did not drink in public until 1922, when he entered newly liberated Izmir and famously ordered a glass of raki at the Kraemer Palace Hotel. Atatürk continued to imbibe until the very end of his life, at times openly displaying his habit to 'let the people see what we eat and drink'.[23] He frequented Istanbul's *gazino*s to listen to his favorite singers such as Müzeyyen Senar (1918–2015), who became known as the Diva of the Republic,[24] and conducted nightly boozing sessions with fellow policymakers until liver cirrhosis felled him in early 1938.[25]

The creation of the Turkish Republic led to a shift in priorities as well as alliances. The *Yeşil Ay*, supported by an eponymous magazine as of 1925 and reinforced by a youth movement—*İçki Aleyhtarı Gençler Cemiyeti* (Youth Against Alcohol Association), founded in 1930—continued its activities. Throughout the 1930s and 1940s, prominent, German-trained medical doctors such as Şükrü Kâmil (1870–1947), Fahrettin Kerim Gökay (1900–87), and Sadi Irmak (1904–90) wrote treatises (often inspired by eugenics) warning about the terrible consequences of drinking, the diseases, immorality, and social dysfunction caused by alcoholism.[26] Yet such voices proved no match for Kemalist regulatory permissiveness. In the late 1920s, the production of alcohol was nationalized and a state monopoly, Tekel, was established.[27]

Modern Turkey came to present a variegated landscape with respect to alcohol. Secular-minded 'Kemalist' Turks learned to drink without concern for, or deliberately in opposition to, religious strictures. Ramadan, to them, became a month of entertainment and relaxation; religious holidays gave way to national holidays, including New Year's Eve and 29 October, the day the founding of the Republic is commemorated. Alcohol also became part of popular culture; in 1932, fully 96 percent of the films shown in Istanbul included characters who drank.[28] Many drinkers justified their transgression by arguing that it is wine specifically, not alcohol overall, that is forbidden, or that drunkenness and not drinking is taboo.[29] Yet Turkey continued and continues today to be a relatively dry nation, where alcohol remains socially unintegrated outside the code of hospitality, family rituals, and the traditions of sociability, all of which are linked to tea.[30]

Of the three main alcoholic beverages in the Middle East—wine, raki, and beer—the first initially suffered a great blow in the new Turkey following the loss of its main production areas, the Balkans and the Greek islands. Its principal producers, the Greeks, had either been killed, fled during the Greco-Turkish War, or left for Greece in the ensuing population exchange, taking their skills with them. In the 1930s, government-sponsored cooperative enterprises sought to remedy this situation, but a lack of expertise initially made for low-quality wines.[31] Kavaklıdere, Doluca, Sevilen, and Tekel (now Kayra and Mey), brands that still dominate the wine market today, were all established in this period, often with the assistance of Turks who had studied in Europe.[32] The exodus of the remaining Greeks in the 1960s further diminished taste and expertise in viticulture. In recent times, winemaking has returned, with the assistance of Turks educated in the United States, Italy, or France and keen to revive old traditions. Today, wine is produced all over Turkey, from Thrace and the Aegean coast to Cappadocia in the interior of Anatolia. Yet wine still labors under its explicit Koranic interdiction, and, mainly linked to modern tourism and the nouveau riche, it now constitutes only 6 percent of total domestic alcohol consumption.[33]

Raki did not suffer the stigma of wine. The secular-minded intellectuals who had favored wine in late Ottoman times, switched to drinking raki under the Republic as more and more of them hailed from Anatolia. Raki thus quickly gained a status as indigenous, authentic, and 'patriotically accepted'. It also won out over imported fare such as cognac, either because it was cheaper or because it allowed Muslims to circumvent the Koranic prohibition on wine and its derivatives.[34] Raki, also called *aslan sütü* (lion's milk), continues to be bound up with (male) Anatolian Turkishness and Kemalist secularism.[35]

Since the 1960s, beer has overshadowed raki, and it now accounts for some 60 percent of total consumption.[36] Beer long remained associated with foreignness and superficial modernization, especially in the last years of the Ottoman Empire, when the Young Turk government began to emphasize patriotism.[37] This changed with the construction of a 'national' brewery in Ankara in 1934, at the behest of Atatürk himself, who praised beer as healthier than stronger liquor. Within three years, the plant was producing more than 340,000 liters annually. Overall consumption went up from *c.* 2,187,000 liters in 1934 to 8,346,000 liters in 1940.[38] In time, two brands—Efes and Tuborg—came to dominate the market. Efes, founded in 1969 and now part of the Anadolu Efes group, is far and away the market leader, with 83 percent of total sales in 2012. Tuborg, which opened a brewery in Izmir in 1967, is a distant second. Consumption of beer, aided by aggressive advertisement appealing to youth culture and aspirational lifestyles, went up dramatically in the 1980s and 1990s, eventually stabilizing in recent years at an annual per capita level of some twelve liters.[39]

In the Republican period, Istanbul's Grand'rue became İstiklal Caddesi (Independence Avenue), and Beyoğlu definitively took over as the center of entertainment, for the dwindling number of Christians as much as for a growing number Muslim Turks. Mid-century bohemian Istanbul counted among its habitués artists, musicians, filmmakers, and literati, men such as poet and neo-Bektashi Neyzen Tevfik (1879–1953), who led a life of heavy drinking. The American John Freely, who spent a lifetime in Istanbul after arriving in the city in 1960, speaks of 'Istanbul's alcoholic intellectuals, drunken poets', who frequented the drinking venues of the city's 'Latin Quarter', Beyoğlu. A landmark in this universe was Çiçek Pasajı (the Passage of Flowers), off İstiklal Caddesi, an L-shaped arcade that had opened in 1876 and was home to several *meyhane*s which catered to workmen, taxi drivers and merchants, who would consume hearty food along with raki and beer served in pint-size glasses known as Argentines, sitting on stools around beer barrels topped with marble slabs.[40]

However, by the midpoint of the century, cosmopolitan Beyoğlu was no longer what it used to be. As said, its decline began in the late 1920s with the departure of Istanbul's non-Muslims and following increasingly onerous state intervention. The anti-Greek riots of 1955, in which thousands of minority-owned businesses were vandalized, led to the exodus of most of the remaining Hellenes in town. The final blow came with the Cyprus Crisis of 1964, which caused another outburst of anti-Greek violence. The few remaining Greeks packed up and left Beyoğlu a ghost town.[41] The *gazinos* survived, yet the gradual 'Anatolization' of the city, caused by an influx first of provincial entrepreneurial types during the aftermath of the Second World War, and then of peasants in the 1950s and 1960s, changed their character. They became more indigenously Turkish, with folk 'arabesk' music replacing Western tunes.[42] Otherwise, the disappearance of the Christian element from Istanbul north of the Golden Horn made itself felt in the dilapidation, neglect, and loss of variety that ensued. By the late 1970s, establishments like Café Küllük on Bayezid Square and Cennet Bahçesi in Cihangir had disappeared. All the patisseries and cafés opened by Russians in the 1920s had closed their doors, too.

The military coup of 1980, which was meant to end the spiral of political violence in the country, inaugurated fundamental societal change. It cleared the way for the reappearance of Islam in Turkish politics, a modern Islam, pious yet pragmatic, ready to accommodate a neoliberal openness to the word. The protagonist of this trend and the founder of the center-right Motherland Party (*Anavatan Partisi*) that espoused it was Turgut Özal, an economist and a Naqshbandi adept who, following the coup, served first as deputy prime minister responsible for the economy, then as prime minister, and between 1989 and 1993 as president of the republic. Under the watchful eyes of the military, Islam reentered politics, resulting in the restoration of religious education, a greater role for religious broadcasting on TV, and the introduction of interest-free banking. At the same time, the country embraced neoliberalism, reducing the role of the state and offering a wide berth to private enterprise.[43] Led by an emergent Muslim business elite centered in the heartland, conservative yet consumerist, and considering material success a sign of God's favor, Turkey opened to the world.

The new political and economic climate had a paradoxical effect. On the one hand, advocates of the new religious sensibility raised concerns about the detrimental effect alcohol had on the health of the nation. Beer, previously seen as healthy, was targeted in particular. Alarmed at the dramatic rise in beer consumption and its spread to coffeehouses and sandwich shops, lawmakers, arguing that it was a gateway drug for young people, sought to reclassify beer as alcoholic. In 1984, they succeeded in doing so despite heavy resistance from the beer lobby. Faced with a precipitous drop in sales, the industry began to rebrand its product, making beer part of cultural events featuring music and other forms of entertainment. They also reconfigured its association with dark, men-only haunts to family-oriented social events.[44] The *gazinos*, which had experienced their heyday in the 1960s and 1970s, suffered as well. Most closed down and became shopping malls or parking garages. Attempts to revive them in the 1990s failed.[45]

In the same decade, as the neoliberal policies initiated by the Özal government began to bear fruit and Turkey, having spawned a new bourgeoisie, became a middle-income country, Istanbul's Beyoğlu and Cihangir districts underwent an enormous transformation. Whole neighborhoods were gentrified in an effort to restore a lost world by rehabilitating a 'cosmopolitan' Christian past and recreating a (carefully selected and mythologized) 'Levantine' Belle Époque. In the process, the *meyhanes* were transformed into restaurants which now mostly serve mediocre, overpriced food to foreign tourists. Today, İstiklal Caddesi bisects a gentrified area that reminds one of the former Grand'rue de Péra only in its nostalgically invoked multiculturalism.

Erdoğan's Turkey and Alcohol

Drinking has become an overtly political act since the Islamist government came to power in 2002. To drink in a society ruled by the Justice and Development Party (AKP) sends a message: I am secular, modern, and Westernized.[46] Conversely, abstinence stands for tradition, faith, and family values. A new terminology came into being: 'white' Turks (*Beyaz Türkler*)—Kemalist, secular, progressive, Westernized, urban—versus 'black' Turks (*Kara Türkler* or *Siyah Türkler*), Anatolian peasants, undereducated, traditional, and religious. 'White' Turks drink; 'black' Turks do not. Drinking or not drinking thus has become a symbolic battleground, pitting secular Turks who uphold the right of people to make their own lifestyle choices against their more traditional fellow citizens who believe that drinking is a sin and should be outlawed by the state. All this reflects a general debate in Turkish society about the role of religion in public life that in the late spring of 2013 erupted in violence.[47]

This trend started under the premiership of Necmettin Erbakan (1996–7), who personified the first wave of neo-Islam in Turkey. He failed to have alcohol banned in government-owned restaurants, but municipalities under the control of his Welfare Party went dry during this period. When Erbakan was ousted by the military, then still the guardian of Atatürk's secular legacy, Recep Tayyip Erdoğan picked up the baton. During his tenure as mayor of Istanbul between 1994 and 1998, alcohol was banned from all recreational facilities run by the municipality. Erdoğan has been a champion of faith-based sobriety ever since. With the electoral victory of the AKP in 2002, changes were seen at the national level. In a 2014 speech referring to those who opposed his policies, Erdoğan proclaimed: 'They say: we are artists, we are writers, we have capital, our vote is not equal with that of Ahmet or Mehmet in Kayseri' … They drink their whisky on the Bosporus … and hold the rest of the people in contempt.'[48] In his speeches, President Erdoğan is also wont to dismiss Atatürk and his successor, İsmet İnönü, as the 'two drunken founders of the nation'.

Erdoğan's government has run a vigorous crusade against drinking. In 2002, it privatized the government-run raki industry. Three years later, it launched a sustained campaign to limit the supply and consumption of alcohol. In keeping with the hygienist tone of many anti-alcohol campaigns, the tenor is paternalistic and moralistic: alcohol is a social ill that, like drugs and cigarettes, threatens 'family values'. The state appeals to patriotic values, claiming to act in the interest of protecting young people and defending the nation. Aware that alcohol cannot just be eradicated, it also presents itself as 'regulatory' rather than 'prohibitionist'.[49]

The campaign started with restrictions on advertising, prohibiting commercials that associate alcohol with youthfulness, athleticism, and social status. This forced the Efes-sponsored basketball team Efes Pilsen Spor Kulübü to change its name to Anadolu Efes Spor Kulübü.[50] At the same time, alcohol was banned from all government facilities, places of worship, construction sites, and storage facilities of hazardous material. It also became much harder to obtain and renew liquor licenses. Provincial authorities were invited to establish 'alcohol zones', akin to European red-light districts. These appropriately came to be called *kırmızı sokaklar* or *kırmızı bölgeler*, 'red streets' or 'red zones'. Many are on the edge of towns, in unattractive locations. Soon, alcohol bans were put in place in sixty-one of Turkey's eighty-one provinces.[51] A law adopted in 2011 also placed restraints on showing scenes of a sexual nature and involving the use of alcohol in films and TV series. This censorship, which, given the vagueness of the directives, tends to take the form of self-censorship, has led to the blurring of many scenes in the visual media.[52]

In September 2012, a new round kicked off with a law that banned the sale of alcohol and cigarettes 'by breaking its packaging or dividing them', making it effectively impossible to sell by the glass in restaurants.[53] Many alcohol-serving establishments closed as a result. Six months later, the *Yeşilay* society hosted a Global Alcohol Policy Symposium in Istanbul in conjunction with the World Health Organization, an event that drew over 1,200 representatives from fifty-three countries.[54] In his address to the forum, Erdoğan declared *ayran*, a salty mixture of yoghurt and water, rather than raki the national drink of Turkey. Little over one month later, the Turkish parliament, citing public health reasons, passed a bill that banned retail sales of alcohol between 10pm and 6am, halted all promotion of alcohol-related products, and forbade the sale of liquor within 100 meters of schools and houses of worship.[55]

These measures coincided with the Gezi Park protests of June 2013. The authorities sneeringly called the demonstrators foreign-inspired beer drinkers and moved against them with great brutality. Many 'raised a glass in defiance' in response, and T-shirts appeared emblazoned with the words '*Şerefine Tayyip*' ('Cheers to you, Tayyip').[56] In 2014, a new law forbade drink shops and bars to advertise alcoholic products with outside neon signs, logos, marquees, and such.[57] Three years later, the municipality of Antalya on the Mediterranean coast 'regulated' (that is, banned) drinking not just in places of worship, train stations, and bus terminals, but in all public places, shopping malls, parks, gardens, picnic areas, historical sites, and even the interior of vehicles.[58] In 2019, a raki festival that had been held annually since 2010 in the southeastern city of Adana found itself at the center of controversy and was cancelled, ostensibly for reasons of safety—to prevent terrorist from targeting large groups of attendees—but really for not being in line with 'Turkish traditions and customs'.[59] In another sign of the times, the old Bomonti factory was demolished in July 2020.[60] Finally, in April 2021, coinciding with Ramadan, the authorities declared a seventeen-day ban on the sale of alcohol in retail stores. The excuse they gave was that alcohol was a vector of COVID-19, but many suspected that in reality it was part of the ongoing anti-alcohol campaign.[61]

The AKP-ruled Turkish state has been most energetic in trying to tax alcohol out of existence. In 2002, a special consumption tax (ÖTV)—created for luxury items, gasoline, and 'harmful' products—made the tax on alcohol go up from the existing rate of 18 to 48 percent, with a further increase to a whopping 63 percent in 2009. In 2010, under heavy criticism, the government eliminated this impost on some alcoholic beverages, such as wine, only to add a lump-sum tax on each bottle. The beer tax, meanwhile, went up by almost 800 percent between 2002 and 2015. The price of raki in the same period quintupled, outpacing inflation by almost 300 percent. Since then, consumption taxes on alcohol have only increased. At the time of writing, the price of a regular bottle raki stands at 550 lira, equaling almost US$30, which means that the monthly minimum wage in Turkey would buy fifteen bottles of raki. Nearly 90 percent of that goes to the government as tax revenue.[62]

These tax hikes have put alcohol out of reach for most, causing the country's per capita consumption to drop by one-third in the last few years. The number of cafés and restaurants selling alcohol fell by 21 percent between 2005 and 2008. Total raki consumption decreased from 48.8 million liters in 2011 to 35.4 million liters in 2017.[63]

Another result of this policy is a tremendous increase in homemade alcohol, stimulated, ironically, by a law enacted in 2008 that allowed for an annual production and consumption of 350 liters of fermented spirits, wine, and beer per person. Especially retired men have in recent years turned distilling raki into a hobby.[64] In late 2017, the government cracked down on this as well by mandating that methyl alcohol, widely used in home brewing, must contain a certain amount of denatonium benzoate, an extremely bitter chemical compound that effectively makes it undrinkable. Alcohol poisoning now occasionally takes its toll as a result. The illegal production of spirits meanwhile goes well beyond private use. The Turkish police these days regularly catch large shipments of bootlegged alcohol.[65]

As said, the kind of alcohol one drinks—raki, beer, or wine—in modern Turkey marks one's class as well as one's choice of a secular versus a pious lifestyle.[66] Raki has suffered in the new millennium, and not just from the break-up of Tekel, which controlled the production and importation of alcoholic beverages until 2003, when it opened the market to hard liquor imports. The secular symbolism attached to the drink has made it a target of the AKP, while its association with virility has made the new urban youth dismiss it as stodgy, even primitive, grandfather's tipple. Total consumption consequently declined by half between 2000 and 2015, ceding first place to beer.[67]

A century of Kemalism notwithstanding, alcohol in modern Turkey remains unintegrated, with much of the country given to the assumption that drinking it is a social curse that inevitably leads to short-term drunkenness and long-term alcoholism. Many Turks are now careful not to be seen drinking in public for fear that they might be reported by AKP members, thus jeopardizing their jobs or prospective state contracts.[68] The places where alcohol is served vary widely. The greatest concentration is in zones of 'permissiveness' in large cities such as Istanbul and Izmir; on the Aegean and Mediterranean coast, particularly in the tourist hubs Kuşadası and Bodrum; and in the European part of Turkey, as well as on the southeastern Black Sea Coast, toward Georgia, with Trabzon and Artvin as its centers.[69] The country's interior is practically dry, with towns like Siirt, Bitlis, Muş, and Mardin virtually devoid of bars. Larger cities in inner Anatolia may have one to three hotels that serve alcohol, often in a separate location from the 'family section'. In smaller towns, one has to resort to a Tekel shop or grocery store with a shelf of raki and a few overpriced bottles of wine gathering dust, or find a bar typically located in side streets and without any sort of signage following the law of 2013.[70]

In the heartland, a similar furtiveness is reflected in that drinking establishments are located at the upper levels of anonymous buildings, in shady gambling halls, or outside the cities, out of view. A particular form is the *pavyon* (dance halls or discotheques), which were originally nightclubs catering to the elite, often attached to major hotels. After the 1950s they degenerated into striptease joints lining provincial roads where call girls (*konsomatris;* Fr. *consommatrices*) lured middle-class men into ordering expensive drinks.[71] All this makes drinking in Turkey's interior an often-lonely male affair that takes place in the shadows, somewhere between the public and the private sphere, yet belonging to neither. Women, it is said, as a rule do not drink, although there are urban zones where those who do enjoy a measure of anonymity.[72]

Twentieth-century Iran

Throughout the first half of the twentieth century, there were holdouts of traditional drinking in Iran. In the 1910s, the chiefs of the Bakhtiyari tribes living in the Zagros Mountains are said to have become 'excessively fond of wine since they contracted the habit of going so often to the capital', as a result of which 'each of their fortresses contained a store of Russian wine'.[73] In 1916, F. Hale, the manager of the Anglo-Persian Bank in Birjand, was treated to whisky and sodas by Hisam al-Dawla, the amir of this remote town in the eastern desert.[74] G. E. Hubbart, a British official employed by the Commission that in 1913–14 drew the borders between Iran and the Ottoman Empire, tells an amusing story about a 'wealthy and influential' merchant in Muhammara (modern Khorramshahr on the Shatt al-'Arab, the waterway that separates Iran from Iraq) who had 'acquired from his English friends such as taste for whiskey that he [found] it hard to get through the morning without his "tot"'. During a gathering following a funeral, the merchant, like everyone else, had brought a little teapot. Unlike the others, whose teapots were filled with water to moisten their lips after chanting verses from the Koran, he brought his filled with whisky. When the odor betrayed him, the mullah in attendance severely rebuked the merchant in front of the assembly. Unfazed, he asked a respectable fellow merchant to taste the liquid. The latter did and, barely able to conceal the 'agony of his burnt gullet', declared it to be water, at which point the merchant got up and walked out indignantly, hugging his teapot while decrying 'such infamous slanderers'.[75]

Such holdouts coexisted with the gradual onset of changing attitudes, as noted in Chapter 7, in the form of incipient concerns among physicians and publicists about the physical and mental harm alcohol causes. Yet nonreligious regulation was slow in coming. The Constitutional Revolution of 1905–9, otherwise an important moment in the collective awareness of modern Iran, did not result in a comprehensive policy vis-à-vis alcohol beyond some desultory attempts at state intervention. In 1909, the Armenian chief of Police in Tehran, Yefrem Khan, introduced an excise tax on the sale of alcohol as well as directives licensing the right to operate distilleries and granting permits only to cabarets run by non-Muslims and foreign nationals. These measures drove some alcohol manufacturing underground but otherwise just encouraged bribery and subterfuge. Proposals were also made to concentrate alcohol in one particular location and to double its price through taxation, but a weak state and the strength of vested interests prevented any of these from being put into practice.[76] The aftermath of the Constitutional Revolution also saw some clerical concerns and popular petitioning against public prostitution and related vices in Tehran, including the use of alcohol, all of it tinged with growing concerns about public health and hygiene.[77] And during the First World War, the authorities of Rasht in Russia-dominated Gilan sought to shutter taverns and gambling halls.[78]

That last measure is likely to have been directed at the many non-Muslims living in the north at the time. The Russian diplomat Ivan Yakovlevich Korostovetz, who served in Iran in 1914–15, notes in his memoirs that he had had rarely seen an inebriated Iranian other than Armenians, Georgians, and Russians. Muslim Iranians remained a most sober people, 'except for those who had become acquainted with Western ways while visiting Europe and who now consumed 'Shiraz wine, arrack, and brandy in the privacy of their homes'.[79]

Iran, in sum, remained a largely traditional society until a mid-level military officer in the nation's Cossack Brigade named Riza Khan staged a coup and seized power in 1921. Four years later, he ended Qajar rule and had himself crowned shah, becoming Riza Shah. An ardent nationalist determined to regulate society by bringing order and strength to his country, he set out to modernize Iran through social discipline. In 1921, barely in power, the new government sought to tackle alcohol through traditional, religiously inspired prohibition. Among its first proclamations was a ban on imports, then, a few days later, on overall consumption. Liquor (along with opium) was outlawed and alcohol-purveying shops were forced to close. Presumably inspired by Prime Minister Sayyid Ziya Tabataba'i, Riza Shah's fellow conspirator, the measure was designed in part to enhance Iran's religious profile, thus forestalling Bolshevik influence, as well as to keep Iran's Cossack Brigade away from alcohol.[80] Sayyid Ziya made sure that at receptions for foreign diplomats only fruit juice and *dugh* (a sour yoghurt drink) were served. One session of the parliament thus became known as the *dugh* session.[81] However, the ban was short-lived. Upon Tabataba'i's forced resignation in May 1921, liquor stores were allowed to resume operation.[82] Within a year, the import ban had been 'considerably diluted', largely for reasons of revenue, as the British resident in Tehran put it.[83]

Riza Shah had much in common with Atatürk, whom he admired for his modernizing drive, but differed from the Turkish ruler in that his secularism was instinctive rather than ideological. Riza Shah had his own winemaker but was not known to imbibe—rumor had it that he was given to opium—and he certainly did not follow his Turkish neighbor in consciously bringing alcohol out from the shadows.[84] Subsequent restrictions on drinking such as were undertaken after 1921 reflected nationalist zeal and a quest for self-sufficiency rather than religious concerns. In December 1922, a ministerial decree mandated that those joining the (newly constituted) army be free from opium and alcohol dependence.[85] In 1924, all distilleries in Tehran were concentrated in five locations outside the city.[86] Late 1926 saw the proclamation of a new ban on the importation of luxury items, including alcoholic beverages.[87] In 1926–7, tariffs on alcohol reached 100 percent, putting it beyond the means of most people.[88]

The result of these measures was a steep decline in liquor imports, which dropped from 5,603,000 *qirān*s in 1925–6 to

3,949,000 *qirāns* in 1926–7.[89] Yet none of this led to a decrease in the level of alcohol consumption as such; indeed, all indications are that it went up, evidently riding on an increase in relatively cheap, domestically produced alcohol. After falling precipitously from *c.* 5,000 hectoliters in 1920 to some 1,300 in 1921, consumption as recorded by way of tax figures shot up to almost 2,000 hectoliters in 1922 and 1923, and then back to nearly 5,000 hectoliters the following year, to reach *c.* 5,500 hectoliters in 1929.[90]

As always, most of this was consumed indoors. Friedrich Rosen, a German diplomat stationed in Iran in the early twentieth century, described entertainment among the well-to-do as follows: 'The guests would be received in the state rooms of men's apartments, and treated to a variety of salted and roasted seeds, nuts, pistachios, almonds, etc., and small glasses of very fine tea and arak.' Echoing many earlier observers of life in Iran, Rosen also commented on the propensity among those Iranians who drank to do so generally 'with the idea of getting totally intoxicated', since the 'sin ... is anyhow committed, therefore it is advisable to make the best of it'.[91]

The medicalization of alcohol, apparent in Ottoman lands much earlier, came to Iran as well in this period. Western-educated Iranian doctors wrote theses that pointed out the dangers of alcohol and referred to anti-alcohol campaigns in Western countries, including the United States, which at the time was in the throes of Prohibition.[92] An example is Dr. Sa'id Malik (Luqman al-Mulk) from Tabriz. Educated at the Luqmaniyya School in that city, he subsequently studied medicine in Paris, where he wrote a dissertation titled 'Eye disease resulting from alcohol and tobacco use'. He would go on to become a lecturer at Iran's earliest institute of higher learning, the Dār al-Funun in Tehran, and eventually served as minister of health. Another physician, 'Ali Akbar Jalali, in 1945 submitted a dissertation on the human nervous system to the Medical Faculty of the University of Tehran, which reflects the changed attitude toward alcohol. He acknowledged that alcohol was not as much of a problem in Iranian society as opium. He nevertheless warned that, in recent years, alcohol consumption had spread. Whereas previously religion and the force of shame had forced people to drink in hidden places, he intoned, they now consumed it openly and brazenly. Drawing on the latest, mostly French, research, Jalali argued that alcohol produces all kinds of ailments, some of which are hereditary, affecting the brain and prematurely bringing about old age, and are responsible for criminal behavior. His recommendations for remedies for the creeping onslaught of alcoholism ranged from restrictions on the sale of alcohol to the closing of wine shops.[93]

The burgeoning women's press of the time was part of this new discourse as well. The March–April 1928 issue of *Payk-i Sa'ādat-i Nisvān* ('The Messenger of Female Happiness'), a women's journal published in Rasht, opened with an article titled 'War has to be waged against opium'. The piece clearly reflects a prevailing concern about opium addiction being the greater scourge on society, which the author called a 'national disease'. Yet it also warned about alcoholism, claiming that the pressures of modern life could easily lead both rich and the poor alike down the path of opium or alcohol. The difference, the author insists, is that the well-off tend to consume good-quality alcohol, whereas people without means drink stuff of low quality, often on an empty stomach, and suffer greater harm for it.[94] The *Sālnāma-yi Pārs* of 1935 warned that despite its many medicinal applications, alcohol was a poisonous substance, adding that it would be erroneous to consider arak and other hard liquor harmful while seeing wine somehow as an exception.[95]

Iran Under Muhammad Riza Pahlavi (1941–79)

By the time Riza Shah was forced to abdicate in 1941, Tehran's Lalehzar Street had opened. Originating as a garden, the Bagh-i Lalehzar, this famous street had been laid out in the 1870s at the orders of Nasir al-Din Shah after his return from his first European trip. In the early Riza Shah period, and especially after the installation of electricity, Lalehzar Street developed into the entertainment district of the capital, a symbol of modernity filled with fancy shops, cinemas, theaters, cabarets, and European-style restaurants. During the Second World War, when Iran was occupied by Russian, British, and American armed forces, soldiers from the latter two countries frequented the street, as did the many Polish refugees who spent the war years in Iran. Throughout the Pahlavi period, poets and proletarians, bazaar merchants, and intellectuals mixed and mingled in the district, which at the time was located on the faultline between traditional and modern Tehran. *Mutribs* (traditional singers) would perform there, and drinking arak was part of the entertainment provided. By the 1970s, the once-elegant street was in decline, though, its family-friendly restaurants giving way to popular cabarets and seedy bars mainly frequented by men looking for cheap entertainment and booze.[96]

Arak was also the mainstay of the bars that sprang up elsewhere in Tehran at the time, no longer the 'dark and dank wine cellars run by Jews in the old days', but still rather inhospitable other than to (lonely) men.[97] Iran's bars, known as *piyāla-furushi* (lit. sale of drinking glasses), had come into being in the late Qajar period. Substituting for the traditional 'speakeasies', the *kharābāts*, and *maykhānas*, it would become more common in the reign of Muhammad Riza Pahlavi, first in Tehran and later in provincial cities.[98] Those who wished to purchase alcohol for home consumption could also turn to the dimly lit, rather unwelcoming liquor stores that were to be found throughout the city in the 1970s. The modern international hotels that opened in the 1960s invariably had their own bars, catering to foreigners as well as to Westernized Iranians keen to flaunt their modern lifestyle by swilling gin and tonics, and whisky.

Vodka especially was prevalent among Tehran's upper classes, served in iced decanters and with bowls of caviar beside splashing fountains under weeping willow trees in walled garden cafés, as Kennett Love, *New York Times* correspondent in Iran in the early 1950s, put it.[99] In later years, it came to be seen as a traditional, somewhat old-fashioned drink, still associated—like raki in Turkey—with an expressly anticlerical 'secular' mindset and lifestyle. The sons of the vodka drinkers, who aspired to a modern lifestyle and were indifferent to religion rather than keen to fight it, gravitated either to wine if they were Francophiles, or to whisky if they belonged to the growing number of people enamored of Anglo-Saxon ways.

Beer drinking, too, gained in popularity at the time, with domestic brands such as Shams and Majidiyya finding a ready clientele.[100] Shams, introduced in *c.* 1949, was produced at an Armenian-owned brewery located in Majidiyya, in northeastern

Tehran. A distillery called Vodka 55, located in Qazvin, produced what was popularly known as '*araq sagi*', or 'doggy araq', not because of the infidel image of the dog in Islam, but on account of its logo.[101] All in all, 8,000 people were directly employed in the business by the early 1950s, and thousands more gained their livelihood from manufacturing, distributing, and selling alcohol.[102] By the early 1960s, twenty factories in Iran produced alcoholic drinks, with 382 workers putting out 7.92 million bottles of vodka and arak, 96,256 bottles of cognac, and 462,630 bottles of wine. There were also four beer breweries with 183 workers who produced 7.68 million bottles of beer.[103] In later editions of the *Iran Almanac*, the source of this information, there are no more references to the production of alcoholic beverages, perhaps in deference to religious pressure not to publicize national alcohol consumption. If so, this was a harbinger of things to come.

The association of drinking with modernity did not remain confined to the capital. In the 1970s, Hashtgerd, a town located some 70km west of Tehran, just beyond Karaj and inhabited by an ancient Armenian community, was known for its open-air wine gardens distantly reminiscent of the Heurige, restaurants-cum-winehouses on the outskirts of Vienna.[104] In Tabriz, too, consuming alcohol was seen as modern, a rebuke to traditional religion and its superstitions. The city's (few) Armenian-run taverns in the 1960s were gathering places for leftist intellectuals and teachers, who would bring their students to teach them how to drink beer. One of the local watering holes at the time was even run by two immigrant women from the Caucasus who had originally come to Tabriz with the Soviet army during the Second World War. *Maykhāna-yi Nanu* (Nanu's Winehouse), named after one of the owners, was the hangout of bazaaris, whose religious beliefs did not prevent them from getting drunk on '*araq sagi*.[105] Cities farther in the interior, meanwhile, would have at least one liquor store, with the ones located in the eastern half of the country typically run by men from the Indian Subcontinent.

Alcohol, openly consumed in an urban setting, thus became part of Iran's modern scene, even if, overall, the country continued to be a 'most sober nation,' where for the most part people lived and died without ever tasting alcohol.[106] Strangely enough, alcohol

257

hardly figures in modern Iranian fiction. In post-Second World War cinema, by contrast, it is ubiquitous. Particularly in the so-called *film-fārsi* genre, which refers to movies made in the three decades preceding the revolution, the swaggering tough-guy protagonists typically spend ample time swilling arak in a *maykhāna* or cabaret.[107] Muhammad Riza Shah put few obstacles in the way of alcohol. Like his father, he had little patience for what he called reactionaries in black, the Shiʻi clergy, but he also saw them as indispensable allies against communism.[108] In deference to religious sensibilities, in 1948 the sale of alcohol was forbidden in the shrine cities of Qom and Mashhad.[109] The other exception occurred in early 1953, at the height of Mohammad Mossadegh's tenure as prime minister, whose fragile National Front coalition was heavily dependent on religious forces led by firebrand cleric Ayatollah Kashani. On 8 February, Kashani's parliamentary faction sponsored a bill banning the manufacture, sale, and use of alcoholic beverages. The bill passed unanimously after only five hours of debate. Still, Iran's deteriorating economy, suffering under a British embargo, made for a compelling argument against the measure. There was also some concern about economic relations with the vodka-exporting Soviet Union. In a compromise, it was decided that the bill would not take effect until six months later.[110] When the six months were up, the economy had only gotten worse, and so on 11 August 1953 the law was postponed by another year. Eight days later, Mossadegh was toppled in a British- and American-sponsored coup, and any further anti-alcohol action was deferred for another quarter of a century.[111]

The shah himself personified a preference for Western ways yet favored Persian food and hardly drank. During state dinners he did little more than bring the wine glass to his lips. A glass of whisky or wine was all he might consume after dinner.[112] Yet his entire persona oozed disdain for what he saw as the obscurantism of traditional religion. This came out most vividly during the celebrations of 2,500 years of Persian kingship held at Persepolis in 1971, where the main dinner included sixty-year-old champagne, fine French wines, and vintage cognac.[113] This bash, intended as a coming-out party for the shah and his country as being modern and fully developed, also spawned a domestic wine industry that was supposed to represent 'modern' Iran by conforming to international standards. In its aftermath, two wines, Château Sardasht and Château Riza'iyya, were launched, both from Azerbaijan and of better quality than the customary sweet fare.[114] Jimmy Carter's New Year's champagne toast in Tehran on 31 December 1977, in which the American President expressed admiration for the shah and his leadership and called Iran an 'island of stability in one of the more troubled areas of the world', shortly before the Iranian Revolution was about to erupt, was unmistakably symbolic in retrospect.

The Islamic Revolution and the Islamic Republic

This situation—in which alcohol was publicly available yet not common, its consumption limited, as before, to the upper classes and the haute bourgeoisie—remained in place until the end of Pahlavi rule in 1979.

Khomeini, the charismatic religious leader who brought the revolution to its successful conclusion, naturally was averse to alcohol. His insistence that there were more wine bars than bookstores in Iran was manifestly untrue, but his *bon mot* did suggest the role debauchery played in his thinking.[115] Yet not many in the non-Persian-speaking world know that the Ayatollah, apart from being the father of the Iranian Revolution, was a poet—and a mystically inclined one at that. His mystical interpretation of Islam was hardly reflected in his Machiavellian political practice, but it appears in some of his political declarations and is on full display in his poetry, where he shows himself an adept of Hafez by reflecting his disdain for formalistic and formulaic Islam as well as the hypocrisy of its narrow-minded clergy. Khomeini shuns the 'seminary and the mosque' they represent, and instead becomes a 'son of the tavern', who seeks the company of those who stand for true Islam, the antinomian *qalandars*:

> Open the door of the wine-house to me day and night
> For I have enough of the mosque and the school.
> I have worn out the cloth of asceticism and of hypocrisy
> and now I wear a mystic apparel given by the old guide of the
> wine-house.

And:

259

O *qalandars*, make of the wine-house a Paradise
[for] we converse with the Paradise bird who is drunk with wine …
Cupbearer! Pour rose-colored wine in my cup:
this jar full of wine is the reason for our honor.

And:

Cupbearer! Open the door of the tavern to me
Destroy my desires for study, discussion, asceticism and hypocrisy.[116]

Among modern Iranians, always ready to poke fun at their clerics, the joke runs that Khomeini's name consist of three ingredients of profane delight: Khom-mey-ney—*khom* (barrel); *mey* (wine); *ney* (reed/flute).

None of this made headlines during the Revolution, which offered a foretaste of what was to come with respect to alcohol. On 9 August 1978, coinciding with Ramadan, a mob attacked the famous Shah Abbas Hotel in Isfahan, and two days later the cinemas and liquor stores lining the city's Chahar Bagh Avenue were torched.[117] Tehran's liquor stores, too, were ransacked and burned. Followers of Khomeini torched the Moulin Rouge Cabaret on Lalehzar Street.[118] The Vodka 55 distillery was destroyed on 30 December. One month later, a crowd stormed the Majdiyya brewery and set it ablaze.[119] Ekkehard Zitzman, whom we encountered in the previous chapter as the last brewer in the Arabian Peninsula, temporarily managed to protect his Tehran brewery from a similar mob by covering the windows of his Volkswagen van with brown paper to disguise its contents. But after six months, a turbaned mullah materialized at the gate and told him that the brewing had to stop.[120]

The Islamic government which took over a short while later moved against alcohol not, as its Turkish counterpart did, by stealth but in full combat mode. Shortly after the triumph of the revolution and the installation of the Islamic Republic in February 1979, Muslims were banned from selling as well as consuming alcohol. (Armenian and Assyrian Christians remained exempted from the ban and are allowed to produce their own alcohol.) Soon there were reports about violators being flogged.[121] On 21 May, the importation of alcohol was halted. Less than a week later, the staff of the Iranian embassy in Washington, DC emptied the contents of the 4,000 bottles of wine and liquor held in the cellar.[122] On 12 November of the same year, Iran's Revolutionary Guards took over the Intercontinental Hotel in downtown Tehran. In a symbolic gesture, they brought up high-quality European wines, including fine champagne, from the cellars and poured these along with 250,000 cans of beer out into the gutter behind the hotel.[123] In 1982, Koranic punishment as set forth in the *hudud* and *qisās* laws was implemented for those caught drinking: eighty lashes for violators and death for repeat offenders. A three-month prison term for those found to be imbibing in public places was added the following year.[124]

Unsurprisingly, this entire process was riddled with hypocrisy. Nothing was more galling to Tehran's denizens than the ban on alcohol, their exasperation compounded by the fact that the bootlegging operations that quickly sprang up were often run by the very same neighborhood vigilante cadres (*Komitehs*) that took it upon themselves to eradicate alcohol. These were known to operate with two successive roadblocks, one selling eager motorists illicit liquor and the other pulling them over, confiscating the same liquor and giving them lashes.[125]

Outwardly, Iran has been a model Muslim country for over four decades now. Yet it is also a thoroughly secularized society— arguably at least as much as neighboring Turkey. The revolution notwithstanding, the dynamic of the shah's modernization has continued apace, resulting in a highly literate, predominantly young society fully connected to the global 'economy of desire'. The government, partly unwilling and partly unable to stem the flow of information, has reacted to this with continued rhetoric mixed in with clear-eyed pragmatism. The populace tends to react with cynicism while taking full advantage of the second stance to indulge their consumerist appetites.[126]

Since 1979, Iranians once again had to turn to the privacy of their homes to quench their thirst. Factories producing alcoholic drinks were shuttered, as were liquor stores; the popular vodka brand 'Quchan'—referring to the bibulous, partly Kurdish town in Khorasan mentioned in Chapter 7—disappeared from shelves, and those determined to keep their drinking going were relegated to their own kitchens and bathtubs. As a result, home production got

underway on an enormous scale. Raisins, which pre-revolution had
been an export product, became a scarce article, transforming much
of the country's grape cultivation into the cultivation of raisins.[127]

'Privacy', meanwhile, remains a flexible concept. The upper-
middle classes now hold lavish and expensive alcohol-fueled weddings
in well-appointed party halls, dozens of which have sprung up in the
desert south of Tehran, out of sight on rural roads. The authorities,
seemingly resigned to Iranians' irrepressible urge to party, collude
for the most part, with security forces checking in to collect bribes
and not much else.[128] All this is reminiscent of Prohibition in the
United States of the 1920s, even with regards to the 'alcohol that
got away'—medicinal alcohol—which in Prohibition-era America
continued to be sold by the 15,000 pharmacists who had applied for
a permit to sell.[129] Similarly, in Iran, pharmacies lining the road to
ski resorts north of Tehran at one point reportedly festooned their
facades with banners advertising 'medicinal' alcohol (*alkul-i tibbi*),
for passersby.[130] According to a report issued in 2011 by the official
Iranian news agency *Mehr News*, some 80 million liters of alcohol are
currently bootlegged in the country each year.[131]

The harm—including casualties—done by illegal alcohol
consumption, and especially that of industrial alcohol, is
considerable, and has led to the arrest of bootleggers and alarming
articles about addiction in the press.[132] In the period of March
2016–March 2017, reportedly 153 people succumbed to poisoned
alcohol.[133] In the autumn of 2018, at least forty-two people died,
more than a dozen lost their eyesight, and 100 ended up in the
hospital from drinking methanol alcohol. In March 2020, between
300 and 500 Iranians were killed, and thousands were injured
from consuming bootleg alcohol following a rumor that it would
be an antidote to the coronavirus.[134] The reason for this surge in
fatalities may have been the collapse of the Iranian currency (the
riyāl) and the resulting spike in the price of illegally imported
alcohol, prompting an increase in homemade alcohol.[135] Official
statistics put the percentage of drinkers in Iran at 10 percent.[136]
According to other sources, some 5 million people drink alcohol,
with each person above the age of fifteen consuming one liter of
pure alcohol annually.[137]

How little some things have changed is suggested by the words of a cleric who, in 2011, excoriated the rampant alcohol consumption in his country: 'Not even the Westerners drink alcohol like we do. They pour a neat glass of wine and sip it. We here pour a four-liter barrel of vodka on the floor and drink it until we go blind ... We are all the masters of excess and wastage.'[138]

Punishment is meted out to those whose drinking is too flagrant to be ignored, or who engage in repeat recidivism. In July 2020, for instance, a man with a prior criminal record, including repeated alcohol consumption and driving under the influence, was executed in Mashhad for having consumed alcohol in prison.[139]

Meanwhile, alongside condemnation, lamentation and, occasionally, draconic punishment, the state has adopted harm reduction as a more effective approach. In the 2000s, a committee headed by the Minister of the Interior was set up to prevent and combat the use of alcohol. In the last few years, dozens of private alcohol clinics have opened as well, with state approval. The government, meanwhile, has given its blessing to the creation of a Western-style network of Alcohol Anonymous groups.[140] The creation of an office for alcohol misuse in 2013, and the fact that in 2014 the first Iranian Congress of Alcohol Abuse was held in Tehran, suggests a deliberate approach that combines deterrence with prevention through harm reduction, as is true of the government's stance on the use of opiates.[141]

Pakistan

Pakistan, outwardly a country under strict Islamic law, used to be different. The British traveler-adventurer Richard Burton, reporting from Sind in the mid-nineteenth century, claimed a 'particular prevalence of intoxication' in the region. This mostly concerned the use of hemp products (*bang*), but alcohol was around as well. According to Burton, 'From the highest to the lowest order of the people, the fair sex included, only the really religious can withstand the attraction of a glass of cognac'. He further claimed that when they felt like carousing, people would first drink *bang* and then proceed to spirits, always in that order for maximum effect. The poorer classes, he continued, were 'compelled to drink the pichak or dregs of the different alcohols and wines'. He also mentions several indigenous, low-quality wines such as *anguri*, made with Sind grapes in Hyderabad, Shwan, and Shikarpur; *soufi*, 'extracted from aniseed with Gur brandy and considered a superior kind of drink'; *mushki*, 'perfumed with musk and other perfumes'; *turanji*, 'extracted from citrus peel'; and *misri*, 'made with sugar candy and perfumed'.[142]

Burton notwithstanding, in the rural parts of what would become Pakistan in 1947, drinking among Muslims was uncommon. If the poorer classes consumed alcohol, it was *gur*, a 'fiery spirit, preferred by the natives to all other liquors except brandy'.[143] The real drinking took place in the cities, especially in Lahore and Karachi. Lahore had its entertainment district, Hira Mandi (originally called Shahi Mohallah), near the Badshahi Mosque, long associated with prostitution and famous for its *nauch*, or dancing girls.[144] Elsewhere, drinking was mostly a colonial affair. In Lahore itself there were the modern hotels along the Mall, such as the Elphinstone and the Stiffles.[145] The Murree Brewery Company—founded near Murree, a town in the western Himalayas—mainly served British officers.[146] And until well after 1947, Karachi, to the extent that it was 'modern', was very much a colonial British city. The hotels built there in the late nineteenth century—the Palace Hotel, the Beach Luxury, and, later, the Intercontinental, or, for jazz, the Marina Hotel—uniquely served foreigners and the local well-to-do, as did a variety of bars with well-stocked cellars, cabaret performances, and music ensembles.[147]

Pakistan, the 'land of the pure', had a fraught identity from the moment it came into being in 1947: it was meant to be at once a Muslim haven and a place where all religions would be tolerated and respected. In 1956, it officially became the first Islamic Republic in the world. Yet until the 1970s, drinking in Pakistan, whether in traditional form, as described by Burton, or in 'modern' ways (the legacy of the British) was not really an issue. Indeed, the founder of the nation, Muhammad Ali Jinnah, might serve as a poster boy for the wetness of the elite. A scion of an Isma'ili (Sevener Shi'i) Khoja family who later converted to Twelver Shi'ism, the British-educated

ALCOHOL IN THE MODERN AGE

Jinnah incarnated the colonial Anglophile dandy who drank Scottish whisky and ate pork sausages.[148]

Subsequent rulers were even more given to the bottle. General Ayyub Khan, president from 1958 to 1969, was a 'notorious drinker and womanizer'.[149] The country's next ruler, Yahya Khan (in office 1969–71), was a clean-living officer of impeccable integrity until he came to power in 1969, at which point he became a debauched drunk with a 'lust for female flesh'. During the 1971 war with India that led to the partition of Pakistan from Bangladesh, he is said to have consumed at least a bottle and a half of Black Dog whisky a day, and on the day of Pakistan's surrender in Dacca he was so drunk that he had to be dragged out of his bedroom to make the announcement, which as a result had to be postponed.[150] Zulfikar Ali Bhutto (in office 1971–7), another avowedly secular ruler, famously proclaimed, 'Yes, I do drink alcohol, but at least I don't drink the blood of the poor'.[151]

Karachi, the country's largest city and its major port, was a cosmopolitan melting pot for three decades after independence. With an ethnically and religiously diverse population ranging from a Westernized elite to a large proletariat, its downtown Saddar district was filled with bars, billiard rooms, nightclubs, and brothels. The city long coasted on its traditional decadent colonial past, enriched by an influx of mostly left-leaning Mohajers, Muslim migrants from India. In the 1970s, the city boasted 119 cinemas and numerous cabarets, six of which featured striptease acts.[152] As late as 1978, the Saddar district teemed with discotheques, billiard rooms, dance schools, and bookshops; new bars and clubs catering to the middle and lower-middle classes sprang up in the district, and on Tariq Road the film industry thrived. Even an Urdu version of *Playboy*— *Ishtraq*, Pakistan's first and only adult magazine—appeared on the newsstands of major cities in January 1976.[153]

The Indian subcontinent's traditional shrine culture remained alive as well, to the point where in the 1960s and 1970s shrines enjoyed greater popularity than mosques. The transgressive notion of intoxication symbolizing one's love for and by the Almighty that was linked to this culture received a boost as young people gravitated to *qawwali* music, a blend of traditional Persian Sufi music and the singing traditions of the subcontinent. A commercialized version of the *qawwali* chant, meanwhile, became popular among the urban middle and lower-middle classes.[154]

A breakthrough moment for the *qawwali* business came in 1972 when Aziz Mian (Meeruthi), a gifted singer with a degree in Urdu literature, wrote a *qawwali* titled *Mein sharabi* ('I am a drunkard'). Performing in a hypnotic, rapturous chant alternating with sonorous monologues, Aziz Mian did not employ wine in his songs as just a metaphor for divine love, but openly praised alcohol and other intoxicants on their own terms. His performances often degenerated into drunken brawls. Benefiting from a burgeoning state-supported film industry, Aziz Mian eventually turned and expanded *Mein sharabi* into an album, *Teri soorat* ('Your face' / 'Mein sharabi'), which within months went on to sell over a million copies. In early 1976, Bhutto invited Aziz Mian to perform for him in Islamabad and share a drink.[155]

Underneath it all, change was inexorable. In keeping with a recognizable pattern across the developing world, Pakistan's urban centers in the 1960s and 1970s saw a great influx of rural folk drawn by a pressing demand for unskilled and semi-skilled labor. This wave transformed the cities, ruralizing them and redrawing their divisions along new lines: left-right, rural-urban. Religious rifts especially came out in the open; many of the new arrivals were drawn to a puritanical Islam whipped up by the mullahs, who decried the debauchery of the city and its godless elites. Alcohol and gambling were lightning rods for this rhetoric. The first riots and attacks against bars and nightclubs took place in 1968, under Ayyub Khan.[156]

Nadeem Farooq Paracha, a journalist working for *Dawn*, Pakistan's main English-language newspaper, in a passionate memoir, documents his country's transformation from the freewheeling days of Jinnah and Ayyub Khan's liberal and secular dictatorship to the existential despair that set in with Zia-ul-Haq. Paracha recalls that, when he grew up in the 1970s, only the elderly prayed five times a day in his family, and that the only mosque in the area was far less popular than the Sufi shrines. He also refers to the dramatic changes in the wake of working and middle-class folk going to Saudi Arabia and the Emirates to work in 'those strange, spiritually dry, but rich lands of the limousine-driving Bedouins', and how the undreamt-of amounts of money they earned plus the sudden rise in status back home that came with it helped them 'give up their old version of the faith and take up what their Arab paymasters insisted was true Islam'. Paracha's female cousins, he recalls, suddenly adopted the burqa and became 'invisible' to him.[157]

The country's hybrid identity underwent a full-blown identity crisis in the face of economic failure and military defeat, especially vis-à-vis its archenemy India. From the 1960s onward, the Jama'at Islami, the party founded by Abu'l-A'la Mawdudi, Pakistan's leading advocate for strict Islamic rule, blamed the country's decline on the nefarious effects of 'wine and women'.[158] The 1962 constitution enacted under Ayyub Khan had already given Islam a far greater role in social and political affairs, tilting the balance between religion and state in favor of religion.[159] The civil war of 1971—leading to defeat and the loss of East Pakistan, which became Bangladesh—turned the crisis into an existential one. Just as their defeat by the Israelis in 1967 had led to soul-searching among the Arabs, making them turn to Islam as solace-cum-remedy for their plight, so did Pakistani Islamism gain momentum in the wake of the break-up of the country.

Inheriting a country impoverished by a ruinously secessionist war, Bhutto began to court the Saudis and their petrodollars. This generosity came at the price, though. The Saudis recruited Pakistanis to set up branches of the Muslim Brotherhood in their own country. Bhutto played a double game: he coaxed the Saudis while trying to stave off their direct interference in Pakistan. At the same time, just like Anwar Sadat in Egypt, he sought to blunt the newly assertive religious parties by mollifying them, surrendering to them the right to interpret Islam however they pleased. Fashioning himself as the 'people's leader', *Quaid-i awam*—a calque on Jinnah's title, *Quaid-i azam*, or 'great leader'—he appealed to the poor, the devotees of rural, shrine-centered traditional Islam, seeking to mobilize them for his project of restructuring state and society. By fostering shrine culture, visiting the sites under the glare of cameras, and spending money on their beautification, Bhutto used the power of popular Sunnism as a bulwark against Salafism. He thus ended up competing with the high ulama, who were inherently suspicious of folk Islam. Ultimately, the mix of quasi-socialism and populism Bhutto offered satisfied no one. It alienated small traders and shopkeepers backed by disgruntled industrialists, and the concessions he made to the Islamists only made the latter hungry for more.[160]

To appease his new constituents, Bhutto stepped away from his socialist and secular policies. A new constitution, adopted in 1973, explicitly proclaimed Pakistan to be an Islamic republic and made further concessions to the country's religious lobby. The following year, alcohol was banned from army mess halls. Bhutto also organized a first Islamic summit, forging strong bonds with the countries of the Persian Gulf. While he sought to enhance his religious legitimacy, his new Arab friends were determined to wean Pakistan off socialism. When Bhutto swept the 1977 elections, the Pakistan National Alliance (PNA) reacted with protests, demanding his resignation. Crowds of Islamically charged young men rioted in Karachi's central district, breaking into liquor stores and smashing their wares. Bhutto's reaction was further appeasement. In April 1977, shortly before his fall and accused of being a womanizing sot who was desperate to hold on to power, he met with representatives of the religious parties and consented to make Friday instead of Sunday the day of rest. He half-heartedly also agreed to close casinos, nightclubs, and horseracing tracks as well as to ban the sale and consumption of alcoholic drinks.[161]

Bhutto never meant it; his successor, Zia-ul-Haq, a man of a radically different disposition, did. Zia-ul-Haq, who came to power by staging a coup that deposed Bhutto in the summer of 1977, yoked nationalism to Islam in unprecedented ways. Supported by Pakistan's Westernized elite, who detested Bhutto's quasi-socialist populism, he propagated an anti-communist, anti-Zionist, anti-Shi'a, and anti-secular agenda paired with a pro-business attitude not unlike what would be pursued later on by President Erdoğan in Turkey. Saudi generosity continued unabated and, in fact, intensified in the 1980s, looking to counter both the communist threat that had become acute with the Soviet invasion of Afghanistan and the specter of Iran's revolutionary Shi'ism spreading east. During Ramadan (August) 1978, the rules of fasting were strictly enforced in public. In February 1979, as the revolutionary forces in neighboring Iran claimed victory, Zia-ul-Haq announced a *nizam-i Islam* (Islamic order) for Pakistan. A ban on alcohol consumption was inserted into the country's penal code. Anyone found intoxicated exposed himself to Islamic punishment, including flogging, and those wishing to drink were now required to present credentials demonstrating their non-Muslim status.[162] The country's bars and breweries were shuttered. The long tradition of the *nauch* girls came to an end as well, and with it the allure of Lahore's Heera Mandi quarter.[163] Aziz Mian's concerts now were routinely raided by the police, and members of the audience were arrested for 'drunken behaviour'. The grittily authentic Aziz Mian, the 'Nietzschean qawwal', responded by taunting the government, imbuing his lyrics with references to official hypocrisy. He kept performing into the 1990s, but eventually his own alcoholism got the better of him: he died in 2000 during a concert tour in, of all places, Iran.[164] The religious establishment thus became the 'custodian of public morality', and the puritanical form of Sunni Islam that took hold squeezed out culture and creativity, until 'Karachi, like the rest of Pakistan, was a cultural desert'.[165]

Drinking in Pakistan went underground following these developments, prompting the appearance of 'speakeasies', bootlegging, and moonshine, which resulted in people dying from drinking tainted whisky.[166] If Zia-ul-Haq's dictatorship took the fun out of Pakistani society, it also made it turn inward. The film industry collapsed, shopping malls replaced cinemas, and people ended up finding entertainment and relaxation at home.[167] Breweries, now officially only allowed to cater to non-Muslim citizens, disappeared, too. Pakistan's Christian, Hindu, and Parsi communities were too small to sustain domestic production. One brewery that did survive was Murree. Having modernized its Rawalpindi plant with German technology, Murree Breweries still produce an award-winning beer, as well as a variety of liquors and non-alcoholic beverages. In 2013, it circumvented its inability to export directly to neighboring India by granting a production license to a Bangalore-based entrepreneur.[168] In 2018, a Chinese company, Hui Coastal Brewery and Distillery Limited, was given a license to set up a brewery in Baluchistan Province. Its beer became popular because of its relatively high alcohol content.

Unsurprisingly, Pakistanis never stopped drinking, despite the grim cultural climate, the intimidation, the police patrols, and the threat of punishment, including the eighty lashes introduced by Zia. In fact, consumption is said to have gone up, along with corruption and black-market operations, with foreign consulates selling off their monthly allowed quota to bootleggers, and Muslims obtaining sale permits through connections and then simply running their shops in the name of their Hindu or Christian employees.[169]

Of course, the rich were hardly affected by all this. They mostly did as they pleased, organizing booze-fueled parties in the privacy of their homes and gardens. The poor, who lived in the public glare, had to be more circumspect so as not to make a nuisance of themselves and disturb the façade of sobriety.[170] As in Iran and Egypt, every neighborhood has its 'semi-official' bootlegger who delivers any type of alcohol at the door. Newspapers still carry advertisement for alcohol clinics.[171] In Karachi (as elsewhere in Sindh province), where one can buy alcoholic beverages rather easily, licensed 'wine shops' are aplenty, and bootleggers dealing in smuggled whisky, vodka, and beer brands operate freely.[172]

Indeed, the city counts some 100 wine stores tucked away in the bazaar, a number wildly out of proportion to its non-Muslim population, officially catering only to non-Muslims but effectively selling paper-wrapped booze to anyone who enters with a fake national identity card or a computerized ID number belonging to a dead soul. Whisky is especially popular because the small bottles in which it is sold make it easier to conceal than beer. The police facilitate the smooth running of the business. As in Ottoman Istanbul, they are paid off to engage in *nazar-andazi* (looking the other way), making sure not to patrol near wine shops, or indulging themselves. Everyone thus keeps up a carefully constructed façade, and a win-win situation prevails as a result.[173] As in Iran, home delivery is also an option. In today's Pakistan, 'drinks can be ordered to the door quicker than pizza', says Sadaqat Ali, who runs a chain of clinics designed to treat alcoholics. Since creating 'Willing Ways' in 1980, he has treated many of the one million Pakistanis he estimates are alcoholics, including judges, politicians, and sportsmen. 'Most aren't keen to seek treatment because drinking is still taboo,' he says. 'We need to change that'.[174]

CONCLUSION

This book has viewed alcohol through the lens of Islam and Islam through the lens of alcohol. In the process, I have tried not to homogenize or essentialize the religion, faith-cum-culture, as the sole determinant of 'Muslim' identity. There is more to people's identity than religion, even in the Islamic world. Islam's ban on *umm al-khabā'ith*—the mother of abominations—is always invoked and justified in terms of religion, so that the choice of whether to drink or not to drink automatically becomes a religious one, appealing to the 'Muslim' element in one's identity. Yet, as the foregoing pages have shown, within the Islamic world a great deal of variety has always existed, and the cliché that Muslims do not drink because their religion forbids it, and that those who do violate its tenets, is as misleading as it is simplistic. I have accordingly examined Islam as a set of practices beyond the straitjacket of 'cult of regulation, restriction and control' that it is so often pressed into, by Muslims as much as by outsiders.[1] I have tried to stay away from dichotomies that pit abstemious Muslims against drinking non-Muslims, or which posit a public-private divide, with Muslim authorities tolerating a 'contingent' private sphere in which formally proscribed behavior was allowed to exist so long as it remained indoors and did not disturb the public order. We have seen many Muslims who not only drank but did so proudly and openly, assuming personal agency by 'defying' the Islamic law and its strictures. All along I have refrained from calling those Muslims who insist that alcohol has no place in Islam

271

while they consume it themselves just 'hypocritical'. 'Hypocrisy' is ubiquitous in any society in any period in world history. Theory and practice are never aligned; they must diverge at some point if life is to be livable. Dismissing behavior as 'hypocritical' also obscures motives and motivations. I have finally surveyed this vast topic not by striving for completeness but rather by examining the history of drinking in specific Muslim-majority locales, empires in the past, and selected nation-states in the present, and I invite future scholars to address the many gaps and lacunae left unexplored here.

Alcohol viewed in this manner corroborates Bauer's and Ahmed's central idea that meaning in Islam comes into being through contradiction, opposition, and ambivalence; that supposedly secular and even objectionable behavior is part of Islam's kaleidoscopic way of manifesting itself in the world. (Defiant) drinking arguably does not render a Muslim less Muslim; in a way, it makes him more Muslim, for it reminds his co-religionists that any faith that wishes to endure will have to focus more on inner conviction than on outward compliance. At least in premodern times, the interplay between theory and practice with respect to alcohol reveals a capacious faith that embraced contradiction and ambiguity as constitutive elements, well beyond the stark dichotomy of halal versus haram, (permissible versus impermissible) based on an exclusive focus on the textual-legalism that in modern times has gained currency in many Muslim societies. All this is true with the caveat that the ambiguity and paradox inherent in Islam represent an abstract image of the faith-cum-culture, one that predominantly exists in paint and on paper. Those who fell afoul of authorities keen to apply the law on drinking and who suffered harsh treatment, including flogging and death, probably would have shown little appreciation for the idea of ambiguity and ambivalence.

This study's main conclusion is, of course, that the ban on alcohol in Islam has always been 'honored more by compliance than by transgression'.[2] Throughout history, few people in the Muslim world, especially ordinary people in rural areas, drank. Whereas European peasants and common city folk routinely consumed alcohol, especially during (religious) holidays, ordinary Muslims drank water or fruit juice, and most never tasted liquor in their lives. This is especially true for the pious middling segments of society, but it also holds for the lower classes, who tended to use other drugs, especially opium and hashish, to while away boredom, to find oblivion from miserable lives and, above all, as a form of self-medication. No matter how we define both terms, the 'Muslim world' was never a 'drinking culture'. Even today, Middle Easterners and Muslims in general continue to drink far less alcohol than people anywhere else in the world.[3]

Yet this study has also found that, while most Muslims never touched alcohol, alcohol and oenophilia are by no means absent from Islamic history and society, and that its high society and literature are drenched in alcohol. Throughout Islam's formative period, many khans, sultans, and shahs imbibed, surrounded by their boon companions and courtiers, and quite a few were raving alcoholics who drank themselves into oblivion. So ingrained was alcohol that, in Rowell's words, the question becomes less 'how to reconcile the two than how to conceive of "classical Islam" without wine'.[4] Alcohol, in other words, takes us to the heart of Islam.

The antecedents of these conditions are easy to find. Pre-Islamic Mesopotamia and late antique Iran were the lands of wine-soaked royal banquets, of alcohol-induced divination, and of prophecy inspired by intoxicating drinks. Islam spread precisely to some of the world's oldest wine-growing regions—the southern Caucasus, western Iran, and eastern Anatolia—exposing the conquering Arabs to new forms of pleasure and giving them the wealth to enjoy it.[5]

The Koranic engagement with alcohol reflects the power of these antecedents. If the Prophet was inspired by alcohol, it was by way of proscription, to be sure. But it was a reluctant, gradual proscription, at once absolute and relative, providing loopholes, the ability to engage in subterfuge, and the chance to have one's guilt absolved through repentance. Rather than flatly condemning it as a substance, the Koran approaches alcohol sequentially, referring to its various aspects, differentiating between levels of existence and circumstance without seeking to reconcile them. It relegates—elevates, sublimates—the enjoyment of wine without guilt to the hereafter. Just as the virgins of Paradise remain virgins despite unbridled sexual activity, so alcohol in paradise can be enjoyed without any negative consequences. (Tellingly, those who enter paradise are promised celestial wine but not celestial pork or the opportunity to engage in gambling.)[6] Whether or not we attribute the Koran's inconsistencies regarding wine as a reflection of the problems Muhammad had with drunkenness among his followers, Islam's holy writ ultimately condemns wine for its effect, intoxication, which interferes with the faith by impeding the exercise of its religious commands, especially prayer. Muslims have labored under this ambiguity ever since.

Small wonder, then, that drinking did not go away under Islamic proscription. Alcohol indeed figures prominently in early Islamic sources, which surely means that Muslims at the time drank a lot. Some willfully transgressed the rules, but many likely remained ignorant of the strictures of what long remained an ill-defined faith professed by people whose familiarity with its tenets was tenuous at best.[7] Regardless of motives, the abundance of references to early Muslim drinking puts paid to the ahistorical reading cherished by Muslims and often unthinkingly adopted by Westerners, according to which 'Islam', when it conquered the lands of the Middle East, overwhelmed and eliminated everything that had gone before: Zoroastrianism, Judaism, and Christianity, not to mention all manner of pagan religions. In fact, Islam became deeply enmeshed with these preexisting traditions, becoming the majority faith in most of the lands it conquered only gradually. Rather than a corpus of set injunctions, passed on as an accruing body and faithfully followed by its adherents, the Muslim faith proved to be a living organism capable of accommodating, absorbing, and assimilating many things, including pre-Islamic Persian and Greek drinking customs.

A few generalizations can be made about drinking by Muslims beyond the truism that most never did. The most obvious is that the topic is very much gendered. With some noteworthy exceptions— the Ilkhanids and, to some extent, the Indian Mughals, the Iranian Safavids, and the women of Shiraz—the (written) sources present drinking as a male affair. In the visual arts of especially the Persianate world, too, women play a significant role, albeit mainly in an idealized form. Elsewhere, it is difficult to find women other than 'loose' ones in connection with alcohol until recent times, the age of global youth culture.

Another common feature is that Muslims tended to be excessive drinkers. This is an Orientalist trope, to be sure, endlessly repeated by foreign observers. But the aggregate evidence suggests that 'Muslims' did tend to imbibe heavily for the sole purpose of quick inebriation. Such excess neatly follows an age-old perceived dichotomy between moderation and temperance (equaling self-restraint) as opposed to indulgence and incontinence as a metaphor for civilization versus barbarism. The distinction indeed is as old as Herodotus, who praised wine as a civilized drink yet dismissed the immoderate 'Scythian' way of consuming it as barbaric.[8] One does not have to invoke a lack of sophistication as an explanatory factor for this tendency. That drunkenness was often the point rather relates to the fact that alcohol in Islamic culture was not synonymous with sociability. In the steppe tradition of Central Asia, collective drinking tended to be a male bonding event. And as in the Greek symposium tradition, alcohol might enliven court sessions. But given its status as a forbidden (or at least specious) substance, alcohol in Islam could never become a ceremonial drink accompanying the rituals of birth, marriage, and death, much less a recreational drink, an accompaniment to food to enhance the convivial atmosphere of the meal, the way it did in Mediterranean and Christian-European cultures. As foreign visitors noted time and again, meals in the Islamic Middle East were typically taken in silence and rather quickly, to be rounded off with a glass of water or a yoghurt drink, with tea or coffee to follow.

A third shared characteristic concerns evasion and excuse. Like people the world over confronted with a forbidden fruit, Muslims have traditionally found myriad ways to evade Islam's strictures on alcohol and rationalize their drinking habits. Practice, it turns out, was far more improvisational than the formal proscription would lead one to assume, and there were enough casuistic loopholes for those intent on finding them to do so. The stricter the rules, the more intricate the ways around them must be. The fact that the Koran only explicitly refers to red wine (*khamr*) has always been the most readily available one, allowing one to argue that any other alcohol-containing beverage, if taken in moderation, is not strictly forbidden. Vodka, raki, and in modern times champagne and beer have widely been deemed permissible for this reason, especially in the Hanafi tradition. There was also the age-old 'medical alibi', imbibing alcohol with reference to its healing faculties. Finally, drinking in Islam, like sin in general, is not something irredeemable, but a violation for which solutions exist. The most obvious one is seeking forgiveness through repentance. Consuming alcohol manufactured by a non-Muslim, too, helps to alleviate the burden of premeditated intentionality. Traditional Islam embraced such contradictions without losing its unity.

The fourth and final form of shared behavior involves the *dhimmis*—Jews, Christians, and, in Iran, Zoroastrians—who were officially exempt from the liquor laws in the sense that they had permission to manufacture and consume their own. The rule that forbade them from selling wine to Muslims was routinely violated, allowing urban Muslims in search of alcohol who wanted to drink to patronize *maykhānas*, watering holes tucked away in side alleys in the Christian or Jewish part of town, at an appropriate distance from mosques. The role *dhimmi*s played was indispensable: they were suppliers, covertly or overtly, as well as potential scapegoats.[9]

Wine drinking, we saw, remained an integral part of court life, especially in the eastern half of the Islamic world in the so-called classical age, the period up until the thirteenth-century Mongol onslaught. In the Umayyad and Abbasid empires, wine was common at the caliphal courts and among elites. Beyond these circles, control and regulation were always uneven and variable, dependent on the ruler and his predilections, his whims and moods, and his need to prop up his standing as a good Islamic ruler, as well as prevailing political and economic conditions. Since Islam's rejectionist stance on alcohol automatically obviated reform through moderation, attempted restriction always took the form of bans and (often draconian) punishment for violators. Bans were ostensibly intended to combat and curtail religiously proscribed behavior, but as numerous examples suggest, they typically grew out of a preoccupation with the preservation of public order, the ultimate rationale of Islamic law. They also were invariably honored in the breach more than in the observation and never worked for long.

The frequency and sequential nature of anti-alcoholic decrees suggest that they were largely formulaic, episodic, and temporary,

Fig. 16: At Champigny—giving wine to Algerian troops, early 1900s.

Fig. 17: Asahi advertisement in *Baghdad Times*, 1922.

Fig. 18: Ankara Birası poster, 1930s.

Fig. 19: Drunken man in basket, Istanbul or Bursa, 1960s.

Fig. 20: Emptying bottles during the Iranian Revolution.

Fig. 21: Yeni Rakı in Çandarli, Turkey, 2013.

Fig. 22: Efes beer advertisement, Istanbul, 2013.

Fig. 23: Iranian Kurdish smugglers prepare to load cases of alcohol onto their horses before riding over the border to Iran from Iraq Sunday, 4 January 2004 near the border in Iraq.

Fig. 24: Bar Trésor, Meknes, Morocco.

Fig. 25: Homemade wine in Iran, 2019.

Fig. 26: Steamrollers crush liquor bottles on outskirts of Karachi, 2019.

Fig. 27: Grapes for homemade wine, Takestan, Iran, 2021.

Fig. 28: An Egyptian man walks past a shop that sells alcohol, Cairo, 2013.

running up against irrepressible urges as well as powerful interests. As the chroniclers all but acknowledged in their records of the recurrent bans, eradicating alcohol from society proved impossible.[10] As for interests, none was more powerful than the tax revenue that the alcohol business generated for the ever-insolvent state. Taverns hence operated until they were forced to close, after which they soon were allowed to open again, according to the adage that the law of the (Ottoman) sultan was valid for three days.[11] Punishment might be draconian, but pragmatism often prevailed. The ulama would inveigh against drinking and at times be instrumental in having it officially sanctioned, but they ultimately had to bow to a state with a secular will to power on which they depended for positions and emoluments. Self-styled custodians of the faith, they were in fact counselors, and rulers with their own interests and concerns might or might not heed their exhortations.

Consistency is hard to find in all of this. But insisting on consistency in the past mostly reflects the bias of the modern 'rational' mind, which demands it and (falsely) claims to have achieved it in the present. In the premodern East and West, in the Christian world as much as in Islamic lands, societies were infinitely less regulated and 'disciplined' than what the denizens of the modern world are used to. People, most of them illiterate, were effectively left to their own devices; regulations, to the extent that they were issued, were pious incantations, erratically enforced and often practiced in the breach with little consequence, in part because the state lacked the capacity to enforce them but, more basically, because it profited from the liquor business. As in premodern Europe, in traditional Islamic societies the sacred and the profane also commingled in easy, unremarkable, and mostly unremarked fashion—not as a self-conscious, 'knowing' approach to life in the 'postmodern' sense of the term, but as an implicitly accepted outgrowth of reality as it exists 'on the ground': messy, unruly, impossible to control, and all of it reflecting the totality of the divinely created universe.[12]

This type of capaciousness, juxtaposition and entwinement is fully on display in classical Islamic art, which abounds in bawdiness and alcoholic excess, at times to a shocking degree. It is abundantly visible in the visual arts, where drinking scenes are quite common.

No reticence or restraint can be observed in the image of Sultan Jahangir holding a wine cup or Shah 'Abbas being served wine by his *sāqi*, confirming Ahmed's contention that such scenes are not extra-Islamic, nor symbols of defiance, but, in the very contradictory message they convey, reflective of Islamic practice. To dismiss this type of portrayal as un-Islamic would be to dismiss a vast literature, belles lettres as well as advisory treatises, in which wine plays a central role.

Much artistic—especially poetic—expression in Islam is indeed imbued with 'free thinking': a humanistic interpretation of the universe guided by reason as well as animated by the belief that all aspects of creation are God's work. And wine plays a pivotal role in this. At times, it is presented through 'disassociation', enabling authors who describe, and even celebrate, drinking to shield themselves from being rebuked for their complicity in sinful behavior. But, overall, a remarkable openness permeates the poetic and painterly corpus of especially the eastern, Persianate half of the Islamic world. Islamic culture has always prioritized the ideal over reality. The image of wine connects the two in intricate ways. Wine at times may refer to the mystical attempt to sublimate and annihilate the self. Or it may be reflective of reality, representing nothing more than a real or imagined scene without any mystical overtones. In Sufi poetry, wine is often a metaphor for deep emotions, consolation for the fickleness of fate and the finality of life, the only remedy against despondency in the face of this fact. It is the drink of paradise, linking the world of the seen to that of the unseen. The ruby-red liquid swirling in the goblet represents divine radiance; the drunkenness it produces symbolizes the mystic's intoxicating love for God; the *maykhāna* becomes the treasure trove of hidden Truth; and the free-spirited Sufi thumbs his nose at the the *muhtasib*, the hypocritical morality officer, who drinks himself. Rather than operating on the margins of society, such ideas existed side by side with formal religion, and were part of the marketplace of ideas in the 'classical' period and long thereafter.

At the turn of the second millennium, existing drinking customs were reinforced with the arrival of waves of Central Asian nomads—ethnic Turks and, later, Mongols—who brought with them new types of booze and even more excessive habits of ingesting it. Most khans and sultans of Inner Asian origin were real topers, no less engaged in perpetual boozing than the rulers of premodern and early modern Europe, including Russia. That they did so without apparent guilt—indeed, with bravado—is amply reflected in contemporary chronicles that recorded endless descriptions of rulers carousing with their boon companions. The advice literature written at the time presents sovereigns as entitled to their fun and entertainment so long as it does not come at the expense of good governance. As exemplified by Sultan Babur and his entourage, elite drinking combined the expectations of the lifestyle of the tribal chief leading a band of brothers, and a spiritual, even sacral dimension reminiscent of the ancient libation rite. The king was supposed to drink, both as a sign of his stature as a 'big man' and as a way of demonstrating that he occupied his own autonomous moral space.[13] As always, the sources make a clear distinction between elites and commoners. The former, the powerful and privileged, were entitled to drink; the lower classes officially were not, though they were allowed to violate the law under cover of darkness, so long as the social order was not threatened. Both groups thus could have their wine and drink it too: the powerful from a sense of entitlement, the poor from a sense of being irredeemable.

All this is abundantly visible in the three main Islamic empires of the early modern era: the Ottomans, the Safavids, and the Mughals, and their various (functional) alcoholic rulers. The best-documented case is that of the early Safavids, whose drinking combined ancient pre-Islamic traditions, the ways of the Central Asian steppes, and, following the introduction into their ranks of numerous Georgians and Armenians as soldiers and administrators, the rituals of Christianity. The Safavids remained wedded to the open steppes longer than the Mughals, and far longer than the Ottomans, who became relatively stationary after taking Constantinople in 1453. That, and their remarkable curiosity about foreign customs and Christian symbols, explains why Safavid rulers invited not just their boon companions to their drinking sessions but outsiders—European guests, diplomats, merchants, and missionaries—even allowing them to quaff from the royal goblet. Mughal rulers did invite Portuguese Jesuits to sit and debate religion with them, but their gatherings never involved alcohol. Inviting foreigners, much less sharing a goblet of wine with them, would have been unthinkable in Istanbul. The Topkapı Palace maintained a highly choreographed ritual that left little room for spontaneity and none whatsoever for frivolous pastimes in the presence of non-Muslim guests.

Much of this type of 'traditional' drinking endured, some of it into modern times. Safavid shahs continued to drink even as they retreated into the privacy of their palaces; many a nineteenth-century provincial magistrate indulged in wine or arak; quite a few North African sultans and beys were given to the bottle. Transformative change nevertheless set in around the turn of the nineteenth century, following increased contact and interaction with Europe. In the case of Egypt and Algeria, the intrusion, precipitated by military assault and occupation, was radical and abrupt. Elsewhere, change was more gradual and insidious, taking the form of indirect control and a creeping influence of Western ways rather than 'imposed' consumption patterns. This is especially the case for Iran, which was farther away from European influence, with a much smaller non-Muslim population, and lacking cosmopolitan port cities.

Everywhere, military, political, and economic pressure forced nineteenth-century Middle Eastern governments to open their domestic markets to European consumer goods at reduced toll tariffs, including new types of alcohol. The most obvious examples of such 'alco-imperialism' are to be found in Algeria, where French settler colonialism brought a rapid spread of viticulture and a notable change in drinking patterns, as well as in nineteenth-century Istanbul and Egypt, where the Capitulations enabled British nationals, including resident Ionian Greeks and Maltese, to expand the liquor business beyond traditionally 'Christian' quarters. But 'alco-imperialism' in a Muslim-majority environment was never straightforward, and it has its explanatory limits. The laws of capitalism did not quite work the way they did elsewhere: in the Islamic world, foreign firms did not create and control their own consumer base. The phenomenon of Westerners just pushing alcohol (or opium)—whether to maximize profits or, more nefariously, to turn the 'natives' into docile addicts—does not apply to the Islamic world. Western powers knew better than simply to encourage drinking in majority-Muslim societies, as they did in the Americas, Africa, and India. Capitalism here had to make concessions to culture. Even in Algeria, where they had full political control, the French pursued a *politique des égards*, navigating between Muslim sensibilities, the alcoholic prerogatives of non-Muslims, and the interests of their own domestic producers. Nor did Muslims need to be pressured by Europeans to fall for bubbly, translucent, aesthetically pleasing champagne.

Everywhere, alcohol consumption went up following growth in supply interacting with increased demand on the part of elites who, regardless of their stance on 'infidels' and foreign intervention, tended to imitate the lifestyle that came with 'modernity'. Following the example set by shahs and sultans tiptoeing around port, Bordeaux, and champagne, a new and 'modern' class of Muslim drinkers emerged. These were members of the upper classes who flaunted their worldliness by openly flouting the religious rules and, in some cases, showing their contempt for religion by drinking openly and defiantly. In time, nonreligious education and growing wealth bred attitudes that were no longer simply governed by the strictures of Islam but increasingly left room for personal choice in outward behavior, which in turn led to a loosening of social control on the observation of the fast. In the process, new identities beyond religious ones were forged, and the seeds of the nation-state and allegiance to it were sown. The Muslim world as we know it today came into being in this period, a self-conscious civilization positioning itself against the West, marked by a new dichotomy between 'religious' and 'traditional' elements on the one hand, and 'secular' and 'modern' forces on the other.

This new dichotomy caused the discourse surrounding alcohol to shift. The religious authorities reacted to the intrusion of modern mores in ways that were predictably traditional and negative. The state, in turn, ever more interventionist in its proscriptive as well as prescriptive interaction with society, increasingly took a 'modern' approach—that is, fiscal and health-related rather than religiously inspired and punitive—to alcohol. Influenced by European and American models, the state now sought to curb and contain through admonition and exhortation, no longer just invoking traditional religious morality but increasingly articulating its concerns in terms of health and hygiene. In the process, the celebratory, Sufi-type approach to alcohol as expressed in poetry and painting—exuberant, irreverent, skirting blasphemy—faded out as poets and painters ceased to produce such work and older material was increasingly censored and, in some cases, relegated to oblivion.

A newly emerging national identity, largely secular in tone and tenor, played a role as well in the new language developing around alcohol. Its traditional embeddedness in Islamic societies receded into the background, and drinking increasingly came to be associated with the non-Muslim world, the West. Resistance to it was now often voiced in anti-colonial terms, with some even arguing that Europeans intentionally sought to subjugate Muslims by fomenting alcohol use within their societies. In the late Ottoman Empire, this resulted in *dhimmis*, now formally endowed with rights and operated under the protective umbrella of foreign powers, becoming targets for their outsize role in the liquor business (and in commerce in general). As it became clear that the empire was on the verge of collapse, many of those who subscribed to an emerging form of Ottoman identity—a mix of rekindled Islamic sentiment and gathering (secular) nationalism—blamed the country's decline on foreign powers and their domestic collaborators, Greeks and Armenians. As calls went out for the revival of the Ottoman economy under Muslim control, non-Muslims stood accused of profiteering and unfair competition. The First World War made matters even worse, turning domestic Christians into presumed members of a fifth column aiding and abetting enemy interests.

In the half-century between the 1920s and the 1970s, most Middle Eastern lands turned from protectorates or European-controlled mandate states to independent nations which were increasingly ruled by secular leaders, such as Atatürk and Riza Shah. Military officers, such as Nasser in Egypt and the Baath leaders in Syria and Iraq, took control of Arab lands under the banner of pan-Arabism. None acted like Atatürk, who, even if he did not actively encourage his people to drink, taught them not to hide their drinking. They rather showed themselves indifferent to alcohol, except where it was a source of income, as reflected in their efforts to attain economic self-sufficiency through import substitution by supporting a domestic liquor industry.

Gradually, the secular tide turned, and not just in Iran, where the proclamation of an Islamic Republic in 1979 portended a radical break with the past and drove drinking underground. Throughout the second half of the century, the Middle East saw mass migration toward the cities, resulting in a degree of ruralization and, with it, a recrudescence of traditional norms. Leaders from the Maghreb to the Indian subcontinent made concessions to Islamic sentiment just to stay in power. Anwar Sadat encouraged Islamism in his country to exorcise Nasser's leftist legacy. Saddam Hussein tried to gain support from his people by currying favor with the devout during the Iran-Iraq War. In Pakistan, Zulfiqar Ali Bhutto, forced to make concessions to his main creditors, the Saudis, imposed restrictions on drinking halfway through his tenure. His Islamist successor, Zia-ul-Haqq, even more dependent on petrodollars, turned Pakistan into the Islamic republic it had officially become in 1956.

In the decades that followed, new manifestations of 'Islamization' and the creeping conservatism it represents gained momentum. The institution of halal holiday facilities in places like Tunisia and Turkey is a good spatial example of this process. In Algeria, Tunisia, and Iraq, Salafists put pressure on bars and liquor stores to close, and have even attacked alcohol-serving hotels. Nowhere has a policy of restrictive measures against alcohol, limiting its availability and pricing it out of reach for most, been more methodical than during the two decades of President Erdoğan's regime in Turkey.

The Muslim world has come out of two centuries of 'modernization' in a state of part oblivion, part willful amnesia with respect to the way it has dealt with alcohol in the past. The balancing act between censure and complicity, reflecting a 'live and let live' toleration, a capacity for ambiguity, and the implicit acceptance of a parallel normative system is half-forgotten or deliberately ignored in our puritanical age. Alcohol in the Islamic world is now associated with mental and physical deficiency, depravity, and social malaise: in sum, Western decadence, which represents temptation as much as it invites rebuke. In modern Arab and Turkish novels and movies, it is portrayed as a source of marital conflict, male loneliness, and depression. Modern Middle Eastern literature retains nothing of the ethereal register of the *khamriyya*, or of Sufi poetry, which celebrated intoxication as a metaphor for divine love and called the true believer to the *maykhāna* rather than the mosque. In the Persian-speaking world, Hafez and Khayyam are sacrosanct; censors are reluctant to touch their works, and readers continue to draw inspiration from the immortal wisdom cast in their surpassing verse. But elsewhere in the Islamic world, classic Arabic, Persian, and Turkish texts that talk openly and positively about alcohol and sex now often are republished in bowdlerized versions; full reprints and new editions tend to appear in Cologne, Uppsala, or Los Angeles rather than Cairo, Tehran, and Istanbul.[14]

Of course, alcohol itself has not gone away. Indeed, in some ways it is more conspicuously present than ever, bound up—as it is everywhere on the planet—with global mobility, foreign tourism, and a youth culture seeking fun, freedom, and social status. Decades of neoliberal policy have resulted in expensive nightclubs and fancy bars in Cairo's upscale Zamalek district, all venues catering to those able to afford their hefty cover charges. Even in countries that are officially dry, alcohol is widely available. Tehran's private party culture is second to none, and alcohol is home delivered by one's personal *sāqi* the same way pizza is. For those who know where to look, Karachi abounds in liquor stores tucked away in the bazaar. Shopkeepers in Muslim countries wrap bottles of alcohol in newspaper, and restaurants may serve vodka in Sprite bottles.

In the modern Islamic world, rules and regulations concerning the sale and consumption of alcohol vary from country to country. The degree to which Islam informs the legal system generally determines its availability. In Baath-controlled Syria, alcohol continues to be freely available. In Tunisia, Turkey, and Egypt, alcohol is sold year-round except during Ramadan. In Afghanistan, Pakistan, and Malaysia, only non-Muslims can obtain alcohol by presenting proof of (religious) identification. (In Afghanistan, the rules have tightened since the Taliban took over again in the summer of 2021.)[15] Absolute interdiction is the rule in Saudi Arabia, Iran, and Mauritania. In Qatar and Sharjah, the most conservative of the Arab Emirates, exorbitantly high prices are designed to limit consumption.[16] The northern emirates, by contrast—'Ajman, Umm al-Quwayn, Ra's al Khayma, and Fujayra—are far more relaxed in their liquor laws. Various countries have made concessions to global culture in recent years. Iran, for one, has shown a remarkable sense of realism by allowing Alcohol Anonymous meetings, and by setting up rehabilitation centers in the last decade. The organizers of the 2022 World Cup in Qatar initially agreed to allow alcohol to be sold near stadiums a few hours before matches, and to lower alcohol prices to reasonable levels for the international fans whose attendance is needed to make the spectacle a success.[17] Since late 2020, drinking alcohol without a license is no longer a criminal offense in Dubai, although one is still needed to purchase and possess it.[18] And even Saudi Arabia under Muhammad bin Salman, eager to become a tourist and 'events' destination, is now said to be considering relaxing the rules on alcohol.[19]

Yet old concerns and anxieties regarding alcohol are still very much alive, even if they operate in new contexts. Questions such as the permissibility of vinegar, whether Islam allows its followers to work in shops that sell alcohol, or whether it permits the use of cosmetics that contain small amounts of alcohol continue to preoccupy (pious) Muslims, with questions, answers, and debate regularly conducted online.[20] At the same time, Muslims still engage in motivated reasoning to justify their drinking. Muslim societies continue to struggle with the paradox of how far to go in censoring a commodity that is at once illicit and irrepressible, of how to keep the visible invisible. Alcohol indeed is still about concealment and exposure, about the 'haunting presence of negated objects and spaces'.[21] The result—a 'don't ask, don't tell' attitude and an 'out of sight' approach—is most notably visible in the relocation of alcohol-serving restaurants to highways outside urban centers, as can be seen in Turkey and Algeria, or in the full-fledged hypocrisy of the Saudi elite escaping the stiflingly dry environment at home by visiting Bahrain on the weekends and indulging in the pleasures of European capitals during the summer. Akin to Michel Foucault's interpretation of Victorian sex, conspicuous through its supposed absence, ubiquitous yet rarely mentioned other than in winks and whispers, alcohol is everywhere in Islam; the more it is hidden and the more it is banned, the more it is talked about, the more it is on people's minds—and lips. Today, it reflects the tension between traditional morality, communal and binding, versus a modern, imported, capitalist (a)morality that is individual, casual, and optional. The result is the formation of multiple personalities employing situational strategies of acting in the world.

The traditional 'Sufi' approach to alcohol is gone in the Muslim world, yet alcohol is still a metaphor for rebelliousness to some. As the Algerian journalist and chronicler Kamel Daoud says, addressing his Western readers,

> For you, a glass of wine is taste, perfumes, gown, and palace. For me, it is dissidence, disobedience, infraction, and shame. Among us [Muslims], he laments, bacchanalian poetry has always been more voluminous and elaborate than actual wine. There are more delicate poems about wine than types of wine. And even where they were written one had to play games, take recourse to metaphors, talk about getting sloshed as if one talked about an encounter with the divine. Today, alas, even that is past memory; one no longer sings about wine; wine has fallen silent; of poor quality, acid, it is drunk in the shadows, behind the walls of seedy bars.[22]

The same Kamel Daoud eloquently speaks of a colonization from within: the straitjacket that his 'Arabness' imposes on him, preventing him from rediscovering himself, from embracing not just his Muslim identity but also his Roman and Ottoman past; acknowledging the Spanish, Christian, and Jewish influences on the land of his birth and residence, Algeria, which, even while facing the sea, finds it hard to retrieve its Mediterranean identity.[23]

The Muslim world still faces the task of 'decolonizing' itself, of ridding itself of a self-imposed restrictiveness now that the time-honored practices that provided an outlet for human instinct and need are forgotten, relegated to the realm of denial-cum-self-delusion. In past times, there was the text, and it had a way of reasserting itself in the face of defiance. Yet drinking—even drinking in excess—was 'accepted', treated as unremarkable, seen as integral to power and even as symbolic of the mystical bond of humans with the divine, so long as the elite was involved and so long as its lower-class variant did not spill too much out into the open. The intrusion of European ways led to an increasing self-awareness about inexplicable contradictions between practice and theory, a self-awareness that was followed by a growing focus on the norm as laid down in the text during the modernizing twentieth century. The flexibility, the 'live and let live' mindset, the capacity for ambiguity that had marked premodern Muslim life got lost and became overwhelmed by full-fledged denial and hypocrisy. In a modern world that measures everything morally, and which demands consistency between theory and practice, this fullness is unlikely to come back any time soon.

IMAGE CREDITS

1. Arthur M. Sackler Gallery, Smithsonian Institution, Washington, DC: Purchase—Smithsonian Unrestricted Trust Funds, Smithsonian Collections Acquisition Program, and Dr. Arthur M. Sackler, S1986.231

2. Illustrated folio from a manuscript of Divan of Hafiz, Harvard Art Museums/Arthur M. Sackler Museum, The Stuart Cary Welch Collection, Gift of Mr. and Mrs. Stuart Cary Welch in honor of the students of Harvard University and Radcliffe College. Jointly owned by the Harvard Art Museums and the Metropolitan Museum of Art. Photo © President and Fellows of Harvard College, 1988.460.2.

3. © Victoria and Albert Museum, London.

4. BM 1612938610. © The Trustees of the British Museum. All rights reserved.

5. Courtesy of Sussan Babaie.

6. © RMN-Grand Palais/Art Resource, NY.

7. Detroit Institute of Arts, USA © Detroit Institute of Arts/Gift of Robert H. Tannahill in memory of Dr W.R. Valentiner/Bridgeman Images.

8. Harvard Art Museums/Arthur M. Sackler Museum, The Edwin Binney, 3rd Collection of Turkish Art at the Harvard Art Museums, 2011.91.

9. © Staatsbibliothek zu Berlin, Orientabteilung, Diez A fol. 73, f. 23.

10. Courtesy of Darüşşafaka Society.

289

11. The Museum of Fine Arts, Houston, The Hossein Afshar Collection at the Museum of Fine Arts, Houston. Photograph © The Museum of Fine Arts, Houston; photographer: Will Michels.

12. From Şeyh Muhammed ibn Mustafa el-Misri, *Tühftet ul-Mülk*, 1817. No known copyright restrictions.

13. 'S.A. Brasserie Bomonti—Bomonti Bira Fabrikası'. Salt Research, Photograph and Postcard Archive. Available at: https://archives. saltresearch.org/handle/123456789/ 119261

14. From *Diken* magazine, 1918. No known copyright restrictions.

15. From *Ayine*, 1922, no. 32. Available at: https://digitale-sammlungen. ulb.uni-bonn.de/ulbbnioa/periodical/titleinfo/8011703. No known copyright restrictions.

16. Library of Congress, Grantham Bain Collection, LC-DIG-ggbain-17044. Available at: https://www.loc.gov/pictures/item/ 2014697198/. No known copyright restrictions.

17. From *Baghdad Times*, 27 November 1922, no. 3223. Available at: https://gpa.eastview.com/crl/mena/newspapers/bagt19221127- 01.1.1. No known copyright restrictions.

18. Courtesy of the Tarih Vakfi Foundation.

19. No known copyright restrictions.

20. Political Studies and Research Institute, Tehran. No known copyright restrictions.

21. Photo by author.

22. Photo by author.

23. AP Photo/Julie Jacobson.

24. Courtesy of Philippe Chaudat.

25. Photo by author.

26. Reuters/Alamy stock photo.

27. Courtesy of Masoud Amini.

28. GIANLUIGI GUERCIA/AFP via Getty Images.

NOTES

INTRODUCTION

1. Laufer, 'On the Possible Oriental Origins'.
2. Gruner, *Treatise*, pp. 409–10. Whether al-Razi counts as a Muslim remains undecided.
3. Obsopoeus, *How to Drink*, pp. xii–xiii.
4. Brückner, *Fatwas zum Alkohol*, p. 69.
5. Maraqten, 'Wine Drinking', p. 104; Rowell, *VSintage Humour*, p. xxxvii.
6. Fulton, 'Fīrūzābādī's Wine List'.
7. Schrad, *Vodka Politics*.
8. Mamou, 'Pays musulmans'.
9. Honchell, 'Story of a Drunken Mughal', p. 5.
10. Southgate, *Narrative*, vol. 2, p. 317.
11. Van Gelder, 'Muslim Encomium', p. 222.
12. Rowell, *Vintage Humour*, p. li.
13. Kueny, *Rhetoric of Sobriety* is a good example of the tendency to examine Islam's legal take on alcohol without connecting theory to practice.
14. See Tattersall and Desalle, *Natural History of Wine*, pp. 19–20; Hames, *Alcohol in World History*, p. 34; and Varriano, *Wine: A Cultural History*, pp. 221–6. Attention to the topic is currently growing, though. In addition to Turkey, North Africa has been receiving scholarly attention in the last few years, as is evidenced in the recent appearance of Koyuncu, *Osmanlı İmparatorluğu'nda İçki Üretimi*; Georgeon, *Au pays du raki*; White, *Blood of the Colony*; Znaien, *Les raisins*; Biçer-Deveci and Bourmaud, eds, *Alcohol in the Maghrib*; and special issues of *Middle Eastern Studies* and *Revue du Monde Musulman et de la Méditerranée*.
15. Taheri, *Spirit of Allah*, p. 259.
16. Osborne, *The Wet and the Dry*, p. 15.
17. al-Muqri, *al-Khamr wa'l-nabidh*, p. 10.
18. Schirmbeck, *Islamische Kreuzzug*, p. 16–17.
19. Bauer, *Culture of Ambiguity*, pp. 28–9, 72.
20. Bezouh, *Ils ont trahi Allah*, pp. 117–25; and Ghanim, *Sexual World*, p. 170.
21. Shakosh, 'Bint al-girān'.
22. Bauer, *Culture of Ambiguity*, pp. 24–5.

23. Ibid., pp. 130ff.
24. Ahmed, *What Is Islam?*, pp. 152ff.
25. Ibid., pp. 345, 357.
26. Bauer, *Culture of Ambiguity*, p. 130.
27. Ahmed, *What Is Islam?*, p. 281.
28. Bauer, *Culture of Ambiguity*, pp. 166–7.
29. Ahmed, *What Is Islam?*, p. 67.
30. Ibid., p. 409.
31. See, for example, Ruthven, 'More Than a Religion'.
32. Abbasi, 'Did Premodern Muslims Distinguish?'.
33. Losensky, *Welcoming Fighani*, pp. 291–2.
34. Opwis, 'Shifting Legal Authority', pp. 66–7, 77–8.
35. Lukacs, *Inventing Wine*, pp. 68, 84, 96.
36. See, for instance, Ludington, *Politics of Wine in Britain*; and Idem, 'Drinking for Approval'.
37. Haller, 'Cosmopolitan Mediterranean', p. 32; Hanley, 'Grieving Cosmopolitanism'; and Eldem, 'Ottoman Galata'.
38. Examples are Beyhaqi, *History of Beyhaqi*; Babur, *Baburnama*; and I'timād al-Saltana, *Ruznāma*.
39. Berkey, 'Tradition', p. 44; and Szombathy, *Mujūn*, pp. 2–6.
40. Lewicka, *Food and Foodways*, p. 518.
41. Álvarez Dopico, 'Vino y tavernas', p. 209.

1. ISLAM AND ALCOHOL

1. McGovern, *Uncorking the Past*, p. 82; Idem, *Ancient Wine*, pp. 64–8; McGovern et al., 'Early Neolithic Wine of Georgia'.
2. Spengler, *Fruit From the Sands*, p. 195.
3. Magdy, 'Egypt Uncovers Brewery'.
4. Norrie, 'History of Wine', pp. 35–6.
5. Clement and Weber, *Vins d'Orient*, introd., p. 8; Heskett and Butler, *Divine Vintage*, pp. 30–1.
6. Weststeijn, 'Josef verhaal'.
7. Floor and Javadi, *Persian Pleasures*, pp. 170–1.
8. Herodotus, *Histories*, vol. 1, p. 668. For alcohol as a truth-telling device in various cultures, see Slingerland, *Drunk*, pp. 13–33.
9. Feins, 'Wine and Islam', p. 21.
10. Melikian-Chirvani, 'From the Royal Boat', p. 13.
11. Hillenbrand, '*La Dolce Vita*', p. 13.
12. Brookshaw, 'Lascivious Vines', pp. 106–7.
13. Tabari, *History*, vol. xxvii, p. 128.
14. Sherrat, 'Alcohol and Its Alternatives', p. 17.
15. Weststeijn, 'Aardse en hemelse wijngaarden'.
16. Shahîd, *Byzantium and the Arabs*, vol. 2, pp. 139–58.
17. Kueny, *Rhetoric of Sobriety*, pp. 89ff.
18. Feins, 'Wine and Islam', p. 38.
19. Maraqten, 'Wine Drinking', pp. 97–8.
20. Kueny, *Rhetoric of Sobriety*, p. 66.

21. Wensinck, 'Wine in Islam'.
22. Wensinck, 'Khamr', p. 994.
23. Kueny, *Rhetoric of Sobriety*, pp. 15–17.
24. Weiss, *Spirit of Islamic Law*, pp. 4–5.
25. Buckley, 'Muhtasib', p. 60; Stilt, *Islamic Law in Action*, p. 40. Rabb, *Doubt in Islamic Law*, p. 173.
26. Kueny, *Rhetoric of Sobriety*, pp. 26, 44; Wensinck, 'Khamr'.
27. Shi'ism knows three main branches. Twelver Shi'ism, named after the twelve Imams it follows, is the state religion of Iran and the country's dominant faith, and the majority branch in Iraq. Other variants, much smaller in number, are the Zaydis, who believe in five Imams, and the Isma'ilis, 'Seveners'.
28. Kulayni, *al-Kafi*, vol. 6, p. 336; Majlisi, *Bihār al-anwār*, vol. 76, pp. 327ff; Id. Hilyat *al-muttaqin*, pp. 481–2; Kueny, *Rhetoric of Sobriety*, pp. 44–6, 50.
29. Haider, 'Contesting Intoxication'; Reinhart, *Before Revelation*, pp. 133–5; Melchert, *Formation of the Sunni Schools*, pp. 49–50.
30. Haider, 'Contesting Intoxication', pp. 71ff; Kueny, *Rhetoric*, pp. 53–88.
31. See Hurr al-'Āmilī, *Wasā'il al-Shi'a*, vol. 1, p. 18; vol. 3, pp. 468, 470; vol. 8, p. 38.
32. Shaykh al-Saduq, *Man lā yahduruhu al-faqih*, vol. 1, p. 43; Hurr al-'Amili, *Wasā'il al-Shi'a*, vol. 3, p. 471; vol. 10, p. 38. Some declared it pure as a substance, but most insisted that it is *najis*.
33. Stilt, *Islamic Law in Action*, pp. 92–4.
34. Weber, 'Le vin dans la tradition', p. 75.
35. Cook, *Commanding Right*, p. 494.
36. al-Muqri, *al-Khamr wa'l-nabidh*, pp. 77ff.; Shefer-Mossensohn, *Ottoman Medicine*, pp. 90–2; Gruner, *Treatise on the Canon*, pp. 313–14, 409–13.
37. Coulson, *History of Islamic Law*, p. 82.
38. Rosen, *Justice of Islam*, p. 41.
39. Cook, *Commanding Right*, pp. 9, 71.
40. Ibid., pp. 11–12, 99–100, 138.
41. Ibid., p. 363.
42. Ibid., 42–3, 52–3, 128, 132–4, 394, 524. An exception is the radical early Islamic sect of the Kharijites who tended to be uncompromising on this point. See Ibid., pp. 394–5.
43. Ibid., pp. 77–8; 489; and 238–9 for the Zaydis.
44. Ibid., pp. 427ff.
45. Denny, 'Tawba'; Stern, *Al-Ghazzali on Repentance*, pp. 5–6, 22.
46. *The Qur'an*, p. 67.
47. Stewart, *Islamic Legal Orthodoxy*, p. 47.
48. Ker Porter, *Travels in Georgia*, pp. 347–8.
49. Denny, 'Tawba'.
50. Shuraydi, *Raven and the Falcon*, p. 171.
51. Ibid., pp. 35–5.
52. *The Qur'an*, p. 341.
53. Vrolijk, 'Vijftig Moslims aan de zwier', pp. 221–3.
54. Kulayni, *al-Kafi*, vol. 8, p. 88.
55. Cook, *Commanding Right*, pp. 436, 481–2.
56. Crone, *God's Rule*, pp. 316–17.
57. Alshech, 'Do Not Enter Houses'; Lange, 'Vom Recht sich zu verhüllen'.
58. Kadri, *Heaven on Earth*, p. 222.

59. Cook, *Commanding Right*, p. 57.
60. Hagemann, Mewes, Verkinderen, 'Studying Elites', p. 5; Szombathy, *Mujūn*, pp. 20–9.
61. Ahmed, *What Is Islam?*, pp. 283–4.
62. Zubaida, *Beyond Islam*, p. 164.
63. Bauer, *Culture of Ambiguity*, passim.

2. ALCOHOL IN THE PREMODERN ISLAMIC WORLD (C. 600 TO C. 1400)

1. Broshi, 'Wine in Ancient Palestine', p. 166.
2. Von Kremer, *Aegypten*, vol. 1, p. 217.
3. Sijpesteijn, *Shaping a Muslim State*, p. 301.
4. Shabushti, *al-Dāyirāt*, pp. 4, 63, and passim.
5. Tannous, *Making of the Medieval Middle East*, pp. 464–71; Kilpatrick, 'Monasteries', pp. 22–5.
6. Mas'udi, *Muruj al-dhahab*, vol. 3, p. 77; Muqri, *al-Khamr wa'l nabidh*, p. 96.
7. Tannous, *Making of the Medieval Middle East*, pp. 280–2.
8. Hillenbrand, '*La Dolce Vita*', p. 93.
9. Harb, 'Wine Poetry', p. 224.
10. Fowden, *Art and the Umayyad Elite*, pp. 31–83.
11. Hamilton, *Walid and His Friends*, pp. 93.
12. Mas'udi, *Muruj al-dhahab*, vol. 3, pp. 225–6.
13. Isbahani, *Kitāb al-aghāni*, vol. 6, p. 107; Qayrawani, *Qutb al-surur*, p. 282.
14. Isbahani, *Kitāb al-aghāni*, vol. 6, p. 99; Qayrawani, *Qutb al-surur*, p. 282; Judd, 'Reinterpreting al-Walīd', p. 440.
15. Qayrawani, *Qutb al-surur*, p. 285; Hillenbrand, '*La Dolce Vita*', pp. 89, 95; Judd, 'Reinterpreting al-Walīd', pp. 448, 451–52, 458; Whitcomb, 'Khirbat al-Mafjar'.
16. Qayrawani, *Qutb al-surur*, p. 321.
17. Ibid., pp. 328, 333; Mas'udi, *Muruj al-dhahab*, vol. 3, p. 279; Chejne, 'Boon Companion', p. 329; Kennedy, *When Baghdad Ruled the World*, p. 15.
18. Ahsan, *Social Life*, p. 156.
19. Qayrawani, *Qutb al-surur*, p. 343; Chejne, 'Boon Companion', p. 329.
20. Kai Kā'ūs, *Mirror for Princes*, p. 197; Chejne, 'Boon Companion', p. 330.
21. al-Muqri, *al-Khamr wa'l-nabidh*, p. 114; Rowell, *Vintage Humour*, pp. xxviii–xxxi.
22. Tannous, *Making of the Medieval Middle East*, p. 470.
23. Shabushti, *al-Dirāyāt*, p. 11; Vadet, 'Ibn Ḥamdūn'.
24. Zettersteen, Bosworth, and Van Donzel, 'al-Wāthiḳ Bi 'llāh'.
25. Tabari, *History*, vol. xxxiv, pp. 158–9, 178–9; Kennedy, *When Baghdad Ruled the World*, pp. 264–7.
26. Qayrawani, *Qutb al-surur*, p. 490; Forstner, *al-Mu'tazz billāh*, pp. 17, 64–6.
27. Zettersteen and Bosworth, 'al-Mutahdī'; Melchert, 'Religious Policies', p. 334.
28. Qayrawani, *Qutb al-surur*, p. 498.
29. Ibn Khallikan, *Ibn Khallikan's Biographical Dictionary*, vol. 2, pp. 304–6.
30. Osti, 'Caliph', p. 50.
31. Kennedy, *Prophet and the Age*, pp. 193–4; Szombarty, *Mujūn*, p. 175.
32. Melchert, *Formation of the Sunni Schools*, pp. 143–8.
33. Cook, *Commanding Right*, pp. 116–19; Mouline, *Clerics of Islam*, p. 29.
34. Tellier, 'Judicial Authority', pp. 123–8; Idem, 'Umayyads and the Formation', pp. 2–7.

35. Cook, *Commanding Right*, p. 448; Buckley, 'Muhtasib', p. 98.
36. Buckley, 'Muhtasib', pp. 60–5, 69; Stilt, *Islamic Law in Action*, p. 40.
37. Lange, 'Changes in the Office', pp. 158–9, 161–3.
38. Lange, *Justice, Punishment*, pp. 56, 82, 185, 227.
39. Isnard, *La vigne en Algérie*, 1, pp. 261–2, 265.
40. Sánchez, 'La triada mediterránea', pp. 115–16 ; Clément, 'Vignes et vins', p. 87.
41. Dozy, *Histoire des Musulmans*, vol. 3, pp. 254, 268.
42. Pérès, *Poésie andaluse*, pp. 367–8.
43. Lévi-Provencal, *Califat umaiyade*, p. 169.
44. Dozy, *Histoire*, vol. 4, pp. 22–4.
45. Ibid., pp. 69–70.
46. Ibid., pp. 122.
47. Heine, *Weinstudien*, p. 127.
48. Bennison, *Almoravid and Almohad Empires*, pp. 39, 50.
49. Escartín Gonzáles, *Estudio económico*, pp. 10–11, 50–2.
50. Wasserstein, 'Jonah Theme', pp. 236–7.
51. Dursteler, '"Abominable Pig'," p. 231.
52. Ibid., pp. 227–8.
53. Lewicka, *Food and Foodways*, p. 522.
54. Adorno, *Itinéraire*, pp. 70–1.
55. Von Harff, *Pilgrimage*, pp. 118–19.
56. Ibid.
57. Lewicka, *Food and Foodways*, pp. 485–6; Biesterfeldt, '*Mizr fī Miṣr*', p. 384.
58. Behrens-Abouseif, *Azbakiyya*, p. 9–10, 40; Leiser, *Prostitution*, pp. 147, 157, 161.
59. Lewicka, *Food and Foodways*, pp. 72–3, 78.
60. Goitein, *Mediterranean Society*, vol. 1, pp. 122–3; vol. 4, p. 254.
61. Leiser, *Prostitution*, pp. 105–6.
62. Amitai, *Holy War and Rapprochement*, pp. 95–6, 98.
63. The name Bahri refers to the island al-Rawda in the Nile—called *bahr*, sea or river—where the Mamluks had their headquarters.
64. Fayyala, *Mazāhir al-fasād*, pp. 106–10.
65. Petry, *Criminal Underworld*, pp. 124, 131.
66. Lewicka, *Food and Foodways*, p. 537.
67. Aigle, 'Inscriptions de Baybars', pp. 61–2; Eadem, 'Legitimizing a Lowborn Regicide', pp. 61–3.
68. Eddé, 'Babyars et son double', pp. 74–5.
69. Behrens-Abouseif, 'Baptistère de Saint Louis', p. 6. Edward Lane, *Manners and Customs*, pp. 406–19, recounts the stories of Baybars's life as told as popular romance in early nineteenth-century Cairo. His story has remained popular on the streets of Damascus, where he is buried, to this day. See Aigle, 'Legitimizing a Lowborn Regicide', p. 61.
70. Fuess, 'Zulm by Maẓālim', p. 123.
71. Yürekli, 'Bahrī Memlûk Hükümdarlarının Eğlence', pp. 147–8.
72. Thorau, *Lion of Egypt*, p. 268; Guo, 'Paradise Lost'.
73. Petry, *Criminal Underworld*, pp. 125–7; Idem, 'Travails of Prohibition', pp. 26–8; Fayyala, *Mazāhir al-fasād*, pp. 146–7, 150.
74. Borsch and Sabra, 'Refugees', p. 73.
75. Leiser, *Prostitution*, pp. 127–9.

76. Levanoni, *Turning Point*, pp. 189–90.
77. Fulton, 'Fīrūzābādī's Wine List', p. 579.
78. Soshan, *Popular Culture*, p. 17.
79. Ibid., pp. 49–50.
80. Irwin, 'Eating Horses', p. 3.
81. Lewicka, *Food and Foodways*, pp. 498, 530–1.
82. Ibid., pp. 544–5.
83. Ibid., pp. 531–2, 545; Petry, *Criminal Underworld*, p. 128, n. 7. Reportedly some 10,000 were found.
84. Lewicka, *Food and Foodways*, pp. 532, 544; Stilt, *Islamic Law in Action*, p. 92; Petry, 'Travails of Prohibition', p. 30.
85. Petry, *Twilight of Majesty*, p. 15.
86. Koh, 'Qāytbay's Journey', p. 73.
87. Yürekli, 'Bahrī Memlûk Hükümdarlarının Eğlence', p. 146.
88. Lewicka, *Food and Foodways*, p. 537.
89. Ibid., p. 538.
90. Shoshan, *Damascus 1480–1500*, pp. 67–9; Petry, 'Travails of Prohibition', pp. 29–31.
91. Yarshater, 'Theme of Wine-drinking', p. 43.
92. Samarqandi, *Chahár Maqála*, p. 35; tr. in Browne, *Literary History*, vol. 2, p. 38.
93. Gardizi, *Ornament of Histories*, pp. 101–2.
94. Beyhaqi, *History*, vol. 1, pp. 218, 229, 232–3, 255, 262; vol. 2, pp. 96, 122.
95. Ibid., vol. 1, pp. 326–9.
96. Ibid., vol. 1, pp. 281–2; Gardizi, *Ornament of Histories*, pp. 103.
97. Beyhaqi, *History*, vol. 2, p. 361.
98. Safi, *Politics of Knowledge*, pp. 1–42.
99. Ibid., pp. xxiv–xxv; Tor, '"Sovereign and Pious"', pp. 39ff.; Peacock, *Great Seljuq Empire*, pp. 250–2.
100. Nishapuri, *History*, p. 51.
101. Tor, '"Sovereign and Pious"', p. 48.
102. Yürekli, 'Bahrī Memlûk Hükümdarlarının Eğlence', p. 145.
103. Tor, '"Sovereign and Pious"', p. 46.
104. Ibid., p. 48; Peacock, *Great Seljuqs*, p. 176.
105. Jackson, *Mongols and the Islamic World*, p. 93.
106. Smith, 'Dietary Decadence', p. 3.
107. Amitai, *Holy War*, p. 107.
108. Rashid al-Din, *Compendium*, vol. 3, p. 743.
109. Brack, 'Mongol Mahdi', pp. 618–19.
110. Melville, 'Year of the Elephant', p. 205. Not to be outdone, his main rival, the aforementioned Mamluk ruler Nasir Muhammad took similar measures in Syria.

3. WINE IN ISLAMIC PAINTING, POETRY, AND *ADAB* LITERATURE

1. Szombathy, *Mujūn*, pp. 41, 200.
2. Al-Azmeh, 'Freidenkertum'.
3. Rowell, *Abu Nuwas*, p. xlix.
4. Davis, *Mirror of my Heart*, pp. xviii–xix.
5. Lewisohn, *Beyond Faith and Fidelity*, p. 118.
6. Balafrej, *Making of the Artist*, p. 63.

7. Floor, 'Culture of Wine Drinking', p. 172.
8. Babaie, 'Visual Vestiges of Travel', p. 113.
9. Canby, *Rebellious Reformer*, pp. 158–64.
10. Ibid., pp. 174–5; Babaie, 'Visual Vestiges of Travel', p. 122.
11. Babaie, 'Visual Vestiges of Travel'.
12. Ahmed, *What Is Islam?*, pp. 415–24.
13. Ibid., pp. 66–70, 420–2, 442. For a similar analysis of the meaning of the wine cup in Mughal society and art, see Khare, 'Wine-cup'. The Prophet Khidr refers to the Koran 18:65–82, where Moses meets an unnamed 'servant of God'. In later lore, he became known as a prophet named Khidr who attained immortality by drinking from the spring of eternal life.
14. Diba and Ekhtiyar, *Royal Persian Paintings*, p. 159.
15. Davis, 'Wine and Persian Poetry', p. 59.
16. Davis, introduction to Gorgani, *Vis & Ramin*, pp. xiv–xv.
17. Homerin, 'Arabic Religious Poetry', p. 83.
18. Nawâjī, *La joie du vin*, p. 41.
19. Rowell, *Vintage Humour*, p. 17.
20. Davis, *Faces of Love*, p. xxvi.
21. Weber, 'Le vin dans la tradition', pp. 54–83.
22. Hamori, *On the Art of Medieval Arabic Literature*, pp. 38, 52.
23. Harb, 'Wine Poetry', p. 223.
24. Brookshaw, 'Lascivious Vines', p. 93.
25. Isbahani, *Kitāb al-aghāni*, vol. 6, p. 107.
26. Keyvani, 'Khamriya'; Kennedy, *Wine Song*, pp. 36–7; Idem, *Abu Nuwas*, pp. 2–3.
27. Beaumont, 'Trickster and Rhetoric', pp. 6–7.
28. Losensky, 'Sāqi-nāmah'.
29. Nateq, *Hafez*, pp. 291–301. Examples are *ābdār, chamani, rekābdār, meygosār*.
30. Van Ruymbeke, 'Le vin, interdiction'.
31. Davis, 'Wine and Persian Poetry', p. 62.
32. Yarshater, 'Theme of Wine-drinking', p. 52–3.
33. Losensky, *Welcoming Fighani*, p. 291.
34. Rosenthal, 'Fiction and Reality', p. 11, n. 20.
35. Harb, 'Wine Poetry', p. 223.
36. Ibid. The 'Iraqi' stand for 'Hanafi' in legal literature.
37. Ibid., pp. 225–6.
38. Rowell, Abu Nuwas, pp. xxvi–xxxii.
39. Ibid., p. xl.
40. Ibid.
41. Ibid., pp. xl–xlv, l.
42. Kennedy, *Wine Song*, p. 18.
43. Bauer, *Culture of Ambiguity*, p. 167.
44. Losensky, *Welcoming Fighani*, pp. 291–2.
45. Davis, 'Wine and Persian Poetry', p. 62.
46. Ergin, 'Rock Faces'.
47. Papas, *Thus Spake the Dervish*, p. 16.
48. Ibid., Introduction; Covel, 'Extracts', p. 153; Rycaut, *History*, p. 266.
49. Papas, *Thus Spake the Dervish*, pp. 44–5.
50. Goshiri, 'Alienation', p. 230.

51. Feuiebois-Pierunek, *De l'ascèse au libertinage*, pp. 395–7.
52. Noorani, 'Heterotopia', p. 350.
53. Ibid., p. 351.
54. Stetkevych, 'Intoxication', pp. 211, 223–4; Losensky, 'Sāqi-nāmah'.
55. Davis, *Faces of Love*, p. 10.
56. Ibid., p. 133.
57. Losensky, *Welcoming Fighani*, pp. 291–2.
58. Davis, *Faces of Love*, p. 23.
59. Ibid., p. 35.
60. Lewis, 'Hafez and Rendi', p. 35.
61. Davis, *Faces of Love*, p. 33.
62. For the likelihood that Khayyam's poetic oeuvre is a collective work composed over centuries rather than the creation of one individual, see Cole, *Rubáiyát*, pp. 2–5, 80–2.
63. Aminrazavi, *Wine of Wisdom*, p. 141.
64. Davis, 'Wine and Persian Poetry', p. 55.
65. Aminrazavi, *Wine of Wisdom*, pp. 112, 121.
66. Keyvani, 'Ḵamriya'.
67. Aminrazavi, *Wine of Wisdom*, pp. 8–14.
68. Ibn al-Mu'tazz, *Kitāb fusul al-tamāthil*, pp. 48–54, 67–72, 86ff., 189ff., 229.
69. Barbouchi, 'Vin et ivresse', p. 250.
70. Nawajī, *La joie du vin*, p. 71; Harb, 'Wine poetry', p. 219.
71. Pellat, 'Adab'.
72. Salvatore, 'Secularity', p. 37.
73. Lecomte, *Ibn Qutayba*, pp. 113–5; and Ibn Qutayba, *Kitāb al-ashriba*.
74. Tafazzoli, 'Dadestan ī menog ī xrad'.
75. Kai Kā'ūs, *Mirror for Princes*, pp. 57–60; and Nizam al-Mulk, *Book of Government*, p. 119.
76. Marlow, 'The Khāṣṣa and the 'Āmma', pp. 32–3.
77. Dahlén, 'Kingship and Religion'.
78. Nizam al-Mulk, *Book of Government*, p. 119.
79. Kai Kā'ūs, *Mirror for Princes*, pp. 57–60.
80. Ibid., p. 84.
81. Marino, 'Raconter l'ivresse'.
82. Anon., *Book of Virtues*, pp. 142–3.
83. Davis, *Faces of Love*, p. 117.
84. Rowell, *Vintage Humour*, pp. xliv–xlv.
85. Kennedy, *Wine Song*, p. 223.
86. Nasir al-Din Tusi, *Nasirean Ethics*, pp. 176–8.
87. Al-Rawandi, *Rāhat al-sudur*, pp. 416–28; Yavari, *Advice for the Sultan*, p. 77.

4. ALCOHOL IN THE EARLY MODERN ISLAMIC EMPIRES: THE OTTOMANS AND THE MUGHALS

1. For the element of trust and social solidarity in tribal drinking, see Slingerland, *Drunk*, pp. 134–41.
2. Kastritsis, 'Tales of Viziers and Wine', pp. 228, 235; Kafadar, *Between Two Worlds*, pp. 110–11.

3. Lewis, *Book of Dede Korkut*, pp. 42, 88.
4. Yürekli, 'Bahrī Memlûk Hükümdarlarının Eğlence', p. 144.
5. Fleet, *European and Islamic Trade*, p. 74.
6. Lowry, 'Impropriety and Impiety'.
7. Fleet, *Europe and Islamic Trade*, pp. 74–5; Kastritsis, 'Tales of Viziers', p. 246.
8. Lowry, 'Impropriety and Impiety'.
9. White, *Three Years in Constantinople*, vol. 3, p. 98.
10. D'Ohsson, *Tableau*, vol. 4, tome 1, pp. 54–6.
11. Kastritsis, 'Tales of Viziers', pp. 242, 248.
12. Brocquière, *Travels*, pp. 242–3; Lowry, 'Impropriety and Impiety'.
13. Babinger, *Mehmed the Conqueror*, p. 61.
14. Fleet, *European and Islamic Trade*, pp. 74, 76.
15. D'Ohsson, *Tableau*, vol. 4, tome 1, p. 56.
16. Lewicka, *Food and Foodways*, p. 547.
17. Georgeon, *Au pays du raki*, p. 105.
18. Busbecq, *Turkish Letters*, p. 180.
19. D'Ohsson, *Tableau*, vol. 4, tome 1, pp. 56–7; Koyuncu, *Osmanlı İmparatorluğu'nda İçki Üretimi*, pp. 64–5; Bakhit, *Ottoman Province*, p. 141.
20. Fresne-Canaye, *Voyage*, pp. 115–16, 120–1; Rabaud, 'L'image des sultans', p. 84. Cantemir, *History*, p. 218, claims that he never missed a prayer, though.
21. Roth, *Duke of Naxos*, pp. 18–19, 46–7; D'Ohsson, *Tableau*, vol. 4, tome 1, pp. 58–9.
22. Southgate, *Narrative*, vol. 2, p. 320.
23 Garzoni, *Relazione*, pp. 33–4; Dursteler, 'Bad Bread', pp. 211–2. In the nineteenth century, the people of Istanbul still remembered Selim II as *bekri* (the drunkard). See White, *Three Years*, vol. 3, p. 99.
24. Gerlach, *Tage-Buch*, pp. 85, 88–9; Billerberg, [*Most Rare and Straunge Discourses*], unpag. (p. 2); Bonifacio Antelmi, 'Relazione' 1576; Giacomo Soranzo, 'Relazione' 1576; Giovanni Corer, 'Relazione', 1578, in Pedani-Fabris, ed., *Relazioni*, pp. 199, 205, 228.
25. Rabaud, 'L'image des sultans', p. 118.
26. Zilfi, *Politics of Piety*, p. 137; Sheikh, *Ottoman Puritanism*, pp. 11–12.
27. The profitability of the trade is suggested by the fact that its practitioners offered Mehmed III's grand vizier, Koca Sinan Pasha, 1,500,000 akçes to keep the wine houses of Istanbul open. See Koyuncu, *Osmanlı İmparatorluğu'nda İçki Üretimi*, pp. 69, 110.
28. Ibid., pp. 66–8, 70, 109.
29. Ibid., pp. 69–70, 110; and Agostino Nani, reports 2 May, 23 May, and 12 July 1601, in *Calendar of State Papers*, pp. 457, 461 463–6.
30. Girolamo Cappello, 'Relazione', 1600, in Pedani-Fabris, ed., *Relazioni*, pp. 397–8; Dursteler, 'Bad Bread', p. 212.
31. D'Ohsson, *Tableau*, vol. 4, tome 1, pp. 60–1.
32. Vatin and Veinstein, *Le sérail ébranlé*, p. 224; Koyuncu, *Osmanlı İmparatorluğu'nda İçki Üretimi*, p. 70.
33. Giustanina, 'Relazione', 1627, in Pedanis-Fabris, ed., *Relazioni*, p. 543.
34. Na'îmâ, *Târih-i Na'îmâ*, vol. 2, pp. 755–6; Hammer-Purgstall, *Geschichte*, vol. 3, pp. 119–20.
35. Na'îmâ, *Târih-i Na'îmâ*, vol. 2, p. 792; Hammer-Purgstall, *Geschichte*, vol. 3, p. 132.
36. Hammer-Purgstall, *Geschichte*, vol. 3, p. 207.

37. Contarini, 'Relazione', p. 367; Cantemir, *History*, pp. 249–50; D'Ohsson, *Tableau*, vol. 4, tome 1, p. 61; Hammer-Purgstall, *Geschichte*, vol. 5, p. 289.

38. Cantemir, *History*, p. 254; Hammer-Purgstall, *Geschichte*, vol. 3, pp. 213, 216.

39. Smith, Remarks, pp. 121–3; Covel, 'Extracts from the Dairies', p. 269; Hammer-Purgstall, *Geschichte*, vol. 6, pp. 255–6; Zilfi, *Politics of Piety*, pp. 129ff.; Baer, *Honored by the Glory*, pp. 94–5, 102–3, 116–18; Faruk Köse, 'Fatwa Collection', pp. 35ff.

40. Cantemir, *History*, p. 438.

41. DNA, Consulaat Smyrna, Inv. nr 1-2, 21 Aug. 1691, fol. 269.

42. Hammer-Purgstall, *Staatsverfassung*, vol. 1, p. 329–30; Koyuncu, *Osmanlı İmparatorluğu'nda İçki Üretimi*, pp. 84–5.

43. Shaw, 'Ottoman Tax Reforms', p. 442.

44. Koyuncu, *Osmanlı İmparatorluğu'nda İçki Üretimi*, pp. 88–92, 115.

45. Mehmed Efendi, *Paradis des infidèles*, pp. 49, 228–9; Göçek, *East Encounters West*, pp. 42, 79–80.

46. Upham, *History*, vol. 2, p. 258; Schmidt, '"Guided by the Almighty"', p. 343; Webb, *The Earl and his Butler*, p. 23.

47. Hammer-Purgstall, *Geschichte*, vol. 8, p. 96.

48. Ibid., p. 177.

49. Upham, *History*, vol. 2, pp. 263–5.

50. Sakaoğlu, *Bu Mülkün Sultanları*, p. 403.

51. Dallaway, *Constantinople*, p. 41. The same sultan was also known as dimwitted.

52. Hobhouse, *Journey*, vol 2, p. 279; Başaran, *Selim III*, p. 98.

53. Tott, *Mémoires*, vol. 1, pp. 252–3; Olivier, *Voyage*, vol. 1, p. 324; Başaran, *Selim III*, pp. 96–9, 106.

54. Dallaway, *Constantinople*, p. 43; Hobhouse, *Journey*, vol 2, p. 279.

55. D'Ohsson, *Tableau*, vol. 4, tome 1, p. 51.

56. Rycaut, *History*, pp. 314–16; Smith, *Remarks*, p. 121.

57. Schmidt, '"Guided by the Almighty"', p. 343.

58. Contarini, *Travels to Tana*, p. 139.

59. Pouqueville, *Voyage*, vol. 2, p. 117.

60. Montagu, *Best Letters*, pp. 102–4.

61. Porter, *Turkey*, vol. 1, pp. 334–5.

62. Lubenau, *Beschreibung*, vol. 1, p. 260.

63. Thévenot, *Relation*, vol. 1, p. 62.

64. Busbecq, *Turkish Letters*, pp. 9–10; also see Rycaut, *History*, p. 166.

65. Southgate, *Narrative*, vol. 2, p. 318.

66. Pouqueville, *Voyage*, vol. 2, p. 137.

67. Busbecq, *Turkish Letters*, pp. 110–12, 149–50; Rycaut, *History*, pp. 384–5. For the sobriety of ordinary soldiers, see Senior, *Journal Kept in Turkey*, p. 140; and Georgeon, *Au pays du raki*, pp. 84–5.

68. De Billerbeg, [*Most Rare and Straunge Discourses*], unpag. (p. 2).

69. Rycaut, *History*, pp. 196–8; Goffman, *Izmir*, pp. 114–15; Boyar and Fleet, *Social History*, p. 195; Grehan, *Everyday Life*, p. 134.

70. Thévenot, *Relation*, vol. 1, p. 62; Webb, *Earl and His Butler*, p. 23; Frank, *Histoire de Tunis*, p. 84; Masters, 'Aleppo's Janissaries', p. 165. The British medic William Wittman in 1800 witnessed how in Jaffa in Palestine two men were beheaded for selling wine to Ottoman soldiers. See Wittman, *Travels*, vol. 1, p. 140.

71. Wishnitzer, *As Night Falls*, pp. 84–6.

72. Başaran, *Selim III*, pp. 61–2.
73. Mustafa Âli, *Ottoman Gentleman*, p. 131; Evliya Efendi in Freely, *Stamboul Sketches*, pp. 143–4; Hobhouse, *Journey*, vol. 2, p. 279; Koçu, *Eski İstanbul'da Meyhaneler'*, p. 16.
74. Bassano, *Costumi*, p. 36 (79).
75. Toft, 'Preserving Public Health', p. 213; Mustafa Âli, *Ottoman Gentleman*, pp. 132–3.
76. Freely, *Stamboul Sketches*, p. 145.
77. Lâtifı, *Evsâf-ı İstanbul*, pp. 57–8.
78. Tournefort, *Relation*, vol. 2, p. 223.
79. Eldem, 'Istanbul', p. 150.
80. Tott, *Mémoires*, vol. 1, pp. 252–3.
81. Seetzen, *Tagebuch*, 24 Jan. 1803, p. 96.
82. Southgate, *Narrative*, vol. 2, p. 324.
83. Trépanier, *Food Ways*, p. 118.
84. Maundrell, *Journey*, pp. 12–3.
85. Rycaut, *History*, pp. 131, 149; Burckhardt, *Travels*, p. 201.
86. Covel, 'Extracts From the Diaries', pp. 244–5.
87. Pouqueville, *Voyage*, vol. 1, p. 34; Hobhouse, *Journey*, vol. 1, p. 139.
88. The term raki (T. rakı), like arrack or arak, comes from the Arabic word for sweat (*'araq*), which refers to the dripping that occurs in distilling.
89. Mrgić, 'Wine or Raki', p. 633.
90. Pashley, *Travels*, vol. 1, p. 10.
91. Pouqueville, *Voyage*, vol. 1, p. 391.
92. Browne, *Travels*, pp. 374–5; Bel, 'Ottomans', pp. 190–1.
93. Sestini, *Voyage*, pp. 34–5; Faroqhi, 'Producing Grapes'; Perry, *View of the Levant*, p. 121.
94. Yılmaz, 'What About a Little Fun?', p. 156; Olnon, *'Brought Under the Law'*, pp. 59, 60, 76, 255.
95. Kinglake, *Eothen*, p. 50.
96. Tavernier, *Les six voyages*, vol. 1, p. 87; Fontanier, *Voyages* (1836), p. 112.
97. Olnon, *'Brought Under the Law'*, p. 198.
98. Smyrnelis, 'Colonies européennes', pp. 180–1.
99. D'Arvieux, *Mémoires*, vol. 1, pp. 117–18; DNA, Consulaat Smirna 16, Letter European consuls, 22 October 1782, fols 56–9.
100. Masters, 'Aleppo', pp. 46–7.
101. Ibid., p. 48; Russell, *Natural History*, vol. 1, p. 81; D'Arvieux, 'Mémoires', p. 344.
102. Yılmaz, 'What About a Little Fun?', pp. 154–5.
103. Mather, *Pashas*, p. 78; Darling, *Janissaries of Damascus*, p. 13.
104. Bakhit, *Ottoman Province*, p. 141.
105. Rafeq, 'Public Morality', p. 182.
106. Evstatiev, 'Qādīzādeli Movement', p. 225.
107. Valentia, *Voyages*, vol. 2, p. 350.
108. Tobi, *Juifs et musulmans*, pp. 145–8.
109. Palgrave, *Personal Narrative*, vol. 2, pp. 264, 327; Wellsted, *Travels in Arabia*, vol. 1, pp. 139, 144–5, 434. Wahhabi-inspired Omanis considered the Banu Riyam irascible, slothful and amoral.
110. Niebuhr, *Beschreibung*, vol. 1, p. 56.
111. Burckhardt, *Travels*, vol. 1, p. 361.
112. Freitag, *History of Jeddah*, pp. 301–2.

113. Begum, *Pilgrimage*, p. 35.
114. Von Maltzan, *Drei Jahre*, vol. 1, pp. 298–9.
115. Heine, 'Nabīḏh'.
116. Burckhardt, *Travels*, vol. 1, pp. 361–2.
117. Von Maltzan, *Drei Jahre*, vol. 2, p. 236. Tamisier, *Voyage*, vol. 1, p. 303, in 1834 confirms that the Meccans consumed liquor made from grapes brought from Ta'if.
118. Doughty, *Travels*, vol. 1, p. 151.
119. Lewicka, *Food and Foodways*, p. 547.
120. Ibid.; Winter, *Egyptian Society*, p. 13.
121. Meshal, 'Antagonistic Sharī'as', pp. 189, 198, 205; Idem, *Sharia and the Making*, p. 146.
122. Winter, *Egyptian Society*, p. 230.
123. Olivier, *Voyage*, vol. 3, pp. 17–18.
124. Luth, *La vie quotidienne en Égypte*, p. 180.
125. Maillet, *Description de l'Égypte*, p. 229; Browne, *Travels*, p. 63; Lane, *Manners and Customs*, p. 96; Boyar and Fleet, *Social History*, p. 189; Yılmaz, 'What About a Bit of Fun?', p. 163.
126. Damurdashi, *Damurdashi's Chronicle*, pp. 121–3.
127. Foresien, *Peregrinations*, p. 99; Rycaut, *History*, p. 306.
128. Villamont, *Voyages*, p. 651; Gerlach, *Tage-Buch*, p. 334; Maillet, *Description de l'Égypte*, p. 107.
129. Wild, *Neue Reisebeschreibung*, p. 178.
130. Vansleb, *Present State of Egypt*, pp. 65, 67–68, 154–5.
131. Gonsales, *Hierusalemsche Reyse*, vol. 2, pp. 93, 94, 99.
132. Jackson, *Algiers*, p. 66.
133. Peyssonnel, *Relation d'un voyage*, p. 107.
134. D'Arvieux, *Mémoires*, vol. 4, p. 4.
135. MacGill, *Account of Tunis*, pp. 182–3.
136. Álvarez Dopico, 'Vino y tavernas', pp. 221–2, 225ff, 232.
137. Znaien, *Les raisins*, p. 57.
138. Poiron, *Mémoires*, p. 26.
139. Álvarez Dopico, 'Vino y tavernas', pp. 225ff.; Boujarra, 'al-Zāhira al-khamriyya', p. 40; Znaien, *Les raisins*, p. 98.
140. Boujarra, 'al-Zāhira al-khamriyya', pp. 56–9.
141. Frank, *Histoire de Tunis*, pp. 83–4.
142. MacGill, *Account of Tunis*, pp. 20–1, 182–3; Frank, *Tunis*, p. 71.
143. Windus, *Journey to Mequinez*, pp. 86, 153–4; Braithwaite, *History*, pp. 74, 292.
144. Terrasse, *Histoire du Maroc*, pp. 198, 212, 231.
145. Pidou de Saint Olon, *Estat présent*, p. 8.
146. Pidou de Saint Olon, *Relation*, p. 157; Idem, *Estat présent*, pp. 64, 67; Busnot, *Histoire du règne*, pp. 47–8; Langier de Tassy, *Histoire du royaume d'Alger*, p. 116.
147. Busnot, *Histoire du règne*, pp. 105–8.
148. Windus, *Journey to Mequinez*, p. 147.
149. Braithwaite, *History*, p. 4.
150. La Véronne, *Vie de Moulay Isma'īl*, pp. 42, 111.
151. Jackson, *Account of Morocco*, p. 35.
152. Haringman, *Beknopt dag-journaal*, p. 24.
153. Bernier, *Libertin*, pp. 248–9, 443.

154. Gonzáles de Clavijo, *Narrative*, pp. 147–9, 154–63.
155. Thackston, *Century of Princes*, p. 97.
156. Gonzáles de Clavijo, *Narrative*, p. 97, 244–8.
157. Thackston, *Century of Princes*, p. 118.
158. Khandamir, *Habib al-siyar*, vol. 4, p. 17; Barthold, *Four Studies*, p. 113; Manz, *Power*, pp. 211–12.
159. Barthold, *Four Studies*, p. 114; Lentz et al., 'Shahrukh', p. 97.
160. Babur, *Baburnama*, p. 206; Subtelny, *Timurids in Transition*, pp. 78–9.
161. Khandamir, *Habib al-siyar*, vol. 4, p. 384; Subtelny, 'Late Medieval Persian *Summa*', pp. 603–4.
162. Geleynssen de Jongh, 'Corte verclaringe', fol. 36v.
163. Dale, *Gardens of the Eight Paradises*, p. 143.
164. Ibid., pp. 179–83.
165. Babur, *Baburnama*, pp. 295, 301–2, 305, 311.
166. Bhargava, 'Narcotics and Drugs', pp. 123–4.
167. Honchell, 'Story of the Drunken Mughal', pp. 12–14, 18.
168. Dale, *Gardens of the Eight Paradises*, p. 282. *'Id* (holiday) refers to Ramadan; *ma'jūn* is a paste of opiates and additives.
169. Babur, *Baburnama*, pp. 233, 235–6.
170. Ibid., p. 305.
171. Ibid., pp. 373–6, 387; Bhargava, 'Narcotics and Drugs', pp. 125–6.
172. Qandhari, *Tarikh-i Akbari*, p. 172.
173. Gentil, *Mémoires*, p. 397.
174. Jahangir, *Jahangirnama*, p. 39; Nicoll, *Shah Jahan*, pp. 36–7, 46, 55, 78; Khare, 'Wine Cup'.
175. Bhargava, 'Narcotics and Drugs', p. 127.
176. Roe, *Embassy*, vol. 1, p. 119; vol. 2, p. 362.
177. For an analysis of possible motives, see Lefèvre, *Pouvoir impérial*, pp. 42–3.
178. Foster, *Early Travels in India*, p. 116.
179. Manucci, *Storia do Mogor*, vol. 1, pp. 158–9.
180. Pelsaert, *Kroniek*, p. 302.
181. Manucci, *Storia do Mogor*, vol. 1, pp. 162–3, 153–74.
182. Balabanlilar, *Emperor Jahangir*, pp. 96–7.
183. Pelsaert, *Kroniek*, p. 285; Gandhi, *The Emperor Who Never Was*, pp. 55, 57.
184. Jahangir, *Jahangirnama*, pp. 25, 184–5, 275–6; Chatterjee, 'Lives of Alcohol', p. 202.
185. Nicoll, *Shah Jahan*, pp. 83, 115; Gandhi, *The Emperor Who Never Was*, pp. 39–40, 231.
186. Ibid., p. 227.
187. Ibid., p. 230.
188. Bernier, *Libertin*, pp. 97–8.
189. For an evaluation of this reputation, see Sheikh, 'Aurangzeb as Seen From Gujarat'.
190. Eaton, *India in the Persianate Age*, p. 334.
191. Shah Navaz Khan and 'Abdul Hayy, *Maathir ul-Umarā*, vol. 1, pp. 806–7.
191. Manucci, *Storia do Mogor*, vol. 2, pp. 5–6; Sheikh, 'Aurangzeb as Seen From Gujarat', p. 574.
193. For a recent attempt to 'rehabilitate' Aurangzeb, see Brown, 'Did Aurangzeb Ban Music?'
194. Quoted in Umar, *Urban Culture*, p. 243.
195. Manucci, *Storia do Mogor*, vol. 2, pp. 5–6.

196. Van Santen, *Op bezoek*, p. 76.
197. Manucci, vol. 3, p. 245. Before he took power, Bahadur Shah was known as Shah 'Alam.
198. Irvine, *Later Mughal Rulers*, vol. 1, p. 196.
199. Malik, *Reign of Muhammad Shah*, pp. 285, 367.
200. Grose, *Voyage*, vol. 1, p. 151.

5. ALCOHOL IN THE EARLY MODERN ISLAMIC EMPIRES: THE SAFAVIDS

1. Contarini, *Travels*, p. 132.
2. Mudarrisi Tabataba'i, *Farmānhā-yi Turkamānān*, p. 76.
3. Khandamir, *Tārikh-i habib al-siyar*, vol. 4, p. 132.
4. The quote is from Kaempfer, *Exotic Attractions*, pp. 10, 195. Also see Membré, *Mission*, p. 42; d'Alessandri, 'Narrative', p. 223; and Aubin, *L'ambassade*, pp. 58–9.
5. Bardsiri, *Tazkira-yi Safaviyya*, p. 387.
6. Jodogne, 'La vita del Sophi', p. 228; Tenreiro, *Itinerário*, pp. 105–6; Couto, 'Festins', pp. 572–80.
7. *Rakı Ansiklopedisi*, 'Rakı', p. 375.
8. Ja'fariyan, ed., *Tārikh-i Qizilbāshān*, pp. 79–80.
9. Junabadi, *Rawzat al-Safaviyya*, p. 358.
10. Maybudi, *Munshā'āt-i Maybudi*, p. 233.
11. Khandamir, *Tārikh-i Shāh Ismā'il*, p. 118.
12. Ghafari-Qazvini, *Tārikh-i jahān-ārā*, p. 274; Budaq Qavini, *Javāhir al-akhbār*, p. 128; Anon., *Jahāngushā-yi khāqān*, p. 383; Rumlu, *Ahsan al-tavārikh*, p. 161; Petry, *Twilight of Majesty*, pp. 175–6. This practice existed in various Eurasian tribal societies, from prehistoric Britain to ancient China.
13. Qummi, *Khulāsat al-tavārikh*, vol. 1, pp. 154–5; Khurshah, *Tārikh-i Nizāmshāhi*, pp. 18, 79.
14. Bacqué-Grammont, *Les Ottomans*, p. 86; Matthee, *Pursuit of Pleasure*, p. 50.
15. Tenreiro, *Itinerário*, pp. 105–6. Tenreiro estimated Tahmasb's age to be sixteen.
16. Nava'i, ed., *Shāh 'Abbās*, vol. 1, pp. 117–19.
17. Gaudereau, 'Relation', in Kroell, ed., *Nouvelles d'Ispahan*, p. 64.
18. Alonso, 'Misiones', p. 273.
19. Pires, *Suma Oriental*, p. 27.
20. Shafi' Tihrani, *Mir'āt-i vāridāt*, p. 109.
21. The word *shira* in Persian denotes the residue of opium left in the pipe after it is smoked. But in Safavid times, when opium was ingested rather than smoked, *shira* referred to wine; hence the translation 'winehouse'. See Borhan, *Burhān-i Qāti'*, p. 764.
22. Floor and Javady, *Persian Pleasures*, pp. 275–9.
23. Khuzani Isfahani, *Chronicle*, vol. 2, p. 581; Olearius, *Vermehrte Newe Beschreibung*, p. 527.
24. Chardin, *Voyages*, vol. 9, pp. 360–1; Kaempfer, *Exotic Attractions*, p. 300.
25. Floor, *German Sources*, pp. 578–9.
26. [Villotte/Frizon], *Voyages*, p. 124.
27. Chardin, *Voyages*, vol. 9, p. 360.
28. Matthee, *Pursuit of Pleasure*, pp. 48, 52, 63, 66.
29. Mashizi, *Tazkira-yi Safaviyya-yi Kirmān*, p. 448; Mustawfi Bafqi, *Jāmi'a-yi mufidi*, vol. 3, p. 196–7; DNA, VOC 1297, Gamron to Heren XVII, 1 April 1675, fol. 1011r.

30. Tavernier, *Les six voyages*, vol. 1, pp. 103–4.
31. Zak'aria of Agulis, *Journal*, pp. 148–9.
32. Chardin, *Voyages*, vol. 3, p. 218; vol. 4, pp. 69–70.
33. Tavernier, *Les six voyages*, vol. 1, p. 277. In modern Turkey there is still a strong association between fish and alcohol. See Knudsen, 'Between Life Giver and Leisure'.
34. Herbert, *Travels*, p. 306.
35. Floor and Javady, *Persian Pleasures*, p. 265.
36. Tavernier, *Les six voyages*, vol. 1, p. 662.
37. Windler, 'Regelobservanz', pp. 57-8; and [Chick], *Chronicle*, vol. 1, pp. 515–16.
38. Kaempfer, *Exotic Attractions*, pp. 297–301.
39. Chardin, *Voyages*, vol. 3, pp. 216–17, gives between one and three pints; Manucci, *Storia di Mogor*, vol. 1, p. 40, mentions two and a half *canada*s, or almost four liters. Tsar Peter the Great's similar receptacle, the 'Great Eagle', held 1.25 liters of vodka, not wine.
40. Chardin, *Voyages*, vol. 3, pp. 216–17; Tavernier, *Les six voyages*, vol. 1, p. 500; Speelman, *Journaal*, p. 271; Manucci, *Storia di Mogor*, vol. 1, p. 40; Hoppe, 'Diplomatischen Missionen', p. 161. For the Russian 'Great Eagle', see Schrad, *Vodka Politics*, pp. 42–6.
41. Père Sanson, Isfahan, 8 April 1691, in Kroell, ed., *Nouvelles d'Ispahan*, p. 30.
42. Sanson, *Estat de la Perse*, pp. 112–35.
43. Matthee, 'Politics of Protection', pp. 256–7.
44. Połczyński, 'Relacyja', p. 91.
45. Bedik, *Man of Two Worlds*, pp. 222–3.
46. Details in Matthee, 'Safavid Iran', pp. 75–8.
47. Manucci, *Storia di Mogor*, vol. 1, p. 41.
48. Speelman, *Journaal der reis*, p. 148.
49. ARSI, Gall. 97ⁱⁱ, Claude Ignace, Isfahan to Claude Bouchier, Rome, 10 Nov. 1665, fols. 331–2.
50. A third non-eyewitness description is by Maertial de Thorigne, who resided in Aleppo and compiled reports from various locales in the East. See Richard, *Raphaël du Mans*, pp. 153–66.
51. Tavernier, *Les six voyages*, vol. 1, pp. 498–504; Dauliers Deslandes, *Les beautés de la Perse*, pp. 30–37; Kroell, ed., *Nouvelles d'Ispahan*, pp. 18–19; Richard, *Raphaël du Mans*, vol. 1, pp. 154ff.
52. Tavernier, *Les six voyages*, vol. 1, pp. 551–4, who speculates that the victim may have owed the 'lesser' punishment to the intercession of a harem lady.
53. Lettre du Réverend Père H. B. à Mons. Comte de M., in *Lettres édifiantes et curieuses*, vol. 4, p. 118.
54. Dunlop, ed., *Bronnen*, pp. 747–9; Rota, *La vita*, pp. 92, 354.
55. DNA, VOC 1106, Overschie, Isfahan to Heren XVII, 8 May 1633, unfol.
56. Tavernier, *Les six voyages*, vol. 1, pp. 522–3.
57. DNA, VOC 1248, Gamron to Batavia, 30 Aug. 1664, fol. 3046.
58. IOR, G/36/106/106, Gombroon to Surat, 29 April 1672, fol. 96; ibid., Gombroon to Surat, 27 Nov. 1672, fol. 38.
59. Details in Matthee, 'Administrative Stability', pp. 84–5.
60. Manucci, *Storia di Mogor*, vol. 1, p. 30.
61. Matthee, *Pursuit of Pleasure*, p. 73.
62. Shah Tahmasb, *Tazkira*, pp. 29–30.
63. Qiriqlu, 'Bardāsht'hā-yi Sufiyān', p. 108.

64. Qummi, *Khulāsat al-tavārikh*, vol. 1, p. 386.

65. Ja'fariyan, *Naqsh-i khāndān*, pp. 278–88.

66. Qummi, *Khulāsat al-tavārikh*, vol. 1, pp. 314–15; Rumlu, *Ahsan al-tavārikh*, pp. 405–6.

67. Budaq Qazvini, *Javāhir al-akhbār*, pp. 166–7; 'Abdi Bayg, *Takmilat al-akhbār*, pp. 76–7; Qummi, *Khulāsat al-tavārikh*, vol. 1, pp. 225–6.

68. Matthee, *Pursuit of Pleasure*, pp. 78–9.

69. Membré, *Mission*, p. 25.

70. Roxburgh, *Persian Album*, pp. 245–9.

71. Soudavar, 'Between the Safavids and the Mughals', p. 51.

72. Jawhar, *Tezkereh al Vakiāt*, p. 73.

73. For this, see Matthee, *Pursuit of Pleasure*, pp. 74ff.

74. Della Valle, *Delle conditioni*, pp. 6, 48, 52, 109–10; Pinçon, 'Relation', p. 155.

75. Del Niño Jesūs, *A Persia*, p. 117.

76. Tectander, *Abenteuerliche Reise*, p. 65.

77. De Orta Rebelo, *Un voyageur portugais*, pp. 124–5.

78. Khuzani Isfahani, *Chronicle*, p. 794; Della Valle, *Viaggi*, vol. 2, pp. 143–4.

79. [Chick], *Chronicle*, vol. 1, pp. 255–6.

80. Khuzani Isfahani, *Chronicle*, p. 949.

81. Ja'fariyan, *Safaviyya dar 'arsa-yi din*, vol. 1, p. 380.

82. Qazi b. Kashif al-Din Muhammad, *Jām-i jahān-nāma*, pp. 27–31.

83. Husayni, *Tārikh-i Shāh Safi*, pp. 22–3; Tafrishi, *Mabāni-yi tārikh*, p. 220.

84. [Chick], *Chronicle*, vol. 1, p. 350; Krusinski, *History*, vol. 1, p. 47.

85. Diary Jan Smidt, in Dunlop, ed., *Bronnen*, pp. 738, 741, 746–7.

86. Tavernier, *Les six voyages*, vol. 1, pp. 517–18.

87. Tafrishi, *Tārikh-i Shah Safi*, pp. 22–3; and Matthee, *Pursuit of Pleasure*, pp. 52–3.

88. Tavernier, *Les six voyages*, vol. 1, p. 579; Kamal ibn Jalal, *Tārikh-i mukhtasar*, p. 129.

89. Qazvini, *Tārikh-i jahān-ārā-yi 'Abbasi*, pp. 412–6; details in Matthee, *Pursuit of Pleasure*, pp. 85–6.

90. Vala Isfahani, *Khuld-i barin*, p. 480

91. Matthee, *Pursuit of Pleasure*, pp. 85–90.

92. Chardin, *Voyages*, vol. 5, pp. 215–16; details in Matthee, *Pursuit of Pleasure*, pp. 89–90.

93. Qummi, *Opposition to Philosophy*, pp. 18, 20.

94. Sabzavari, *Rawzat al-anvār-i 'Abbāsi*, pp. 143–80.

95. Chardin, *Voyages*, vol. 10, p. 88.

96. Bembo, *Travels*, p. 302; Sebastian, *Breve relación*, p. 217.

97. IOR, G/37/107, Rolt, Gombroon to Surat, 17 April 1675, fol. 88.

98. DNA, VOC 1323, Casembroot to Gamron, 2 March 1678, fol. 688.

99. Kaempfer, *Exotic Attractions*, pp. 198–9.

100. DNA, VOC 1501, Notulen Van Leene, 21 March 1691, fol. 508.

101. Nasiri, *Dastur-i shahriyārān*, pp. 39–40. In provincial cities, the proclamation was engraved above the entrance portals of mosques.

102. [Villotte/Frizon], *Voyages*, pp. 313–14.

103. DNA, VOC 1549, Verdonck, Gamron to Heren XVII, 9 Dec. 1694, fol. 617r; [Chick], *Chronicle*, vol. 1, pp. 470–1.

104. [Gaudereau], *Relation*, p. 38.

105. Krusinski, *History*, vol. 1, p. 72.

106. De Bruyn, *Reizen*, pp. 127 and 434.

107. Bell of Antermony, *Travels*, vol. 1, p. 135.

108. Yeşilot, *Şah'in Ülkesinde*, p. 118.

6. CHANGING DRINKING HABITS IN THE NINETEENTH CENTURY—PART
   ONE: THE OTTOMAN EMPIRE AND NORTH AFRICA

1. Hattox, *Coffee and Coffeehouses*, p. 78
2. Schrad, *Smashing the Liquor Machine*, p. 72.
3. Findley, *Turkey, Islam, Nationalism*, p. 91.
4. Badem, *Ottoman Crimean War*, pp. 331–43.
5. For more on this, see Aydin, *Idea of the Muslim World*, chs. 1 and 2.
6. Georgeon, *Le mois plus long*, p. 98.
7. Lane-Poole, *Life of Stratford Canning*, vol. 1, p. 504, vol. 2, pp. 75–6. This demeanor
   earned the sovereign the epithet *gâvur sultan*, or 'infidel sultan', among his more
   traditional subjects.
8. Georgeon, 'Le sultan caché', pp. 95–6.
9. Ibid., pp. 106–7; Walsh, *Residence*, vol. 2, pp. 275–6.
10. Southgate, *Narrative*, vol. 2, pp. 335–6.
11. Ibid.; Šedivý, *Metternich*, pp. 630–1.
12. Eldem, 'In Vino Modernitas', pp. 530, 534, 539, 544–5. For Husrev Pasha, see
    Moltke, *Briefe*, pp. 102ff.
13. White, *Three Years*, vol. 3, p. 100; Farman, *Constantinople*, p. 22; Šedivý, *Metternich*,
    p. 640.
14. White, *Three Years*, vol. 3, pp. 100–1.
15. De Kératry, *Mourad V*, p. 70; Greppi, 'Souvenirs', p. 379 ; Mansel, *Levant*, p. 54.
16. [Mordtmann], *Stambul*, vol. 1, p. 15.
17. Greppi, 'Souvenirs', pp. 381–3 ; [Mordtmann], *Stambul*, vol. 1, p. 20; vol. 2, pp. 160–
    2, 271; Millingen, *La Turquie*, pp. 250–8, 299ff.; *Islâm Ansiklopedisi*, 'Abdülaziz',
    pp. 180, 183.
18. Dumont, 'L'homme malade', pp. 512–5; Şiviloğlu, *Emergence*, pp. 229ff.
19. Pears, *Life of Abdul Hamid*, pp. 37–44.
20. Georgeon, 'Le sultan caché', pp. 119–20.
21. Müller, *Letters*, p. 90; Şiviloğlu, *Emergence*, p. 248; Rakı Ansiklopedisi, 'Abdülhamid',
    p. 11. The sultan told Lady Layard that he did not drink wine. See Layard, *Twixt Pera
    and Therapia*, p. 54.
22. Georgeon, *Abdülhamid II*, pp. 434–5.
23. Georgeon, *Le mois plus long*, pp. 193–4.
24. See Arpacı, 'Sağlam Nesiller ya da Dejenerasyon', p. 37; Engin, *Sultan Abdülhamid*,
    pp. 62–5; and Wishnitzer, 'Eyes in the Dark', pp. 248–9.
25. Müller, *Letters*, p. 90; Georgeon, *Abdülhamid II*, p. 448; *Rakı Ansiklopedesi*,
    'Abdülhamid', pp. 13–14.
26. De Amicis, *Constantinople*, p. 215.
27. Tevfîq, *Ein Jahr in Konstantinopel*, p. 12.
28. Fontanier, *Voyages* (1834), pp. 90–1; Mordtmann, *Skizzen*, p. 297.
29. Eldem, 'French View', pp. 174–9.
30. Grunzel, *Bericht*, p. 20.
31. Rougon, *Smyrne*, p. 361; Köse, *Westlicher Konsum*, p. 160.
32. White, *Three Years*, vol. 3, p. 97.
33. Southgate, *Narrative*, vol. 2, p. 329; Rougon, *Smyrne*, p. 362.

34. Ubicini, *Lettres*, vol. 1, p. 404.
35. Rougon, *Smyrne*, p. 362; Köse, *Westlicher Konsum*, pp. 146–7, 160.
36. Grunzel, *Bericht*, p. 165.
37. De Kay, *Sketches*, p. 360.
38. Moltke, *Briefe*, pp. 102, 104. 'Çamlıca' currently refers a Turkish soft drink.
39. De Kay, *Sketches*, p. 360; Farman, *Constantinople*, pp. 19–22.
40. Brewer, *Residence*, p. 368. At least 4,000 are said to have been killed.
41. Koyuncu, *Osmanlı İmparatorluğu'nda İçki Üretimi*, p. 106; Georgeon, *Au pays du raki*, p. 141.
42. Southgate, *Narrative*, vol. 2, p. 328.
43. [Mordtmann], *Stambul*, pp. 134–5.
44. Southgate, *Narrative*, vol. 2, p. 328.
45. Lane-Poole, *Life of Stratford Canning*, vol. 2, pp. 75–6.
46. MacFarlane, *Constantinople*, pp. 47–8. Katiboğlu ended up being sent to Mytilene (Lesbos) where he was beheaded.
47. Walsh, *Residence*, vol. 2, pp. 311–12.
48. White, *Three Years*, vol. 3, pp. 96–9, 101.
49. [Porter], *Constantinople*, vol. 2, p. 6. Porter's source was Stratford Canning.
50. Smith and Dwight, *Missionary Researches*, p. 30.
51. Southgate, *Narrative*, vol. 2, pp. 327–8; and Porter, *Turkey*, vol. 1, p. 335; Galizzi, *Souvenirs*, p. 78.
52. Georgeon, *Au pays du raki*, p. 153.
53. *Revue commerciale du Levant*, pp. 196–201; 'Raki et apéritifs' (1903, 2me semestre), p. 119.
54. Boyar, 'Late Ottoman Brothel', pp. 170–4. As of 1845, a bridge, the *Cisr-i Cedid* (New Bridge), linked Karaköy with Galata, but those wishing to cross had to pay a toll (the *mürüriye*).
55. Neumann, 'Contribution'.
56. Southgate, *Narrative*, vol. 2, p. 324.
57. Tevfîq, *Ein Jahr in Konstantinopel*, p. 9.
58. Ibid., pp. 10, 51–8, 71–8; Koçu, *Eski Istanbul'da Meyhaneler*, pp. 15–16, 30–4, 54–5.
59. Avcı, 'Shifts in Sexual Desire', pp. 769–71.
60. Tevfîq, *Ein Jahr in Konstantinopel*, pp. 60–5; Koçu, *Eski Istanbul'da Meyhaneler*, p. 15.
61. Tevfîq, *Ein Jahr in Konstantinopel*, pp. 5, 87; Koçu, *Eski Istanbul'da Meyhaneler*, pp. 32–4; Bareilles, *Constantinople*, pp. 82–3.
62. Fuhrmann, *Port Cities*, p. 192.
63. Koçu, *Eski Istanbul'da Meyhaneler*, pp. 115–16.
64. Eren, *Geçmişten Günümüze Anadolu'da Bira*, pp. 71–2.
65. Ibid., pp. 61, 64–5.
66. Mylès, *Fin de Stamboul*, pp. 102–10.
67. Bareilles, *Constantinople*, pp. 47–8.
68. Muhidine, *Istanbul*, p. 97.
69. *Rakı Ansiklopedisi*, 'Gazinolar', pp. 225–9.
70. Eldem, 'Ottoman Galata', p. 35.
71. Georgeon, 'Ramadan à Istanbul', pp. 47–9
72. Neumann, 'Contribution', p. 2.
73. Reinelt, *Reise*, p. 140–3.
74. Georgelin, *Smyrne*, p. 33; Martini, *Crépuscule*, p. 20.

75. Fuhrmann, *Port Cities*, pp. 175–81.
76. Reinelt, *Reise*, pp. 150, 160, 164.
77. Rougon, *Smyrne*, p. 362.
78. Georgelin, *La fin de Smyrne*, p. 112.
79. Fuhrmann, 'Down and Out'.
80. Bali, ed., *Survey*, pp. 106–9.
81. Martini, *Crépuscule*, p. 30.
82. Galizzi, *Souvenirs*, pp. 23–6, 45, 55, 62.
83. Southgate, *Narrative*, vol. 2, p. 322; Beauchamp, *La vie d'Ali Pacha*, pp. 249–50; Philippe, *Acre*, p. 59; Skinner, *Adventures*, vol. 2, p. 134. Ahmed Pasha is said to have given up on drinking after returning from the hajj in 1791.
84. Kırmızı, 'Drunken Officials'.
85. *Revue commerciale du Levant* 261, 'Vins et spiritueux' (31 December 1908), p. 807; and pp. 322–7.
86. Dallaway, *Constantinople*, p. 266; Seetzen, *Tagebuch*, p. 671.
87. Georgelin, *La fin de Smyrne*, pp. 112–3.
88. Knudsen, 'Between Life Giver and Leisure', p. 406.
89. *Die heutige Türkei*, vol. 2, p. 130.
90. Fontanier, *Voyages* (1829), vol. 1, p. 244.
91. Rich, *Narrative*, vol. 2, p. 59.
92. Ibid., pp. 153, 211.
93. d'Beth Hillel, *Travels*, p. 42.
94. Mélikoff, 'Le problème Kizilbash', pp. 64ff.; Eadem, *Hadji Bektach*, pp. 204–10.
95. Jessup, *Fifty-Three Years*, pp. 730–1.
96. Bel, *Paysages viticoles*, pp. 42–3; Eldem, 'French View', p. 181.
97. Georgeon, *Au pays du raki*, pp. 147–9.
98. Tancoigne, *Voyage*, pp. 95, 145–6.
99. Pashley, *Travels*, vol. 1, pp. xxviii and xxx; Lindsay, *Letters*, vol. 2, p. 295.
100. Shaw, 'Ottoman Tax Reforms', p. 442; Birdal, *Political Economy*, p. 121.
101. Wishnitzer, *When Night Falls*, pp. 104–5.
102. Wishnitzer, 'Eyes in the Dark', pp. 248–9.
103. Shaw, 'Ottoman Tax Reforms', pp. 442–3; Köse, *Westlicher Konsum*, pp. 151 and 170; and Fuhrmann, 'Beer'.
104. Aksan, *Ottoman Wars*, p. 360.
105. Senior, *Journal*, pp. 214, 131–6, 185; Rosenthal, *Politics of Dependency*, pp. 107–13.
106. Dwight, *Constantinople*, pp. 194–5.
107. Edman, 'Temperance and Modernity'.
108. Besim Ömer, *Mükeyyefat ve Müskirat*; Vanizade, *Müskirat*; Georgeon, *Au pays du raki*, pp. 180–2.
109. Nuri, *Müskirat ve İşretin Sebeb Olduğu*.
110. Kuneralp, 'Aspects de la vie sociale', p. 351.
111. Sestini, *Viaggio*, p. 160.
112. Al-Jabarti, *Napoleon in Egypt*, pp. 45, 93.
113. Seetzen, *Seetzen's Reisen*, vol. 3, p. 180.
114. Lane, *Manners and Customs*, p. 96.
115. Burton, *Personal Pilgrimage*, vol. 1, pp. 133–40; Didier, *Nuits du Caire*, p. 358; Hamont, *L'Égypte sous Méhémet-Ali*, vol. 1, p. 516.
116. Šedivý, *Metternich*, pp. 464–5.

117. *Histoire de l'Égypte*, p. 81; St. John, *Egypt and Mohammed Ali*, vol. 1, pp. 58–63; vol. 2, p. 393.
118. Tamisier, *Voyage*, vol. 1, pp. 148–9.
119. Toledano, *State and Society*, pp. 244–7.
120. Fahmy, *In Quest of Justice*, pp. 196–7, 204–5, 202–4.
121. Ezzat, 'Law and Moral Regulation', pp. 681–3.
122. Fahmy, *In Quest of Justice*, pp. 202–5, 208–10.
123. Gautier, *L'Orient*, vol. 2, p. 209; Behrens-Abouseif, *Azbakiyya*, pp. 78–90, 98; Kozma, *Policing Egyptian Women*, pp. 84, 86–7.
124. Gautier, *L'Orient*, vol. 2, p. 209; Behrens-Abouseif, *Azbakiyya*, p. 98; Kozma, *Policing Egyptian Women*, p. 84; Cormack, *Midnight in Cairo*, p. 31.
125. Kozma, *Policing Egyptian Women*, pp. 91–2.
126. Zwemer, 'Mohammedans and Their Drink', pp. 366–7.
127. Johnston, 'Prohibition of Alcohol', p. 428.
128. Hammad, 'Regulating Sexuality', pp. 203–6.
129. Blunt, *My Diaries*, vol. 1, pp. 33–5.
130. Ibid., Cromer, *Modern Egypt*, vol. 2, pp. 251–2; Low, *Egypt in Transition*, pp. 279–80; Foda, 'The Pyramid and the Crown'; Foda, *Egypt's Beer*, p. 17.
131. Lucas, *Alcoholic Liquors*, pp. 1–5, 10.
132. Johnston, 'Prohibition of Alcohol', p. 737.
133. Foda, 'Anna and Ahmad', pp. 119–23.
134. Rohlps, *Adventures*, p. 161.
135. Von Maltzan, *Drei Jahre*, vol. 4, p. 46; Kenbib, *Juifs et musulmans*, pp. 30, 32.
136. White, *Blood of the Colony*, pp. 36–7, 96. Many of the settles were from Spain, Italy, and Malta.
137. Ibid., p. 82.
138. Isnard, *La vigne en Algérie*, vol. 2, pp. 45, 47.
139. White, *Blood of the Colony*, p. 97.
140. Peyronnet, *Le vignoble nord-africaine*, pp. 11, 148.
141. Thierry-Mieg, *Six semaines*, p. 357.
142. Cited in Studer, 'The Same Drink', p. 30.
143. Wagner, *Reisen*, vol. 1, p. 239.
144. Studer, 'It Is Only Gazouz'.
145. Thierry-Mieg, *Six semaines*, pp. 322, 353.
146. Studer, 'It Is Only Gazouz', pp. 418–19.
147. CADN, 1AE/138/35, Tunisie française, 21 November 1901, Maurice Leclercq, 'Assimiler les Arabes'; Znaien, 'Le vin et la viticulture', pp. 142, 144; Idem, *Les raisins*, pp. 51–3.
148. Munji, *Mazāhir al-fasād*, pp. 8, 12.
149. Larguèche, *Les ombres de Tunis*, pp. 36, 264, 268, 270–1; Munji, *Mazāhir al-fasād*, p. 10.
150. Znaien, *Les raisins*, p. 127.
151. Miège and Hugues, *Les Européens à Casablanca*, pp. 30, 36, 107.
152. Javier Martínez, 'Drinking Dis-ease', pp. 62ff. For the population figures, see Rivet, *Histoire du Maroc*, p. 229.

7. CHANGING DRINKING HABITS IN THE NINETEENTH CENTURY—PART TWO: QAJAR IRAN

1. This has been argued by Hamadeh, *The City's Pleasures*, pp. 234–5.
2. Fraser, *History of Nadir Shah*, p. 227; Hanway, *Account*, vol. 4, p. 268.
3. Floor, *Rise and Fall*, p. 69.
4. Ferrières-Sauveboeuf, *Mémoires historiques*, vol. 2, pp. 62–3.
5. Werner, 'Taming the Tribal Native', pp. 226–7.
6. Rustam al-Hukama, *Rustam al-tavārikh*, pp. 331ff. Rustam al-Hukama may have been a pseudonym for the prominent late Qajar court historiographer Riza Quli Khan Hidayat.
7. Mirza Muhammad Kalantar-i Fars, *Ruznāma*, pp. 72–3; tr. in Busse, *History of Persia*, pp. 9–10, who renders *shāhidan*, which clearly refers to ephebes, as 'women'.
8. Olivier, *Voyage*, vol. 5, pp. 189; vol. 6, p. 117.
9. Southgate, *Narrative*, vol. 2, pp. 17, 22–3, 322. Also see Dubeux, *La Perse*, p. 26.
10. Gordon, *Persia Revisited*, p. 53.
11. Bellew, *From the Indus*, pp. 428, 430.
12. MacGregor, *Narrative*, vol. 2, p. 86; Napier, 'Diary of a Tour', p. 86.
13. Bellew, *From the Indus*, p. 430.
14. Wills, *Persia as It Is*, pp. 153–5. Gordon, *Persia Revisited*, p. 59, echoed Wills' verdict on wine from Hamadan.
15. Korf, *Vospominaniia*, pp. 128–9.
16. Bérézine, *Voyage*, p. 221.
17. Vámbéry, *Meine Wanderungen*, p. 231.
18. Wills, *Land of the Lion and the Sun*, p. 363; Issawi, *Economic History of Iran*, pp. 60–1.
19. Wills, *Persia as It Is*, pp. 154–5.
20. Olivier, *Voyage*, vol. 5, pp. 280–1.
21. Flandin, *Voyage*, vol. 2, pp. 404 and 414–15; Southgate, *Narrative*, vol. 2, pp. 17, 22–3, 322; Collins, *In the Kingdom*, p. 57.
22. Kitto, *People of Persia*, p. 172.
23. Southgate, *Narrative*, vol. 2, p. 322.
24. Wills, *Land of the Lion and the Sun*, pp. 141–2, 363.
25. CADN, 685PO/A/78, Crampon to Tehran, 27 July 1868, fol. 225.
26. Wills, *Persia as It Is*, pp. 156–8.
27. Vámbéry, *Meine Wanderungen*, p. 231.
28. Southgate, *Narrative*, vol. 2, p. 325.
29. Stern, *Dawnings of Light*, pp. 121, 132.
30. Sa'idi Sirjani, *Vaqā'i-yi ittifāqiyya*, p. 172.
31. Wills, *Land of the Lion and the Sun*, pp. 141–2, 363
32. *Guzārish'hā-yi nazmiyya*, pp. 25, 33, 36, 49–50, 68, 79, 103, 116, 143–4, 155–6, 196, 197, 243, 371, 379, 394, 250, 254, 283, 284, 301, 311, 316, 347.
33. Fraser, *Narrative*, p. 422.
34. Bérézine, *Voyage en Perse*, p. 221.
35. Von Kotzbue, *Narrative*, pp. 122–3.
36. Flandin, *Voyage*, vol. 2, pp. 404 and 414–15.
37. Von Kotzbue, *Narrative*, pp. 197–8; Bérézine, *Voyage*, p. 221.
38. Southgate, *Narrative*, vol. 2, p. 324.
39. Ibid., p. 326.

40. Ibid., pp. 326–7.
41. Anon. [Ritter von Riederer], *Aus Persien*, p. 86.
42. Rivadeneyra, *Viaje al interior*, vol. 2, p. 70.
43. Southgate, *Narrative*, vol. 2, pp. 326–7.
44. Ferrier, *Caravan Journeys*, p. 151. The Iranians had lost Herat at the time, yet still claimed it as theirs.
45. Mumtahin al-Dawla, *Khātirāt*, p. 289.
46. Arfa, *Memories*, pp. 212–14.
47. Lomnitskii, *Persiia i Persy*, pp. 121–2.
48. Waring, *Tour to Sheeraz*, pp. 67–8.
49. Bérézine, *Voyage*, p. 221.
50. Stern, *Dawnings*, p. 148.
51. Kitto, *People of Persia*, pp. 109–11.
52. I'timad al-Saltana, *Ruznāma*, pp. 828, 830.
53. Gleave, 'The Clergy and the British', p. 50; Martin, 'The British in Bushehr', p. 59.
54. Sipihr, *Mir'āt al-vaqā'i-yi Muzaffari*, pp. 26–7.
55. Tsadik, 'Jews in the Pre-constitutional Years', pp. 248, 252–3.
56. Southgate, *Narrative*, vol. 2, p. 322.
57. Keppel, *Personal Narrative*, vol. 2, pp. 57–9.
58. Von Kotzbue, *Narrative*, pp. 105, 110–11, 122–3.
59. D'Beth Hillel, *Travels*, p. 87.
60. Conolly, *Journey*, vol. 2, pp. 2, 16–17, 20–1.
61. Ferrier, *Caravan Journeys*, pp. 151–2, 186–7.
62. Perkins, *Residence*, p. 226.
63. Flandin, *Voyage*, vol. 1, p. 171.
64. Southgate, *Narrative*, vol. 2, p. 17.
65. Stuart, *Journal*, pp. 138, 206.
66. Napier, 'Diary of a Tour', p. 78.
67. Ibid., p. 95.
68. Fraser, *Narrative*, pp. 391–2.
69. O'Donovan, *Merv Oasis*, vol. 1, p. 438.
70. Baker, *Clouds in the East*, p. 286.
71. Curzon, *Persia*, vol. 1, p. 108, thought it 'extremely nasty'.
72. Fraser, *Narrative*, pp. 577–8.
73. Baker, *Clouds in the East*, p. 276.
74. Curzon, *Persia*, vol. 1, p. 102.
75. Yate, *Khorasan and Sistan*, p. 179.
76. Curzon, *Persia*, vol. 1, p. 101.
77. I'timad al-Dawla, *Ruznāma*, pp. 247–8.
78. Floyer, *Unexplored Balūchistan*, pp. 256–7, 318, 331.
79. Wills, *Land of the Lion and the Sun*, pp. 243–6.
80. Saravi, *Tārikh-i Muhammadi*, p. 285.
81. Von Kotzbue, *Narrative*, pp. 256–8.
82. Fath 'Ali Shah, *Divān;* Dubeux, *La Perse*, p. 388, called him 'assez sobre'.
83. Arjomand, 'Mujtahid of the Age', p. 90.
84. 'Azud al-Dawla, *Tārikh-i 'Azudi*, p. 81.
85. Smith and Dwight, *Missionary Researches*, p. 322.
86. Bélanger, *Voyage*, vol. 2/ii, pp. 376–87.

87. Porter, *Travels in Georgia*, p. 349.
88. Rivadeneyra, *Viage al interior de Persia*, vol. 2, p. 155.
89. Bambad, *Sharh-i hāl*, vol. 3, p. 114.
90. Sheil, *Glimpses*, pp. 327–8.
91. Brugsch, *Im Land der Sonne*, p. 203.
92. Sheil, *Glimpses*, p. 200.
93. Burgess, *Letters from Persia*, p. 60.
94. Stuart, *Journal*, p. 169.
95. Southgate, *Narrative*, vol. 2, pp. 32, 79, 321; Wilbraham, *Travels*, p. 17; and, for the English porter, Fowler, *Three Years*, vol. 1, p. 48.
96. Sercey, *La Perse*, pp. 206–7; Flandin and Coste, *Voyage*, vol. 1, p. 316.
97. I'timad al-Saltana, *Ruznāma*, pp. 300, 778; Dust 'Ali Khan, *Yāddāsht'ha*, p. 23; and, for the wider context, Matthee, *Pursuit of Pleasure*, pp. 179ff.
98. Dust 'Ali Khan, *Yāddāsht'hā*, pp. 74–5; Qaziha, *Marāsim-i darbār*, pp. 5–9.
99. Wilson, *Persian Life*, p. 171.
100. Smirnov, *Zapiski*, p. 61; Dawlatabadi, *Hayāt-i Yahyā*, vol. 1, p. 149.
101. Brydges, *Account*, p. 423. Brydges surmised that the shah liked being read to and listening to music.
102. I'timad al-Saltana, *Ruznāma*, pp. 34, 76, 95, 109, 119, 120, 128, 152, 155, 171, 208, 263, 343, 367, 414, 445, 447, 508, 656, 670, 752, 924, 925, 935, 1005, 1013.
103. Ibid., p. 678.
104. Ibid., p. 545.
105. Gasteiger, *Handelsverhältnisse*, pp. 32–3; Vámbéry, *Meine Wanderungen*, pp. 236–7.
106. I'timad al-Saltana, *Ruznāma*, p. 642.
107. Mukhbir al-Saltana, *Khātirāt*, p. 383; Wills, *Persia as It Is*, p. 301, who in the 1880s reckoned that the number of Englishmen in the country was well under 100.
108. MAE Corr. pol., Perse 37, Tholozan to Nasir al-Din Shah, 'Notes sur l'apauvrissement monétaire de la Perse et sur le moyens d'y remédier', 20 October 1875, fol. 366r-v.
109. I'timad al-Saltana, *Ruznāma*, p. 710.
110. Curzon, *Persia*, vol. 2, p. 507.
111. Perkins, *Residence*, p. 225.
112. Sercey, *La Perse*, p. 151.
113. Wagner, *Travels*, vol. 3, pp. 110–11.
114. Ibid., p. 80.
115. CADN, 685PO/A/78, annex to letter Crampon to Tehran 15 May 1868, fol. 118; and Idem, 8 June 1868, fol. 144.
116. Lomnitskii, *Persiia i Persy*, pp. 62, 379.
117. Fraser, *Narrative*, p. 422.
118. Wills, *Persia as It Is*, p. 153.
119. Ouseley, *Travels*, vol. 3, pp. 249, 317.
120. AAE, Corr. pol., n.s., Perse 47, 'Rapport sur le mouvement commercial de l'année persane, 21 mars 1902 à 20 mars 1903'.
121. Taqizada, *Zindigi-yi tufāni*, p. 45.
122. AAE, Corr. pol., n.s., Perse 6, Nicolas, Tabriz, 10 Aug. 1909, fol. 200.
123. Kuss, *Handelsratgeber*, p. 121.
124. AAE, Corr. pol., n.s., Perse 49, 'Notes sur Guilan', fol. 57.
125. Ibid., 'Notes sur les conséquences économiques de la guerre en Guilan', fols. 5 and 27.
126. DNA, VOC 2511, Koenad, Gamron to Boucher [Bushehr], 5 May 1740, fol. 1017.

127. Sheil, *Glimpses*, p. 157.
128. Gasteiger, *Handelverhältnisse*, p. 33.
129. AAE, Corr. comm., Tauris, 1869–70, fol. 432v.
130. AAE, Corr. comm., Audibert, 'Commerce de Tauris', Tabriz, 12 June 1896.
131. NA, FO 1894, DCR, 'Report for the year 1893–94 on the Trade of Shiraz', p. 13.
132. AAE, Corr. pol., n.s., Perse 47, 'Rapport sur le mouvement commercial de l'année persane bars-il, 21 mars 1902 à 20 mars 1903'.
133. Ibid.
134. Kuss, *Handelsratgeber*, p. 121.
135. Ibid.
136. Arfa', *Memories*, pp. 233–4.
137. Wishard, *Twenty Years*, p. 90.
138. Taqizada, *Zindigi-yi tufāni*, p. 44.
139. Schayegh, *Who Is Knowledgeable*, pp. 92, 179.
140. Kashani, 'Dar bayān-i ikhtilāl'.
141. Floor, 'Premières règles', p. 177.

8. ALCOHOL IN THE MODERN AGE: NEW DRINKS AND DRINKING CUSTOMS—PART ONE: THE ARAB WORLD

1. Hammad, *The Parisian*, pp. 6–7.
2. Zwemer, 'Mohammedans and Their Drink', p. 367.
3. Tuominen, 'Clash of Values', p. 43.
4. Courtwright, *Forces of Habit*, p. 178.
5. The French plied Moulay 'Abd al-Hafiz with large quantities of bubbly on the cruiser that took him to Marseille as part of a series of tastings that induced him to agree to his country becoming a French protectorate. See Sainte Aulaire, *Confession*, pp. 255–62; and Javier Martínez, 'Drinking Dis-ease', pp. 61–2.
6. Harry, *Tunis la blanche*, pp. 222–31.
7. Aubin, *Le Maroc*, p. 349; Javier Martínez, 'Drinking dis-ease', p. 64; Flamand, *Mellah en pays berbère*, p. 81; Gottreich, *Mellah of Marrakesh*, p. 78.
8. White, *Blood of the Colony*, pp. 82, 129, 137.
9. Peyronnet, *Le vignoble nord-africain*, pp. 219–20.
10. Ibid., p. 8; White, *Blood of the Colony*, pp. 9, 206, 211.
11. Znaien, *Les raisins*, pp. 31–2, 40.
12. *Le Petit Matin*, 25 July 1934; Peyronnet, *Le vignoble nord-africain*, p. 106; Znaien, 'Drinking', p. 48.
13. Znaien, *Les raisins*, pp. 72–7, 335.
14. Ibid., pp. 331–4.
15. Sebag, *Tunis*, p. 404–28.
16. Znaien, 'Drinking', pp. 53–4.
17. Ibid., p. 47.
18. White, *Blood of the Colony*, p. 161.
19. Znaien, *Les raisins*, pp. 223, 226.
20. *La Voix de Tunisie*, 8 May 1931, in CADN, ITU/1/V, Tunisie 1889, Fd. de la Résidence, 'Débit des boissons', #1889, fol. 343.
21. Znaien, 'Drinking', p. 46.
22. Taraud, *La prostitution coloniale*, pp. 85–6.

23. Munji, *Mazāhir al-fasād*, pp. 31–2.
24. Znaien, *Les raisins*, pp. 100–3, 106–7, 122–4, 138–9.
25. CADN, ITU/1/V, Tunisie 1889, Pierre Mareschal, 'La faiblesse de la répression de l'alcoolisme tunisien', 1941; Ibid., Dir. Service de Sécurité à Mr Mons. Rés. Gén. de France à Tunis, 8 September 1948, fols 399–403; Znaien, *Les raisins*, pp. 228–30.
26. Znaien, *Les raisins*, pp. 175–81, 188–90, 259ff.
27. White, *Blood of the Colony*, pp. 186–7.
28. Znaien, *Les raisins*, pp. 141, 144n.
29. CADN, Maroc SGP 2MA/1 140, petition Action Marocain, 22 Jan. 1937; Znaien, 'Drinking', pp. 47, 54.
30. Javier Martínez, 'Drinking Disease', pp. 63ff.
31. White, *Blood of the Colony*, p. 197.
32. 'Algeria Pushing Cut', *New York Times*, 14 November 1971.
33. White, *Blood of the Colony*, pp. 218–21, 227–9.
34. Botje, *Het duivelshuis*, pp. 146–7.
35. Lobe, 'Mit Allah gegen Alkohol'.
36. Mandraud, 'L'Algérie glisse vers une prohibition'; Eadem, 'En Algérie'; 'De moins en moins de bars'; Haddar, 'L'Algérie vers la prohibition'; Djebara, 'En Algérie'.
37. Ouali, 'En Algérie'.
38. See https://gco-dz.com/fr/content/8-distributeurs.
39. 'Vineyards and Vine-Growers'; 'The Other Grape'; Dhenin, 'Rise and Fall'.
40. White, *Blood of the Colony*, p. 233.
41. Daum, 'Mémoire interdite'.
42. Djebara, 'En Algérie'; Othmani, 'Algérie Underground'.
43. Znaien, *Les raisins*, p. 385.
44. Abdelmoula, 'Tunisie'.
45. Dahmani, 'Alcool'; Ghorbal, 'Celtia'.
46. Al-Hilali, 'Can Dry Hotels Boost?'.
47. Nsehe, 'Morocco's Multi-millionaire'.
48. Géné, 'Sur la route du vin'; Michbal, 'Maroc'; Dumas, 'Maroc'.
49. 'Glug if You're Not Local'; Dumas, 'Maroc'.
50. 'Alkoholkonsum in Marokko'; Bouman, 'Marokkanen drinken meer'.
51. Ram, *Intoxicating Zion*, p. 99.
52. Russell Pasha, *Egyptian Service*, pp. 178–9.
53. For this so-called Battle of Wazzir, see Ruiz, 'Many Spectacles'.
54. Cormack, *Midnight*, pp. 32, 40, 59–60.
55. Van Nieuwkerk, *A Trade Like Any Other*, pp. 43–5.
56. Foda, 'Pyramid and the Crown', pp. 151–3.
57. This was part of a massive Belgian investment spree led by Baron Éduard Louis Joseph Empain, the engineer-industrialist who designed the Paris metro as well as Cairo's fin-de-siècle suburb of Heliopolis.
58. Foda, *Egypt's Beer*, pp. 21–32, 48–50, 126.
59. 'Bāb al-masā'il', pp. 278–82. Launched in Beirut in 1876, *al-Muqtataf* was published in Cairo as of 1884.
60. Foda, 'Anna and Ahmad', pp. 119–23.
61. Ibid., pp. 130–1.
62. Heyworth-Dunn, *Religious and Political Trends*, p. 40.

63. Foda, 'Anna and Ahmad', p. 147.
64. Cooper, *Cairo in the War*, pp. 114–16, 191.
65. Abaza, *Changing Consumer Cultures*, ch. 4.
66. Van Nieuwkerk, 'Popularizing Islam', pp. 239, 240.
67. Al Aswany, *Yacoubian Building*, pp. 33–4.
68. Foda, *Egypt's Beer*, pp. 42–5, 110, 149, 155–6.
69. Ibid., pp. 163ff. A Heineken representative in the 1950s described what he called the Stella taste as 'a somewhat straw-like and moldy odor'. SAA 834, 1086, Verslag van het bezoek van G. Vermeulen aan Cairo, 31 October–25 November 1954, p. 2; Reisrapport P. R. Feith, Cairo/Sudan, 21 January–8 February 1955, p. 4.
70. Foda, *Egypt's Beer*, p. 192.
71. Roussillon, 'Republican Egypt Interpreted', p. 386.
72. Busch, 'Lessons of Egypt's Perplexing Whiskey Tariffs'.
73. Van Nieuwkerk, 'Popularizing Islam', pp. 242–3.
74. Ibrahim, 'Minority at the Bar', pp. 372–3, 376, 379.
75. Mahfouz, *Palace of Desire*, pp. 297–306.
76. Rios, 'Drinking in Egypt'; Jensen, 'Poor of Cairo'; 'Egypt Foaming Over Beer Sales'.
77. 'Drinkies'; Samuel, 'De-Islamisering van Egypte'.
78. SAA 834, 1121, 'Beknopt overzicht van de door de Heer van Schaik in de periode van 2 maart tot 2 april 1960 bezochte markten in het Nabije en Midden Oosten', p. 3.
79. Karam, *Wines of Lebanon*, pp. 64–7.
80. Bradley, 'Islamic Fundamentalism Rises'.
81. Karam, *Wines of Lebanon*, pp. 79–80, 95–99, 101, 103, 127, 151, 154; Saleh, 'Pursuits of Quality', p 246.
82. Arsan, *Lebanon*, p. 309.
83. Iddon, 'Battle of the Bottle'.
84. Martyr, 'Beirut Nightlife Grinds to a Halt'.
85. Donges Staudt, *Living in Romantic Baghdad*, p. 52.
86. Roosevelt, *War in the Garden of Eden*, p. 136.
87. Gaury, *Three Kings*, p. 42; Lyon, *Kurds, Arabs and Britons*, p. 142.
88. 'Qā'idāt al-tashri'āt al-'Iraqiyya'.
89. Gaury, *Three Kings*, p. 180.
90. Gillman, 'Mild Ale on the Main'.
91. Baram, *Saddam Husayn*, p. 77.
92. Within a month of Kuwait becoming dry in 1965, a lively bootlegging business had sprung up in the country, resulting in many dying or going blind from alcohol poisoning. See 'Kuwait: Oil'.
93. AFP, 'Iraq's Bashiqa'; Garland, 'Iraqis Drink Up'; Abu Zeed, 'Arak Distillery'.
94. Freeman, 'Saddam Hussein's Palaces'; Ghattas, *Black Wave*, p. 231.
95. Baram, *Saddam Husayn*, pp. 79–80.
96. Ibid., pp. 79–80, 219–20, 261–2, 288–9, 321–2; Lewis, 'Iraq Bans Public Use'; Lacey, 'New Target in Basra'.
97. Lacey, 'New Target in Basra'; Wong, 'Struggle for Iraq'.
98. Ackermann, 'Beers in Baghdad'.
99. Ibid.; and Iddon, 'Battle of the Bottle'.
100. Abu Zeed, 'Iraq's Salahuddin Province'.
101. Saadoun, 'Armed Groups'.
102. Kullab, 'In a Baghdad Bar'.

103. Garland, 'Iraqis Drink Up'; 'Iraq's Bashiqa'.
104. Abu Zeed, 'Arak Distillery'.
105. 'Ajil min Zakhu'.
106. Bullard, *Two Kings in Arabia*, pp. 42–3, 260.
107. Palgrave, *Personal Narrative*, vol. 1, p. 49.
108. Bullard, *Two Kings in Arabia*, p. 260.
109. Rundell, *Vision or Mirage*, p. 48.
110. Carsten, *Beschreibung von Arabien*, vol. 1, p. 56.
111. Rathjens, 'Tâghût gegen Scheri'a', p. 184.
112. Dahlgren, *Contesting Realities*, p. 35.
113. MacFarquar, *Media Relations Department*, p. 108.
114. Ibid., pp. 105–8; Werr, 'South Yemen's Only Brewery'.
115. Dahlgren, *Contesting Realities*, p. 82.
116. Ibid., pp. 256–8; Werr, 'South Yemen's Only Brewery'; MacFarquar, *Media Relations Department*, pp. 105–8. In 1998, Zitzmann was recruited as the master brewer for the new Al-Gouna brewery in Egypt. See 'Eine Brauerei in El Gouna'.
117. Spiegel, 'Yemen's Hidden Alcohol Problem'.

9. ALCOHOL IN THE MODERN AGE: NEW DRINKS AND DRINKING CUSTOMS—PART TWO: TURKEY, IRAN, AND PAKISTAN

1. Georgeon, *Au pays du raki*, pp. 190–3; *Revue commerciale du Levant*, Jan.–June 1914, p. 78.
2. Georgeon, *Au pays du raki*.
3. Kechriotis, 'Enthusiasm Turns to Fear'.
4. Ginio, *Ottoman Culture of Defeat*, pp. 191ff. Yet even towns such as Bursa and Ayvalik, on the Aegean, saw incidents of violence.
5. Mansel, *Levant*, p. 199, 204; Mazower, *Salonica*, pp. 298–301.
6. Koçu, *Eski İstanbul'da Meyhaneler*, pp. 101; *Rakı Ansiklopedisi*, 'Gazinolar', p. 183.
7. MacArthur-Seal, 'States of Drunkenness', p. 273.
8. For the story of Thomas, who in 1894 had escaped racism in his home country by going to Europe, ended up in Russia, and, after moving to Istanbul, successfully ended up owning various drinking establishments in town before going bankrupt, see Alexandrov, *Black Russian*, Chs. 6–9.
9. Mufty-Zade K. Zia Bey, *Speaking of the Turks*, pp. 151–60; Sperco, *Turcs d'hier*, pp. 140–5; Mylès, *La fin de Stamboul*, pp. 188–95; King, *Midnight*, pp. 89–132. An estimated number of 40,000 Russian exiles is given in Johnson, ed., *Constantinople To-day*, p. 205. For an (improbably high) number of 200,000, see Üsdiken, *Pera'dan Beyoğlu'na*, p. 237.
10. Armstrong, *Turkey in Travail*, p. 97.
11. Shiragian, *Legacy*, pp. 4–6, 14, 35–6.
12. Johnson, *Constantinople To-day*, p. 263; Macarthur-Seal, 'Intoxication', pp. 301–3; Idem, *Britain's Levantine Empire*, pp. 181–2.
13. Alexandris, *Greek Minority*, pp. 57, 63, 80, 81; Zia Bey, *Speaking of the Turks*, pp. 81–2, 101, 109, 112–13, 126–7, 146ff.
14. MacArthur-Seal, 'States of Drunkenness', pp. 275–7.
15. The movement still exists. See the *Yeşilay* website: https://www.yesilay.org.tr/tr/
16. Spode, 'Forel', pp. 221–2.

17. Evered, 'Anti-alcoholism'.
18. Ibid.
19. Saç, 'Wine Production', pp. 24–7; Evered and Evered, 'Geopolitics of Drinking', pp. 52–7; Idem, 'From Rakı to Ayran', pp. 43–4.
20. Karahanoğulları, Birinci Meclisin İçki Yasağı, pp. 15–25, 145–50; Evered and Evered, 'Between Promotions', pp. 87–8.
21. MacArthur-Seal, 'States of Drunkenness', pp. 277–9.
22. Ibid.; Saç, 'Wine Production', pp. 33–4; Karahanoğulları, Birinci Meclisin İçki Yasaği, pp. 145–50; Biçer-Deveci, 'Wie die Prohibition'.
23. Mango, Atatürk, pp. 47, 349.
24. Rakı Ansiklopedisi, 'Gazinolar'.
25. Mango, Atatürk, pp. 46–7, 97, 292, 513, 518–19; Georgeon, Au pays du raki, pp.263–8.
26. Arpacı, 'Sağlam Nesiller ya da Dejenerasyon', pp. 40ff.; Georgeon, Au pays du raki, pp. 255–61.
27. Evered and Evered, 'Geopolitics of Drinking', pp. 52–7; Idem, 'From Rakı to Ayran', pp. 43–4; Saç, 'Wine Production', pp. 75, 84ff., 96.
28. King, Midnight, p. 158.
29. Georgeon, Le mois le plus long, pp. 143–5, 233–4, 260–73.
30. Gangloff, Boire en Turquie, pp. 80–6, 257.
31. Saç, 'Wine Production', pp. 40ff., 65–8.
32. Neuville, 'Mise en place'.
33. Gangloff, Boire en Turquie, pp. 119–20, and annexe, pp. vi–ix; 'Wine Sector in Turkey'.
34. Köse, Westlicher Konsum, pp. 164–5; Georgeon, 'Ottomans and Drinkers', pp. 16–18.
35. Çetingüleç, 'Turkish National Booze'.
36. Gangloff, Boire en Turquie, pp. 29–32.
37. Köse, Westlicher Konsum, pp. 164–5; and Georgeon, 'Ottomans and Drinkers', pp. 16–18.
38. Eren, Geçmişten Günümüze Anadolu'da Bira, pp. 129–32.
39. Gangloff, Boire en Turquie, annexe, pp. iv–v; Evered and Evered, 'Between Promotions', pp. 92ff.
40. Freely, Stamboul's Ghosts, pp. 25–6, 83–9; Id., Stamboul Sketches, pp. 197–202; Muhidine, 'Hommes inutiles'; Idem, Istanbul rive gauche, pp. 202–3, 268–9, 304–17; Eldem, 'Ottoman Galata'.
41. Türker, Pera'dan Beyoğlu'na, pp. 84–9, 97–101.
42. Beken, 'Musicians, Audience, and Power', pp. 110ff.
43. Baran, Torn Country, pp. 35–7; White, Muslim Nationalism, pp. 7–9, 35–7.
44. Evered and Evered, 'Between Promotions', pp. 104ff.
45. Rakı Ansiklopedisi, 'Gazinolar', p. 229.
46. Gangloff, Boire en Turquie, p. 173. AKP stands for Adalet ve Kalkınma Partisi.
47. Arango, 'Resisting by Raising a Glass'.
48. Bucak, 'Turkey's Erdoğan'.
49. Gangloff, Boire en Turquie, pp. 128–33; Evered and Evered, 'From Rakı to Ayran', p. 40.
50. Evered and Evered, 'From Rakı to Ayran', pp. 47–8.
51. 'Alcohol the Battleground'.
52. Karakaş, 'TV Dizilerinin Perde Arkası'.
53. 'Turkish AKP Alcohol Law'.
54. Evered and Evered, 'Between Promotions', pp. 110–1.

55. 'Alcohol in Turkey'.
56. Arango, 'Resisting by Raising a Glass'; Evered and Evered, 'From *Rakı* to *Ayran*', pp. 40–1.
57. Seibert, 'With Turkish Liquor Ban'.
58. 'Governor Office Bans Alcohol'; Koylu, 'Turkish Bans'.
59. Osterlund, 'Southern Turkish City'.
60. 'Tarihi Bomonti Bira Fabrikası'nın Yıkımına Başlandı'.
61. Soyglu, 'Covid-19'.
62. 'Tarihi Bomonti Bira Fabrikası'nın Yıkımına Başlandı'; 'AKP, Alcohol and Government-engineered Change'; 'Turkish Consumers Dazed'.
63. Çetingüleç, 'Turkish National Booze'.
64. Ibid.; Çetingüleç, 'Turkey's Homemade Booze Boom'.
65. 'Bootlegged Alcohol'; 'Turkish Police'; 'Mindestens 44 Toten'.
66. White, *Muslim Nationalism*, p. 132.
67. Gangloff, *Boire en Turquie*, pp. 69–72, annexe, pp. ii–iii; White, *Muslim Nationalism*, pp. 120–1, 132–3.
68. Baran, *Torn Country*, p. 100.
69. Gangloff, *Boire en Turquie*, pp. 167–8.
70. Ibid., pp. 19, 35, 168–9.
71. *Rakı Ansiklopedisi*, 'Pavyonlar', pp. 444–5. Today the dancers are mainly so-called *natasha*s from the former Soviet Union.
72. Gangloff, *Boire en Turquie*, pp. 150–5, 158, 160–3, 170.
73. Macbean Ross, *Lady Doctor*, p. 132.
74. Hale, *From Persian Uplands*, p. 117.
75. Hubbart, *From the Gulf to Ararat*, pp. 42–3.
76. Floor, *Fiscal History of Iran*, pp. 405–6.
77. Gahan, 'Sovereign and the Sensible', pp. 225, 227–9.
78. Qutbi, *Asnād-i jang*, pp. 203ff.
79. Korostovetz, *Persian Arabesques*, pp. 114–15.
80. Makki, *Tārikh-i bist sāla*, vol. 1, pp. 298–9; Balfour, *Recent Happenings*, p. 241; Shahri, *Tārikh-i ijtimā'i*, vol. 4, pp. 378–9. Balfour argued that the measure was likely taken 'rather from policy than from conviction, since the Seyd and several members of this Council were by now means averse to the pleasures of the table'.
81. Makki, *Tārikh-i bist sāla*, vol. 1, p. 334; and Ilahi, *Sayyid Ziyā*, pp. 101–2.
82. Shahri, *Tārikh-i ijtimā'i*, vol. 4, pp. 380–1.
83. NA, Iran, Political Diaries (IPD):6:416, E8057/8057/34, N°314: 'Persia. Annual Report, 1922. XII – Medical Affairs (2), Sanitary and Allied Questions', p. 64.
84. Koelz, *Persian Diary*, p. 192.
85. NA, IPD:6:648 (E1285/255/34, N° 599: 'Encl. in N°1: Intelligence Summary N° 51, Dec. 22, 1923'), p. 2.
86. Floor, *Fiscal History of Iran*, p. 407.
87. AAE, Corr. comm., Tehran to Paris, 8 January and 10 February 1927, fols. 65ff.
88. AAE, Corr. pol., n.s. Perse 62, fol. 116.
89. *Tableau générale du commerce*, 'Importations'.
90. *Baladiyya-yi Tihrān. Duvvumin sālnāma*, p. 207.
91. Rosen, *Oriental Memories*, pp. 135, 139.
92. 'Hurmat-i muskirāt dar Inglis'.
93. Jalali, 'Ta'sir-i alkul'.

94. *Payk-i saʿādat-i nisvān*, pp. 4–6; new edn., pp. 134–6.

95. *Sālnāma-yi Pārs* 1314/1925, pp. 88–9.

96. Lewisohn, 'Rise and Fall of Lalehzar'; Bresley and Fatemi, *Iranian Music*, pp. 1, 21.

97. Golshiri, 'Victory Chronicle', p. 18.

98. Shahbazi, 'Piyāla-furushi'.

99. Love, 'Iran Postpones Prohibition'.

100. Fragner, 'Drinking Wine in Iran', pp. 254–5.

101. Shahbazi, 'Ābjawsāzi-yi Majidiyya'; 'Aragh sagi'; 'Maykada-yi Qazvin'. After 1979, 'doggy ʿaraq' became the term for moonshine in Iran.

102. 'Tehran Skeptics Scoff at Dry Law'.

103. *Iran Almanac* (1963), p. 24.

104. Fragner, 'Drinking Wine in Iran', p. 256.

105. Razmi, 'Coffeehouses of Tabriz', pp. 115–16.

106. Rosen, *Oriental Memories*, p. 139.

107. Naficy, *Social History of Iranian Cinema*, vol. 1, p. 303; and vol. 2, p. 294.

108. Milani, *The Shah*, p. 100.

109. Mihrabi, 'Hashtād sāl qānun-guzāri'.

110. Ibid.; Daniel, 'Prohibition Is Approved'.

111. Love, 'Iran Postpones Prohibition'.

112. Cooper, *Fall of Heaven*, p. 39, 'Alam, *Yāddāsht'hā*, vol. 6, p. 180.

113. Steele, *Shah's Imperial Celebrations*, p. 47. To be more precise, the menu included Dom Pérignon Rosé 1959 for the official toast; Château Haut-Brion Blanc 1964; Château Lafite Rothschild 1945; Moët & Chandon 1911 (the best between 1874 and 1921); and Musigny Comte Georges de Vogüé 1945. See Milani, *The Shah*, p. 325; and George, 'What the Shah of Iran Drank'.

114. Fragner, 'Drinking Wine in Iran', p. 257.

115. 'Sahifa-yi Imām Khumayni'.

116. Seyed-Gohrab, 'Khomeini the Poet-mystic'.

117. Buchan, *Days of God*, pp. 211–12.

118. Kandell, 'Tehran Entertainment District'.

119. Shahbazi, 'Abjawsāzi-yi Majidiyya'; and 'Maykada-yi Qazvin'; told in Golshiri, 'Alienation'.

120. MacFarquar, *Media Relations Department*, p. 108.

121. 'Three Iranians Flogged'.

122. 'Iranian Embassy Empties 4,000 Bottles'.

123. Ghattas, *Black Wave*, pp. 75–6.

124. Mihrabi, 'Hashtād sāl qānun-guzāri'.

125. 'Joyless Revolution'.

126. Zubaida, *Beyond Islam*, pp. 172–3.

127. 'Rasidan bih khud-kafāʾi', *Iran Times*, p. 13.

128. Erdbrink, 'As Taboos Break Down'.

129. Okrent, *Last Call*, pp. 193, 197.

130. Personal communication.

131. Zarindast, 'Illegal Alcohol'; 'That Sweet Iranian Spirit'; Esfandiari and Zarghami, 'Iranian Officials Warn'.

132. See, for instance, 'Raʾis-i pizishki-yi qānun'; and 'Kharid va furush'.

133. Mihrabi, 'Hashtād sāl qānun-guzāri'.

134. Jackson, 'Bootleg Alcohol Kills 194 People'; Hannon, 'Hundreds Die in Iran'.

135. 'Afzāyish-i marg'; and 'Dastgiri-yi shakhs-i muttaham'.
136. Mueller, 'Tainted Bootleg Alcohol'.
137. 'Muʿāvin-i vizārat-i kishvar-Irān'.
138. 'Illegal Alcohol Booming in Iran'.
139. 'Difaʿ-i quvva-yi qazā'iya-yi Irān'.
140. Mueller, 'Tainted Bootleg Alcohol'.
141. Namaghi and Perry, 'Perception'; Lankarani, and Afshari, 'Alcohol Consumption'; Al Ansari, et al., 'Alcohol Policy'; Taylor, 'Iran Is Opening 150 Alcoholism Treatment Centers'.
142. Burton, *Sindh and the Races*, pp. 106–7.
143. Baillie, *Kurrachee*, p. 41.
144. Neville, *Lahore*, pp. 53–60.
145. Ibid., p. 16.
146. Murree Brewery Website; and Paracha, *End of the Past*, pp. 128–9.
147. Mooraj, 'Karachi Before Prohibition'.
148. Wolpert, *Jinnah of Pakistan*, p. 79; Walsh, *Nine Lives*, p. 51.
149. Paracha, *End of the Past*, p. 42.
150. Dewan, *Private Life*, pp. 12, 18, 60, 120–2. In 1973, he reverted to a more sober regime of one bottle a day at his doctor's advice, and he later became a teetotaler.
151. Hanif, 'Pakistan Has a Drinking Problem'. Asadullah Alam, the shah's confidant, in his diary relates how Bhutto, visiting Iran in October 1973, coinciding with Ramadan, announced that he was fasting, 'which came as a conservable shock to HIM', but then proceeded to drink a 'considerable quantity of wine and whisky' during dinner. When asked how he reconciled this with his fasting, he said, 'Today I fasted, and tomorrow I shall fast again. But as for nighttime, now that's a different matter altogether'. See Alam, *The Shah and I*, p. 327.
152. Hasan, 'From the Demise of Cosmopolitanism', pp. 174–5.
153. Ibid.; Paracha, *Pakistani Antihero*, pp. 216–17. By the end of 1976, sales of *Ishtraq* had gone up from 15,000 to 65,000 copies. *Ishtraq* was banned and revived several times beginning in April 1977, until its license was definitively revoked in 1979.
154. Paracha, *Pakistan Antihero*, p. 176; Idem, *Soul Rivals*, p. 70.
155. Paracha, *Pakistan Antihero*, pp. 155, 164–71.
156. Paracha, *End of the Past*, p. 42.
157. Ibid., pp. 21, 23, 27, 42, 47, 48.
158. Nasr, *Vanguard*, p. 171.
159. Paracha, *End of the Past*, p. 42.
160. Paracha, *Pakistan Antihero*, p. 160; Idem, *Soul Rivals*, pp. 70–1; Nasr, *Islamic Leviathan*, pp. 78–9.
161. Nasr, *Islamic Leviathan*, pp. 80–1; Paracha, *Pakistan Antihero*, pp. 50, 122–5, 160, 206–11.
162. President's Order No. 4 of 1979.
163. Abi-Habib, 'They Once Danced for Royalty'.
164. Paracha, *Pakistan Antihero*, pp. 171–3.
165. Hasan, 'From the Demise', pp. 179 and 181.
166. Paracha, 'Alcohol in Pakistan'. In 2014, liquor stores in the province of Sindh were shut over the Eid holiday, after more than twenty-five people died after drinking homebrew.
167. Paracha, *End of the Past*, pp. 173–4.
168. 'Murree Brewery Soon to Brew in India'; Foreman, 'All Under the Veil'.

169. Paracha, *End of the Past*, pp. 173–6.
170. Hanif, 'Pakistan Has a Drinking Problem'.
171. Kureishi, 'Erotic Politicians'; Walsh, *Nine Lives*, pp. 8, 116.
172. Paracha, 'Alcohol in Pakistan'.
173. Paracha, pp. 134–5; Gomes, 'Real Picture'.
174. 'Islam and Alcohol', *The Economist*.

CONCLUSION

1. Ahmed, *What is Islam?*, p. 120.
2. Goitein, *Mediterranean Society*, vol. 4, p. 253.
3. Abstention rates in the Islamic world are between 80 and 100 percent, with many countries registering more than 95 percent. It is estimated that more than two-thirds of total consumption go unreported, though. See World Health Organization, *Global Status Report*, pp. 40–1, 43.
4. Rowell, *Vintage Humour*, p. liv.
5. Shuraydi, *Raven and the Falcon*, pp. 89–90.
6. Vroijk, *Veertig Moslims aan de zwier*, p. 213.
7. Tannous, *Making of the Medieval Middle East*, pp. 284–5.
8. Dursteler, 'Outrageous Drunkenness', pp. 213–14, 21.
9. Kiyanrad, 'Thou Shalt Not Enter the Bazaar', p. 179.
10. Petry, 'Travails of Prohibition', p. 26.
11. Georgeon, *Au pays du raki*, p. 113.
12. In *c.* 1830, the Frenchman Jean-François Champollion, the scholar who deciphered hieroglyphics, alludes to this in his description of the Azbakiyya Gardens in Cairo during the *mawlid*, or birthday festival, of the Prophet. He was astounded to witness the juxtaposition of 'profane' games and religious exercises, the presence of dancing and singing girls and even prostitutes next to the tents where religious ceremonies were being held. See Behrens-Abouseif, *Azbakiyya*, p. 52. Such scenes continued to exist until a few decades ago at Pakistani Sufi festivals. See Chaudary, *Cultural Analysis of Politics*, pp. 47–86; and Frembgen, '*We Are Lovers of the Qalandar*'.
13. The idea of the inviolable king had a long afterlife. In *c.* 1930, the Finnish anthropologist Edward Westermarck observed how the sharif of Wazzan (Ouezzane) in Morocco was very fond of alcohol and often got soused. When asked how he squared his alcoholism with his Muslim faith, the sharif responded by saying that 'he did not really drink wine, because when the wine touched his saintly lips, it was transformed into honey'. See Westermarck, *Pagan Survivals*, p. 121.
14. For a discussion of how such texts create unease even among Westerners, see Sprachman, *Licensed Fool*, pp. 7–8.
15. 'Afghan Agents Pour 3,000 Litres', *Dawn*.
16. Macfarlane, 'Expatriates'; Karasz, 'A Six-pack of Beer for $26?'.
17. Mills, 'Qatar Planning for World Cup'. They reneged on the promise mere days before the start of the tournament. See Panja, 'Ban on Beer'.
18. Duncan, 'UAE Legal Reforms'.
19. Jones, 'Alcohol-free Saudi Arabia'.
20. Brückner, *Fatwas zum Alkohol*.
21. Ibrahim, 'Drinking in Times of Change', p. 167.
22. Daoud, 'La métaphore', p. 391.
23. Daoud, 'Décoloniser le corps', pp. 24–5.

BIBLIOGRAPHY

Abbreviations

BSOAS   *Bulletin of the School of Oriental and African Studies*
CSSAAME   *Comparative Studies of South Asia, Africa and the Middle East*
EI²   *Encyclopedia of Islam*, second edition, at https://referenceworks.brillonline.
                com/browse/encyclopaedia-of-islam-2
EI³   *Encyclopedia of Islam*, third edition, at https://referenceworks.brillonline.com/
                browse/encyclopaedia-of-islam-3
EIr   *Encyclopaedia Iranica*, at https://referenceworks.brillonline.com/browse/
                encyclopaedia-iranica-online
IJMES   *International Journal of Middle East Studies*
IS   *Iranian Studies*
JAOS   *Journal of the American Oriental Society*
JRAS   *Journal of the Royal Asiatic Society*
MES   *Middle Eastern Studies*
NYT   *The New York Times*

Archives

France:

Paris: Archives des Affaires Etrangères, Paris (AAE)
Nantes: Archives des Affaires Etrangères (CADN)

Germany:

Berlin: Das Archiv des Auswärtiges Amtes (AAA)

Great Britain:

London: British Library: India Office Records (IOR)
National Archives, Kew Garden (NA)

Italy:

Rome: Archivum Romanum Societatis Iesu (ARSI)

BIBLIOGRAPHY

The Netherlands:

The Hague: Nationaal Archief (DNA)
Amsterdam: Stadsarchief (SAA)

Published Sources

Abaza, Mona, *Changing Consumer Cultures of Modern Egypt: Cairo's Urban Reshaping*, Boston, 2006.

Abbasi, Rushain, 'Did Premodern Muslims Distinguish Between the Religious and the Secular? The Dīn-Dunyā Binary in Medieval Islamic Thought', *Journal of Islamic Studies* 31, 2 (2020), pp. 185–225.

Abdelmoula, Mohamed Rami, 'Tunisie. La mort au coin de verre', *Orient XXI*, 18 June 2020, at https://orientxxi.info/magazine/tunisie-la-mort-au-coin-du-verre,3966, accessed 20 June 2020.

Abi-Habib, Maria, 'They Once Danced for Royalty. Now It's Mostly for Leering Men', *NYT*, 5 January 2019.

Abu Zeed, Adnan, 'Arak Distillery Promotes Ambitious New Brand in Defiance of Alcohol Ban', *Al-Monitor*, 12 October 2018, at http://www.al-monitor.com/pulse/originals/2018/10/new-distillery-opened-in-iraq-despite-pressures.html#ixzz5UUGLqwH3, accessed 21 April 2022.

———, 'Iraq's Salahuddin Province Launches War on Alcohol', *Al-Monitor*, 22 July 2018, at https://www.al-monitor.com/pulse/originals/2018/07/saladin-iraq-liquor-alcohol.html?utm_campaign=20180723&utm_source=sailthru&utm_medium=email&utm_term=Daily%20Newsletter, accessed 21 April 2022.

Ackerman, Spencer, 'Beers in Baghdad: Remembering the World's Most Dangerous Bar', *Wired*, 22 December 2011, at https://www.wired.com/2011/12/baghdad-bar/, accessed 21 April 2022.

'A Essaouira, le seul vin bio du Maroc est produit dans les conditions extrêmes', *TelQuel*, 21 September 2018, at https://telquel.ma/2018/09/21/vent-du-desert-dromadaire-et-bio-a-essaouira-le-vignoble-de-lextreme_1611437/?utm_source=tq&utm_medium=normal_post, accessed 20 April 2022.

Adorno, Anselme, *Itinéraire d'Anselme Adorno en terre sainte (1470–1471)*, tr., ed., and ann. Jacques Heers and Georgette de Groer, Paris, 1978.

'Afghan Agents Pour 3,000 Litres of Alcohol into Kabul Canal', *Dawn*, 2 January 2022, at https://www.dawn.com/news/1667231, accessed 29 June 2022.

Afushtah'i Natanzi, Mahmud b. Hidayat Allah, *Nuqavāt al-āsār fī zikr al-akhyār*, Tehran, 1994.

'Afzāyish-i marg bi-dalil-i istifāda az mashrubāt-i taqallubi dar Iran: Masraf-i alkul bidād mikunad', *San'at*, 24 Mordad 1396/15 August 2017.

Ahmad Hussein, Ali, 'The Rhetoric of Hudhalī Wine Poetry', *Oriens. Journal of Philosophy, Theology and Science in Islamic Societies* 43 (2015), pp. 1–53.

Ahmed, Shahab, *What is Islam? The Importance of Being Islamic*, Princeton, NJ, 2016.

Ahsan, M. M., *Social Life Under the Abbasids 170–289 AH, 786–902 AD.*, London, 1979.

Aigle, Denise, 'Les inscriptions de Baybars dans le Bilad al-Sham. Une expression de la légitimité du pouvoir', *Studia Islamica* 96, 1 (2003), pp. 87–115.

———, 'Legitimizing a Lowborn Regicide Monarch. The Case of the Mamluk Sultan Baybars and the Ilkhans of the Thirteenth Century', in Isabelle Charleux et al., eds., *Representing Power in Ancient Inner Asia. Legitimacy, Transmission and the Sacred*, Bellingham, WA, 2010, pp. 61–94.

BIBLIOGRAPHY

'Ājil min Zākhu /Mansurat tahaddud min qatl ashāb al-mahallāt al-mahruqa fi hāl fathihā thāniyya', at http://www.ankawa.com/forum/index.php?topic=547603.0, accessed 15 October 2022.

Akalin, Besim Ömer, *Mükeyyifat ve Müskiratdan Müskirat*, Istanbul, 1888.

'Alam, Asadullah, *Yāddāsht'hā-yi 'Alam*, 7 vols, ed. A. Alikhani, Bethesda, MD, 1992–2014.

Al Ansari, Basma, Anne-Marie Thow, Masoud Mirzaie, Carolyn A. Day, and Katherine M. Conigrave, 'Alcohol Policy in Iran: Policy Content Analysis', *International Journal of Drug Policy* 73 (2019), pp. 185–98.

Al Aswany, Alaa, *The Yacoubian Building*, Cairo, 2004.

Al-Azmeh, Aziz, 'Freidenkertum und Humanismus. Stimmungen, Motive und Themen im Zeitalter der Abbasiden (8.–13. Jahrhundert)', in Ralf Schöppner ed., *Vielfalt statt Reformation. Humanistische Beitrage zum Dialog der Weltanschauungen*, Aschaffenburg, Germany, 2017, pp. 234–55.

'Alcohol in Turkey. Not So Good for You', *The Economist*, 1 June 2013.

'Alcohol the Battleground in East-West Conflict', *The Guardian*, 23 December 2005.

Alexandris, Alexis, *The Greek Minority of Istanbul and Greek-Turkish Relations 1918–1974*, Athens, 1983.

'Algeria Pushing Cut in Vineyards', *NYT*, 14 November 1971.

Alilat, Farid, 'L'alcool en Algérie, business is business', *Jeune Afrique*, 2 December 2014, at http://www.jeuneafrique.com/38730/societe/l-alcool-en-alg-rie-business-is-business/, accessed 12 October 2017.

Al-Jabarti, *Napoleon in Egypt. Al-Jabartī's Chronicle of the French Occupation*, tr. Shmuel Moreh, Princeton, NJ, 1993.

'Alkoholkonsum in Marokko wächst', *Maghreb-Post*, 6 April 2017.

Alonso, Carlos, 'Misiones de orden de San Augustín (1628–1639). Documentación inédita', *Analecta Augustiniana* 28 (1965), pp. 129–80.

Alshech, Eli, '"Do Not Enter Houses Other Than Your Own": The Evolution of the Notion of a Private Domestic Sphere in Early Sunni Islamic Thought', *Islamic Law and Society* 11, 3 (2004), pp. 291–332.

Álvarez Dopico, Clara-Ilham, 'Vino y tavernas en el Túnez beylical a través de los relatos de viajeros, diplomáticos y religiosos', *Cuadernos de Estudios del Siglo XVIII* 19 (2009), pp. 205–43.

Aminrazavi, Mehdi, *The Wine of Wisdom. The Life, Poetry and Philosophy of Omar Khayyam*, Oxford, 2005.

Amitai, Reuven, *Holy War and Rapprochement. Studies in the Relations Between the Mamluk Sultanate and the Mongol Ilkhanate (1260–1335)*, Turnhout, Belgium, 2013.

Āmūzgār, Žāla, 'Cooking in Pahlavi Literature', *EIr*.

Anastassiadou, Meropi, *Salonique, 1830–1912. Une ville ottomane à l'âge des réformes*, Leiden, Netherlands, 1997.

And, Metin, *Istanbul in the 16th Century. The City, The Palace, Daily Life*, Istanbul, 1994.

Anon., [Ritter von Riederer], *Aus Persien. Aufzeichnungen eines Oesterreichers der 40 Monate im Reiche der Sonne gelebt und gewirkt hat*, Vienna, 1882.

Anon., *Jahangushā-yi khāqān*, ed. Allah Ditta Muztar, Islamabad, 1986.

Anon., *The Sea of Previous Virtues (Baḥr al-Favā'id). A Medieval Islamic Mirror for Princes*, tr. Julie Scott Meisami, Salt Lake City, 1991.

Anooshahr, Ali, *The Ghazi Sultans and the Frontiers of Islam. A Comparative Study of the Late Medieval and Early Modern Periods*, London and New York, 2009.

'Aragh sagi', *Wikipedia* at https://en.wikipedia.org/wiki/Aragh_Sagi.

BIBLIOGRAPHY

Arango, Tim, 'Resisting by Raising a Glass', *NYT*, 9 June 2013.

Arfa, Prince. *Memories of a Bygone Age. Qajar Persia and Imperial Russia 1853–1902*, London, 2016.

Armstrong, H. C., *Turkey in Travail. The Birth of a New Nation*, London, 1925.

Arpacı, Murat, 'Sağlam Nesiller ya da Dejenerasyon. Türkiye'de Alkol Karşıtı Düsünce ve Hareket (1910–1950)', *Toplum ve Bilim* 134 (2015), pp. 30–54.

Aubin, Eugène, *Le Maroc dans la tourmente (1902–1903)*, Paris, 2004.

Aubin, Jean, ed., *L'Ambassade de Grégorio Pereira Fidalgo à la cour de Chah Soltan-Hosseyn*, Lisbon, 1971.

Avcı, Mustafa, 'Shifts in Sexual Desire. Bans on Dancing Boys (Köçeks) Throughout Ottoman Modernity (1800s–1920s)', *MES* 53, 5 (2017), pp. 762–81.

Azod al-Dowleh, Soltan Ahmad Mirza, *Tarikh-e 'Azodi. Life at the Court of the Early Qajar Shahs*, tr. and ed. Manouchehr M. Eskandari-Qajar, Washington, DC, 2014.

'Bāb al-masā'il', *al-Muqtataf*, March 1920, pp. 278–82.

Babaie, Sussan, 'Visual Vestiges of Travel: Persian Windows on European Weaknesses', *Journal of Early Modern History* 13, 1 (2009), pp. 105–36.

Babinger, Franz, *Mehmed the Conqueror and His Time*, tr. Ralph Manheim, Princeton, NJ, 1978.

Babur, *The Baburnama, Memoirs of Babur, Prince and Emperor*, tr. and ed. Wheeler Thackston, Washington, DC and Oxford, 1996.

Badem, Candan, *The Ottoman Crimean War, 1853–1856*, Leiden, Netherlands, 2010.

Baer, Marc David, *Honored by the Glory of Islam. Conversion and Conquest in Ottoman Europe*, Oxford, 2008.

Bahadır, Savaşkan Cem, 'Şarap Yasağının XVI. Yüzyıl Divanlarındaki Izleri ve Kanunî Sultan Süleyman Dönemi Şarap Yasağı', *Karadeniz Teknik Universitesi Sosyal Bilimler Enstitüsü Dergisi* 5 (2013), pp. 71–101.

Baillie, Alexander F., *Kurrachee. Past, Present and Future*, Calcutta, 1890.

Baker, Valentine, *Clouds in the East: Travels and Adventures on the Perso-Turkoman Frontier*, London, 1876.

Balabanlilar, Lisa, *The Emperor Jahangir. Power and Kingship in Mughal India*, London, 2020.

———, *Imperial Identity in the Mughal Empire. Memory and Dynastic Politics in Early Modern South and Central Asia*, London and New York, 2012.

Baladiyya-yi Tihrān, Duvvumin sālnama-yi ihsā'iyya-yi shahr-i Tihrān / Deuxième annuaire statistique de la ville de Téhéran, 1925–1929, Tehran, 1930.

Balafrej, Lamia, *The Making of the Artist in Late Timurid Painting*, Edinburgh, UK, 2019.

Balfour, J. M., *Recent Happenings in Persia*, Edinburgh and London, 1922.

Bali, Rıfat N., ed., *A Survey of Some Social Conditions in Smyrna, Asia Minor May 1921*, Istanbul, 2009.

Bambad, Mihdi, *Sharh-i hāl-i rijāl-i Irān dar qarn-i 12, 13, 14 hijri*, Tehran, 4th edn., 1992.

Baram, Amatzia, *Saddam Husayn and Islam, 1968–2003*, Washington, DC and Baltimore, MD, 2014.

Baran, Zeyno, *Torn Country. Turkey. Between Secularism and Islamism*, Stanford, CA, 2010.

Barbouchi, Sarra, 'Vin et ivresse dans *Qutb al-surūr fi awsāf al-anbidha wa'l-khumūr*', *Synergies Monde Arabe* 6 (2009), pp. 249–62.

Bareilles, Bertrand, *Constantinople, ses cités franques et levantines (Pera-Galata-banlieu)*, Paris, 4th edn., 1918.

Barthold, V. V., *Four Studies on the History of Central Asia*, vol. 2, *Ulugh Beg*, Leiden, Netherlands, 1958.

BIBLIOGRAPHY

Başaran, Betül, *Selim III. Social Control and Policing in Istanbul at the End of the Eighteenth Century*, Leiden, Netherlands, 2014.

Basim 'Omar Yuzbaşi, *Mukayyefat ve Müskirat*, Istanbul, 1887–8.

Bassano, Luigi, *I costumi ed i modi particolari della vita de'Turchi*, Rome, 1545.

Bauden, Frédéric, 'The Sons of al-Nāṣir Muḥammad and the Politics of Puppets: Where Did It All Start?', *Mamluk Studies Review* 13, 1 (2009), pp. 53–81.

Bauer, Thomas, *A Culture of Ambiguity. An Alternative History of Islam*, tr. Hinrich Biesterfeldt and Tricia Tunstell, New York, 2021.

Beauchamp, Alphonse de, *Vie d'Ali Pacha, visir de Janina, surnommé Aslan ou le lion*, Paris, 1822.

Beaumont, Adalbert de, 'Voyage en Asie—Nicée', *Revue Orientale et Algérienne* 4 (1852), pp. 418–40.

Beaumont, Daniel, 'The Trickster and Rhetoric in the *Maqāmāt*', *Edebiyât* 5 (1994), pp. 1–14.

Bedik, Bedros, *A Man of Two Worlds. Bedros Bedik in Iran 1670–1675*, tr. and ann. Colette Ouahes and Willem Floor, Washington, DC, 2014.

Begum, Sikandar, *A Pilgrimage to Mecca by the Nawab Sikandar Begum of Bhopal*, London, 1870.

Behrens-Abouseif, Doris, *Azbakiyya and Its Environs. From Azbak to Ismā 'īl 1476–1879*, Cairo, 1985.

———, 'The Baptistère de Saint Louis: A Reinterpretation', *Islamic Art* 3 (1998), pp. 3–14.

Beken, Münir Nurettin, 'Aesthetics and Artistic Criticism at the Turkish Gazino', at https://www.umbc.edu/MA/index/number8/gazino/bek_01.htm, accessed 25 January 2022.

———, 'Musicians, Audience and Power: The Changing Aesthetics of the Music at the Maksim Gazino of Istanbul', PhD dissertation, University of Maryland, 1998.

Bel, Jean-Pierre, 'The Ottomans (1516–Middle of the Nineteenth Century)', in Michael Karam, ed., *Tears of Bacchus. A History of Wine in the Arab World*, London, 2019, pp. 184–98.

———, *Les paysages viticoles de la Bekaa (Liban)*, Paris, 2009.

Bélanger, Charles, *Voyage aux Indes-orientales ... dans les années 1825, 1826, 1827, 1828, 1829*, 4 vols., Paris, 1834–46.

Bell of Antermony, John, *Travels from St. Petersburg in Russia to Diverse Parts of Asia*, 2 vols., Glasgow, 1763.

Bellew, Henry Walter, *From the Indus to the Tigris. A Narrative of a Journey Through the Countries of Balochistan, Afghanistan, Khorassan and Iran, in 1872*, London, 1874.

Benkheira, Mohammed Hocine, 'Ivrognerie, religiosité et sport dans une ville Algérienne (Oran), 1962–1983', *Archives de sciences sociales des religions* 59 (1985), pp. 131–51.

Bennison, Amira K., *The Almoravid and Almohad Empires*, Edinburgh, UK, 2016.

Bérézine, Ilya Nikolaevitch, *Voyage en Perse du Nord*, tr. Jacqueline Calmard Compas, Paris, 2011.

Berindranath, Dewan, *Private Life of Yahya Khan*, New Delhi, 1974.

Berkey, Jonathan P., 'Tradition, Innovation and the Social Construction of Knowledge in the Medieval Islamic Near East', *Past & Present* 46, 1 (1995), pp. 48–65.

Bernier, François, *Un libertin dans l'Inde moghole. Les voyages de François Bernier (1656–1669)*, ed. Frédéric Tinguely, Paris, 2008.

Berque, Jacques, 'L'ambiguité dans le fiqh', in Jacques Berque and Jean-Paul Charnay, eds., *L'Ambivalence dans la culture arabe*, Paris, 1967, pp. 232–52.

Beyhaqi, Abu'l Fazl, *The History of Beyhaqi (The History of Sultan Mas'ud of Ghazna, 1030–1041)*, tr. C. E. Bosworth and Mohsen Ashtiany, 3 vols., Boston, MA and Washington, DC, 2011.

Bezouh, Malik, *Ils ont trahi Allah. Blasphème, homosexualité, masturbation, athéisme … ces tabous qui tuent la religion musulmane*, Paris, 2020.

Bhargava, Meena, 'Narcotics and Drugs: Pleasure, Intoxication or Simply Therapeutic—North India, Sixteenth-Seventeenth Centuries', *The Medieval History Journal* 15, 1 (2012), pp. 103–35.

Biçer-Deveci, Elife, 'Wie die Prohibition Alkoholgegner in der Türkei inspirierte', *Schweizerische Gesellschaft Mittler Osten und Islamische Kulturen*, 4 March 2020, at https://sagw.ch/sgmoik/die-sgmoik/news/details/news/alkoholverbot-eine-westliche-erfindung-wie-die-prohibition-alkoholgegner-in-der-tuerkei-inspirierte/, accessed 5 March 2020.

Biesterfeldt, Hinrich, '"*Mizr fī Miṣr*": Ein Preisgedicht auf das Bier aus dem Kairo des 14. Jahrhundert', Hinrich Biesterfeldt and Verena Klemm, eds., *Differenz und Dynamik im Islam. Festschrift für Heinz Halm zum 70. Geburtstag*, Würzburg, 2012, pp. 383–98.

Billerberg, Franciscus de, [*Most Rare and Straunge Discourses, of Amurathe the Turkish Emperor that now is with the Warres betweene Him and the Persians: The Turkish Triumph, Lately Had at Constantinople.*] *(1584)*, London?, 1584.

Bin Qutayba, Abi Muhammad 'Abd Allah b. Muslim, *Kitāb al-ashriba (wa dhikr al-ikhtilāf fīhā)*, Beirut, 1998.

Birdal, Murat, *The Political Economy of Ottoman Public Debt. Insolvency and European Financial Control in the Late Nineteenth Century*, London and New York, 2010.

Black, Peter Weston, 'Anthropology of Tobacco Use: Tobian Data and Theoretical Issues', *Journal of Anthropological Research* 40, 4 (1984), pp. 475–503.

Blasim, Hassan, *God99*, London, 2020.

Blocker, Jack S., David M. Fahey, and Ian R. Tyrrell, eds., *Alcohol and Temperance in Modern History. An International Encyclopedia*, 2 vols., Santa Barbara, CA, 2003.

Blunt, Wilfrid Scawen, *My Diaries. Being a Personal Narrative of Events 1888–1914*, 2 vols., New York, 1922.

Bonte, Marie, 'Eat, Drink and Be Merry for Tomorrow We Die. Alcohol Practices in Mar Mikhail, Beirut', in Thomas Thurnell-Read, ed., *Drinking Dilemmas. Space, Culture and Identity*, London, 2015, pp. 81–98.

'Bootlegged Alcohol Worth 1 Million Liras Seized', *Hürriyet Daily News*, 17–18 March 2018.

Borsch, Stuart, and Tarek Sabraa, 'Refugees of the Black Death. Quantifying Rural Migration for Plague and Other Environmental Disasters', *Annales de démographie historique* 2 (2017), pp. 63–93.

Bosworth, C. Edmund, *The Ornaments of Histories. A History of the Eastern Islamic Lands AD 650–1041. The Persian Text of Abu Sa'id 'Abd al-Hayy Gardizi*, London, 2011.

Botje, Harm, *Het duivelshuis*, Amsterdam, Netherlands, 1994.

―――――, *In de ban van de Nijl*, Amsterdam, Netherlands, 1991.

Bottéro, Jean, 'Boisson, banquet, et vie sociale', in L. Milano, ed., *Drinking in Ancient Societies, History and Culture in the Ancient Near East*, Padua, Italy, 1994, pp. 1–13.

―――――, 'Le vin dans une civilisation de la bière: La Mesopotamie', in Oswyn Murray and Manuela Tesuşan, eds., *In Vino Veritas*, London, 1995, pp. 21–34.

Boujarra, H., 'al-Dhahira al-khamriyya wa'-l-tatawwuruhā bi'l-bilād al-Tunisiyya fi'l-'ahd al-Turki', *Cahiers de Tunisie* 42 (1990), pp. 27–117.

Bouman, Kaja, 'De Marokkanen drinken meer', *De Groene Amsterdammer*, 22 January 2020.

Boyar, Ebru, 'The Late Ottoman Brothel in Istanbul. A Heterosexual Space for Homosexual Entertainment?', in Ebru Boyar and Kate Fleet, eds., *Entertainment Among the Ottomans*, Leiden, 2019, pp. 160–82.

BIBLIOGRAPHY

Boyar, Ebru and Kate Fleet, *A Social History of Ottoman Istanbul*. Cambridge, UK, 2008.

Brack, Jonathan, 'A Mongol Mahdi in Medieval Anatolia. Rebellion, Reform, and Divine Right in the Post-Mongol Islamic World', *JAOS* 139, 3 (2019), pp. 611–29.

Braithwaite, John, *The History of the Revolutions in the Empire of Morocco Upon the Death of the Late Emperor Muley Ishmael*, London, 1729.

Breen, Benjamin, *The Age of Intoxication. Origins of the Global Drug Trade*, Philadelphia, PA, 2019.

———, 'Drugs and Early Modernity', *History Compass* 15, 4 (2007), pp. 1–9.

Bresley, G. J., and Sasan Fatemi, *Iranian Music and Popular Entertainment. From Motreb to Los Angeles and Beyond*, London and New York, 2020.

Brewer, Josiah, *A Residence at Constantinople in the Year 1827*, New Haven, CT, 1830.

Brinkman, Stefanie, 'Wine in Ḥadīth. From Intoxication to Sobriety', in Fragner, Kauz and Schwarz, eds, *Wine Culture in Iran and Beyond*, pp. 71–136.

Brocquière, Bertrandon de la, *The Travels of Bertrandon de la Broquière to Palestine and His Return via Jerusalem to France in the Years 1432 & 1433*, tr. Thomas Johnes, London, 1807.

Brookshaw, Dominic P., 'Lascivious Vines, Corrupted Virgins, and Crimes of Honor. Variations on the Wine Production Myth as Narrated in Early Persian Poetry', *IS* 47, 1 (2014), pp. 87–129.

Broshi, Magen, 'Wine in Ancient Palestine: Introductory Notes', in Eadem, *Bread, Wine, Walls and Scrolls*, Sheffield, 2001, pp. 144–72.

Browne, E. G., *A Literary History of Persia*, 4 vols., Cambridge, UK, 1906; repr. 1969.

Browne, W. G., *Travels in Africa, Egypt and Syria From the Year 1792 to 1798*, London, 1799.

Brückner, Matthias, *Fatwas zum Alkohol unter dem Einfluss neuer Medien im 20. Jhdt.*, Würzburg, Germany, 2001.

Brydges, Sir Harford Jones, *An Account of the Transactions of His Majesty's Mission to the Court of Persia in the Years 1807–11*, London, 1834.

Bucak, Selin, 'Turkey's Erdoğan Seen Softening Style or Substance as President', *Reuters World News*, 24 August 2014.

Buckley, R. P., 'The Muhtasib', *Arabica* 39, 1 (1992), pp. 59–117.

Budaq Munshi Qazvini, *Javāhir al-akhbār. Bakhsh-i tārikh-i Irān az Aq-Qoyunlu tā sāl-i 928 h.q.*, ed. Muhsin Bahram-Nizhad, Tehran, 1999.

Buisson-Fenet, Emmanuel, 'Ivresse et rapport à l'occidentalisation au Maghreb. Bars et débits de boissons à Tunis', *Égypte/Monde Arabe* 30–1 (1997), pp. 1–13.

Bullard, Reader, *Two Kings in Arabia. Letters From Jeddah 1923–5 and 1936–9*, London, 1993.

Burckhardt, John Lewis, *Travels in Arabia Comprehending an Account of Those Territories in Hedjaz Which the Mohammedans Regard as Sacred*, 2 vols., London, 1829.

———, *Travels in Syria and the Holy Land*, London, 1822.

Burgess, Charles Henry, Edward Burgess, and Benjamin Schwartz, *Letters From Persia 1828–1855*, New York, 1942.

Burhan, Muhammad Husayn b. Khalaf Tabrizi, *Burhān-i Qāti'*, Tehran, 1962.

Burton, Richard T., *Sindh and the Races That Inhabit the Valley of the Indus*, London, 1851; repr. Karachi, 1973.

Busch, Marc L., 'The Lessons of Egypt's Perplexing Whiskey Tariffs', *The Hill*, 16 October 2021, at https://thehill.com/opinion/international/576978-the-lessons-of-egypts-perplexing-whiskey-tariff, accessed 20 October 2021.

Busnot, Dominique, *Histoire du règne de Mouley Ismaël, roy de Maroc, Fez, Tafilet, Souz etc.*, Rouen, France, 1714.

Busse, Heribert, tr., *History of Persia Under Qajar Rule*, New York, 1972.

BIBLIOGRAPHY

Calendar of State Papers and Manuscripts, Relating to English Affairs, Existing in the Archives and Collections of Venice and in Other Libraries of Northern Italy, vol. IX, 1592–1603, ed. Horatio F. Brown, London, 1897.

Canby, Sheila R., 'The Anachronistic Role of Safavid Manuscript Illustration', in Linda Komaroff, ed., *In the Field of Empty Days. The Interaction of Past and Present in Iranian Art*, Los Angeles, 2018, pp. 32–41.

———, 'The Demimonde in Safavid Painting', in Olga M. Davison and Marianna Shreve Simpson, eds., *The Arts of Iran in Istanbul and Anatolia. Seven Essays*, Boston, MA and Washington, DC, 2019, pp. 51–79.

———, *The Rebellious Reformer. The Drawings and Paintings of Riza yi 'Abbasi Isfahanı*, London, 1998.

Cantemir, Demetrius, *The History of the Growth and Decay of the Othman Empire*, London, 1734.

Çelik, Zeyneb, *The Remaking of Istanbul. Portrait of an Ottoman City in the Nineteenth Century*, Seattle, WA, 1986.

Çetinkaya, E. Doğan, *The Young Turks and the Boycott Movement. Nationalism, Protest and the Working Classes in the Formation of Modern Turkey*, London, 2014.

Cetingulec, Mehmet, 'Turkish Homemade Booze Boom Here to Stay', *Al-Monitor*, 15 November 2017, at https://www.al-monitor.com/pulse/originals/2017/11/turkey-boom-in-homemadebooze.html?utm_campaign=20171115&utm_source=sailthru&utm_medium=email&utm_termz=Daily%20Newsletter, accessed 15 November 2017.

———, 'Turkish National Booze Under Government Siege', *Al-Monitor*, 12 January 2018, at https://www.al-monitor.com/pulse/originals/2018/01/turkey-national-booze-under-governmentsiege.html?utm_campaign=20180119&utm_source=sailthru&utm_medium=email&utm_term=Daily%20Newsletter, accessed 19 January 2018.

Chardin, Jean, *Voyages du chevalier Chardin en Perse et en autres lieux de l'Orient*, ed. L. Langlès, 10 vols. and atlas, Paris, 1810–11.

Chatterjee, Prasun, 'The Lives of Alcohol in Pre-colonial India', *The Medieval History Journal* 8, 1 (2005), pp. 189–225.

Chaudary, Muhammad Azam, *Cultural Analysis of Politics, Law and Religion in Pakistan. Some Essays in Interpretive Anthropology*, Cologne, Germany, 2008.

Chejne, Anwar G., 'The Boon Companion in Early 'Abbasid Times', *JAOS* 85, 3 (1965), pp. 327–35.

Chelebi, Evliya, *Travels*, tr. and ed. Willem Floor, Washington, DC, 2009.

[Chick. H.], tr. and ed., *A Chronicle of the Carmelites in Persia*, 2 vols. pag. as one, London, 1939; repr. 2012.

Clément, François, ed., *Les vins d'Orient. 4000 ans d'ivresse*, Nantes, France, 2008.

———, 'Quelques exemples de transgression d'interdit du vin dans l'Islam', in *Actes de la rencontre internationale cultures, manières de boire et alcoolisme*, Rennes, France, 1984, pp. 299–303.

———, 'Vignes et vins dans l'Espagne musulmane', in Clément, ed., *Les vins d'Orient*, pp. 85–137.

Cogan, Killian, 'Istanbul, miroir d'un monde arabe fracturé', *Le Monde Diplomatique*, June 2021, pp. 10–11.

Cole, Juan, *The Rubáiyát of Omar Khayyam. A New Translation From the Persian*, London, 2020.

Congar, Kerem, 'How Turkey's Alcohol and Cigarette Tax Hike Is Devastating Cultural Life', *euronews.culture*, 13 January 2022, at https://www.euronews.com/culture/

BIBLIOGRAPHY

2022/01/13/how-turkey-s-alcohol-and-cigarette-tax-hike-is-devastating-cultural-life, accessed 16 January 2022.

Conolly, Arthur, *Journey to the North of India*, 2 vols., London, 1834.

Contarini, Alvise, 'Relazione di Costantinopole, 1636–1641', in Nicolo Barozzi and Gugliemo Berchet, eds, *Le relazioni degli stati europei lette al Senato degli ambasciadori veneziani*, vol. 5, Venice, Italy, 1871.

Cook, Michael A., *Commanding Right and Forbidding Wrong in Islamic Thought*, Cambridge, UK, 2000.

Cooper, Andrew Scott, *The Fall of Heaven. The Pahlavis and the Final Days of Imperial Iran*, New York, 2016.

Cooper, Artemis, *Cairo in the War, 1939–1945*, London, 1989.

Cormack, Raphael, *Midnight in Cairo. The Divas of Egypt's Roaring '20s*, New York, 2021.

Courtwright, David T., *Forces of Habit. Drugs and the Making of the Modern World*, Cambridge, MA, 2001.

Couto, Dejanirah, 'Les festins à la cour de Chāh Ismāʿîl Safavide vus par les ambassadeurs portugais de la première moitié du XVIe siècle. Fernão Gomes de Lemos (1515) et Balthasar Pessoa (1523)', *Journal Asiatique* 299 (2011), pp. 569–84.

Covel, John, 'Extracts From the Diaries of Dr. Covel 1670–1679', in J. Theodore Bent, ed., *Early Voyages and Travels in the Levant*, London, 1893, pp. 99–287.

Crone, Patricia, *God's Rule: Government and Islam*, New York, 2004.

Curzon, George N., *Persia and the Persian Question*, 2 vols., London, 1892.

Dahlén, Ashk P., 'Kingship and Religion in a Mediaeval Fürstenspiegel. The Case of the *Chahār Maqāla* of Niżāmī Aruẓī', *Orientalia Suecana* 58 (2009), pp. 9–24.

Dahlgren, Susanne, *Contesting Realities. The Public Sphere and Morality in South Yemen*, Syracuse, NY, 2010.

Dahmani, Frida, 'Alcool. La Tunisie championne toutes catégories de la consommation régionale', *Jeune Afrique*, 2 December 2014, at http://www.jeuneafrique.com/38727/societe/alcool-la-tunisie-championne-toutes-cat-gories-de-la-consommation-r-gionale/, accessed 12 October 2017.

Dale, Stephen F., *The Garden of the Eight Paradises. Bābur and the Culture of Empire in Central Asia, Afghanistan and India (1483–1530)*, Leiden, Netherlands, 2004.

D'Alessandri, Vincentio, 'Narrative of the Most Noble Vincentio d'Alessandri', in Charles Grey, tr. and ed., *A Narrative of Italian Travels in Persia in the Fifteenth and Sixteenth Century*, London, 1873, pp. 209–29.

Dallaway, James, *Constantinople Ancient and Modern*, London, 1797.

Damanhuri, al-, *Al-Damanhuri's Chronicle of Egypt 1688–17155. Al-Durra al-musāna fi akhbār al-kināna*, tr. and ann. Daniel Crecelius and ʿAbd al-Wahhab Bakr, Leiden, Netherlands, 1991.

Daniel, Clifton, 'Prohibition Is Approved for Iran. Act Goes into Effect Within 6 Months', *NYT*, 9 February 1953.

Daoud, Kamel, 'Décoloniser le corps, la langue et la mer', in Idem, *Mes indépendances. Chroniques 2010–2016*, Algiers and Arles, 2017, pp. 23–5.

————, 'La métaphore abîmée du vin "arabe"', in Idem, *Mes indépendances. Chroniques 2010–2016*, Algiers and Arles, 2017, pp. 391–2.

Darling, Linda T., 'The Janissaries of Damascus in the Sixteenth Century, or, How Conquering a Province Changed the Ottoman Empire', Otto Spies Memorial Lecture 6, Berlin, 2019.

Darling, Malcolm, *The Punjab Peasant in Prosperity and Debt*, London, 1928.

BIBLIOGRAPHY

d'Arvieux, Laurent, *Mémoires du Chevalier d'Arvieux envoyé extraordinaire du Roy à la Porte ...*, 4 vols., Paris, 1735.

———, 'Mémoires du Chevalier d'Arvieux', in Hussein I. El-Mudarris and Oliver Salmon, eds., *Le consulat de France à Alep au XVIIe siècle*, Aleppo, Syria, 2009, pp. 182–439.

'Dastgiri-yi shakhs-i muttaham-i furush-i mashrubāt-i alkuli- yi taqallubi dar Karaj', *Khabarguzāri-yi Mihr*, 22 Shahrivar 1397/13 September 2018.

Dauliers Deslandes, André, *Les beautés de la Perse*, Paris, 1673.

Daum, Pierre, 'Mémoire interdite en Algérie', *Le Monde Diplomatique*, August 2017, pp. 8–9.

Davidson, Olga M., *Poet and Hero in the Persian Book of Kings*, Ithaca, NY, 1994.

Davis, Dick, *Faces of Love. Hafez and the Poets of Shiraz*, Washington, DC, 2012.

———, introd. and tr., *The Mirror of My Heart. A Thousand Years of Persian Poetry by Women*, Washington, DC, 2019.

———, 'On Not Translating Hafez', *New England Review* 25, 1–2 (2004), pp. 310–18.

———, 'Wine and Persian Poetry', in Najmieh Batmangelij, ed., *From Persia to Napa. Wine at the Persian Table*, Washington, DC, 2006, pp. 55–68.

Dawlatabadi, Yahya, *Hayāt-i Yahyā*, 4 vols., 4th edn., Tehran, 1983.

De Amicis, Edmondo, *Constantinople*, tr. Caroline Tilton, 2 vols., New York and London, 1896.

d'Beth Hillel, Rabbi David, *Travels From Jerusalem Through Arabia, Koordistan, Part of Persia and India*, Madras, India, 1832.

Debre, Isabel, 'UAE Announces Relaxing of Islamic Laws for Personal Freedoms', *Agence Presse*, 7 November 2020, at https://apnews.com/article/dubai-united-arab-emirates-honor-killings-travel-islam-bce74c423897dc77c7beb72e4f51a23a, accessed 8 November 2020.

De Bruyn, Cornelis, *Reizen over Moskovie, door Perzie en Indie*, 2nd edn., Amsterdam, Netherlands, 1714.

De Busbecq, Ogier Ghiselin, *The Turkish Letters of Ogier Ghiselin de Busbecq*, tr. Edward Seymour Forster, Oxford, 1927.

De Kay, James E., *Sketches of Turkey in 1831 and 1832*, New York, 1833.

De Kératry, E., *Mourad V. Prince, sultan, prisonnier d'état, 1840–1878, d'après des témoins de sa vie*, 2nd edn., Paris, 1878.

'De moins en moins de bars et d'alcool en Algérie', *Le Point*, 16 May 2012, at https://www.lepoint.fr/societe/de-moins-en-moins-de-bars-et-d-alcool-en-algerie-16-05-2012-1461992_23.php, accessed 1 January 2022.

De Orta Rebelo, Nicolau, *Un voyageur portugais en Perse au début du XVIIe siècle*, ed. Joaquim Veríssimo Serrão, Lisbon, 1972.

Deeb, Laura and Mona Harb, *Leisurely Islam. Negotiating Geography and Morality in Shi'ite South Beirut*, Princeton, NJ, 2013.

Della Valle, Pietro, *Delle conditioni di Abbàs, rè di Persia*, Venice, 1629; repr. Tehran, 1976.

———, *Viaggi di Pietro della Valle il pellegrino*, 2 vols., ed. Gancia, Brighton, 1843.

Del Niño Jesús, P. Fr. Florencio, *A Persia (1604–1609). Peripecias de una embajada pontificia que fué a Persia a principios del siglo XVII*, vol. 2, Pamplona, Spain, 1920.

Denny, F. M., 'Tawba', *EI²*.

Dhenin, Marianne, 'The Rise and Fall of a North African Wine Giant', *Wine Enthusiast*, at https://www.winemag.com/2022/06/08/algeria-wine-history-africa/, accessed 11 June 2022.

Diba, Layla S., and Maryam Ekhtiar, eds, *Royal Persian Paintings. The Qajar Epoch 1785–1925*, New York and London, 1998.

BIBLIOGRAPHY

Didier, Charles, *Les nuits du Caire*, Paris, 1860.

Dietler, M. 'Alcohol. Anthropological/Archaeological Perspectives', *Annual Review of Anthropology* 35 (2006), pp. 229–49.

'Difā '-i quvva-yi qazā'iya-yi Irān bih jurm-i nushidan-i mashrubāt-i alkuli dar zindān-i markazi-yi Mashhad', BBC Persian, 10 July 2020, at https://www.bbc.com/persian/iran-53361826, accessed 20 July 2020.

Djebara, Fahim, 'En Algérie, les autorités encouragent la production locale ... sauf celle du vin', *Le Monde*, 7 June 2017.

———, 'A Paris, des Algériens écœurés par la guerre contre les terrasses', *Le Monde*, 17 November 2015.

Dmitriev, Kirill, 'The Symbolism of Wine in Early Arab Love Poetry', in Kirill Dmitriev, Julia Hauser, and Bilal Orfali, eds., *Insatiable Appetite: Food as Cultural Signifier in the Middle East and Beyond*, Leiden, Netherlands, 2020, pp. 165–89.

D'Ohsson, Ignatius Mouradgea, *Tableau général de l'Empire Othoman*, 4 vols., Paris, 1787–1820.

Doughty, Charles M., *Travels in Arabia Deserta*, 2 vols., Cambridge, UK, 1888.

Dozy, R., *Histoire des Musulmans d'Espagne jusqu'à la conquête de l'Andalousie par les Almoravides*, 4 vols., Leiden, Netherlands, 1861.

Driessen, Henk, 'Mediterranean Port Cities. Cosmopolitanism Reconsidered', *History and Anthropology* 16, 1 (2005), pp. 129–41.

'Drinkies', at https://www.drinkies.net/, accessed 5 January 2022.

Dubeux, M. Louis, *La Perse*, Paris, 1841.

'Du blues à l'âme', *Le Monde*, 10 April 2004.

Dumas, Laurent Ribadeau, 'Maroc: le vin se vend bien, malgré les interdits', *FranceInfo: Afrique*, 11 July 2013, at https://www.francetvinfo.fr/monde/afrique/maroc/maroc-le-vin-se-vend-bien-malgre-les-interdits_3070037.html, accessed 26 August 2019.

Duncan, Gillian, 'UAE Legal Reforms; New Alcohol Laws Explained', *The National*, 8 November 2020, https://www.thenationalnews.com/uae/courts/uae-legal-reforms-new-alcohol-laws-explained-1.1107842, accessed 5 January 2022.

Dunlop, H., ed., *Bronnen tot de geschiedenis der Oostdindische Compagnie, 1630–1638*, The Hague, 1930.

Dursteler, Eric R., 'Bad Bread and the "Outrageous Drunkenness of the Turks": Food and Identity in the Accounts of Early Modern European Travelers to the Ottoman Empire', *Journal of World History* 25, 2–3 (2014), pp. 203–28.

———, 'The "Abominable Pig" and the "Mother of all Vices": Pork, Wine and the Culinary Clash of Civilizations in the Early Modern Mediterranean', in Kirill Dmitriev, Julia Hauser, and Bilal Orfali, eds., *Insatiable Appetite: Food as Cultural Signifier in the Middle East and Beyond*, Leiden, Netherlands, 2019, pp. 214–4.

Dust 'Ali Khan Mu'ayyir al-Mamalik, *Yāddāsth'ha-i az zindigāni-yi khususi-ye Nāsir al-Din Shāh*, 3rd edn., Tehran, 1993.

Dwight, H. G., *Constantinople, Old and New*, New York, 1915.

Eaton, Richard M., *India in the Persianate Age 1000–1765*, Oakland, CA, 2019.

Eddé, Anne Marie, 'Baybars et son double, de l'ambiguité du souverain idéal', in Denise Aigle, ed., *Le bilād al-Šām face aux mondes extérieurs. La perception de l'autre et la représentation du souverain*, Damascus and Beirut, 2012, pp. 73–86.

Edman, Jonathan, 'Temperance and Modernity. Alcohol Consumption as a Collective Problem 1885–1913', *Journal of Social History* 49, 1 (2015), pp. 20–52.

BIBLIOGRAPHY

'Egypt Foaming Over Beer Sales', *YNetnews*, 15 June 2013, at https://www.ynetnews.com/articles/0,7340,L-4387511,00.html, accessed 31 December 2019.

'Eine Brauerei in El Gouna', *Mein Ägypten*, at https://www.mein-aegypten.com/content/eine-brauerei-el-gouna, accessed 2 January 2022.

El Asmar, Jopesh, *The Milk of Lions. A History of Alcohol in the Middle East*, n. p., 2020.

Eldem, Edhem, 'A French View of the Ottoman-Turkish Wine Market, 1890–1925', in Lucienne Thys-Şenocak, ed., *Of Vines and Wines. The Production and Consumption of Wine in Anatolian Civilizations Through the Ages*, Leuven, Belgium, 2018, pp. 169–209.

————, 'Istanbul: From Imperial to Peripheralized Capital', in Edhem Eldem, Daniel Goffman, and Bruce Masters, eds., *The Ottoman City Between East and West. Aleppo, Izmir, and Istanbul*, Cambridge, UK, 1999, pp. 135–206.

————, 'Ottoman Galata and Pera Between Myth and Reality', in Ulrike Tischler, ed., *From <<milieu de mémoire to <lieu de mémoire>> The Cultural Memory of Istanbul in the 20th Century*, Munich, Germany, 2006, pp. 18–37.

————, 'In vino modernitas: Une fête à Kāğithane en 1833', *Turcica* 52 (2021), pp. 525–59.

Engin, Vahdettin, *Sultan Abdülhamid ve İstanbul'u*, Istanbul, 2001.

Erdbrink, Thomas, 'Decades After Alcohol Ban, Iran Admits It Has a Problem', *NYT*, 11 September 2017.

————, 'As Taboos Break Down, Iranians Party On', *NYT*, 2 June 2018.

Eren, Ercan, *Geçmişten Günümüze Anadolu'da Bira*, Istanbul, 2005.

Ergin, Nina, 'Rock Faces: Opium and Wine. Speculations on the Original Viewing Context of Persian Manuscripts', *Der Islam* 90, 1 (2013), pp. 65–99.

Ernst, Carl W., *Rūzbihān Baqlī: Mysticism and the Rhetoric of Sainthood in Persian Sufism*, Richmond, UK, 1996.

Ernst, Waltraud, ed., *Alcohol Flows Across Cultures Drinking Cultures in Transnational and Comparative Perspective*, London, 2020

————, 'Introduction: Alcohol Flows Across Cultures. Drinking Cultures in Transnational and Comparative Perspective', in Idem, ed., *Alcohol Flows Across Cultures*, pp. 1–19.

Escartín Gonzáles, Eduardo, *Estudio ecónomico sobre el 'Tratato' de Ibn Abdún. El vino e los gremios en al-Andalus antes del siglo XII*, Seville, Spain, 2006.

Esfandiari, G., and M. Zarghami, 'Iranian Officials Warn Alcohol Abuse on the Rise', *Radio Free Europe*, 17 June 2012, at http://www.rferl.org/content/iran-alcohol-abuse-on-the-rise/24617070.html, accessed 22 January 2022.

Estatiev, Simeon, 'The Qāḍīzādeli Movement and the Revival of Takfīr in the Ottoman Age', in Camilla Adang and Hassan Ansari, eds., *Accusations of Unbelief in Islam. A Diachronic Perspective on Takfīr*, Leiden, Netherlands, 2018, pp. 213–43.

Evered, Emine Ö., and Kyle T. Evered, 'A Geopolitics of Drinking. Debating the Place of Alcohol in Early Republican Turkey', *Political Geography* 50 (2016), pp. 48–60.

————, 'Between Promotions and Prohibitions. The Shifting Symbolisms and Spaces of Beer in Modern Turkey', in Ernst, ed., *Alcohol Flows Across Cultures*, pp. 84–122.

————, 'From *Rakı* to *Ayran*. Regulating the Place and Practice of Drinking in Turkey', *Space and Polity* 20, 1 (2016), pp. 39–58.

Ezzat, Ahmed, 'Law and Moral Regulation in Modern Egypt: *Ḥisba* From Tradition to Modernity', *IJMES* 52, 4 (2020), pp. 665–84.

Fahmy, Khaled, *In Quest of Justice. Islamic Law and Forensic Medicine in Modern Egypt*, Oakland, CA, 2018.

Farman, Samuel, *Constantinople in Connexion With the Present War*, London, 1855.

BIBLIOGRAPHY

Faruk Köse, Ömer, 'The Fatwa Collection of an Ottoman Provincial Mufti. Vani Mehmed Efendi', PhD dissertation Boğaziçi University, 2015.

Fath 'Ali Shah, *Divān-i kāmil-i ash 'ār-i Fath 'Ali Shāh Qājār*, Tehran, 1965.

Fathi, Nazila, 'As Liquor Business Booms, Bootleggers Risk the Lash', *NYT*, 4 April 2006.

Fayyala, Rasha Mahmud 'Abd al-'Aziz, *Mazāhir al-fasād al-ijtimā'i fi Misr fi 'asr salātin al-Mamālik, 648–923 h/1250-1517m: al-muskirāt namudhajan*, Alexandria, Egypt, 2019.

Feins, Daniel Scott, 'Wine and Islam. The Dichotomy Between Theory and Practice in Early Islamic History', PhD dissertation, University of Edinburgh, 1997.

Fernandes, Leonor, 'Baybars II al-Malik al-Muẓaffar', *EI³.*

Ferrier, J. P., *Caravan Journeys and Wanderings in Persia, Afghanistan, Turkistan, and Baluchistan. With Historical Notices of Countries Lying Between Russia and India*, London, 1957.

Ferrières-Sauveboeuf, Comte L. de, *Mémoires historiques, politiques et géographiques des voyages … faits en Turquie, en Perse et en Arabie depuis 1782 jusqu'en 1789*, 2 vols., Paris, 1790.

Feuillebois-Pierunek, Ève, *De l'ascèse au libertinage. Les champs de la poésie mystique persane. Sanā'ī (1087?–1130?) et 'Attār (ca. 1145–ca. 1221)*, Paris, 2021.

Fisher, Max, 'Forbidden Drink. Why Alcohol Is Soaring in Officially Booze-free Iran', *The Atlantic*, 28 June 2012, at https://www.theatlantic.com/international/archive/2012/06/forbidden-drink-why-alcoholism-is-soaring-in-officially-booze-free-iran/259120/, accessed 19 September 2020.

Flamand, Pierre, *Un mellah en pays berbère: Demnate*, Paris, 1952.

Flandin, Eugène Napoleon, and Pascal Coste, *Voyage en Perse de MM. Eugene Flandin, peintre, et Pascal Coste, architecte*, 2 vols., Paris, 1851.

Fleet, Kate, *European and Islamic Trade in the Early Ottoman State. The Merchants of Genoa and Turkey*, Cambridge, 1999.

———, 'The Turkish Economy, 1071–1453', in Eadem, ed., *The Cambridge History of Turkey. Vol. 1: Byzantium to Turkey, 1071–1453*, Cambridge, UK, 2009, pp. 227–65.

Floor, Willem, 'The Culture of Wine Drinking in Pre-Mongol Iran', in Fragner, Kauz, and Schwarz, eds., *Wine Culture in Iran and Beyond*, pp. 165–210.

———, *A Fiscal History of Iran in the Safavid and Qajar Periods 1500–1925*, New York, 1998.

———, 'Les premières règles de police urbaine à Téhéran', in C. Adle and B. Hourcade, eds., *Téhéran capitale bicentenaire*, Paris and Tehran, 1992, pp. 173–98.

———, *The Rise and Fall of Nader Shah. Dutch East India Company Reports, 1730–1747*, Washington, DC, 2009.

———, tr. and ed., *German Sources on Safavid Persia*, Washington, DC, 2020.

Floor, Willem, and Hasan Javadi, *Persian Pleasures. How Iranians Relaxed Through the Centuries. Food, Drink & Drugs*, Washington, DC, 2019.

Floyer, Ernest Ayscoghe, *Unexplored Balūchistan*, London, 1882.

Foda, Omar D., 'Anna and Ahmad: Building a Modern Temperance Movement in Egypt (1884–1940)', *Sciences and Missions* 28 (2015), pp. 116–49.

———, *Egypt's Beer. Stella, Identity, and the Modern State*, Austin, TX, 2019.

———, 'Egypt's Beer Industry Toasts Long History', *Al-Monitor*, 3 November 2014, at http://www.al-monitor.com/pulse/originals/2014/10/beer-egypt-stella-heineken-pyramids.html, accessed 10 August 2022.

———, 'Grand Plans in Glass Bottles: The Economic, Social, and Technological History of Beer in Egypt, 1880–1970', PhD dissertation, University of Pennsylvania, 2015.

———, 'The Pyramid and the Crown: The Egyptian Beer Industry From 1897 to 1963', *IJMES* 46, 1 (2014), pp. 139–58.

BIBLIOGRAPHY

————, 'Stella vs. Sadat or How Beer Helps Explain Post-1970 Egypt', *MES* 58, 2 (2022), pp. 310–23.

Fontanier, Victor, *Voyages en Orient, entrepris par ordre du gouvernement français, de l'année 1821 à l'année 1829*, 2 vols., Paris, 1829.

————, *Voyages en Orient, entrepris par ordre du gouvernement français, de 1830 à 1833, 2e voyage en Anatolie*, Paris, 1834.

Foresien, Jean Palerne, *Peregrinations du S. Jean Palerne Foresien*, Secretaire de François de Valois Duc d'Anjou, Paris, 1606.

Forstner, Martin, *Al-Muʿtazz billāh (252/866–255/869. Die Krise des abbasidischen Kalifats im 3./9. Jahrhundert*, Gemersheim, Germany, 1976.

Forsyth, Mark, *A Short History of Drunkenness. How, Why, Where, and When Humankind Has Gotten Merry From the Stone Age to the Present*, New York, 2018.

Foster, William, ed., *Early Travels in India, 1583–1619*, Oxford, 1921; repr. New Delhi, 1968.

Fowden, Garth, *Qusayr ʿAmra. Art and the Umayyad Elite in Late Antique Syria*, Berkeley, CA, 2004.

Fowler, George, *Three Years in Persia: With Travelling Adventures in Koordistan*, 2 vols., London, 1841.

Fragner, Bert G., 'Drinking Wine in Iran Under the Reign of Aryamehr', in Fragner, Kauz, and Schwarz, eds., *Wine Culture in Iran and Beyond*, pp. 251–8.

Fragner, Bert G., Ralph Kauz, and Florian Schwarz, eds., *Wine Culture in Iran and Beyond*, Vienna, 2014.

Frank, Louis, *Tunis. Description de cette régence*, in J. J. Marcel, *Histoire de Tunis*, Paris, 1851.

Fraser, James, *The History of Nadir Shah, Formerly Called Thamas Kuli Khan, the Present Emperor of Persia*, London, 1742.

Fraser, James Baillie, *Narrative of a Journey into Khorasan in the Years 1821 and 1822*, London, 1825.

Freely, John, *Stamboul's Ghosts. A Stroll Through Bohemian Istanbul*, Edinburgh, UK, 2018.

————, *Stamboul Sketches. Encounters in Old Istanbul*, Istanbul, 1974; repr. London, 2014.

Freeman, Colin, 'Saddam Hussein's Palaces', *The Telegraph*, 16 July 2009.

Freitag, Ulrike, *A History of Jeddah. The Gate to Mecca in the Nineteenth and Twentieth Centuries*, Cambridge, UK, 2020.

Frembgen, Jürgen Wasim, *'We Are Lovers of the Qalandar'. Piety, Pilgrimage, and Ritual in Pakistani Sufi Islam*, Karachi, 2021.

Fresne-Canaye, Philippe du, *Voyage du Levant de Philippe du Fresne-Canaye*, ed. M. H. Hauser, Paris, 1897.

Freud, Sigmund, *The Standard Edition of the Complete Psychological Works of Sigmund Freud*, ed. James Strachey, London, 1994.

Frontline PBS, 'Inside an AA Meeting in Iran. A Country Where Alcohol Is Banned', at https://www.youtube.com/watch?v=aCqu_-QQvrA, accessed 10 February 2019.

Fuess, Albrecht, '*Ẓulm* by *Maẓālim*? The Political Implications of the Use of *Maẓālim* Jurisdiction by the Mamluk Sultans', *Mamlūk Studies Review* 13, 1 (2009), pp. 121–47, at https://knowledge.uchicago.edu/record/1289, accessed 26 April 2022.

Fuhrmann, Malte, 'Down and Out on the Quays of İzmir: "European" Musicians, Innkeepers and Prostitutes in the Ottoman Port-cities', *Mediterranean Historical Review* 29, 2 (2009), pp. 169–85.

————, *Port Cities in the Eastern Mediterranean. Urban Culture in the Late Ottoman Empire*, Cambridge, UK, 2020.

BIBLIOGRAPHY

Fulton, A. S., 'Fīrūzābādī's Wine List', *BSOAS* 12, 3–4 (1947–8), pp. 579–85.

Gahan, Jairan, 'Red-light Tehran. Prostitution, Intimately Public Islam, and the Rule of the Sovereign, 1910–1980', PhD dissertation, University of Toronto, 2017.

———, 'The Sovereign and the Sensible: Islam, Prostitution and Moral Order in Tehran, 1911–22', *CSSAAME* 41, 2 (2021), pp. 222–35.

Galizzi, Alfredo Giovanni, *Souvenirs d'un journaliste. Izmir il y a 60 ans*, ed. Rıfat N. Bali, Istanbul, 2016.

Gandhi, Supriya, *The Emperor Who Never Was. Dara Shukoh in Mughal India*, Cambridge, MA, 2020.

Gangloff, Sylvie, *Boire en Turquie. Pratiques et représentations de l'alcool*, Paris, 2011.

Gardizi, Abu Saʿid ʿAbd al-Hayy, *The Ornament of Histories. A History of the Eastern Islamic Lands AD 650–1041*, tr. C. Edmund Bosworth, London, 2011.

Garland, Chad, 'Iraqis Drink Up as Life Returns to Liberated Mosul', *Stars and Stripes*, 9 March 2017, at https://www.stripes.com/news/iraqis-drink-up-as-life-returns-to-liberated-mosul-1.457774, accessed 26 April 2022.

Garzoni, Costantino, *Relazione dell' Impero ottomano del senatore Costantino Garzoni stato all'ambascieria di Costantinopoli nel 1573*, in Eugenio Albèri, ed., *Relazioni degli ambasciatori Veneti al Senato*, vol. III, t. 1, Florence, Italy, 1840.

Gasteiger, Albert Ritter von, *Die Handelsverhältnisse Persiens, in Bezug auf die Absatzfähigkeit Österr. Waaren*, Vienna, 1862.

[Gaudereau, M.], *Relation d'une mission faite nouvellement par monseigneur l'archevesque d'Ancyre en Ispahan en Perse pour la réunion des Arméniens à l'église catholique*, Paris, 1702.

Gaury, Gerald de, *Three Kings in Baghdad. The Tragedy of Iraq's Monarchy*, London, 2008.

———, *Traces of Travel: Brought Home From Abroad*, London, 1984.

Gautier, Théophile, *L'Orient*, 2 vols., Paris, 1977.

Geleynssen de Jongh, Wollebrand, 'Corte verclaringe over Isfahan', in DNA, Coll. Wollebrand Geleynssen de Jongh 28.

Géné, J. P., 'Sur la route du vin marocain', *Le Monde*, 26 September 2010.

Gentil, M., *Mémoires sur l'Indoustan*, Paris, 1822.

George, Stuart, 'What the Shah of Iran Drank', *Local Wine Events*, at https://www.localwineevents.com/wine-food-and-drink-articles/what-the-shah-of-iran-drank/1300, accessed 16 December 2021.

Georgelin, Hervé, *La fin de Smyrne. Du cosmopolitanisme aux nationalismes*, Paris, 2005.

Georgeon, François, *Abdülhamid II. Le crépuscule de l'Empire ottoman*, Paris, 2003; repr. 2017.

———, *Au pays du raki. Le vin et l'alcool de l'Empire ottoman à la Turquie d'Erdoğan (XIVe–XXIe siècle)*, Paris, 2021.

———, 'Ottomans and Drinkers: The Consumption of Alcohol in Istanbul in the Nineteenth Century', in Eugene Rogan, ed., *Outside In: On the Margins of the Modern Middle East*, London, 2002, pp. 7–30.

———, *Le mois le plus long. Ramadan à Istanbul*, Paris, 2017.

———, 'Le Ramadan à Istanbul de l'Empire à la République', in Georgeon and Dumont, eds., *Vivre dans l'Empire ottoman*, pp. 31–113.

———, 'Le sultan caché: réclusion du souverain en mise en scène du pouvoir à l'époque de Abdülhamid II (1876–1909)', *Turcica* 29 (1997), pp. 93–124.

Georgeon, François and Paul Dumont, eds., *Vivre dans l'Empire ottoman. Sociabilités et relations intercommunautaires (XVIIIe–XXe siècles)*, Paris, 1997.

Gerlach, Stephan, *Stephan Gerlachs deß Aeltern Tage-Buch*, Frankfurt a/M, 1674.

BIBLIOGRAPHY

Ghaffari-Qazvini, Qazi Ahmad b. Muhammad, *Tārikh-e jahān-ārā*, Tehran, 1963.

Ghandour Lilian, Chalak A., El-Aily A., Yassin N., Nakkash R., Tauk M. et al., 'Alcohol Consumption in the Arab Region: What Do We Know, Why Does It Matter, and What Are the Policy Implications for Youth Harm Reduction?', *International Journal of Drug Policy* 28, 1 (2016), pp. 10–33.

Ghattas, Kim, *Black Wave: Saudi Arabia, Iran, and the Forty-Year Rivalry That Unraveled Culture, Religion, and Collective Memory in the Middle East*, New York, 2020.

Ghazi, Hamdi, 'L'alcoolisme en Tunisie dans le contexte colonial', *Rawafid* 21 (2016), pp. 91–108.

Ghorbal, Samy, 'Celtia, reine incontestée de la bière en Tunisie', *Jeune Afrique*, 19 April 2017, at http://www.jeuneafrique.com/mag/426274/economie/celtia-reine-incontestee-de-biere-tunisie/, accessed 12 October 2017.

Gignoux, Ph., 'Matériaux pour une histoire du vin dans l'Iran ancien', in Rika Gyselen and Maria Szuppe, eds., *Matériaux pour l'histoire économique du monde iranien*, Paris, 1999, pp. 35–50.

Gillman, Gary, 'Mild Ale on the Main. Part II, or The Iraq Brewery', Gary Gillman's Beer and seq., 12 August 2020, at https://www.beeretseq.com/mild-ale-on-the-main-part-ii-or-the-iraq-brewery/, accessed 15 October 2022.

Gleave, Robert, 'The Clergy and the British. Perceptions of Religion and the *Ulama* in Early Qajar Iran', in Vanessa Martin, ed., *Anglo Iranian Relations Since 1800*, London, 2005, pp. 36–54.

'Global Alcohol Consumption. Drinking Habits. A Map of World Alcohol Consumption', *The Economist*, 14 February 2011.

'Glug if You're Not Local. A Row Over Whether Alcohol Should Be Tolerated for Some or Banned for All', *The Economist*, 18 May 2011.

Göçek, Fatma Müge, *East Encounters West. France and the Ottoman Empire in the Eighteenth Century*, Oxford, 1987.

Goffman, Daniel, *Izmir and the Levantine World, 1550–1650*, Seattle, WA, 1990.

Goitein, S. D., *A Mediterranean Society. The Jewish Communities of the Arab World as Portrayed in the Documents of the Cairo Geniza*, vol. 1, *Economic Foundations*; and vol. 4: *Daily Life*, Berkeley, CA, 1967 and 1983.

Golshiri, Hushang, 'Alienation From the Self-made Revolution: A Short Story', *IS* 30, 3–4 (1997), pp. 225–42.

Gonsales, Anthonius P., *Hierusalemsche reyse*, Antwerp, Belgium, 1673.

Gonzáles de Clavijo, Ruy, *Narrative of the Embassy of Ruy Gonzales de Clavijo to the Court of Timour of Samarcand (AD 1403–6)*, tr. Clements R. Markham, London, 1859.

Good, Peter, *The East India Company in Persia. Trade and Cultural Exchange in the Eighteenth Century*, London, 2022.

Gordon, General Sir Thomas Edward, *Persia Revisited. With Remarks on H.I.M. Mozufer-ed-Din and the Present Situation in Persia*, London and New York, 1896.

Gorgani, Fakhraddin, *Vis & Ramin*, tr. and ed. Dick Davis, Washington, DC, 2008.

Gottreich, Emily, *The Mellah of Marrakesh: Jewish and Muslim Space in Morocco's Red City*, Bloomington, IN, 2006.

Goussaud-Falgas, Geneviève, *Les Français de Tunisie de 1881 à 1931*, Paris, 2013.

Gouvea, António de, *elaça mem que se tratam as guerras e grandes victorias que alcançou o grãde rey da Persia Xá Abbas do grão Turco Mahometto, & seu filho Amethe, as quais resultarão das embaixadas qũe por mandado del rey D. Felippe II de Pdortugal fizerão algũs religiosos da ordem dos Eremeitaas de Santo Agostinho a Persia*, Lisbon, 1611.

BIBLIOGRAPHY

'Governor Office Bans Alcohol in Turkey's Tourism Hub Antalya', *Stockholm Center for Freedom*, 28 April 2017, at https://stockholmcf.org/governor-office-bans-alcohol-in-turkeys-tourism-hub-antalya/, accessed 15 June 2022.

Graham, Bradley, 'Islamic Fundamentalism Rises', *Washington Post*, 5 October 1984.

Green, Nile, 'Kebabs and Port Wine: The Culinary Cosmopolitanism of Anglo-Persian Dining, 1800–1835', in Derryl N. Maclean and Sikeena Karmali, eds., *Cosmopolitanism in Muslim Contexts: Perspectives from the Past*, Edinburgh, UK, 2012, pp. 105–26.

———, *Sufism. A Global History*, Chichester, UK, 2012.

Greene, Molly, *A Shared World: Christians and Muslims in the Early Modern Mediterranean*, Princeton, NJ, 2000.

Grehan, James, *Everyday Life and Consumer Culture in 18th-century Damascus*, Seattle, WA, 2007.

Greppi, Comte, 'Souvenirs d'un diplomate italien à Constantinople (1861–1866)', *Revue d'Histoire Diplomatique* 48 (1910), pp. 372–87.

Grose, John Henry, *Voyage to the East Indies*, 2 vols., new edn., London, 1772.

Gruner, O. Camero, tr. and ed., *A Treatise on the Canon of Medicine of Avicenna*, London, 1930.

Grunzel, Joseph, *Bericht über die wirtschaftlichen Verhältnisse des Osmanischen Reiches*, Vienna, 1903.

Guerra-Doce, Elisa, 'The Origins of Inebriation: Archaeological Evidence of the Consumption of Fermented Beverages and Drugs in Prehistoric Eurasia', *Journal of Archeological Methods and Theory* 22, 3 (2015), pp. 751–82.

Guo, Li, 'Paradise Lost: Ibn Dāniyāl's Response to Baybars' Campaign Against Vice in Cairo', *JAOS* 121, 2 (2001), pp. 219–35.

Guzārish'hā-yi nazmiyya az mahallāt-i Tehrān, 2 vols. pag. as one, Tehran, 1998.

Habermas, Jürgen, *The Structural Transformation of the Public Sphere: An Inquiry Into a Category of Bourgeois Society*, Cambridge, UK, 1989.

Haddar, Yazid, 'L'Algérie vers la prohibition de fait l'alcool : Entre tabou et hypocrisie', *Le Nouvel Observateur*, 30 December 2012.

Hagemann, Hannah-Lena, Katharina Mewes, and Peter Verkinderen, 'Studying Elites in Early Islamic History: Concepts and Terminology', in Hannah-Lena Hagemann and Stefan Heidemann, eds., *Transregional and Regional Elites: Connecting the Early Islamic Empire*, Berlin, 2019, pp. 17–44.

Haider, Najam, 'Contesting Intoxication: Early Juristic Debates About the Lawfulness of Alcoholic Beverages', *Islamic Law and Society* 20, 1–2 (2013), pp. 48–89.

Hale, F., *From Persian Uplands*, London, 1920.

Hallawi, Janan Jasim, *Hawā Qalil*, Beirut, 2009.

Haller, Dieter, 'The Cosmopolitan Mediterranean: Myth and Reality', *Zeitschrift für Ethnologie* 129, 1 (2004), pp. 29–47.

Hammad, Hanan. 'Regulating Sexuality: The Colonial-national Struggle Over Prostitution After the British Invasion of Egypt', in Marilyn Booth and Anthony Gorman, eds., *The Long 1890s in Egypt. Colonial Quiescence, Subterranean Resistance*, Edinburgh, UK, 2014, pp. 195–221.

Hammad, Isabella, *The Parisian*, New York, 2019.

Hamadeh, Shirine, *The City's Pleasures: Istanbul in the Eighteenth Century*, Seattle, WA, 2008.

Hamilton, Robert, *Walid and His Friends. An Umayyad Tragedy*, Oxford, 1988.

Hammer Purgstall, Joseph von, *Des osmanischen Reichs Staatsverfassung*, 2 vols., Vienna, 1815.

———, *Geschichte des osmanischen Reiches*, 10 vols., Pest, Hungary, 1827–35.

BIBLIOGRAPHY

Hamont, Pierre Nicolas, *L'Égypte sous Méhémet-Ali. Populations, gouvernement, institutions publiques, industrie, agriculture, principaux événements de Syrie pendant l'occupation égyptienne, Soudan de Méhémet-Ali*, 2 vols., Paris, 1843.

Hamori, Andras, *On the Art of Medieval Arabic Literature*, Princeton, NJ, 1974.

Hames, Gina, *Alcohol in World History*, Abingdon, UK, 2012.

Hanif, Mohammed, 'Pakistan Has a Drinking Problem', *NYT*, 2 December 2016.

Hanley, Will, 'Grieving Cosmopolitanism in Middle East Studies', *History Compass* 6, 5 (2008), pp. 1346–67.

Hannon, Elliot. 'Hundreds Die in Iran from Bootleg Alcohol Being Peddled Online as Fake Coronavirus Remedy', *Slate*, 27 March 2020, at https://slate.com/news-and-politics/2020/03/hundreds-die-iran-drinking-bootleg-alcohol-methanol-coronavirus-cure-social-media.html, accessed 9 May 2020.

Hanway, Jonas, *An Historical Account of the British Trade over the Caspian Sea: With a Journal of Travels Through Russia Into Persia ... to Which Are Added, the Revolutions of Persia During the Present Century, With the Particular History of the Great Usurper Nadir Kouli*, 4 vols., London, 1753.

Harb, F., 'Wine Poetry (*Khamriyyāt*)', in Julia Ashtiany et al., eds., *The Cambridge History of Arabic Literature, 'Abbasid Belles-Lettres*, Cambridge, UK, 1990, pp. 219–34.

Haringman, H., *Beknopt dag-journaal van een verblyf van agt weeken in het keizerryk van Marocco en landreize naar Mecquinez*, The Hague, 1803.

Harry, Myriam, *Tunis la blanche*, Paris, 1910.

Hasan, Arif, 'From the Demise of Cosmopolitanism to Its Revival: Trends and Repercussions for Karachi', in Nicola Khan, ed., *Cityscapes of Violence in Karachi: Publics and Counterpublics*, Oxford, 2017, pp. 173–86.

Hattox, Ralph, *Coffee and Coffeehouses. The Origins of a Social Beverage in the Medieval Near East*, Seattle, WA, 1985.

Heath, Dwight B., 'Anthropology and Alcohol Studies: Current Islam', *Annual Review of Anthropology* 16 (1987), pp. 99–120.

Heine, Peter, 'Nabīdh', *EI²*.

———, *Weinstudien. Untersuchungen zu Anbau, Produktion und Konsum des Weins im arabisch-islamischen Mittelalter*, Wiesbaden, 1982.

Heitmeyer, Carolyn, 'The Culture of Prohibition in Gujarat, India', in Harald Fischer-Tiné and Jana Tschurenev, eds., *A History of Alcohol and Drugs in Modern South Asia: Intoxicating Affairs*, Abingdon, UK, 2014, pp. 203–18.

Herbert, Sir Thomas, *Travels in Africa, Persia and Asia the Great (1677)*, ed. John Anthony Butler, Tempe, AZ, 2012.

Herodotus, *Histories*, 4 vols., ed. A. D. Godely, Cambridge, MA, 1971.

Heskett, Randall and Joel Butler, *Divine Vintage. Following the Wine Trail From Genesis to the Modern Age*, New York, 2012.

Heyworth-Dunne, J., *Religious and Political Trends in Modern Egypt*, Washington, DC, 1950.

Al-Hilali, Amil, 'Can Dry Hotels Boost Tunisia's Ailing Tourism Sector?', *Al-Monitor*, 10 July 2018, at https://www.al-monitor.com/originals/2018/07/tunisian-controversy-on-helal-tourism.html, accessed 28 April 2022.

Hillenbrand, Robert, '*La Dolce Vita* in early Islamic Syria. The Evidence of Late Islamic Palaces', in Idem, *Studies in Medieval Islamic Architecture*, vol. 1, London, 2001, pp. 58–113.

Hobhouse, John C., *Journey Through Albania and Other Provinces of Turkey, in Europe and Asia, to Constantinople, During the Years 1809 and 1810*, London, 1813.

BIBLIOGRAPHY

Holmes, W. R., *Sketches on the Shores of the Caspian Sea. Descriptive and Pictorial,* London, 1845.

Homerin, Th. Emil, 'Arab Religious Poetry', in Roger Allen and D. S. Richards, eds., *Arabic Literature in the Post-Classical Period,* Cambridge, UK, 2006, pp. 74–86.

Honchell, Stephanie, 'The Story of a Drunken Mughal: Islam, Alcohol and Imperial Ambition', *Social History of Alcohol and Drugs* 29, 1 (2015), pp. 4–28.

Hoppe, Hans, 'Die diplomatischen Missionen des schwedischen Gesandten Ludwig Fabritius nach Moskau und Isfahan gegen Ende des 17. Jahrhunderts', in Hans Hüls and Hans Hoppe, eds., *Engelbert Kaempfer zum 330. Geburtstag,* Lemgo, 1982, pp. 155–166.

'Hurmat-i muskirāt dar Inglis', *Tarbiyat,* 22 Shaʿban 1321/12 November 1903.

Hornby, Lady, *Constantinople During the Crimean War,* London, 1863.

Hurr al-ʿAmilī al-, *Wasāʾil al-Shiʿa,* Qom, Iran, 1993.

Hubbart, G. E., *From the Gulf to Ararat. Imperial Boundary Making in the Late Ottoman Empire,* London, 2016.

Ibn Khallikan, *Ibn Khallikan's Biographical Dictionary,* tr. Mac Guckin de Slane, 2 vols., Paris, 1843.

Ibn al-Muʾtazz, Abi al-ʿAbbas ʿAbd Allah, *Kitāb fusul al-tamāthil fi tabāshir al-surur,* ed. Jurj Qanazi and Fahd Abu Khadra, Damascus, Syria, 1989.

Ibn Qutayba, Abu Muhammad ʿAbd Allah b. Muslim, *Kitāb al-ashriba (wa dhikr ikhtilāf al-nās fihā),* ed. Yasin Muhammad al-Sawas, Damascus, Syria, 1998.

Ibrahim, Mina, 'A Minority at the Bar. Revisiting the Coptic Christian (In-)visibility', *Social Compass* 66, 3 (2019), pp. 366–92.

———, 'Drinking in Times of Change: The Haunting Presence of Alcohol in Egypt', in Elife Biçer-Deveci and Philippe Bourmaud, eds., *Alcohol in the Maghreb and the Middle East Since the Nineteenth Century: Disputes, Policies and Practices,* New York, 2022, pp. 163–84.

Iddon, Paul, 'Battle of the Bottle: Iraq's Love-hate Relationship With Booze', *The New Arab,* 13 June 2017, at https://www.alaraby.co.uk/english/indepth/2017/6/13/battle-of-the-bottle-iraqs-love-hate-relationship-with-booze, accessed 3 January 2022.

Idris, Murad, 'The Politics of *What Is Islam?* What Kind of a Question Is It Anyway?', *CSSAAME* 40, 1 (2020), pp. 198–202.

Ilahi, Sadr al-Din, *Sayyid Ziyā. Mard-i avval ya mard-i duvvum-i kuditā,* Los Angeles, 2011.

———, 'Iran Confronts Its Alcohol Problem', *Los Angeles Times,* 7 July 2012.

———, 'Iranian Embassy Empties 4,000 Bottles of Liquor', *NYT,* 28 May 1979.

'Iraq's Bashiqa Brings Back the Booze to Clear IS Hangover', *Daily Mail,* 18 February 2017, at https://www.dailymail.co.uk/wires/afp/article-4237432/Iraqs-Bashiqa-brings-booze-clear-IS-hangover.html, accessed 28 April 2022.

Irvine, William, *Later Mughals,* 2 vols, London, 1922.

Isbahani, Abuʾl-Faraj al-, *Kitāb al-aghāni,* 21 vols., Cairo n.d.

Isfahani, Muhammad Maʿsum b. Khajigi, *Khulāsat al-siyar. Tarikh-i ruzgār-i Shāh Safi Safavi,* ed. Iraj Afshar, Tehran, 1989.

'Islam and Alcohol. Tipsy Taboo', *The Economist,* 12 August 2012.

'Islamic Pressure Forces Brewery in Aden to Stop Producing Beer', *Reuters,* 24 June 1991, at https://www.joc.com/maritime-news/islamic-pressure-forces-brewery-aden-stop-producing-beer_19910624.html, accessed 28 April 2022.

Isnard, Hildebert, *La vigne en Algérie. Étude géographique,* 2 vols., Paris, 1947.

Issawi, Charles, *The Economic History of Iran 1800–1914,* Chicago, 1971.

Iʿtimad al-Saltana, *Ruznāma-yi khātirat-i Iʿtimād al-Saltana,* 4th edn., Tehran, 1998.

Jackson, G. A., *Algiers, Being a Complete Picture of the Barbary States,* London, 1817.

Jackson, James Grey, *An Account of Morocco and the District of Suse,* London, 1809.

BIBLIOGRAPHY

Jackson, Miriam, 'Bootleg Alcohol Kills 194 People in Iran', *Union Journal*, 22 March 2020, at https://theunionjournal.com/bootleg-alcohol-kills-194-people-in-iran-middle-east-monitor/, accessed 22 March 2020.

Jackson, Peter, *The Mongols and the Islamic World. From Conquest to Conversion*, New Haven, CT, 2017.

Ja'fariyan, Rasul, *Naqsh-i Khāndān-i Karaki dar ta'sis va tadāvum-i dawlat-i Safavi*, Tehran, 2008.

―――, *Safaviyya dar 'arsa-yi din, farhang va siyāsat*, 3 vols. pag. as one, Qom, Iran, 2000.

―――, ed., *Tārikh-i Qizilbāshān-i Safavi dar chandin matn-i tārikhi-mazhabi-yi 'arabi-yi dawra-yi 'Usmāni*, Qom, Iran, 2017.

Jahangir, *The Jahangirnama. Memoirs of Jahangir, Emperor of India*, ed. Wheeler M. Thackston, Washington, DC, 1999.

Jalali, 'Ali Akbar, 'Ta'sir-i alkul bar dastgāh-i pay', PhD dissertation, University of Tehran, Faculty of Medicine, 1945.

Jansen, Willy, 'French Bread and Algerian Wine: Conflicting Identities in French Algeria', in Peter Schollier, ed., *Food, Drink, and Identity: Cooking Eating and Drinking in Europe Since the Middle Ages*, Oxford, pp. 195–218.

Jaubert, P. Amédée, *Voyages en Arménie et en Perse, faite dans les années 1805–1806*, Paris, 1821.

Javier Martínez, Francisco, 'Drinking Dis-ease: Alcohol and Colonialism in the International City of Tangier, c. 1912–1956', in Ernst, ed., *Alcohol Flows Across Cultures*, pp. 61–83.

Jawhar, *The Tezkereh al Vakiāt or Private Memoirs of the Moghul Emperor Hūmayūn Written in the Persian Language by Jouher*, tr. Charles Stewart, London, 1832; repr. New York, 1969.

Jenson, Jon, 'Poor in Cairo Drown Their Sorrows in Moonshine', *Global Post*, 28 January 2010, at https://www.pri.org/stories/2010-01-28/poor-cairo-drown-their-sorrows-moonshine, accessed 31 December 2019.

Jessup, Henry Harris, *Fifty-Three Years in Syria*, New York, 1910.

Jodoigne, Pierre, 'La vita di Giovanni Rota. Edizione critica', in *Studi in onore di Raffaele Spongano*, Bologna, Italy, 1980, pp. 215–32.

Johnson, Clarence Richard, ed., *Constantinople To-day; or, The Pathfinder Survey of Constantinople; a Study in Oriental Social Life*, New York, 1922.

Johnston, Sir Harry H., 'Prohibition of Alcohol in Africa', *The Missionary Review of the World* 42, 6 (1919), pp. 426–30.

Jones, Ror, 'Alcohol-free Saudi Arabia Plans Champagne and Wine Bar at Neom', *The Wall Street Journal*, 17 September 2022.

'A Joyless Revolution', *Newsweek*, 6 August 1979.

Judd, Steven, 'Reinterpreting al-Walīd b. Yazīd', *JAOS* 128, 3 (2008), pp. 439–58.

Junabadi, Mirza Bayg, *Rawzat al-Safaviyya*, ed. Ghulamriza Tabataba'i Majd, Tehran, 1999.

Kadri, Sadakat, *Heaven on Earth. A Journey Through Shari'a Law From the Deserts of Ancient Arabia to the Streets of the Modern Muslim World*, New York, 2012.

Kaempfer, Engelbert, *Exotic Attractions in Persia, 1684–1688. Travels and Observations*, tr. and ed. Willem Floor and Colette Ouahes, Washington, DC, 2018.

Kafadar, Cemal, *Between Two Worlds. The Construction of the Ottoman State*, Berkeley, CA, 1995.

Kai Kā'ūs ibn Iskandar ibn Iskandar, *A Mirror for Princes. The Qābūs Nāma*, tr. Reuben Levy, New York, 1951.

Kamal ibn Jalal, Munajjim Yazdi, *Tārikh-i mukhtasar (Zubdat al-tavārikh)*, ed. Raf'at Khaja-Yar, Tehran, 2019.

Kandel, Jonathan, 'Tehran Entertainment District Is Adapting Itself to the Revolution', *NYT*, 24 June 1979.

BIBLIOGRAPHY

Karahanoğulları, Onur, *Birinci Meclisnin İçki Yasağı (Men-i Müskirat Kanunu)*, Ankara, 2008.

Karakaş, Burcu, 'TV Dizilerinin Perde Arkası: Sansür ve Otosansür', *Gündem*, 5 August 2018, at https://www.dw.com/tr/tv-dizilerinin-perde-arkas%C4%B1-sans%C3%BCr-ve-otosans%C3%BCr/a-44947125, accessed 4 March 2022.

Karam, Michael, *Tears of Bacchus. A History of Wine in the Middle East and Beyond*, London, 2020.

———, *Wines of Lebanon*, London, 2005.

Karasz, Palko, 'A Six-pack of Beer for $26? Qatar Doubles the Price of Alcohol', *NYT*, 1 January 2019.

Kashani, Mirza Taqi Tabib, 'Dar bayān-i ikhtilāl-i nizām-i Irān bih vāsita-yi muskirāt', *Iran*, 10 Safar 1289/29 April 1872.

Kastritsis, Dimitri, 'Tales of Viziers and Wine: Interpreting Early Ottoman Narratives of State Centralization', in Jo van Steenbergen, ed., *Trajectories of State Formation Across Fifteenth-century Islamic West-Asia*, Leiden, Netherlands, 2020, pp. 224–54.

Kazemi, Ranin, 'Doctoring the Body and Exciting the Soul: Drugs and Consumer Culture in Medieval and Early Modern Iran', *Modern Asian Studies* 54, 2 (2020), pp. 554–617.

Kechriotis, Vangelis, 'The Enthusiasm Turns to Fear: Everyday Life Relations Between Christians and Muslims in Izmir in the Aftermath of the Young Turk Revolution', in François Georgeon, ed., '*L'ivresse de la liberté'. La révolution de 1908 dans l'Empire ottoman* (*Turcica* 17), Leuven, Belgium, 2012, pp. 295–316.

Kenbib, Mohammed, *Juifs et Musulmans au Maroc. Des origines à nos jours*, Paris, 2016.

Kennedy, Hugh, *When Baghdad Ruled the World. The Rise and Fall of Islam's Greatest Dynasty*, Cambridge, MA, 2004.

———, *The Prophet and the Age of the Caliphates. The Islamic Near East from the 6th to the 11th Century*, London, 1986.

Kennedy, Philip F., *Abu Nuwas. A Genius of Poetry*, Oxford, 2005.

———, *The Wine Song in Classical Arabic Poetry: Abu Nuwas and the Literary Tradition*, Oxford, 1997.

Keppel, George, *Personal Narrative of a Journey from India to England*, 2 vols., London, 1827.

Khare, Meera, 'The Wine-cup in Mughal Court Culture. From Hedonism to Kingship', *The Medieval History Journal* 8, 1 (2005), pp. 143–88.

'Kharid va furush-i khayli rāhat-i alkul'hā'yi sākht-i Irān dar kishvar', *Quds-Online*, 24 Murdad 1395/14 August 2016, at http://www.qudsonline.ir/news/412379/, accessed 16 October 2020.

Khurshah b. Qubad al-Husayni, *Tārikh-i ilchi-yi Nizāmshāh (Tārikh-i Safaviyya az āghāz tā sāl-i 927 h.q.)*, ed. Muhammad Riza Nasiri and Koichi Haneda, Tehran, 2000.

Khuzani Isfahani, Fazli Beg, *A Chronicle of the Reign of Shah 'Abbas*, 2 vols. pag. as one, ed. Kioumars Ghereghlou, Exeter, UK, 2015.

Khuzani Isfahani, *Afzal al-tavārikh. Ruzgār va zindigāni-yi Shāh Tahmāsb-i avval (930–48 hq.)*, vol. 1, ed. Ihsan Ishraqi, Tehran, 2019.

Khvandamir, Ghiyas al-Din Muhammad, *Tārikh-i habib al-siyar*, 4 vols., ed. Dabirsiyaqi, Tehran, 1984.

Kilpatrick, Hillary, 'Monasteries Through Muslim Eyes: The Diyārāt Books', in David Thomas and Alexander Mallett, eds., *Christian-Muslim Relations: A Bibliographical History*, vol. 2, Leiden, Netherlands, 2010, pp. 19–37.

King, Charles, *Midnight at the Pera Palace. The Birth of Modern Istanbul*, New York, 2014.

Kinglake, Alexander William, *Eothen*, London, 1847.

BIBLIOGRAPHY

Kırmızı, Abdulhamit, 'The Drunken Officials of Abdülhamid II: Alcohol Consumption in the Late Ottoman Bureaucracy', *Revue du Monde Musulman de de la Mediterranée* 151 (2022), pp. 87–104.

Kitto, John, *The People of Persia*, London, 1949.

Kiyanrad, Sarah, 'Thou Shalt Not Enter the Bazaar on Rainy Days! Dhimmī Merchants in Safavid Isfahan: Shiʻite Fiqh Meeting Social Reality', *Journal of Persianate Studies* (2017), pp. 158–85.

Knolles, Richard, *Generall Historie of the Turkes From the First Beginning of That Nation to the Rising of the Othoman Familie*, London, 1603.

Knudsen, Ståle, 'Between Life Giver and Leisure: Identity Negotiation Through Seafood in Turkey', *IJMES* 38, 3 (2006), pp. 395–415.

Koçu, Reşad Ekrem, *Eski Istanbul'da Meyhaneler ve Meyhane Köcekleri*, Istanbul, 2015.

Koelz, Walter N., *Persian Diary, 1939–1941*, Ann Arbor, MI, 1983.

Koh, Choon Hwee, 'Qāytbay's Journey to Bilād al-Shām in 882/1477. Power, Periphery and Royal Peregrinations', MA thesis, University of Beirut, 2014.

Korf, Baron Feodor, *Vospominaniia v Persii 1834–1835*, St. Petersburg, 1838.

Korostovetz, Ivan J., *Persian Arabesques*, tr. Carlo Gastone, Turin, Italy, 2021.

Köse, Yavuz, *Westlicher Konsum am Bosporus: Warenhäuser, Nestlé & Co. Im späten Osmanischen Reich (1855–1923)*, Munich, Germany, 2010.

Koylu, Hilal, 'Turkish Bans on Wikipedia and Public Drinking Rouse Anger', *Al-Monitor*, 1 May 2017, at https://www.al-monitor.com/pulse/originals/2017/05/turkey-recent-bans-spark-contreversy.html, accessed 13 March 2020.

Koyuncu, Derviş Tuğrul, and Ahmet Tabakoğlu, eds, *Osmanlı İmparatorluğu'nda Alkollü İçeceklerin (Arak ve Şarap) Üretimi, Ticareti ve Tüketimi: 1792–1839 İstanbul Örneği*, Istanbul, 2019.

Kozma, Liat, *Policing Egyptian Women. Sex, Law, and Medicine in Khedival Egypt*, Syracuse, NY, 2011.

Kroell, Anne, ed., *Nouvelles d'Ispahan*, Paris, 1979.

Kueny, Kathryn, *The Rhetoric of Sobriety: Wine in Early Islam*, Albany, NY, 2001.

Kulayni, Muhammad b. Yaʻqub al., *Al-Kafi*, tr. Muhammad Sarwar, 8 vols., n.p., 2005.

Kullab, Samya, 'In a Baghdad Bar, a Syrian Serves Cocktails to Fix War Woes', *AP News*, 3 February 2021, at https://apnews.com/article/beirut-lebanon-coronavirus-pandemic-cocktails-baghdad-5ac19f54695f2bb38b310c71885021d0, accessed 7 January 2022.

Kuneralp, Zeki, 'Aspects de la vie sociale et littéraire à Paris à la fin du XIXe siècle d'après un jeune exile politique turc. Lettres écrites de Paris à l'İkdam par Ali Kemal (1895–1899)', in Hamit Batu and Jean-Louis Bacqué-Grammont, eds., *L'Empire ottoman, la République de Turquie et la France*, Istanbul, 1986, pp. 345–57.

Kureishi, Hanif, 'Erotic Politicians and Mullahs', *Granta Magazine* 17 (1985), pp. 139–51.

Kuss, Walther, *Handelsratgeber für Persien*, Berlin, 1911.

'Kuwait: Oil, Oil Everywhere, But Not a Drop to Drink', *TIME*, 22 January 1965.

Lacey, Marc, 'A New Target in Basra: Liquor Stores and Their Owners', *NYT*, 23 May 2003.

Lane, Edward, *The Manners and Customs of the Modern Egyptians*, London, 1860; new edn., 1966.

Lane-Poole, Stanley, *The Life of the Right Honourable Stratford Canning: Viscount Stratford de Redcliffe*, 2 vols., London, 1888.

Lange, Christian, 'Change in the Office of Hisba under the Seljuqs', in Christian Lange and Songül Mecit, eds., *The Seljuqs: Politics, Society and Culture*, Edinburgh, 2011, pp. 157-81.

BIBLIOGRAPHY

————, *Justice, Punishment, and the Medieval Muslim Imagination*, Cambridge, UK, 2008.

————, 'Vom Recht sich zu verhüllen. Dimensionen der Privatsphäre im muslimischen Feqh', in Peter Scholz and Naseef Naeem, eds., *Recht der Staaten im islamischen Kulturraum*, vol. 2, *Jahrbuch für Verfassung, Recht und Staat im islamischen Kontext* (2012– 13), pp. 35–52.

Langier de Tassy, Jacques Philippe, *Histoire du royaume d'Alger*, Amsterdam, 1725.

Lankarani, Kamran Bagheri, and Riza Afshari, 'Alcohol Consumption in Iran', *The Lancet* 384 (29 November 2014), pp. 1927–8.

Larguèche, Abdelhamid, *Les ombres de Tunis. Pauvres, marginaux et minorités aux XVIIIe et XIXe siècles*, Paris, 2000.

Lâtifi (Abdüllatif Hatibzâde), *Evsâf-ı İstanbul*, ed. Nermin Sumer, Istanbul, 1977.

Laufer, Berthold, 'On the Possible Oriental Origins of Our Word Booze', *JAOS* 49, 1 (1929), pp. 56–8.

La Véronne, Chantal, *Vie de Moulay Isma'īl, roi de Fès et de Maroc d'après Joseph de Léon (1708– 1728)*, Paris, 1974.

Layard, Lady, *Twixt Pera and Therapia. The Constantinople Dairies of Lady Layard*, ed. Sinan Kunalp, Istanbul, 2010.

Lecomte, Gérard, *Ibn Qutayba. L'homme, son œuvre, ses idées*, Damascus, Syria, 1965.

Lefèvre, Corinne, *Pouvoir impérial et élites dans l'Inde moghole de Jahāngīr*, Paris, 2017.

Leiser, Gary, *Prostitution in the Eastern Mediterranean World. The Economics of Sex in the late Antique and Medieval Middle East*, London, 2017.

Lentz, Thomas W., and Glenn D. Lowry, 'Shahrukh and the Princely Network', in Idem, *Timur and the Princely Vision. Persian Art and Culture in the Fifteenth Century*, Los Angeles, CA, 1989.

Letsch, Constanze, 'Turkey Alcohol Laws Could Pull the Plug on Istanbul Nightlife', *The Guardian*, 31 May 2013, at https://www.theguardian.com/world/2013/may/31/ turkey-alcohol-laws-istanbul-nightlife, accessed 29 April 2022.

Lettres édifiantes et curieuses, vol. 4, new edn., Toulouse, France, 1810.

Levanoni, Amalia, 'Takfīr in Egypt and Syria During the Mamlūk Period', in Camilla Adang et al., eds., *Accusations of Unbelief in Islam. A Diachronic Perspective on Takfīr*, Leiden, Netherlands, 2018, pp. 155–88.

————, *A Turning Point in Mamluk History. The Third Reign of al-Nāṣir Muḥammad Ibn Qalāwūn (1310–1341)*, Leiden, Netherlands, 2001.

'Levantine Heritage', http://www.levantineheritage.com/bomonti.htm, accessed 16 June 2022.

Lévi-Provençal, É., *Le califat umaiyade de Cordoue (912–1031)*, vol. 2 of Idem, *Histoire de l'Espagne musulmane*, Paris, 1950.

Levy, Avigdor, 'The Ottoman Ulema and the Military Reforms of Sultan Mahmud II', *Asian and African Studies* 7 (1971), pp. 13–39.

Lewicka, Paulina B., *Food and Foodways of Medieval Cairenes. Aspects of Life in an Islamic Metropolis of the Eastern Mediterranean*, Leiden, Netherlands, 2011.

Lewis, Franklin, 'Hafez and Rendi', *EIr*.

Lewis, Geoffrey, tr. and ed., *The Book of Dede Korkut*, London, 1974.

Lewis, Paul, 'Iraq Bans Public Use of Alcohol', *NYT*, 21 August 1994.

Lewisohn, Jane, 'The Rise and Fall of Lalehzar, Cultural Centre of Tehran in the Mid-twentieth century', Tehran Project, UC Irvine, 2015.

Lewisohn, Leonard, *Beyond Faith and Infidelity. The Sufi Poetry and Teachings of Mahmud Shabistari*, Richmond, Surrey, UK, 1995.

Lindsay, A. W. C., *Letters on Egypt, Edom and the Holy Land*, 2 vols., London, 1838.

Lobe, Adrian, 'Mit Allah gegen Alkohol', *Neue Zürcher Zeitung*, 2 December 2013.

Loi sur l'impôt des spiritueux, Constantinople, 1918.

Lomnitskii, S., *Persiia i Persy, Eskizy i ocherki, 1898–1899–1900*, St. Petersburg, 1902.

Losensky, Paul, 'Sāqi-nāmah', *EIr.*

————, 'Song of the Cupbearer by Muhammad Sūfī Māzandarānī', in Ali-Asghar Seyed Gohrab, ed., *The Layered Heart: Essays on Persian Poetry, A Celebration in Honor of Dick Davis*, Washington, DC, 2019, pp. 173–98.

————, 'Vintages of the *Sāqī-nāma*: Fermenting and Blending the Cupbearer's Song in the Sixteenth Century', *IS* 47, 1 (2014), pp. 131–57.

————, *Welcoming Fighānī. Imitation and Poetic Individuality in the Safavid-Mughal Ghazal*, Costa Mesa, CA, 1998.

Love, Kennett, 'Iran Postpones Prohibition for Year. Land of Omar Khayyam Relaxes', *NYT*, 12 August 1953.

Low, Sidney, *Egypt in Transition*, New York, 1914.

Lowry, Heath, 'Impropriety and Impiety Among the Early Ottoman Sultans (1351–1451)', *The Turkish Studies Association Journal* 26, 1 (2002), pp. 29–38.

Lubenau, Reinhold, *Beschreibung der Reisen des Reinhold Lubenau*, ed. W. Sahm, 2 vols., Königsberg, 1914.

Lucas, A., *Alcoholic Liquors and the Liquor Trade in Egypt*, Cairo, 1916.

Ludington, Charles C., 'Drinking for Approval. Wine and the British Court From George III to Victoria and Albert', in Danielle de Vooght, ed., *Royal Taste: Food, Power and Status at the European Courts After 1789*, Farnham, UK, and Burlington, VT, 2011, pp. 57–86.

————, *The Politics of Wine in Britain: A New Cultural History*, Basingstoke, UK, 2013.

Lukacs, Paul, *Inventing Wine. A New History of One of the World's Most Ancient Pleasures*, New York, 2012.

Luth, Jean-Jacques, *La vie quotidienne en Égypte au temps des Khédives*, Paris, 1998.

Lyon, Wallace, *Kurds, Arabs and Britons. The Memoir of Wallace Lyon in Iraq*, ed. D. K. Fieldhouse, London, 2002.

MacArthur-Seal, Daniel-Joseph, *Britain's Levantine Empire, 1914–1923*, Oxford, 2021.

————, 'Intoxication and Imperialism. Nightlife in Occupied Istanbul, 1918–23', *CSSAAME* 37, 2 (2017), pp. 299–313.

————, 'States of Drunkenness: Bar-life in Istanbul Between Empire, Occupation, and Republic, 1918–1923', *Middle Eastern Studies* 58, 2 (2022), pp. 271–83.

Macbean Ross, Elizabeth N., *A Lady Doctor in Bakhtiari Land*, London, 1921.

MacFarlane, Charles, *Constantinople in 1828. A Residence of Sixteen Months in the Turkish Capital and Provinces*, 2 vols., London, 1829.

MacFarquar, Neil, *The Media Relations Department of Hizbollah Wishes You a Happy Birthday. Unexpected Encounters in the Changing Middle East*, New York, 2009.

————, 'Shiite Clerics Clashing Over How to Reshape Iraq', *NYT*, 26 August 2003.

MacGill, Thomas, *An Account of Tunis, of Its Government, Manners, Customs and Antiquities*, Glasgow, 1811.

MacGregor, C. M., *Narrative of a Journey Through the Province of Khorassan and on the N. W. Frontier of Afghanistan in 1875*, 2 vols., London, 1879.

Magdy, Muhammed, 'Egypt Uncovers Brewery That Served Pharaohs', *Al-Monitor*, 19 February 2021, at https://www.al-monitor.com/originals/2021/02/egypt-archaeology-discovery-beer-brewery-pharaos-tourism.html, accessed 4 May 2021.

Mahfouz, Naguib, *Palace of Desire*, Cairo, 2011.

BIBLIOGRAPHY

Maillet, Benoît de, *Description de l'Egypte contenant plusieurs remarques curieuses sur la géographie ancienne et moderne de ce pays*, The Hague, 1740.

Majlisi, Muhammad Baqir al-, *Bihār al-anwār*, vols 75–6, pag. as one vol., Beirut, 2008.

Makki, Husayn, *Tārīkh-i bist sāla-yi Iran. Kuditā-yi 1299*, 3 vols., Tehran, 1944; repr. 1979.

Malik, Zahir Uddin, *The Reign of Muhammad Shah 1719–1748*, New York, 1977.

Mamou, Yves, 'Les pays musulmans deviennent progressivement une région porteuse pour les fabricants d'alcool', *Le Monde*, 23 February 2011.

Mandelbaum, David G., 'Alcohol and Culture', *Current Anthropology* 6, 3 (1965), pp. 281–8.

Mandraud, Isabel, 'En Algérie, la prohibition assèche les bars', *Le Monde*, 31 January 2012.

————, 'L'Algérie glisse vers une prohibition officieuse', *Le Monde*, 31 January 2012; tr. as 'Algeria Slides Into Prohibition', *The Guardian*, 7 February 2012.

Mango, Andrew, *Atatürk. The Biography of the Founder of Modern Turkey*, New York, 1999.

Mansel, Philip, *Constantinople: City of the World's Desire 1453–1924*, London, 1995.

————, *Levant: Splendour and Catastrophe on the Mediterranean*, New Haven, CT, 2011.

Manucci, Nicolai, *Storia do Mogor*, 4 vols., London, 1907.

Manz, Beatrice Forbes, *Power, Politics and Religion in Timurid Iran*, Cambridge, UK, 2007.

Maraqten, Mohammed, 'Wine Drinking and Wine Prohibition in Arabia Before Islam', *Proceedings of the Seminar for Arabian Studies* 23 (1993), pp. 91–115.

Marcus, Abraham, *The Middle East on the Eve of Modernity. Aleppo in the Eighteenth Century*, New York, 1989.

Marino, Danilo, 'Raconter l'ivresse à l'époque mamelouke. Les mangeurs de haschich comme motif littéraire', *Annales Islamologiques* 49 (2015), pp. 55–80.

Marlow, Louise, 'The *khāṣṣa* and the *'āmma*: Intermediaries in the Samanid polity', in A. C. S. Peacock and D. G. Tor, eds., *Medieval Central Asia and the Persianate World. Iranian Tradition and Islamic Civilization*, London, 2015, pp. 31–55.

Martin, Vanessa, 'The British in Bushehr: The Impact of the First Herat War (1838–41) on Relations With State and Society', in Eadem, ed., *Anglo Iranian Relations Since 1800*, London, 2005, pp. 55–66.

Martini, Louis François, *Le crépuscule des Levantines de Smyrne. Étude historique d'une communauté*, Paris, 2018.

Martyr, Kate, 'Beirut Nightlife Grinds to a Halt', *Qantara.de*, at https://en.qantara.de/content/lebanon-beirut-nightlife-grinds-to-a-halt, accessed 3 January 2022.

Mashizi (Bardsiri), Mir Muhammad Sa'id, *Tazkira-yi Safaviyya-yi Kirmān*, ed. Muhammad Ibrahim Bastani-Parizi, Tehran, 1990.

Massena, Florence, 'Lebanon's New Wines Step on Stage', *Al-Monitor*, 9 October 2017, at http://www.al-monitor.com/pulse/originals/2017/10/lebanons-winemakers-gather-inbeirut.html?utm_source=Boomtrain&utm_medium=manual&utm_campaign=20171010&bt_ee=ikEC6lgBKLNbFASqw6l8BA4hdj7QkEf4u8bDfNt8WV+8qMwxjnFK+5V/JmtbyLv3&bt_ts=1507651599651, accessed 12 October 2019.

Masters, Bruce, 'Aleppo's Janissaries: Crime Syndicate or *Vox Populi*?', in Eleni Gara, M. Erdem Kabadayi, and Christoph K. Neumann, eds., *Popular Protest and Political Participation in the Ottoman Empire. Studies in Honor of Suraiya Faroqhi*, Istanbul, 2011, pp. 159–76.

————, 'Aleppo, the Ottoman Empire's Caravan City', in Edhem Eldem, Daniel Goffman, and Bruce Masters, eds., *The Ottoman City Between East and West. Aleppo, Izmir and Istanbul*, Cambridge, UK, 1999, pp. 17–78.

BIBLIOGRAPHY

Mas'udi, Abū al-Hasan 'Alī ibn al-Husayn ibn 'Alī, *The Meadows of Gold. The Abbasids*, tr. and
ed. Paul Lunde and Caroline Stone, London, 1989.

———, (Mas'udi, Abu'l-Hasan 'Ali b. al-Husayn b. 'Ali al-), *Muruj al-dhahab wa ma'ādin al-jawhar*, 4 vols., ed. Muhammad Muhyi al-Din 'Abd al-Hamid, Beirut, 1973.

Mather, James, *Pashas. Traders and Travellers in the Islamic World*, New Haven, CT, 2009.

Matthee, Rudi, 'Administrative Stability and Change in Late-17th-century Iran: The Case of
Shaykh 'Ali Khan Zanganah (1669–89)', *IJMES* 26, 1 (1994), pp. 77–98.

———, 'Alcohol in the Islamic Middle East: Ambivalence and Ambiguity', in Phil
Withington and Angela McShane, eds., *Intoxication and Modernity (Past & Present*,
supplement 9, 2014), pp. 100–25.

———, 'Alcohol and Politics in Muslim Culture: Pre-text, Text and Context', https://
www.intoxicantsproject.org.

———, 'The Ambiguities of Alcohol in Iranian History: Between Excess and Abstention',
in Fragner, Kauz, and Schwarz, eds., *Wine Culture in Iran and Neighboring Countries*,
pp. 137–64.

———, 'Exotic Substances: The Introduction and Global Spread of Tobacco, Coffee, Tea,
Cocoa, and Distilled Liquor, 16th–18th Centuries', in Roy Porter and Mikulas Teich,
eds., *Drugs and Narcotics in History*, Cambridge, UK, 1995, pp. 24–51.

———, 'The Politics of Protection: Iberian Missionaries in Iran During the Reign of Shah
Abbas I (1587–1629)', in Sabine Schmidtke and Camille Adang, eds., *Contacts and
Controversies Between Muslims, Jews and Christians in the Ottoman Empire and Pre-modern Iran*,
Würzburg, Germany, 2010, pp. 245–71

———, *The Pursuit of Pleasure: Drugs and Stimulants in Iranian History, 1500–1900*, Princeton,
NJ, 2005.

———, 'Safavid Iran and the Christian Missionary Experience. Between Tolerance and
Refutation', in Dennis Halft and Emmanuel Pisani, eds., *Les interactions entre Shi'ites
duodécimains et chrétiens, Mélanges de l'Institut Dominicain d'Etudes Orientales* 35 (2020),
pp. 65–100.

Maundrell, H. A., *Journey From Aleppo to Jerusalem at Easter A.D. 1697*, Oxford, 1703.

'Maykada-yi Qazvin', at https://fa.wikipedia.org/wiki/%D9%85%DB%8C%DA%A9%
D8%AF%D9%87_%D9%82%D8%B2%D9%88%DB%8C%D9%86, accessed
19 November 2019.

McGovern, Patrick, *Uncorking the Past: The Quest for Wine, Beer, and Other Alcoholic Beverages*,
Berkeley, CA, 2009.

McGovern, Patrick et al., 'Early Neolithic Wine of Georgia in the South Caucasus',
Proceedings of the National Academy of Sciences of the United States of America 146, 46
(November 2017), at https://www.pnas.org/doi/pdf/10.1073/pnas.1714728114.

McHugh, James, 'Alcohol in Pre-modern South Asia', in Harald Fischer-Tiné and Jana
Tschurenev, eds., *A History of Alcohol and Drugs in Modern South Asia: Intoxicating Affairs*,
Abingdon, UK, 2014, pp. 29–44.

Mehmed Efendi, *Le paradis des infidèles. Un ambassadeur ottoman en France sous la Régence*, ed.
Gilles Veinstein, Paris, 1981.

Mehrabi, Ehsan, 'Hashtād sāl qanun-guzāri dar bārih-yi mashrubāt-i alkuli dar Irān',
Majalla-yi Tablu, 2 Dey 1396/23 December 2017.

Mehrez, Samia, 'Take Them Out of the Ball Game. Egypt's Cultural Players in Crisis',
Middle East Report 219 (Summer 2001), pp. 10–15.

Melchert, Christopher, *The Formation of the Sunni Schools of Law, 9th–10th Centuries C.E.*,
Leiden, Netherlands, 1997.

————, 'Origins and Early Sufism', in Lloyd Ridgeon, ed., *The Cambridge Companion to Sufism*, Cambridge, UK, 2015, pp. 3–23.

————, 'Religious Policies of the Caliphs from al-Mutawakkil to al-Muqtadir AH 235–295/AD 847–908', *Islamic Law and Society* 3, 2 (1996), pp. 316–42.

Melikian-Chirvani, A. S. 'From the Royal Boat to the Beggar's Bowl', *Islamic Art* 5 (1990–1), pp. 3–106.

Mélikoff, Irène, *Hadji Bektach. Un mythe et ses avatars. Genèse et évolution du soufisme populaire en Turquie*, Leiden, Netherlands, 1998.

————, 'Le problème Kizilbash', *Turcica* 6 (1975), pp. 49–67.

Meloni, Julia, and Johan Swinnen, 'Algeria, Morocco, and Tunisia', in Kym Anderson and Vicente Pinilla, eds., *Wine Globalization. A New Comparative History*, Cambridge, UK, 2018, pp. 441–65.

Melville, Charles, '"The Year of the Elephant": Mongol-Mamluk Rivalry in the Hejaz in the Reign of Abu Sa'id (1317–1335)', *Studia Iranica* 21, 2 (1992), pp. 197–214.

Membré, Michele, *Mission to the Lord Sophy of Persia (1539–1542)*, tr. A. H. Morton, London, 1993.

Meshal, Reem A., 'Antagonistic Sharī'as and the Construction of Orthodoxy in Sixteenth-century Cairo', *Journal of Islamic Studies* 21, 2 (2010), pp. 183–212.

————, *Sharia and the Making of the Modern Egyptian. Islamic Law and Custom in the Courts of Ottoman Cairo*, Cairo, 2014.

Michbal, Mehdi, 'Maroc: vivons heureux, buvons cachés', *Jeune Afrique*, 1 December 2014, at http://www.jeuneafrique.com/38728/societe/maroc-vivons-heureux-buvons-cach-s/, accessed 16 October 2017.

Michel, Nicolas, *Une économie de subsistances. Le Maroc précolonial*, 2 vols., Cairo, 1997.

Midhat, Ahmet, *Tedkik Müskirat*, Istanbul, 1886.

Miège, Jean-Louis, *Le Maroc et l'Europe (1822–1960)*, Paris, 1961–4.

Miège, Jean-Louis, and Eugène Hugues, *Les Européens à Casablanca au XIXe siècle (1856–1906)*, Paris, 1954.

Millingen, Frederick (Osman-Seify-Bey), *La Turquie sous le règne d'Abdul-Aziz (1862–1867)*, Paris, 1868.

Mills, Andrew, 'Qatar Planning for World Cup. Fans to Avoid Prosecution for Minor Offences', Reuters, 21 September 2022, at https://www.reuters.com/world/middle-east/exclusive-qatar-planning-world-cup-fans-avoid-prosecution-minor-offences-sources-2022-09-21/, accessed 22 October 2022.

Mills, James H., and Patricia Barton, 'Introduction', in James H. Mills and Patricia Barton, eds., *Drugs and Empires: Essays in Modern Imperialism and Intoxication, c. 1500–c. 1930*, Basingstoke, UK, 2007, pp. 1–18.

Milton, Giles, *Paradise Lost: Smyrna 1922. The Destruction of a Christian City in the Islamic World*, New York, 2008.

'Mindestens 44 toten wegen gepanschten Alkohol in der Türkei', *Stern*, 14 October 2020.

Mirza Muhammad Kalantar-i Fars, *Ruznāma-yi Mirzā Muhammad Kalantar-i Fārs*, ed. 'Abbas Iqbal Ashtiyani, Tehran, 1983.

Moazami, Mahnaz, '*Ḳusraw ī Kawādān ud rēdak-ēw*', *EIr*.

Moltke, Helmut Graf von, *Moltke's Briefe*, 2 vols., ed. W. Andres, Leipzig, Germany, 1922.

Montagu, Lady Mary Wortley, *The Best Letters of Lady Mary Wortley Montague*, ed. Octave Thanet, Chicago, IL, 1890.

Mooraj, Anwer, 'Karachi Before Prohibition', in Hamida Khuhro and Anwer Mooraj, eds., *Karachi. Megacity of Our Times*, 2nd edn., Karachi, Pakistan, 2010, pp. 313–46.

BIBLIOGRAPHY

Mordtmann, A.D., *Skizzen und Reisebriefen aus Kleinasien 1850-1859*, ed. Franz Babinger, Hannover, 1925.

[Mordtmann, A. D.], *Stambul und das modern Türkenthum. Politische, sociale und biographische Bilder von einem Osmanen*, Leipzig, Germany, 1877–8.

Mostaghim, Ramin, 'Iran Confronts Its Alcohol Problem', *Los Angeles Times*, 7 July 2012.

Mottahedeh, Roy, and Kristen Stilt, 'Public and Private as Viewed Through the Works of the Muhtasib', *Social Research* 70, 3 (2003), pp. 735–48.

Mouline, Nabil, *The Clerics of Islam. Religious Authority and Political Power in Saudi Arabia*, New Haven, CT, 2014.

Mrgić, Jelena, 'Wine or *Raki*. The Interplay of Climate and Society In Early Modern Ottoman Bosnia', *Environment and History* 17, 4 (2011), pp 613–37.

'Muʿāvin-i vizārat-i kishvar-Irān mi-guyad "Mayl bih taghyirāt-i asāsi" dar Irān dar hāl-i "afzāyish" ast', BBC Persian, 16 January 2022, at https://www.bbc.com/persian/iran-60014273, accessed 16 January 2022.

Mudarrisi Tabataba'i, Husayn, *Farmānhā-yi Turkamānān-i Qārā Quyunlu va Aq Quyunlu*, Qom, Iran, 1974.

Mueller, Benjamin, 'Tainted Bootleg Alcohol Kills Dozens and Poisons Hundreds in Iran', *NYT*, 2 October 2018.

Mufty-Zade, Zia Bey, *Speaking of the Turks*, New York, 1922.

Muhidine, Timour, 'Hommes inutiles et tavernes d'Istanbul. La vie de bohème', in Nicolas Monceau, ed., *Istanbul. Histoire, promenades, anthologie & dictionnaire*, Paris, 2010, pp. 625–43.

————, *Istanbul rive gauche*, Paris, 2019.

————, 'Les Russes à Constantinople', in Nicolas Monceau, ed., *Istanbul. Histoire, promenades, anthologie & dictionnaire*, Paris, 2010, pp. 600–18.

Mukhbir al-Saltana, Hajj Mihdi Quli Hidayat, *Khātirat va khatarāt. Tawsha-i az tārikh-i shish pādishāh va gusha'i az dawra-yi zindigi-yi man*, 5th edn., Tehran, 1996.

Müller, Mrs. Max, *Letters From Constantinople*, New York and Bombay, 1897.

Mumtahin al-Dawla, *Khātirat-i Mumtahin al-Dawla*, ed. Husayn Quli Khanshiqaqi, 2nd edn., Tehran, 1983.

Munji, b. Muhammad al-, *Mazāhir al-fasād al-ijtimāʿi zamān al-himāyya al-faransiyya*, Tunis, 2004/2005.

al-Muqri, 'Ali, *al-Khamr wa'l nabidh fi'l-Islām*, Beirut, 2007.

'Murree Brewery Soon to Brew in India', *Express Tribune*, 30 November 2013, at http://www.bbc.co.uk/news/world-middle-east-19481835, accessed 9 February 2020.

Murree Brewery Website, http://www.murreebrewery.com/history.html, accessed 6 September 2017.

Mustafa Âli, *The Ottoman Gentleman of the Sixteenth Century. Mustafa Âli's Mevāʾidü'n-nefāʾis fi ḳavāʿidi'l-mejālis, 'Table of Delicacies Concerning the Rules of Social Gatherings'*, tr. Douglas Brookes, Cambridge, MA, 2003.

Mylès, Henri, *La fin de Stamboul. Le décor, les survivances, les fantômes humains, les cendres*, Paris, 1921.

Naficy, Hamid, *A Social History of Iranian Cinema*, 4 vols., Durham, NC, 2011–12.

Na'îmâ Mustafa Efendi, *Târih-i Na'îmâ*, ed. Mehmet İpşirli, 4 vols pag. as one, Ankara, Turkey, 2007.

Napier, G. C., 'Diary of a Tour to Khorasan' and 'Notes on the Eastern Alburz Tracts', *Journal of the Royal Geographical Society* 46 (1876), pp. 62–171.

Nasir al-Din Tusi, *The Nasirean Ethics*, tr. G. M. Wickens, London, 1964.

BIBLIOGRAPHY

Nasiri, Muhammad Ibrahim b. Zayn al-'Ābidin, *Dastur-i shahriyārān*, ed. Muhammad Nadir Nasiri Muqaddam, Tehran, 2004.

Nasr, Seyyed Vali Riza, *Islamic Leviathan. Islam and the Making of State Power*, Oxford, 2001.

Natiq, Huma, *Hāfiz khunyāgari, may va shādi*, Los Angeles, 2004.

Nava'i, 'Abd al-Husayn, ed., *Shāh ʿAbbās. Majmuʿa-yi asnād va mukātibat-i tārikhi hamrāh bā yāddāsht'ha-yi tafsili*, Tehran, 1989.

al-Nawajī, Muhammad, *La joie du vin. L'arène du cheval bai (Halbat al-kumayt)*, tr. and ed. Philippe Vigreux, Paris, 2006.

Necipoğlu, Gülru, 'Framing the Gaze in Ottoman, Safavid and Ottoman Palaces', *Ars Orientalia* 23 (1993), pp. 303–42.

Negari Namaghi, Romina and Douglas G. Perry, 'The Perception of Young Adult Alcohol Consumers Regarding Alcohol Consumption and the Risky Behaviors of Drinking Alcohol in Tehran, Iran', *Journal of Substance Use* 25, 3 (2020), pp. 301–7.

Neumann, Christoph K., 'A Contribution to the Social Geography of Alcohol in Mid-nineteenth-century Istanbul', in Yavuz Köse, ed., *Şehrâyîn: Die Welt der Osmanen, die Osmanen in der Welt. Wahrnemungen, Begegnungen und Abgrenzungen*, Festschrift Georg Majer, Wiesbaden, Germany, 2012, pp. 173–84.

Neuville, François, 'Mise en place d'une vinification et d'une commercialisation modernes des vins en Turquie contemporaine. L'exemple des caves Kavaklidere', in C. L. Le Gars et P. H. Roudié, eds., *Des vignobles et des vins à travers le monde. Hommage à Alain Huetz de Lemps*, Bordeaux, France, 1996, pp. 561–6.

Neville, Pran, *Lahore. A Sentimental Journey*, London, 1993.

Nicoll, Fergus, *Shah Jahan. The Rise and Fall of the Mughal Emperor*, London, 2009.

Niebuhr, Carsten, *Beschreibung von Arabien aus eigenen Beobachtungen und im Lande selbst gesammelte Nachrichten*, 2 vols., Copenhagen, 1772.

Nizam al-Mulk, *The Book of Government or Rules for Kings. The Siyar al-Muluk or Siyasat-nama*, tr. Hubert Darke, London, 1960, repr. 2002.

Noorani, Yaseem, 'Heterotopia and the Wine Poem in Early Islamic Culture', *IJMES* 36, 3 (2004), pp. 345–66.

Norrie, P. A., 'The History of Wine as a Medicine', in Merton Sandler and Roger Pinder eds., *Wine. A Scientific Exploration*, London, 2003, pp. 21–55.

Northedge, Alastair, 'An Interpretation of the Palaces of the Caliph at Samarra (Dar al-Khilafa or Jawsaq al-Khaqani)', *Ars Orientalis* 23 (1993), pp. 143–70.

Nsehe, Mfonobong, 'Moroccan Multi-millionaire Brahim Zniber Dies at 96', *Forbes*, 1 October 2016, at https://www.forbes.com/sites/mfonobongnsehe/2016/10/01/moroccan-multi-millionaire-brahim-zniber-dies-at-96/?sh=2435e7fb465f, accessed 8 April 2022.

Nuri, Osman, *Müskirat ve İsretin Sebeb Olducu—Hastalik be 'Illetler*, Istanbul, 1904.

Obsopoeus, Vincent, *How to Drink. A Classical Guide to the Art of Imbibing*, Princeton, NJ, 2020.

O'Donovan, Edmond, *The Merv Oasis; Travels and Adventures East of the Caspian During the Years 1879–80–81, Including Five Months' Residence Among the Tekkés of Merv*, 2 vols., New York, 1883.

Okrent, Daniel, *Last Call. The Rise and Fall of Prohibition*, New York, 2010.

Olivier, G. A., *Voyage dans l'Empire othoman, l'Égypte et la Perse*, 6 vols., Paris, 1801–7.

Olnon, Merlijn, *'Brought Under the Law of the Land': The History, Demography and Geography of Crossculturalism in Early Modern Izmir and the Köprülü Project of 1678*, Leiden, Netherlands, 2013.

BIBLIOGRAPHY

'Omar bin al-Faridh, *L'Éloge du vin (al khamriya). Poème mystique d'ibn al Faridh*, tr. and ed. Emile Dermenghem, Paris, 2002.

Opwis, Felicitas, 'Shifting Legal Authority From the Ruler to the *'Ulamā* for Drinking Wine During the Saljūq Period', *Der Islam* 86, 1 (2009), pp. 65–92.

Örs, Ilay, 'Coffeehouses, Cosmopolitanism, and Pluralizing Modernity in Istanbul', *Journal of Mediterranean Studies* 12, 1 (2002), pp. 119–45.

Osborne, Lawrence, *The Wet and the Dry: A Drinkers Journey*, New York, 2013.

Osterlund, Paul Benjamin, 'Southern Turkish City Defiant Over Its Raki and Kebab', *Al-Monitor*, 17 December 2019, at https://www.al-monitor.com/pulse/originals/2019/12/turkish-town-of-adana-celebrates-raki-culture-despite-ban.html, accessed 18 December 2019.

Osti, Letizia, 'The Caliph', in Maaike van Berkel et al., eds., *Crisis and Continuity at the Abbasid Court. Formal and Informal Politics in the Caliphate of al-Muqtadir (295–320/908–32)*, Leiden, Netherlands, 2013, pp. 49–64.

'The Other Grape', at https://theothergrape.co.uk/pages/about, accessed 2 June 2022.

Othmani, Beya, 'Algérie Underground (7): Je suis serveuse dans un bar de nuit à Alger', *Le Monde*, 15 May 2015.

Ouali, Amer, 'En Algérie, la vente de boissons alcoolisées échauffe les esprits salafistes', *Le Point*, 30 April 2015, at https://www.lepoint.fr/monde/en-algerie-la-vente-de-boissons-alcoolisees-echauffe-les-esprits-salafistes-30-04-2015-1925333_24.php, accessed 12 January 2022.

Ouseley, Sir William, *Travels in Various Countries of the East; More Particularly Persia*, London, 1821.

Palgrave, William Gifford, *Personal Narrative of a Year's Journey Through Central and Eastern Arabia (1862–1863)*, London, 1865.

Panja, Tariq, 'Ban on Beer Is Latest Flash Point in World Cup Culture Clash', *NYT*, 18 November 2022.

Papas, Alexandre, *Thus Spake the Dervish: Sufism, Language, and the Religious Margins in Central Asia, 1400–1900*, Leiden, Netherlands, 2019.

Paracha, Nadeem Farooq, 'Alcohol in Pakistan: The Prohibition and After', *Dawn*, 15 December 2013, at https://www.dawn.com/news/1060507, accessed 5 February 2022.

———, *Eyewitness Pakistan. An Immediate Eyewitness History of a Troubled Nation*, Lahore, Pakistan, 2016.

———, *The Pakistan Antihero. History of Pakistan Nationalism Through the Lives of Iconoclasts*, Lahore, Pakistan, 2016.

———, *Soul Rivals. State, Militant and Pop Sufism in Pakistan*, Chennai, India, 2020.

Pardoe, Miss, *The City of the Sultan; and Domestic Manners of the Turks in 1836*, 2 vols., London, 1837.

Pargoo, Mahmoud, 'Iran Shifts Approach to Fight Against Alcohol', *Al-Monitor*, 13 November 2015, at http://www.al-monitor.com/pulse/fr/originals/2015/11/iran-alcohol-consumption-authorities-approach.html, accessed 2 May 2022.

Pashley, Robert, *Travels in Crete*, 2 vols., Cambridge, UK and London, 1837.

Payk-i Sa'ādat-i Nisvān repr., ed. Banafsheh Mas'udi and Naser Mohajer, Berkeley, CA and Créteil, France, 2012.

Peacock, A. C. S., *The Great Seljuq Empire*, Edinburgh, UK, 2015.

Pears, Sir Edwin, *The Life of Abdul Hamid*, London, 1917.

BIBLIOGRAPHY

Pellat, Ch., 'Adab ii. Adab in Arabic Literature', *EIr*.

Pelsaert, Francisco, *De geschriften van Francisco Pelsaert over Mughal Indië, 1627*. Kroniek en Remonstrantie, ed. D.H.A. Kolff and H.W. van Santen, The Hague, 1979.

Pérès, Henri, *La poésie andalouse en arabe classique au XIe siècle*, 2nd edn., Paris, 1953.

Perkins, J. A., *A Residence of Eight Years, Among the Nestorian Christians With Notices of the Muhammedans*, Andover, UK, 1843.

Perry, Charles, *A View of the Levant, Particularly of Constantinople, Syria, Egypt and Greece*, London, 1743.

Petry, Carl F., *The Criminal Underworld of a Medieval Islamic Society. Narratives From Cairo and Damascus Under the Mamluks*, Chicago, IL, 2012.

————, 'Travails of Prohibition: Suppression of Alcohol Use in the Mamluk Sultanate', in Amalia Levanoni, ed., *Egypt and Syria Under Mamluk Rule. Political, Social and Cultural Aspects*, Leiden, Netherlands, 2022, pp. 25–37.

————, *Twilight of Majesty. The Reigns of the Mamlūk Sultans al-Ashrāf Qāytbāy and Qānṣūh al-Ghawrī in Egypt*, Seattle, WA, 1993.

Peyronnet, Francis Raymond, *Le vignoble nord-africain*, Paris, 1950.

Peyssonnel, J. A., *Relation d'un voyage sur les côtes de Barbarie, fait par ordre du roi, en 1724 et 1725*, Paris, 1838.

Philip, Thomas, *Acre. The Rise and Fall of a Palestinian City, 1730–1831*, New York, 2013.

Pidou de Saint Olon, François, *Estat présent de l'empire de Maroc*, Paris, 1694.

————, *Relation de l'empire de Maroc*, Paris, 1695.

Pinçon, Abel, 'The Relation of a Journey to Persia Taken in the Years 1598–1599 …', in Sir E. Denison Ross, ed., *Sir Anthony Sherley and His Persian Adventure*, London, 1933, pp. 137–44.

Pires, Tomé, *The Suma Oriental of Tomé Pires*, London, 1944.

Pitel, Laura, 'Turkey's Wine Making Tradition Under Threat From Islamic-rooted Government's New Alcohol Laws', *The Independent*, 25 August 2015.

Poiron, M., *Mémoires concernans l'état présent du Royaume de Tunis*, ed. Jean Serres, Paris, 1925.

Polak, Jacob, *Persien und seine Bewohner*, 2 vols., Leipzig, Germany, 1865.

Połczyński, Michael, 'Relacyja of Sefer Muratowicz: 1601–1602. Private Royal Envoy of Sigismund III Vasa to Shah 'Abbas I', *Turkish Historical Review* 5 (2014), pp. 59–93.

[Porter, David], *Constantinople and Its Environs, in a Series of Letters*, 2 vols., New York, 1835.

Porter, Ker, *Travels in Georgia, Persia, Armenia, and Ancient Babylonia, etc. etc. During the Years, 1817, 1818, 1819, and 1820*, London, 1821–22.

Porter, Sir James, *Turkey; Its History and Progress*, 2 vols., London, 1854.

Pottinger, Henry, *Travels in Beloochistan and Sinde*, London, 1816.

Pouqueville, F. C. H. L., *Voyage en Morée, à Constantinople, et en Albanie … pendant les années 1798, 1799, 1800 et 1801*, 3 vols., Paris, 1805.

Pourjavady, N., 'Love and Metaphors of Wine and Drunkenness in Persian Sufi poetry', in Ali Asghar Seyed Gohrab, ed., *Metaphor and Imagery in Persian Poetry*, Leiden, Netherlands, 2012, pp. 126 36.

'Qā 'idāt al-tashrī'āt al-'Irāqiyya', at http://www.iraqld.iq/LoadLawBook.aspx?SC= 190920052657118, accessed 15 June 2022.

Qandhari, Muhammad Arif, *Tarikh-i Akbari*, Delhi, 1993.

Qayrawani, Abu Ishaq Ibrahim b. al-Qasim al-Raqiq al-, *Qutb al-surur fi awsāf al-anbidha wa'l-khumur*, ed. Sara al-Barbushi b. Yahya, Freiberg a/N, 2010.

BIBLIOGRAPHY

Qazi b. Kashif al-Din Muhammad, *Jām-i jahān-nāma-yi 'Abbāsi. Dar manāfi'-i sharāb*, ed. Ali Hassouri, Uppsala, Sweden, 2014.

Qaziha, Fatima, ed., *Marāsim-i darbār-i Nāsiri (Jashn-i āshpazān (1285–1313 h.q.)*, Tehran, 2003.

Qiriqlu, Kiyumars, 'Bardāsht'hā-yi Sufiyan az qudrat-i fuqahā dar Irān-i avākhir-i sada-yi 11/17. Tasvir-i Mullāh Muhammad Tāhir Qummi dar du risāla-yi jadali Sufiyana', *Faslnāma-yi Mutāli'āt-i Tārikhi. Zamima-yi Majalla-yi Dānishkada-yi Adabiyāt va 'Ulum-i Insāni-yi Mashhad* 5–6 (2004), pp. 103–53.

Qummi, Mullah Muhammad-Tahir, *Opposition to Philosophy in Safavid Iran. Mulla Muhammad-Tahir Qummi's Hikmat al-'Arifin*, ed. Ata Anzali and S. M. Hadi Gerami, Leiden, Netherlands, 2018.

Qummi, Qazi Ahmad b. Sharaf al-Husayni al-, *Khulāsat al-tavārikh*, 2 vols., 2nd edn., ed. Ihsan Ishraqi, Tehran, 2004.

The Qur'an, a New Annotated Translation, tr. A. J. Droge, Sheffield, 2014.

Qutbi, Bihruz, ed., *Asnād-i jang-i avval-i jahāni dar Irān*, Tehran, 1991.

Rabau, Grégory, 'L'image des sultans ottoman de Mehmed II le Conquérant à Ahmed Ier (1451–16) dans la *Continuation de l'Histoire des Turcs* de Thomas Artus (vol. 2)', MA thesis, Université de Poitiers, 2014–15.

Rabb, Intisar A., *Doubt in Islamic law. A History of Legal Maxims, Interpretation, and Islamic Criminal Law*, Cambridge, 2015.

Radjavi, Heydar, *Father Takes a Drink & Other Memories of Iran*, Washington, DC, 2019.

Rafeq, Abdul Karim, 'Public Morality in 18th-century Ottoman Damascus', *Revue du monde musulman et de la Méditerranée* 55–6 (1990), pp. 180–96.

'Ra'is-i pizishki-yi qānuni: I'tiyād bih alkul tahdidi jiddi 'alayhi salāmat-i jāmi'a', *Ittilā'āt*, 10 Dey 1393/21 December 2014, at https://www.ettelaat.com/etiran/?p=94151, accessed 16 October 2020.

Rakı Ansiklopedisi, Istanbul, 2010.

Ram, Haggai, *Intoxicating Zion. A Social History of Hashish in Mandatory Palestine and Israel*, Stanford, CA, 2020.

'Rasidan bih khud-kafā'i dar sākht-e rawgan tabdil-i angur bih kishmish', *Iran Times*, 6 November 1987, p. 13.

Rathjens, Carl, 'Tâghût gegen scheri 'a', *Jahrbuch des Linden-Museums*, new ser. 1 (1951), pp. 172–87.

Rawandi, Muhammad Ibn 'Ali Ibn Sulayman al-, *The Rahat-us-sudur wa Ayat-us-surur, Being the History of the Saljuqs*, ed. Muhammad Iqbal, London, 1921.

Razmi, 'Mashallah, the Coffeehouses of Tabriz', in Floor and Javadi, eds., *Persian Pleasures*, pp. 89–118.

Reinelt, Joseph August, *Reise nach dem Orient zur Erhebung merkantiler Notizen für Oesterreichs Industrie*, Vienna, 1840.

Reinhart, Kevin A., *Before Revelation. The Boundaries of Muslim Moral Thought*, Albany, NY, 1995.

Revue commerciale du Levant. Bulletin mensuel de la chambre de commerce française de Constantinople.

Rich, Claudius James, *Narrative of a Residence in Koordistan and on the Site of Ancient Nineveh*, 2 vols., London, 1836.

Richard, Francis, ed., *Raphaël du Mans missionnaire en Perse au XVIIe s.*, 2 vols., Paris, 1995.

Rios, Lorena, 'Drinking Alcohol Is Always an Open Secret in Egypt', *Munchies*, 19 April 2016, at https://munchies.vice.com/en_us/article/4xbbqj/drinking-alcohol-is-always-an-open-secret-in-egypt, accessed 17 June 2022.

Rippin, Andrew, 'Abrogation', *EI³*.

Rivadeneyra, D. Adolfo, *Viaje al interior de Persia*, 3 vols., Madrid, 1880.

Rivet, Daniel, *Histoire du Maroc de Moulay Idrîs à Mohammed VI*, Paris, 2012.

Riyon, Adolf, *Üç Muzir. Tütün, Müskirat, Cehalet*, Istanbul, 1893.

Roe, Sir Thomas, *The Embassy of Sir Thomas Roe to the Court of the Great Mogul, 1615–1619*, ed. William Foster, 2 vols. pag. as one, London, 1899.

Rohlps, Gerhard, *Adventures in Morocco and Journey Through the Oases of Draa and Tafilet*, London, 1874.

Roosevelt, Kermit, *War in the Garden of Eden*, New York, 1919.

Rosen, Friedrich, *Oriental Memories of a German Diplomatist*, London, 1930.

Rosen, Lawrence, *The Justice of Islam. Comparative Perspectives on Islamic Law and Society*, Oxford, 2000.

Rosenthal, Franz, 'Fiction and Reality. Sources for the Role of Sex in Medieval Muslim Society', in Afaf Lutfi al-Sayyid Marsot, ed., *Society and the Sexes in Medieval Islam*, Malibu, CA, 1979, pp. 3–22.

Rosenthal, Steven T., *The Politics of Dependency. Urban Reform in Istanbul*, Westport, CT, 1980.

Rota, Giorgio, *La vita e i tempi di Rostam Khan (Edizione e traduzione italiana del Ms. British Library Add 7,655)*, Vienna, 2009.

Rougon, Firmin, *Smyrne. Situation commerciale et économique des pas compris dans la circonscription du consulat général de France*, Paris, 1892.

Roussillon, Alain, 'Republic Egypt Interpreted', in M. W. Daly and Carl F. Petry, eds., *The Cambridge History of Egypt*, vol. 2, *Modern Egypt, From 1517 to the End of the Twentieth Century*, Cambridge, UK, 1998, pp. 334–93.

Rowell, Alex, *Vintage Humour. The Islamic Wine Poetry of Abu Nuwas*, London, 2017.

Roxburgh, David J., *The Persian Album 1400–1600. From Dispersal to Collection*, New Haven, CT and London, 2005.

Roy, Oliver, *Globalized Islam. The Search for a New Ummah*, New York, 2006.

Ruiz, Mario M., 'Many Spectacles and Imperial Soldiers in Wartime Egypt', *MES* 45, 3 (2009), pp. 351–71.

Rumlu, Hasan Bik, *Ahsan al-tavārikh*, ed. 'Abd al-Husayn Nava'i, Tehran, 1978.

Rundell, David, *Vision or Mirage. Saudi Arabia at the Crossroads*, London, 2021.

Russell, Alex, *The Natural History of Aleppo*, 2 vols., 2nd edn., London, 1794.

Russell Pasha, Sir Thomas, *Egyptian Service 1902–1946*, London, 1949.

Rycaut, Paul, *The History of the Present State of the Ottoman Empire*, London, 1686.

Saadoun, Mustafa, 'Armed Groups Target Liquor Shops in Iraq', *al-Monitor*, 20 December 2020, at https://www.al-monitor.com/originals/2020/12/liqour-baghdad-iraq-freedom.html, accessed 19 December 2021.

Sabzavari, Mullah Muhammad Baqir, *Rawzat al-Anvār-i 'Abāsi (dar akhlāq-va shiva-yi kishvardāri)*, ed. Isma'il Changizi Ardahani, Tehran, 1998.

Saç, Yavuz, 'Wine Production and Consumption in Turkey 1920–1940', MA thesis, Istanbul Bilgi University, 2010.

Saeidi, Ali, and Tim Unwin, 'Persian Wine Tradition and Symbolism: Evidence From the Medieval Poetry of Hafiz', *Journal of Wine Research* 15, 2 (2004), pp. 97–114.

Safi, Omid, *The Politics of Knowledge in Premodern Islam: Negotiating Ideology and Religious Inquiry*, Chapel Hill: NC, 2006.

Sağlam, Nevzat, 'Bir Semte Adını Verem Bomonti Bira Fabrikası', *Uluslarası Tarih Araştırmaları Dergisi* 1, 1 (2017), pp. 26–56.

BIBLIOGRAPHY

'Sahifa-yi Imām Khumayni', at http://www.tebyan.net/newindex.aspx?pid=58950&vn=9&gpn=137.

Sa'idi Sirjani, ed., *Vaqāyi'-i ittifāqiyya*. *Majma'-yi guzārish'hā-yi khufyā-nivisān-i Inglis dar vilāyat-i junubi-i Irān az sāl-i 1291 tā 1322 q.*, Tehran, 1983.

Saint Aulaire, Comte de, *Confession d'un vieux diplomate*, Paris, 1953.

Sakaoğlu, Necdet, *Bu Mülkün Sultanları*, 13th edn., Istanbul, 2015.

'Salafists Raid Tunisian Hotel Bar for Serving Alcohol', at http://www.npr.org/2012/06/06/154349799/once-tolerated-alcohol-now-creates-rift-in-tunisia, accessed 9 February 2020.

Saleh, Elizabeth, 'The Pursuits of Quality in the Vineyards: French Oenologists at Work in Lebanon', in Rachel E. Black and Robert C. Ulin, eds., *Wine and Culture. Vineyard to Glass*, London, 2013, pp. 245–60.

Salvatore, Armando, 'Secularity Through a Soft Distinction in the Islamic Ecumene? Adab as a Counterpoint to Shari'a', *Historical Social Research* 44, 3 (2019), pp. 33–51.

al-Samarqandi, Ahmad ibn 'Umar ibn 'Ali al-Nizami al-'Arudi, *Chahár Maqála*, Leiden, Netherlands and London, 1910.

Samuel, Mounir, 'De de-islamisering van Egypte: Mohammed gelooft niet meer in God', Blog, 10 January 2018, at https://www.mounirsamuel.nl/islamisering-egypte-mohammed-gelooft-meer-god/, accessed 3 January 2022.

Sánchez, Garcia, 'La triada mediterránea en al-Andalus', in C. San Martin and Ramos Lizana, eds., *Con pan, aceite y vino. La triada mediterránea a través de la historia*, Granada, 1997, pp. 97–127.

Sanson, François, *Estat présent du royaume de Perse*, Paris, 1694.

Saravi, Muhammad Fathullah, *Tarikh-i Muhammadi*, Tehran, 1992.

Schachner, L. A., '"I Greet You and Thy Brethren. Here are Fifteen Shentasse of Wine". Wine Production in the Early Monasteries of Egypt and the Levant', *ARAM Periodical* 17 (2005), pp. 157–84.

Schayegh, Cyrus, *Who Is Knowledgeable Is Strong: Science, Class, and the Formation of Modern Iranian Society, 1900–1950*, Berkeley, CA, 2009.

Schirmbeck, Samuel, *Der islamische Kreuzzug und der ratlose Westen. Warum wir eine selbstbewusste Islamkritik brauchen*, Zürich, Switzerland, 2016.

Schmidt, Jan, '"Guided by the Almighty". The Journey of Stephan Schultz in the Ottoman Empire, 1752–6', in Christine Woodhead, ed., *The Ottoman World*, 2011, pp. 332–46.

Schrad, Mark Lawrence, *Smashing the Liquor Machine. A Global History of Prohibition*, Oxford, 2021.

———, *Vodka Politics. Alcohol, Autocracy, and the Secret History of the Russian State*, Oxford, 2014.

Sebag, Paul, *Tunis. Histoire d'une ville*, Paris, 1998.

Sebastian, Don Pedro Cubero, *Breve relación de la peregrinación que ha hecho de la mayor parte del mundo Don Pedro Sebastian*, Madrid, 1680.

Šedivý, Miroslav, *Metternich, the Great Powers and the Eastern Question*, Pilsen, Czech Republic, 2013.

Seetzen, Ulrich Jasper, *Tagebuch des Aufenthalts in Konstantinopel und der Reise nach Aleppo 1802–1803*, ed. Volkmar Enderlein, Hildesheim, 2012.

———, *Ulrich Jasper Seetzen's Reisen durch Syrien, Palästina, Phönicien, die Transjordan-Länder, Arabia Petraea und Unter-Aegypten*, ed. Friedrich Kruse and H. L. Fleisher, 4 vols., Berlin, 1854–55.

BIBLIOGRAPHY

Seibert, Thomas, 'With Turkish Liquor Ban, Raki Goes Underground', *The Daily Beast*, 13 June 2014, at http://www.thedailybeast.com/with-new-turkish-liquor-ban-raki-goes-underground, accessed 7 May 2022.

Senior, Nassau W., *A Journal Kept in Turkey and Greece in the Autumn of 1857 and the Beginning of 1858*, 1859.

Sercey, Comte Laurent de, *La Perse en 1839–1840. Une ambassade extraordinaire*, Paris, 1928.

Sestini, Domenico, *Viaggio di ritorno da Bassora a Costantinopoli*, n.p., 1788.

———, *Voyage dans la Grèce asiatique*, London and Paris, 1789.

Seyed-Gohrab, A. A., 'Khomeini the Poet-mystic', *Die Welt des Islams* 51, 3–4 (2011), pp. 438–58.

Shabushti, Abu'l Hasan 'Ali b. Muhammad, *Al-Dirāyāt*, ed. Kurkin 'Awwad, 2nd edn., Baghdad, 1966.

Shah Navaz Khan, Nawwāb Samsamuddaula, and 'Abdul Hayy, *Maāthir ul-Umarā*, tr. and ed. H. Beveridge, 3 vols., Kolkata, India, 2003.

Shahnavaz, Shahbaz, 'Ḵaz'al Khan', *EIr*.

Shahbazi, Dariyush, 'Abjaw-sāzi-yi Majidiyya', at http://tehrannameh.com/list/%D8%A2/%D9%A2%D8%A8%D8%AC%D9%88%D8%B3%D8%A7%D8%B2%DB%8C-%D9%85%D8%AC%DB%8C%D8%AF%DB%8C%D9%87, accessed 13 March 2020.

———, 'Piyāla-furushi', at https://www.darioush-shahbazi.com/articles/%D9%BE%DB%8C%D8%A7%D9%84%D9%87-%D9%81%D8%B1%D9%88%D8%B4%DB%8C, accessed 16 December 2021.

Shahîd, Irfan, *Byzantium and the Arabs in the Sixth Century*, vol. 2, pt. 2, Washington, DC, 2009.

Shahri, Ja'far, *Tārikh-i ijtimā'i-yi Tihrān dar qarn-i sizdahum*, 3rd edn., Tehran, 1999.

Shah Tahmasb, *Tazkira-yi Shāh Tahmāsb*, ed. D. C. Philliott, Calcutta, 1912; 2nd edn., repr. Tehran, 1984.

Shakosh, Hassan, 'Bint al-giran', https://www.youtube.com/watch?v=uHBaHQau8b4, accessed 21 February 2020.

Shams, Riyad Majeed, 'The Wine and Arak Industry in Lebanon', PhD dissertation, American University in Beirut, 1970.

Sharma, Sunil, 'Hāfiz's Sāqināmeh: The Genesis and Transformation of a Classical Poetic Genre', *Persica* 18 (2002), pp. 75–83.

Shaw, Stanford. 'The Nineteenth-century Ottoman Tax Reforms and Revenue System', *IJMES* 6, 4 (1975), pp. 421–59.

Sheikh, Mustafa, *Ottoman Puritanism and Its Discontents. Aḥmad al-Rūmi al-Āqḥiṣārī and the Qāḍīzādelis*, Oxford, 2016.

Sheikh, Samira, 'Aurangzeb as Seen from Gujarat. Shi'i and Millenarian Challenges to Mughal Sovereignty', *JRAS*, 3rd ser., 28, 3 (2018), pp. 557–81.

Sheil, Lady, *Glimpses of Life and Manners in Persia*, London, 1856.

Sherrat, A. G., 'Alcohol and Its Alternatives: Symbol and Substance in Pre-industrial Cultures', in P. E. Lovejoy Goodman and A. G. Sherrat, eds, *Consuming Habits: Drugs in History and Anthropology*, London, 1995, pp. 11–46.

Shirazi, 'Abdi Bayg, *Takmilat al-akhbār (Tārikh-i Safaviyya az āghāz tā 978 h.q.)*, ed. 'Abd al-Husayn Nava'i, Tehran, 1990.

Shoshan, Boaz, *Damascus Life 1480–1500. A Report of a Local Notary*, Leiden, Netherlands, 2020.

BIBLIOGRAPHY

Shuraydi, Hasan, *The Raven and the Falcon: Youth Versus Old Age in Medieval Arabic Literature*, Leiden, Netherlands, 2014.

Sijpesteijn, Petra M., *Shaping a Muslim State. The World of a Mid-eighth-century Egyptian Official*, Oxford, 2013.

Simidchieva, Marta, 'Rituals of Renewal: Ṣādeq Hedāyat's "The Blind Owl" and the Wine Myth of Manučehri', *Oriente Moderno* n. s. 22 (2003), pp. 219–41.

Sipehri, 'Abd al-Husayn Khan, *Mir'āt al-vaqāy'-i Muzaffari va yāddāsht'hā-yi Malik al-Muvarrikhin*, ed. 'Abd al-Husayn Nava'i, Tehran, 1989.

Şiviloğlu, Murat R., *The Emergence of Public Opinion. State and Society in the Late Ottoman Empire*, Cambridge, UK, 2018.

Skinner, Thomas, *Adventures During a Journey Overland to India: By Way of Egypt, Syria, and the Holy Land*, 2 vols., London, 1836.

Slingerland, Edward, *Drunk. How We Sipped, Danced, and Stumbled Our Way to Civilization*, New York, 2021.

Slye, Liz, 'Baghdad Gets Its Groove Back: Violence Is Receding and Iraq's Capital Is Partying Again', *Washington Post*, 28 August 2018.

Smirnov, K. N., *Zapiski vospitatelya persidskogo shaha 1907–1914 gody (s prilozheniyami)*, Tel Aviv, 2002.

Smith, Eli and H. G. O. Dwight, *Missionary Researches in Armenia Including a Journey Through Asia Minor, and Into Georgia and Persia*, London, 1834.

Smith, John Masson, 'Dietary Decadence and Dynastic Decline in the Mongol Empire', *Journal of Asian History* 34, 1 (2000), pp. 1–12.

Smith, Thomas, *Remarks Upon the Manners, Religion, and Government of the Turks*, London, 1678.

Smyrnelis, Marie-Carmen, 'Colonies européennes et communautés ethnico-confessionnelles à Smyrne. Coexistence et réseaux de sociabilité (fin du XVIIIe-milieu du XIXe siècle)', in Georgeon and Dumont, eds., *Vivre dans l'Empire ottoman*, pp. 173–194.

Soshan, Boaz, *Popular Culture in Medieval Cairo*, Cambridge, UK, 1993.

Soudavar, Abolala, 'Between the Safavids and the Mughals: Art and Artisans in Transition', *Iran. Journal of the British Institute of Persian Studies* 37 (1999), pp. 49–66.

Southgate, Horatio, *Narrative of a Tour Through Armenia, Kurdistan, Persia and Mesopotamia. With Observations Upon the Condition of Mohammedanism and Christianity in Those Countries*, 2 vols., London and New York, 1840.

Soyglu, Ragib, 'Covid-19: Turkey Bans Alcohol Sales in Stores During Lockdown, Causing Backlash', *Middle East Eye*, 27 April 2021, at https://www.middleeasteye.net/news/covid-turkey-alcohol-ban-lockdown, accessed 27 April 2021.

Speelman, Cornelis, *Journaal der reis van den gezant der O. I. Compagnie Joan Cunaeus naar Perzië in 1651–1652*, ed. A. Hotz, Amsterdam, 1908.

Spengler, Robert N. III, *Fruit From the Sands. The Silk Road Origins of the Foods We Eat*, Oakland, CA, 2019.

Sperco, Willy, *Turcs d'hier et d'aujourd'hui (D'Abdul Hamid à nos jours)*, Paris, 1961.

Spiegel, Judith, 'Yemen's Hidden Alcohol Problem', *Jerusalem Post*, 17 January 2011.

Spode, Hasso, *Die Macht der Trunkenheit. Kultur- und Sozialgeschichte des Alkohols in Deutschland*, Opladen, Germany, 1993.

Sprachman, Paul, *Licensed Fool. The Damnable, Foul-Mouthed Obeyd-e Zakani*, Costa Mesa, CA, 2012.

St. John, James Augustus, *Egypt and Mohammed Ali, or Travels in the Valley of the Nile*, 2 vols., London, 1834.

BIBLIOGRAPHY

Staudt, Ida Donges, *Living in Romantic Baghdad: An American Memoir of Teaching and Travel in Iraq, 1924–1947*, Syracuse, NY, 2012.

Stephanov, Darin, 'Sultan Mahmud II (1808–1839) and the First Shift in Modern Ruler Visibility in the Ottoman Empire', *Journal of Ottoman and Turkish Studies Association* 1, 1–2 (2014), pp. 128–48.

Stern, Henry A., *Dawnings of Light in the East … in Persia, Coordistan and Mesopotamia*, London, 1854.

Stern, M. S., *Al-Ghazzali on Repentance*, New Delhi, India, 1990.

Stetkevytch, Suzanne Pinckney, 'Intoxication and Immortality: Wine and Associated Imagery in al-Ma'arri's Garden', in J. W. Wright and Everett K. Rowson, eds., *Homoeroticism in Classical Arabic Literature*, New York, 1997, pp. 210–32.

Stewart, Devin J., *Islamic Legal Orthodoxy. Twelver Shiite Response to the Sunni Legal System*, Salt Lake City, UT, 1998.

Stilt, Kristen, *Islamic Law in Action. Authority, Discretion, and Everyday Experiences in Mamluk Egypt*, Oxford, 2011.

Stuart, Lieutenant-Colonel Charles, *Journal of a Residence in Northern Persia and the Adjacent Provinces of Turkey*, London, 1854.

Studer, Nina S., 'The Infantilization of the Colonized: Medical and Psychiatric Descriptions of Drinking Habits in the Colonial Maghreb', in R. Ouissa et al., eds., *Reconfiguration – Politik und Gesellschaft*, Wiesbaden, 2022, pp. 135–51.

———, 'It Is only Gazouz: Muslims and Champagne in the Colonial Maghreb', *Asiatische Studien / Études Asiatiques* 73, 3 (2019), pp. 399–424.

———, 'The Same Drink? Wine and Absinthe Consumption and Drinking Cultures Among French and Muslim Groups in Nineteenth-century Algeria', in Ernst, ed., *Alcohol Flows Across Cultures*, pp. 20–43.

Subtelny, Maria E., 'A Late Medieval Persian *Summa* on Ethics: Kashifi's *Akhlāq-i Muḥsini*', *IS* 36, 4 (2003), pp. 601–14.

———, *Timurids in Transition: Turko-Persian Politics and Acculturation in Medieval Iran*, Leiden, Netherlands, 2007.

Sutter Fichtner, Paula, *Terror and Toleration: The Habsburg Empire Confronts Islam, 1526–1850*, London, 2008.

Szombathy, Zoltan, *Mujūn. Libertinism in Mediaeval Muslim Society and Literature*, Exeter, UK, 2013.

al-Ṭabari, *The History of al-Ṭabari*, vol. XXVII, *The 'Abbasid Revolution A.D. 743–750 / A.H. 126–132*, tr. John Alden Williams, Albany, NY, 1989.

———, *The History of al-Ṭabari*, vol. XXXIV: *Incipient Decline*, tr. Joel Kramer, Albany, NY, 1985.

Tableau générale du commerce avec les pays étrangers pendant l'année 1305, xi / 2, 'Importations', Tehran, 1927.

Tafazzoli, Ahmad, 'Dadestan ī menog ī xrad', *EIr*.

Tafrishi, Abu'l Mafakhir b. Fazl Allah al-Husayni Savana-Nigar, *Tārikh-i Shāh Safi*, ed. Muhsin Bahramnizhad, Tehran, 2010.

Tafrishi, Muhammad Husayn al-Husayni, *Mabādi-yi tārikh-i zamān-i navvāb-rizvān-i makān (Shāh Sāfi)*, in Abu'l Mafakhir b. Fazl Allah al-Husayni Savana-Nigar Tafrishi, *Tārikh-i Shāh Safi*, pp. 207–74.

Taheri, Amir, *The Spirit of Allah. Khomeini and the Islamic Revolution*, London, 1986.

Talbot, Michael, *British-Ottoman Relations, 1661–1807. Commerce and Diplomatic Practice in Eighteenth-Century Istanbul*, Woodbridge, UK, 2017.

BIBLIOGRAPHY

Tamisier, Maurice, *Voyage en Arabie. Séjour dans le Hedjaz. Campagne d'Assir*, 2 vols., Paris, 1840.

Tancoigne, J. M., *Voyage à Smyrne, dans l'archipel et l'île de Candie, en 1811, 1812, 1813 et 1814*, Paris, 1817.

Tannous, Jack, *The Making of the Medieval Middle East: Religion, Society, and Simple Believers*, Princeton, NJ, 2018.

Taqizada, Sayyid Hasan, *Zindigi-yi tufāni (khātirāt)*, Tehran, 2000.

Taraud, Christelle, *La prostitution coloniale. Algérie, Tunisie, Maroc (1830–1962)*, Paris, 2003.

'Tarihi Bomonti Bira Fabrikası'nın Yıkımına Başlandı', *Cumhuriyet*, 19 July 2020, at https://www.cumhuriyet.com.tr/haber/tarihi-bomonti-bira-fabrikasinin-yikimina-baslandi-1752543, accessed 19 July 2020.

Tattersall, Ian, and Rob Desalle, *A Natural History of Wine*, New Haven, CT, 2015.

Tavernier, Jean-Baptiste, *Les six voyages de Jean Baptiste Tavernier en Turquie, en Perse et En Indes*, 2 vols., Paris, 1678.

Taylor, Adam, 'Iran Is Opening 150 Alcoholism Treatment Centers Even Though Alcohol Is Banned', *Washington Post*, 9 June 2015.

Tectander, Georg, *Eine abenteuerliche Reise durch Russland nach Persien 1602–1604*, ed. Dorothea Müller-Ott, Tulln, 1978.

Tefvîq, Mehmed, *Ein Jahr in Konstantinopel. Fünfter Monat. Die Schenke oder die Gewohnheitstrinker von Konstantinopel*, tr. Theodor Menzel, Berlin, 1909.

'Tehran Skeptics Scoff at Dry Law', *NYT*, 15 February 1953.

Tenreiro, António, *Itinerário da Índia por terra a este reino de Portugal*, ed. Rui Manuel Loureiro, Portimão, Portugal 2020.

Terrasse, Henri, *Histoire du Maroc des origines à l'établissement du Protectorat français*, Casablanca, Morocco, 1950.

Terem, Etty, *Old Texts New Practices. Islamic Reform in Modern Morocco*, Stanford, CA, 2014.

Thackston, Wheeler, *A Century of Princes. Sources on Timurid History and Art*. Cambridge, MA, 1989.

'That Sweet Iranian Spirit', *Frontline, Tehran Bureau*, 10 April 2012, at http://www.pbs.org/wgbh/pages/frontline/tehranbureau/2012/04/dispatch-that-sweet-iranian-spirit.html, accessed 13 March 2020.

Thevenot, Jean de, *Relation d'un voyage fait au Levant*, Paris, 1669.

Thierry-Mieg, Ch., *Six semaines en Afrique. Souvenirs d'un voyage*, Paris, 1861.

Thorau, P., *The Lion of Egypt. Sultan Baybars I and the Near East in the Thirteenth Century*, London and New York, 1992.

'Three Iranians Flogged for Violations of Laws', *NYT*, 26 February 1979.

Tillier, Mathieu, 'Judicial Authority and Qāḍīs' Autonomy under the 'Abbāsids', *Al-Masāq* 26, 2 (2014), pp. 119–31.

———, 'The Umayyads and the Formation of Islamic Judgeship', in Andrew Marsham, ed., *The Umayyad World*, London, 2020, pp. 168–82.

Tobi, Yosef Yuval, *Juifs et Musulmans au Yémen de l'avènement de l'islam à nos jours*, Paris, 2019.

Toft, Amir A., tr., 'Preserving Public Health', in Hakan T. Karateke and Helga Anetshofer, eds., *The Ottoman World. A Cultural History Reader, 1450–1700*, Oakland, CA, 2021, pp. 210–19.

Toledano, Ehud R., *State and Society in Mid-nineteenth-century Egypt*, Cambridge, UK, 1990.

Tor, D. G. '"Sovereign and Pious." The Religious Life of the Great Seljuq Sultans', in Christian Lange and Songül Mecit, eds., *The Seljuqs. Politics, Society and Culture*, Edinburgh, UK, 2011, pp. 39–62.

BIBLIOGRAPHY

Tott, Baron de, *Mémoires du Baron de Tott sur les Turcs et les Tatares*, 4 vols., Amsterdam, 1784.

Tournefort, M. Pitton de, *Relation d'un voyage au Levant*, 2 vols., Lyon, France, 1717.

Treaster, Joseph B., 'Inverting the Pyramid in Egypt. A Beer Maker Blossoms With Its Nonalcoholic Brew', *NYT*, 28 December 1999.

Trépanier, Nicolas, *Foodways & Daily Life in Medieval Anatolia. A New Social History*, Austin, TX, 2014.

Troadec, Anne, 'Baybars and the Cultural Memory of Bilād al-Shām. The Construction of Legitimacy', *Mamluk Studies Review* 18 (2014–15), pp. 113–47.

Tsadik, Daniel, 'Jews in the Pre-constitutional Years. The Shiraz Incident of 1905', *IS* 43, 2 (2010), pp. 239–63.

Tuominen, Pekka, 'The Clash of Values Across Symbolic Boundaries: Claims of Urban Space in Contemporary Istanbul', *Contemporary Islam* 7 (2013), pp. 33–51.

'Turkish AKP Alcohol Law Raises Question Marks', *Hürriyet Daily News*, 23 September 2012.

'Turkish Police Seize Several Tons of Illegal Alcohol', *Al-Monitor*, 3 February 2021, at https://www.al-monitor.com/originals/2021/02/turkey-bootleg-alcohol-liquor-police-seize-taxes-illegal.html, accessed 19 December 2021.

Ubicini, M. A., *Lettres sur la Turquie*, 2 vols., Paris, 1853.

Umar, Muhammad, *Urban Culture in Northern India During the Eighteenth Century*, Delhi, India, 2001.

Üsdiken, Behzat, *Perad'an Beyoğlu'na 1840–1955*, Istanbul, 1999.

Ussher, John, *A Journey From London to Persepolis*, London, 1865.

Vadet, J.C., 'Ibn Ḥamdūn', *EI²*.

Vala Qazvini Isfahani, Muhammad Yusuf, *Khuld-i barin (Irān dar ruzgār-i Safaviyān)*, ed. Mir Hashim Muhaddis, Tehran, 1993.

Valentia, George, *Voyages and Travels to India, Ceylon, the Rea Sea, Abyssinia, and Egypt in the Years 1802, 1803, 1804, 1805, and 1806*, 3 vols., London, 1809–11.

Vámbéry, Hermann, *Meine Wanderungen und Erlebnisse in Persien*, Pest, Hungary, 1867.

Van Gelder, Geert-Jan, *God's Banquet. Food in Classical Arabic Literature*, New York, 2000.

———, 'A Muslim Encomium on Wine. The Racecourse of the Bay (*Halbat al-Kumayt*) by al-Nawagi (d. 859/1455) as a Post-classical Arabic Work', *Arabica* 42, 2 (1995), pp. 222–34.

Vanizade Halid, *Müskirat*, Istanbul, 1891.

Van Nieuwkerk, Karin, 'Female Entertainers in Egypt. Drinking and Gender Roles', in Dimitra Gefou-Madianou, ed., *Alcohol, Gender and Culture*, London, 1992, pp. 35–47.

———, '"Repentant" Artists in Egypt. Debating Gender, Performing Arts and Religion', *Contemporary Islam* 2, 3 (2008), pp. 191–210.

———, *'A Trade Like Any Other'. Female Singers and Dancers in Egypt*, Austin, TX, 1995.

Van Ruymbeke, Christine, 'Le vin, interdiction et licence, dans la poésie persane', *Acta Orientalia Belgica* 10 (1997), pp. 173–86.

Van Santen, Hans, *Op bezoek bij de Groot-Mogol. Twee hofreizen van de VOC naar de Groot-Mogol in India, 1662 en 1711–1713*, Leiden, Netherlands, 2016.

Vansleb, F., *The Present State of Egypt; or, A New Relation of a Late Voyage into that Kingdom. Performed in the Years 1672 and 1673*, London, 1678.

Varriano, John, *Wine. A Cultural History*, London, 2010.

Vatin, Nicolas, and Gilles Veinstein, *Le Sérail ébranlé. Essais sur les morts, dépositions et avènements des sultans ottomans XIVe–XIXe siècles*, Paris, 2003.

Villamont, Jacques de, *Les Voyages du seigneur de Villamont*, Lyon, France, 1620.

BIBLIOGRAPHY

[Villotte, Jacques/Nicolas Frizon], *Voyages d'un missionnaire de la Compagnie de Jésus en Turquie, en Perse, en Arménie, en Arabie, & en Barbarie*, Paris, 1730.

'The Vineyards and Vine-Growers of Western Algeria', at https://gco-dz.com/en/content/6-vignobles-vignerons, accessed 2 June 2022.

Von Harff, Arnold, *The Pilgrimage of Arnold von Harff Knight From Cologne, Through Italy, Syria, Egypt, Arabia, Ethiopia, Nubia, Palestine, Turkey, France and Spain Which He Accomplished in the Years 1496 to 1499*, ed. Malcolm Letts, London, 1946.

Von Kotzbue, Moritz, *Narrative of a Journey Into Persia in the Suite of the Imperial Russian Embassy of 1817*, London, 1819.

Von Maltzan, Heinrich Freiherr, *Drei Jahre im Nordwesten von Afrika. Reisen in Algerien und Marokko*, 4 vols., Leipzig, Germany, 1863.

————, *Meine Wallfahrt nach Mekka in der Küstengegend und im Innern von Hedschas*, 2 vols., Leipzig, Germany, 1865.

Vrolijk, Arnoud. 'Vijftig moslims aan de zwier. Drankgebruik en spijt in een middeleeuws Egyptisch boek', in Remke Kruk and Sjef Houpermans, eds., *Een vis in een fles raki. Literatuur en drank in verschillende culturen*, Amsterdam, 2005, pp. 211–24.

Wagner, Moritz, *Reisen in der Regentschaft Algier in den Jahren 1837, 1838, und 1839*, 3 vols., Leipzig, Germany, 1841.

————, *Travels in Persia, Georgia and Koordistan, With Sketches of the Cossacks and the Caucasus*, 3 vols., London, 1856.

Walsh, Declan, *The Nine Lives of Pakistan. Dispatches From a Precarious State*, New York, 2020.

Walsh, Robert, *Residence at Constantinople During a Period Including the Commencement, Progress, and Termination of the Greek and Turkish Revolutions*, 2 vols., London, 1836.

Waring, Scott, *A Tour of Sheeraz by the Route of Kazroon and Feerozabad, With Various Remarks on the Manners, Customs, Laws, Language, and Literature of the Persians*, London, 1807.

Wasserstein, David J., 'A Jonah Theme in the Biography of Ibn Tumart', in Farhad Daftary and Joseph W. Meri, eds., *Culture and Memory in Medieval Islam. Essays in Honour of Wilferd Madelung*, London, 2003, pp. 232–49.

Webb, Nigel and Caroline, *The Earl and His Butler in Constantinople. The Secret Diary of an English Servant Among the Ottomans*, London and New York, 2009.

Weber, Edgar, 'Le vin dans la tradition arabo-musulman', in Clemént, ed., *Les vins d'Orient*, pp. 53–84.

Weiss, Bernard G., *The Spirit of Islamic Law*, Athens and London, 1998.

Wellsted, Lieut. J. R., *Travels in Arabia*, 2 vols., London, 1835.

Wensinck, 'Khamr', *EI²*

Werner, Christoph, 'Taming the Tribal Native: Court Culture and Politics in Eighteenth-century Shiraz', in Albrecht Fuess and Jan Peter Hartung, eds., *Court Cultures in the Middle East, Seventh to Nineteenth Centuries*, London and New York, 2011, pp. 226–7.

Werr, Patrick. 'South Yemen's Only Brewery Stays in Business Despite Islamic Distaste for Alcohol', *Los Angeles Times*, 17 June 1990.

Westermarck, Edward, *Pagan Survivals in Mohammedan Civilisation*. London, 1933; repr. Amsterdam, 1973.

Weststeijn, Johan, 'Aardse en hemelse wijngaarden in de Koran', *ZemZem, Tijdschrift over het Midden Oosten, Noord-Afrika en de islam* 17, 1 (2021), pp. 125–36.

————, 'Het Jozefverhaal en de Perzische mythe van de wijnbouw', *ZemZem, Tijdschrift over het Midden Oosten, Noord-Afrika en de islam* 12, 1 (2016), pp. 97–109.

White, Charles, *Three Years in Constantinople or Domestic Manners of the Turks in 1844*, 3 vols., London, 1845.

BIBLIOGRAPHY

White, Jenny, *Muslim Nationalism and the New Turks*, Princeton, NJ, 2013.

White, Owen, *The Blood of the Colony. Wine and the Rise and Fall of French Algeria*, Cambridge, MA, 2021.

Wickham, Chris, *Framing the Early Middle Ages: Europe and the Mediterranean, 400–800*, Oxford, 2005.

Wilbraham, Captain Richard, *Travels in the Transcaucasian Provinces of Russia and Along the Southern Shore of Lakes of Van and Urumiah in the Autumn and Winter of 1837*, London, 1839.

Wild, Johann, *Neue Reisebeschreibung eines Gefangenen Christen wie derselbe … zum sibenden mal verkaufft worden … 1604–11. Von der Türcken und Araber järlichen Walfahrt von Alcairo nach Mecha*, Nuremberg, Germany, 1613.

Wills, C. J., *The Land of the Lion and the Sun (Modern Persia)*, 2nd edn., London, 1891.

Windler, Christian, 'Regelobservanz und Mission. Katholische Ordensgeistliche im Safavidenreich (17. und frühes 18. Jahrhundert)', in A. Karsten and H. von Thiessen, eds., *Normenkonkurrenz in historischer Perspektive*, Berlin, 2015, pp. 39–63.

Windus, John, *A Journey to Mequinez / Un voyage à Meknès*, ed. Dominique Meunier, Paris, 2005.

'Wine Sector in Turkey' (Turkish Ministry of Food and Agriculture), at https://www.trade.gov.tr/data/5b8fd55613b8761f041fee87/Wine.pdf, accessed 4 February 2022.

Winter, Michael, *Egyptian Society Under Ottoman Rule, 1517–1798*, London, 1992.

Wishard, John G., *Twenty Years in Persia; A Narrative of Life Under the Last Three Shahs*, New York, 1908.

Wishnitzer, Avner, *As Night Falls: Eighteenth-century Ottoman Cities After Dark*, Cambridge, UK, 2021.

————, 'Eyes in the Dark. Nightlife and Visual Regimes in Late Ottoman Istanbul', *CSSAAME* 37, 2 (2017), pp. 245–61.

Wittman, William, *Travels in Turkey, Asia Minor, Syria, and Across the Desert into Egypt During the Years 1799, 1800, and 1801, in Company With the Turkish Army and the British Military Mission*, 2 vols., London, 1803.

Wollina, Torsten, 'Between Beirut, Cairo, and Damascus: al-Amr bi al-Maʿrūf and the Sufi/Scholar Dichotomy in the Late Mamluk Period (1480s–1510s)', *Mamluk Studies Review* 20 (2017), pp. 55–92.

Wolpert, Stanley, *Jinnah of Pakistan*, New York and Oxford, 1984.

Wong, Edward, 'The Struggle for Iraq. Basra's Killings of Vendors in Iraqi City Drive Alcohol Sales off Streets', *NYT*, 19 February 2004.

Wood, Josh, 'Militants Set Their Attacks on Alcohol in Lebanon', *NYT*, 25 January 2012.

Woodall, G. Carole, 'Awakening a Horrible Monster. Negotiating the Jazz Public in 1920s Istanbul', *CSSAAME* 30, 3 (2010), pp. 574–86.

World Health Organization, *Global Status Report on Alcohol and Health 2014*, at https://www.iccp-portal.org/system/files/resources/9789240692763_eng.pdf.

Yarshater, Ehsan, 'The Theme of Wine-drinking and the Concept of the Beloved in Early Persian Poetry', *Studia Islamica* 13, 1 (1960), pp. 43–53.

Yate, C. E., *Khorasan and Sistan*, Edinburgh, UK and London, 1900.

Yavari, Neguin, *Advice for the Sultan. Prophetic Voices and Secular Politics in Medieval Islam*, Oxford, 2014.

Yeşilay, at https://www.yesilay.org.tr/tr/, accessed 6 March 2020.

Yilmaz, Fikret, 'What About a Bit of Fun? Wine, Crime and Entertainment in Sixteenth-century Western Anatolia', in Suraya Faroqhi and Arzu Öztürmen, eds., *Celebration, Entertainment and Theatre in the Ottoman World*, London, 2014, pp. 145–72.

BIBLIOGRAPHY

Yürekli, Tulay, 'Bahrī Memlûk Hükümdarlarının Eğlence ve Alışkanlık Unsuru Olarak Şarap', *Avrasya Uluslararası Araştırmalar Dergisi* 7, 20 (2019), pp. 143–53.

Zak'aria of Agulis, *The Journal of Zak'aria of Agulis*, tr. and ed. George A. Bournoutian, Costa Mesa, CA, 2003.

Zak'aria of K'anak'er, *The Chronicle of Deacon Zak'aria K'anak'er*, tr. and ed. George Bournoutian, Costa Mesa, CA, 2004.

Zaman, Muhammad Qasim, *Islam in Pakistan*, Princeton, NJ, 2018.

Zarindast, Karen, 'Illegal Alcohol Booming in Iran', BBC, 15 September 2011, at http://www.bbc.co.uk/news/world-middle-east-14939866, accessed 29 February 2020.

Zetterstéen, K. V., C. E. Bosworth, and E. van Donzel, E., 'al-Muhtadi', *EI²*.

———, 'al-Wāthik Bi'llāh', *EI²*.

Zilfi, Madeline C., *The Politics of Piety: The Ottoman Ulema in the Postclassical Age (1600–1800)*, Minneapolis, MN, 1988.

Znaien, Nessim, 'L'alcool en Tunisie depuis 2011. Une révolution?', *Khayyam*, 21 May 2018, at https://khayyam.hypotheses.org/32, accessed 15 June 2022.

———, 'Boire en Tunisie sous le Protectorat (1881–1956)', *Le Carnet de l'IRMC* 20 (2017), at https://irmc.hypotheses.org/2168, accessed 27 June 2022.

———, 'Drinking and Production Patterns of Wine in North Africa During French Colonisation, c. 1830–1956', in Ernst, ed., *Alcohol Flows Across Cultures*, pp. 44–60.

———, *Les raisins de la domination. Une histoire de l'alcool en Tunisie à l'époque du Protectorat (1881–1956)*, Paris, 2021.

———, 'Le vin et la viticulture sous le Protectorat. Entre synapse et apartheid', *French Cultural Studies* 26, 2 (2015), pp. 140–151.

Zubaida, Sami, *Beyond Islam, A New Understanding of the Middle East*, London, 2011.

———, 'Middle Eastern Experiences of Cosmopolitanism', in S. Vertovec and R. Cohen, eds., *Conceiving Cosmopolitanism*, New York, 2002, pp. 32–41.

Zwemer, Samuel M., 'Mohammedans and the Drink Question', *The Missionary Review of the World* 42, 5 (1919), pp. 365–8.

INDEX

'Abbad II al-Mu'tadid, 45
'Abbas I, Shah, 127, 130, 131, 132, 138-9, 187, 278
'Abbas II, Shah, 127, 131-34, 135, 140, 141
'Abbas Mirza, 189-90
Abbasids, 18, 36, 39-44, 59, 69
'Abdallah b.Yasin, 45
'Abd al-Malik, Sultan, 111, 112
'Abd al-Malik al-'Aziz 'Uthman, Sultan (Ayyubids), 49
'Abd al-Malik b. Marwan, Caliph (Umayyads), 37
'Abd al-Malik al-Muzaffar, Caliph (Spain), 44
'Abd al-Nasir, Gamal, 218-19
'Abd al-Rahman, Caliph (Spain), 39
'Abd al-Rahman III, Caliph (Spain), 44
'Abd al-Rahman Sanchuelo, Caliph (Spain), 44
Abdülaziz, Sultan (Ottomans), 150, 152
Abdülhamid I, Sultan (Ottomans), 97
Abdülhamid II, Sultan (Ottomans), 152-4, 166

Abdülmecid, Sultan (Ottomans), 150, 151-2
absinthe, 173, 175, 207, 209
Abu'l-'Abbas ibn al-Muqtadir see al-Radi
Abu'l-'Abbas al-Saffah, Caliph (Abbasids), 39
Abu 'Ali, 40
Abu Bakr, Caliph, 24
Abu Hasan 'Ali I, 110
Abu'l Hasan Khan, 188
Abu'l-Husayn Mirza, 115
Abu'l Fath Khan, 178
Abu Ja'far, 57
Abu Mihjan al-Thaqafi, 69
Abu Nuwas, 5, 7, 30, 40, 68, 69-70, 72-3, 78, 84
Abu Sa'id, 61
Adana, 249
Aden, 232-3
Aden Sirra (Seera) beer factory, 233
Adornes, Anselm, 47
Adrianople see Edirne
Aegean Islands, 104, 154, 243, 250, 93, 97

365

INDEX